Human Rights in Action

The Erik Castrén Institute Monographs on International Law and Human Rights

General Editor

Martti Koskenniemi

VOLUME 11

University of Helsinki

The titles published in this series are listed at the end of this volume.

Human Rights in Action

Learning Expert Knowledge

By

Miia Halme-Tuomisaari

MARTINUS
NIJHOFF
PUBLISHERS

LEIDEN • BOSTON
2010

This book is printed on acid-free paper.

Library of Congress Cataloging-in-Publication Data

Halme, Miia.
Human rights in action : learning expert knowledge / by Miia Halme-Tuomisaari.
p. cm. -- (The Erik Castren Institute monographs on international law and human rights, 1568-2765 ; v. 11)
Includes bibliographical references and index.
ISBN 978-90-04-18445-9 (hardback : alk. paper) 1. Human rights--Finland. 2. Human rights--Scandinavia. 3. Human rights--Anthropological aspects. I. Title.
JC599.F5H35 2010
323.094897--dc22

2010028712

ISSN 1568-2765
ISBN 978 90 04 18445 9

THE MONOGRAPH SERIES

The Series of *International Law Monographs* by the *Erik Castrén Institute of International Law and Human Rights* seeks to bring to the reader high-quality research in international law with particular emphasis on the theoretical and historical aspects of the topics dealt with. The Series encourages doctrinal and practical criticism, a multi-disciplinary approach and broad syntheses. Manuscripts that seek to renew the field's intellectual energy and political commitment are welcome. The Series is based on a conviction that theoretical ambition and practical relevance cannot be dissociated from each other and that even as it looks for a rejuvenation of the field it insists on speaking to both academic and practising lawyers.

Martti Koskenniemi
General Editor

CONTENTS

Foreword ... ix
Acknowledgements ... xiii

Chapter One: Introduction ... 1
Chapter Two: Emergence of the Human Rights Phenomenon in Finland ... 33
Chapter Three: The Scandinavian Network of Human Rights Experts ... 75
Chapter Four: Training for Expertise ... 117
Chapter Five: From Translation to Advocation through Law ... 171
Chapter Six: Profile of Expertise ... 201

Conclusions ... 247
Bibliography ... 253
Index ... 275

FOREWORD

Human rights are often thought of in terms of large legal or moral principles, grand blueprints for social or institutional reform. We use the vocabulary of human rights to address the most varied questions of social morality and law and to propagate different, often conflicting political projects. We do this so often that is has become a commonplace to note that human rights sound like the religion of a secular society. Like faith, they intrude in the most varied human relationships, from politics to the workplace, from families to hospitals, from government to the university. The relations between women and men, consumers and producers, aliens and citizens, between representatives of overlapping communities, generations, and religions are routinely addressed in human rights terms. Human rights are everywhere as discourse, as community, and as artifacts, as Miia Halme-Tuomisaari argues in the path-breaking, insightful and even exciting study of what she calls the "human rights phenomenon".

Not all have been happy with the increasing ubiquity of human rights. If rights are everywhere, then that is as good as their being really nowhere. Others worry about the abstraction of rights: it is so much easier to agree on large principles than on what they should mean in practice. Few would reject what is being said in the 1948 Universal Declaration on Human Rights – despite (or because of?) the difficulty of determining what it actually commits us to. It is not only that rights are formulated in such general terms that they can be associated with almost any imaginable policy. In a world of limited resources – that is, in *our world* – rights can often only be realized at the cost of other rights. The self-determination of an indigenous or religious community may often require limiting the freedom of its members. Action to give reality to the right to be free from poverty for some would certainly cut into the right of property of others. Free speech clashes with the right of privacy, as we know from our societies, just like the exercise of the freedom of movement by some may appear to encroach on the right to security of others. As many have noted, perhaps with desperation, from our sharing a human rights vocabulary, it does not follow that we would agree what to do, what consequences rights should have in our lives. The language itself refers always to further debate about what ought to be done – a debate that is often waged under the supervision of human rights experts whose priorities may thus determine what rights come to mean "in action".

Halme-Tuomisaari's starting-point here is that in addition to being a vocabulary and a blueprint of social reform, human right are also a set of artifacts (declarations, treaties, laws, perhaps even colourful sweaters bought from indigenous communities) and a community of practice – namely the practice of human rights expertise. As a shared way of speaking and a repository of common symbols, human rights socialise us in communities of activists or academics, sharing not only a particular type of knowledge but also typical forms of behaviour and easily identifiable preferences, forms of both insight and blindness. In this book Halme-Tuomisaari has chosen to lift her gaze here from human rights as a legal or moral language to human rights as a community of men and women joined by "human rights expertise". If it is true that what human rights mean is largely mediated by what those who are regarded as "human rights experts" say or think it should mean, then surely, a study of "human rights in practice" must be a study of what it is experts do, what they say, how they behave and what counts for their recognizing each other as experts in this particular field.

"Ask not what the human rights experts say – ask what they do." Not only is this the only realistic way to approach human rights expertise – it also gives a good sense of what "human rights" mean as vocabulary and a doctrine, one that is authoritatively guarded by those who are its "experts". Halme-Tuomisaari uses the sharp gaze of a trained anthropologist-lawyer to provide us with a close reading of the meaning of human rights expertise through surveying the behaviour of a community of Scandinavian human rights experts with whom she spent a considerable amount of time, participating in their meetings and discussions, taking notes and asking questions. And now she has come back to tell "how it is out there, in human-rights-land". There she met both experienced leaders and young apprentices, men and women, North Europeans and others, witnessing how the relationships between them developed in the course of their shared education project. The result is an elegant and insightful account of how one is socialised to becoming a "human rights expert". What preferences and hierarchies are internalised during the process? What opinions are learned, what unlearned? Like most good anthropological studies, her work makes the familiar alien – after having read her intimate account we can no longer think of human rights quite as we once did. It no longer appears just as a reflection of great principles but a terrain for ambition and desire, fear and sympathy, enthusiasm and frustration. In a word, it appears as an altogether human practice.

Above all, however, Halme-Tuomisaari's constructively critical engagement with a Nordic community of human rights experts is both liberating and empowering at the same time. We feel liberated inasmuch as we now (finally) learn that human rights is not a religion that requires faith in some determinate social preferences but rather an all-too-human practice of grappling with an indeterminate social present, with all that this means regarding its intellectual, psychological, economic, geographic, gendered and other stakes. We feel empowered because her narrative breaks the illusion that the field is one of pre-existing truths and rigid hierarchies that one would only have to accept in order to speak authoritatively in it. In fact, everyone can be a "human rights expert" because what Halme-Tuomisaari calls the "human rights phenomenon" is not a closed world of authoritative truths or institutions. It is neither more nor less than what the ambitious men and women who have decided to live in and through human rights, have been prepared to invest in that effort.

New York, 3 September 2010
Martti Koskenniemi

ACKNOWLEDGEMENTS

This project has benefited from the contributions of a great number of individuals and research communities. Of these, the most important has been the Erik Castrén Institute of International Law and Human Rights of the University of Helsinki. I thank the Institute leader, professor Martti Koskenniemi, and all of my colleagues for endless vigorous debate, a stimulating intellectual environment and friendship – as well as the numerous quotes they provided me with on the ingenious uses made today of the human rights discourse. Thanks also to the persons who handle practical issues and thus make research, and life, easier and more enjoyable. Scholars from the department of Anthropology at the University of Helsinki have provided insightful and challenging comments, and the Finnish Centre of Excellence in Global Governance Research has offered an inspiring inter-disciplinary context in which to present and receive feedback on my research. Many thanks to all the participants of these contexts.

During this study I have presented papers in different workshops, seminars and conferences in Finland and elsewhere.[1] I have also had the good fortune of holding courses as well as visiting lectures. These experiences have resulted in exciting debates, which have helped me significantly as I have developed my approaches. Numerous persons contributed to my analysis on the manner the human rights phenomenon had emerged in Finland, facilitated my visits to the UN and provided sources on American internationalism, among others. Warm thanks for these. In the preparation of this manuscript I have benefitted from the research assistance, copy-editing and general help by Suvi Huotari, Anna Szegedi, Mary Morgan, Susan Liu and Merje Jõgi, Sara Norja and Ville Peltokorpi. Warm thanks to them all.

This project has enjoyed generous funding from the Finnish Graduate School in Human Rights Research (2002–2006). Many thanks to the School's leader Martin Scheinin. In addition funding has

[1] Here the most important have been the papers presented at the Anthropology and Law Workshop at Birkbeck College, London (25–27 April, 2005), and the session 'Human Rights: Global Legal Pluralism Revisited' of the Law and Society Association - RCSL Conference 'Law and Society in the 21st Century' at Humboldt University, Berlin (25–27.7.2007).

been provided by the Law Faculty of the University of Helsinki, the Finnish Centre of Excellence in Global Governance Research (2006–2011), and the Finnish Academy Project 'Human Rights: Law, Religion and Subjectivity' (2009–2012). Shorter funding periods and travel grants have been received from the University of Helsinki. Earlier versions of Chapters 2 and 5 have been featured in previously published articles.[2]

This study was originally defended as a doctorate thesis at the Department of Anthropology at the University of Helsinki in spring 2008. Many thanks to Professors Sally Engle Merry and Teemu Ruskola for acting as my preliminary examiners; and a most heart-felt thanks to professor Sally Engle Merry for being the opponent in my public examination – an exciting exchange which pushed me to improve this manuscript as well as motivated me in my future projects. Finally, an enormous thanks to the organizers and participants of the empirical context of this study, addressed through the pseudonym of the Scandinavian Network of Human Rights Experts (SCANET), for allowing me to carry out this research.

I dedicate this book to my parents, my husband and our son.
In Helsinki, 15 February, 2010
Miia Halme-Tuomisaari

---

[2] 'Laki ja Ihmisoikeudet: etnografinen lähestymistapa.' In *Oikeus-lehti*, Symposium on Law and Anthropology, 1/2007, 32–43; 'From the Periphery to the Centre: Emergence of the Human Rights Phenomenon in Finland.' In *Finnish Yearbook of International Law* 2007 (Ed. Creutz, Katja). Brill Academic Publishers, Leiden, 2010, 257–281.

CHAPTER ONE

INTRODUCTION

> *All human beings are born free and equal in dignity and rights. They are endowed with reason and conscience and should act towards one another in a spirit of brotherhood.*
>
> Article 1, Universal Declaration of Human Rights, 1948

In February 2006 two Finnish parliamentarians proposed a constitutional amendment to separate the Lutheran church from the Finnish state. The very proposal may surprise an outsider: is this technologically advanced and prosperous Northern state not thoroughly secularized but instead continually holds formal allegiance to some sacred domain? How does this comply, for example, with the demands that Turkey, a Muslim state, become secularized before EU membership? That this is indeed accurate – the Lutheran church holds likewise the state church status in Norway, Iceland and Denmark – and further treated as commonplace was reflected in the forceful opposition and absent support the proposal received as it was discussed in the Finnish Parliament. Although one parliamentarian mentioned Turkey, she simultaneously declared to oppose the proposal. The subsequent discussion focused on values. Participating parliamentarians, primarily senior representatives of the Christian and agrarian parties, emphasized the historic link between Christian values and the Finnish state. They further argued that these values form continually the nation's ideological foundation. Their arguments were historically accurate. Prior to independence in 1917, only Christians could ascertain civil rights in the autonomous Grand Duchy of Finland. Also, only the law on religious freedom of 1923 allowed Finns to abandon the state church. Yet relatively few resigned, and by the new millennium over 85% of Finns were still church-members. 2003 brought radical change: as new legislation on religious freedom facilitated leaving the church – before, a personal parish visit was required, now a mere e-mail sufficed – resignation numbers exploded. Whereas in 2001 and 2002 around 15 000 Finns left the church, in 2007 the figure was over 37 000. Of those resigning, the vast majority are under 40, which increases the number of children born without church-membership. If resignations continue to increase, Lutheran church members will according to estimates become a minority by 2015 – a scenario that would challenge the very status of the state church.

In many ways this development is understandable. After all, most Finns hardly ever actually attend the church they almost mechanically belong to. Consequently, instead of radical change in values, recent developments signal a longer decline or alteration of religious sentiment. This applies also more generally to the modern era characterized by individualism, equality, rationality, liberalism and secularization. That Finns increasingly embrace these values was reflected in the Presidential election of 2000 won by Tarja Halonen, an urban single mother living in a common-law marriage – not a church-member but a member of a well-known organization for sexual minorities – over Esko Aho, a church-belonging head of a nuclear family.[1] Against this background paramount of the above Parliament discussion emerges how it embodied a rare public exchange depicting Christian values as common to all Finns. Particularly recent initiatives to renew school curricula demonstrate how, despite continued formal links between church and state, in public policy-making Christian values have lost their universal status. Instead policy-making signals them to reflect the ideology of one particular religion that must compete on an equal footing with the values of all other ideologies. That is, all ideologies but one: human rights as articulated by the Universal Declaration of Human Rights (UDHR). Virtually every recent school curriculum reform emphasizes that human rights form the foundational values of contemporary Finnish education. Whereas requiring non-church members to participate in religious education has become unacceptable and unlawful in Finnish schools, no limitations are mentioned in regards to human rights. To the contrary, no mentions exist of instances permitting a student *not* to attend human rights education. Human rights are the new common values into which policy makers want to socialize the next generation of Finns.

[1] The election was very tight and showed clear division between urban and rural areas, the first supporting Halonen, the latter Aho. In 2006 Halonen was selected for another term after a tight competition with Sauli Niinistö, an enormously popular right-wing male candidate. Reflecting ideological change was the fact that whereas church membership and religion were among key themes of the 2000 campaign – particularly that Halonen was not a church member was highlighted – no emphasis rested on the issue in the 2006 election.

Human Rights as New Universal Values

This study examines human rights in action. It investigates the authority structures and patterns of flow that accompany the abstract human rights discourse in a concrete setting formed by the educational activities of the Scandinavian Network of Human Rights Experts, SCANET. Through examination of SCANET interactional patterns this study asks, what kinds of conceptions of knowledge, expertise and learning they give rise to. Do these conceptions realize the ideals of emancipation and equality embedded in the human rights discourse? SCANET analysis gains its context from the favourable ideological and societal position enjoyed by the human rights discourse in Finland. This position results from ongoing societal change which increasingly treats Christian values as articulated by the Lutheran church as particular conceptions that can be trumped by the secular, universal values articulated by the human rights discourse. In Finland human rights are cherished particularly by young urban adults, the group that both leads public opinion and resigns most actively from the Lutheran church.[2] Societal change is likewise visible in the Finnish media, as for example the country's largest and hugely influential newspaper Helsingin Sanomat advocates openly for the separation of church and state as well as approaches religion critically in its articles.[3]

By contrast, human rights are praised by politicians, interest groups from sexual minorities to the disabled, journalists, columnists, food critics and osteopaths. Interest groups advocate weekly for their realization around the University of Helsinki, whereas religious coalitions are markedly absent.[4] Allegiance to human rights represents the shift from ideological homogeneity to pluralism and openness; it marks the emancipation of the individual inquisitive mind from religious and ideological authority. This ideological shift continues a general post-World War II era development, in which human rights have emerged as the favoured discourse of international law, politics

---

[2] Mikkola, Teija; Niemelä, Kati & Petterson, Juha: The Questioning Mind: Faith and Values of the New Generation. Church Research Institute, Tampere, 2007.

[3] Rahkonen, Juho: Kirkko median kuvastimessa: Kristinuskon ja kirkollisten asioiden käsittely sanomalehdissä. Kirkon tutkimuskeskus, Tampere, 2007, 37.

[4] When a human rights NGO representative was prevented from campaigning in the University main building, an article followed at the university paper. Henrikki Timgren: 'Ihmisoikeudet eivät sovi päärakennukseen.' In *Yliopistolainen* 7/2004, 5.

and transnational activism. Human rights have become "glorified Esperanto",[5] they provide "values for a godless age".[6]

The link between secularization and the increasing importance of human rights reflects the observations of Paul Johnson, who notes how

> Among the advanced races, the decline and ultimately the collapse of the religious impulse would leave a huge vacuum. The history of modern times is in great part the history of how that vacuum had been filled... In place of religious belief, there would be secular ideology.[7]

E.H. Carr observed the same already prior to World War II, describing that

> An ethical standard was required which would be independent of any external authority, ecclesiastical or civil; and the solution was found in the doctrine of a secular 'law of nature', whose ultimate source was the individual human reason.[8]

Particularly after the Cold War human rights have increasingly filled this vacuum, simultaneously replacing nationalism as the principal ideology behind "imagined communities".[9] Like nationalism, the human rights ideology creates a paradox of objective modernity to the eyes of a historian and a sense of subjective antiquity to its supporters.[10] It is further characterized by an imagined community formed around deep, horizontal comradeship, paired with the realization that it is impossible to personally know each of the persons belonging to the community.[11]

However, differing from nationalism, the human rights ideology does not envision itself as finite; whereas Anderson notes how no nation imagines itself coterminous with mankind, this very

---

[5] Klabbers, Jan: 'Glorified Esperanto? Rethinking Human Rights.' In *Finnish Yearbook of International Law, 2002* (Ed. Tuori, Taina). Martinus Nijhoff Publishers, Leiden, 2004, 63–77.

[6] Klug, Francesca: Values for a Godless Age: The Story of the United Kingdom's New Bill of Rights. Penguin Books, London, 2000.

[7] Johnson, Paul: Modern Times: A History of the World from the 1920's to the 1990's. Phoenix, London, 1992, 48.

[8] Carr, E. H.: The Twenty Years' Crisis 1919–1939: An Introduction to the Study of International Relations. Palgrave, Hamsphire, 2001[1939], 25.

[9] Anderson, Benedict: Imagined Communities: Reflections on the Origin and Spread of Nationalism. Revised Edition. Verso, London, 2003 [1983].

[10] *Ibid.*, 5.

[11] *Ibid.*, 6–7.

notion – the community of *everyone*[12] – is constitutive of the human rights ideology. Greg Urban has emphasized the role discourses play in creating communities and spreading ideologies. In his discussion of the American Declaration of Independence, Urban notes how its discourse is "designed to be persuasive, to have an effect".[13] He then recalls Jacques Derrida's discussion on how regarding Declarations "[t]he signature invents the signer", giving rise to the community in whose name "the people, the "good" people (a decisive detail because it guarantees the value of the intention and the signature) have signed the document".[14] Urban assesses this account as incomplete, as "[w]hat is crucially missing from the performativity account is an understanding of cultural motion, of the circulation of discourse that is necessary for a significant number of individuals to come to articulate their membership in a group, of a "we" ".[15]

These findings apply to the community that has emerged around the UDHR over the past six decades. On the one hand, its foundations were laid in 1948 when the 'good people' representing 'all the peoples of the world' adopted the UDHR at the United Nations General Assembly. On the other, the emergence of an empirically observable 'human rights community' was preceded by decades of circulation of the human rights discourse. This study construes that in this circulation the decisive performative account has been education. The importance of education was highlighted already by the Preamble of the UDHR, which states that:

> Now, Therefore THE GENERAL ASSEMBLY proclaims THIS UNIVERSAL DECLARATION OF HUMAN RIGHTS as a common standard of achievement for all peoples and all nations, to the end that every individual and every organ of society, keeping this Declaration constantly in mind, shall strive by *teaching and education* to promote respect for these rights and freedoms.[16]

---

[12] Universal Declaration of Human Rights, 1948. http://www.un.org/Overview/rights.html (4.4.2006).

[13] Urban, Greg: Metaculture: How Culture Moves through the World. University of Minnesota Press, Minneapolis, 2001, 104.

[14] Derrida, Jacques: 'Declarations of Independence.' In *Negotiations: Interventions and Interviews 1971–2001*. Stanford University Press, Stanford, 2002, 49.

[15] Urban: Metaculture, *supra* note 13, 95.

[16] UDHR, *supra* note 12; italics added.

The importance of education was repeated in the 1993 UN World Conference of Human Rights[17] as well as the UN Decade of Human Rights Education from 1995 to 2004.[18] In 1998 Mary Robinson, former UN High Commissioner for Human Rights, highlighted education as the highest priority of the human rights phenomenon; she viewed it as fundamental in empowering individuals to defend their rights and those of others. This emphasis placed on education in the human rights phenomenon can be associated to the ideas of the Enlightenment which assigned intellectuals a pivotal role in the spread of progressive ideas.[19] It likewise resonates with the 'civilizing mission' of international law.[20] Yet the rhetoric of education entails a decisive, in the human rights field often overlooked, separation of individuals into those holding competence over the knowledge to be distributed, and those for the benefit of whom knowledge needs to be disseminated; the separation of people into 'experts' and 'students'.[21] This forms an intrinsic hierarchy between these groups, thus challenging the egalitarian ethos of the human rights discourse. Although 'all human beings are born free and equal in dignity and rights' and are 'endowed with reason and conscience', only some are competent to educate others on the exact content of universal rights.

Education is a potent tool of societal change, and consequently questions on what is taught, how, and by whom generate ongoing controversy worldwide. Minorities strive for teaching in their native languages, and religious groups aspire to have teaching that concurs with their doctrine. In the US education was a central tool in the assimilationist policies directed at Native Americans, and today an intense controversy plagues many Southern US states on whether schools should teach the Darwinian theory of Evolution, or the Biblical story of Creationism. In Finland education has a distinct tradition due to its link to the spread of the Lutheran faith in the 17th century. Then the

---

[17] Vienna Declaration, adopted on 25 June 1993, A/Conf. 157/23, http://www2.ohchr.org/english/law/vienna.htm (21.12.2005).

[18] United Nations Decade for Human Rights Education (1995-2004). http://www.unhchr.ch/html/menu6/1/edudec.htm (6.5.2007).

[19] Gramsci, Antonio: Selections from the Prison Notebooks. International Publishers, New York, 1989 [1971] 5–43.

[20] Koskenniemi, Martti: 'Human Rights, Politics and Love.' In *Mennesker & rettigheter 4*, 2001, 33–45.

[21] Hannerz, Ulf: Cultural Complexity: Studies in the Social Organization of Meaning. Columbia University Press, New York, 1992.

ability to read, and hopefully understand, the Bible was construed as pivotal for achieving contact with God. This rendered reading ability a prerequisite for obtaining a marriage permit from the church – a compelling incentive as civil marriages were not recognized in Finland. Consequently, although the law on mandatory education was only passed in 1921, some form of education was practically compulsory centuries earlier. Until the early 20th century few public schools existed particularly in the remote rural areas inhabited by large portions of Finns, and thus an important legacy emerged of Lutheran ministers acting as educators. This legacy has left a lasting impact on the Finnish public consciousness, as is reflected in literature, for example. Most Finns still learn at schools how in *Seitsemän veljestä* – the novel "Seven Brothers" written and published in the late 19th century by Aleksis Kivi and continually one of the most famous Finnish novels – the thick-headed brothers struggle in their reading sessions led by a stern Lutheran minister. Two elements of this educational legacy hold significance for this study. First, as Lutheran ministers were traditionally among the most influential members of the Finnish society, also educators enjoyed high status. Although the status of teachers has since declined remarkably, as has also the status of Lutheran ministers, high status continues to resonate with the Finnish population. This is reflected in the common expression *kansankynttilä*, which literally translates as 'a candle for the common people'. The second decisive element relates to the conception of learning internalized by common Finns: learning was primarily mechanical adoption of knowledge disseminated by an authority without public reflection or dissent. The "Seven Brothers" illustrates tangibly how peasants were not to negotiate with the minister.

Human Rights Experts as Educators

In this study the individuals acting as educators are human rights experts. Although their actions are explored in an explicit educational context, SCANET, their educational role is understood to occupy a more general role in the contemporary human rights phenomenon. For this study the 'human rights phenomenon'[22] is understood to

[22] The concept 'phenomenon' is utilized for example by Mark Mazover as well as Saladin Meckled-Garcia and Basak Cali; see Mazover, Mark: 'The Strange Triumph of Human Rights, 1933–1950.' In *47 The Historical Journal 2*, 2004, 379–398;

consist of three elements: discourse, community and artifacts.[23] All three elements have faced expansion, and, whereas this study makes no claims for exhaustive treatment of the process, it is briefly overviewed in the subsequent chapters. To summarize, this study places the human rights discourse as articulated by the UDHR at the heart of expansion. At the end of World War II the discourse was revolutionary in its articulation of formal global equality, and thus it persuasively pulled newly independent people – previously excluded from the diplomatic discourses of the League of Nations[24] – into the incipient human rights community. Adding to the attraction was the potency of the discourse to make claims in a language that "*can't be reduced* to a mere "value judgment"".[25] Six decades after the adoption of the UDHR, an infinite community of NGOs, experts, policy makers, volunteers, educators, politicians and ordinary citizens has emerged around the discourse.[26] Human rights education has importantly contributed to this development, as it has both made people around the world aware of the discourse, and instructed them on how to articulate differing claims through it. The expansion of the human rights community has been accompanied by the proliferation of human rights artifacts[27] – entities that exist objectively in empirical and ontological

---

Meckled-Garcia, Saladin & Cali, Basak (Eds.): The Legalization of Human Rights. Routledge, London, 2006.

[23] Many other scholars talk of the 'human rights movement'; see Steiner, Henry J. & Alston, Philip: International Human Rights in Context: Law, Politics, Morals. Second Edition. Oxford University Press, Oxford, 2000; Simpson, A. W. Brian: Human Rights and the End of Empire: Britain and the Genesis of the European Convention. Oxford University Press, Oxford, 2001; Sellars, Kirsten: The Rise and Rise of Human Rights. Sutton Publishing, Phoenix Mill, 2002; Mutua, Makau: Human Rights: A Political & Cultural Critique. University of Pennsylvania Press, Philadelphia, 2002; Merry, Sally Engle: 'Anthropology and Activism: Researching Human Rights across Porous Boundaries.' In *28 Political and Legal Anthropology Review 2*, 2005, 240–258; Mahoney, Jack: The Challenge of Human Rights: Their Origin, Development, and Significance. Blackwell Publishing, Malden, 2007.

[24] See discussion in Wallin, Risto: Yhdistyneet kansakunnat organisaationa: Tutkimus käsittellisestä muutoksesta maailmanjärjestön organisoinnin periaatteissa. Jyväskylän yliopisto, Jyväskylä, 2005.

[25] Kennedy, Duncan: A Critique of Adjudication. Harvard University Press, Cambridge, 1997, 305.

[26] Keck, Margaret E. & Sikkink, Kathryn: Activists beyond Borders: Advocacy Networks in International Politics. Cornell University Press, Ithaca, 1998.

[27] Jean-Klein, Iris & Riles, Annelise: 'Introducing Discipline: Anthropology and Human Rights Administration.' In *28 Political and Legal Anthropology Review 2*, 2005, 173–203.

terms – including international instruments, policies, institutions, journals and educational programs.

Combined, these developments have also dramatically expanded the human rights discourse. Instead of focussing on distinct claims, the discourse possesses a generality that allows all claims to be forwarded through it. Few people today would claim that human rights adjudicate solely the relationships of sovereign states and their subjects, although this was arguably their initial juridical significance. Instead, human rights have become free-floating signifiers:[28] concepts the exact content of which each individual speaker can define for herself and which can further be utilized to argue, for example, for the improved treatment of chimpanzees. Human rights have become all-inclusive and therefore are threatened to be synonymous with everything and nothing. This challenges the potency of the discourse to act as trumps. The human rights phenomenon entails an important structural authority position with which to combat this challenge, namely the systemic agency of human rights experts. Marshall Sahlins elaborates the concept in relation to historical events, characterizing it as an institutional or structural form of empowerment that conveys authority to particular persons by the structural relays of the larger organization of society.[29] In the human rights phenomenon systemic agency is held primarily by human rights experts who act as educators on what human rights are; what remains within, what falls outside the discourse. Through their systemic agency human rights experts act as intermediaries who translate the discourse to meet local concerns.[30] The Finnish context exemplifies this, as experts are consulted by legislators and policy makers, and relied on by different interest groups. In the issue of state church, both sides cited predominant human rights experts to add potency to their claims.

The systemic agency of human rights experts has given rise, to utilize the concept Jean Lave and Etienne Wenger use to describe learning processes, to a "community of practice" constituted of a "set of relations among persons, activity, and world over time and in relation with

[28] Mehlman, Jeffrey: 'The "Floating Signifier": From Lévi-Strauss to Lacan.' In *Yale French Studies 48*, 1972, 30–37; Laclau, Ernesto: Emancipation(s). Verso, London, 1996.

[29] Sahlins, Marshall: Apologies to Thucydides: Understanding History as Culture and Vice Versa. The University of Chicago Press, Chicago, 2004, 155–156.

[30] Merry, Sally Engle: Human Rights & Gender Violence: Translating International Law into Local Justice. The University of Chicago Press, Chicago, 2006.

other tangential and overlapping communities of practice".[31] In this community human rights experts are *full members*. Today this community is both significantly large in size as well as diverse in its practices and motivations. Yet in Finland the community enjoys a monolithically favourable societal position: human rights experts are in the media described as "always being on the side of the weak ones", and they are greeted by acquaintances as "doing something good". In terms of their systemic agency, constitutive for this community of practice is its access to the "thousands of articles, referees, supporters and granting bodies". This allows the conceptions of its members on the limits of the human rights discourse to trump "those of the "average man who happens to hit the truth", naively postulated by Galileo", as has been phrased by Bruno Latour in regards to the formation of facts in the natural sciences.[32] In terms of influence, decisive emerges the community's association to institutions enjoying a recognized and esteemed position inside the human rights phenomenon, such as different UN bodies.

This study explores a formal context, SCANET, in which human rights experts act as educators. As education has the capacity to challenge the emancipation of the individual inquisitive mind from external authority, this study asks: what kind of a *teaching curriculum* – formal and explicit curriculum for intended learning[33] – does the observed context embody? How does this curriculum correspond to the *learning curriculum* – learning that occurs through general participation in an educational activity instead of formal teaching – observable in SCANET?[34] What kind of conceptions of learning, knowledge and expertise does SCANET create; what kinds of patterns of flow emerge in it?[35] In this study these questions will be addressed, to continue with the terms of Lave and Wenger, from the perspective of a *legitimate peripheral participant* – a student and a newcomer into the community of practice of human rights experts. This study analyses whether the status of peripheral participants is *dynamic*, allowing for gradual evolution into full membership, or one characterized by "*unrelatedness* or

[31] Lave, Jean & Wenger, Etienne: Situated Learning: Legitimate Peripheral Participation. Cambridge University Press, Cambridge, 1991, 98.

[32] Latour, Bruno: Science in Action. Harvard University Press, Cambridge, 1987, 44.

[33] Lave & Wenger: Situated Learning, *supra* note 31, 40–41.

[34] *Ibid.*

[35] Hannerz: Cultural Complexity, *supra* note 21.

irrelevance to ongoing activity".[36] These questions assist particularly in the search for answers on how an educational context such as SCANET realizes the ideals of individualism, equality, rationality, and secularity embedded in the human rights discourse.

Education in SCANET

This study discusses its empirical context through the pseudonym of the Scandinavian Network of Human Rights Experts, SCANET. Scholars have differing approaches for the use of pseudonyms: while for example Annelise Riles utilizes them in her analysis of Fijian NGO workers without supplementary explanation,[37] Sally Engle Merry discusses the CEDAW committee with its real name.[38] In her analysis of a Northern Irish village Nancy Scheper-Hughes utilized a pseudonym, but in retrospect condemns their "cute and conventional use". She claims this "time-honored practice" to "fool few and protect none – save, perhaps the anthropologist", and continues:

> I fear that the practice makes rogues of us all – too free with our pens, with the government of our tongues, and with our loose translations and interpretations of village life.[39]

Such concerns should not be dismissed lightly. For this venture the use of pseudonyms has not stemmed principally from desires to conceal SCANET participant identities – after all, many discussed elements of human rights expert capacities, such as newspaper interviews, are public, and thus no reasons exist to protect anonymity. Rather pseudonyms assist in gaining greater distance and upgrading the analytical level by treating SCANET above all as a characteristic example of artifacts and communities of the human rights phenomenon.

SCANET, formed in 2002, is a loose coalition of scholars and practitioners for whom legal education turned out to be characteristic. Its members represent the Scandinavian and Nordic region, meaning

---

[36] Lave & Wenger: Situated Learning, *supra* note 31, 37; italics in original.

[37] Riles, Annelise: The Network Inside Out. The University of Michigan Press, Ann Arbor, 2001.

[38] Merry: Human Rights & Gender Violence, *supra* note 30.

[39] Scheper-Hughes, Nancy: Saints, Scholars, and Schizophrenics: Mental Illness in Rural Ireland. Updated and Expanded Edition. University of California Press, Berkeley, 2002, 12.

Sweden, Norway, Denmark, Finland and Iceland, and in its organizing rationale SCANET is characteristic of the artifacts that have in recent years emerged within the human rights phenomenon. SCANET members include some of the most influential Nordic human rights experts, among others professors and senior scholars in universities as well as leaders and researchers in Scandinavian and Nordic human rights institutes. Many SCANET members act as consultants for their governments in policy-making and legislation as well as participate in the work of numerous interest groups; many hold UN expert positions such as treaty body memberships. In Finland, due to the recent emphasis of human rights education, human rights experts including SCANET members are increasingly relied on as educators and providers of educational material for elementary and higher education, a development which increases their societal influence. SCANET operates through various forms such as upkeeping an e-mail list which distributes information of developments and activities in the human rights field as well as offers research and travel grants. However, the most important feature of its operations is the organizing of educational activities – courses of some days to a week, organized in changing localities – which intend to help researchers in their ongoing PhD research. These activities are participated in by both permanent SCANET experts as well as visiting experts from well-known universities primarily in Europe and North America. Students of these activities are PhD candidates and in some instances post-doctorate researchers who have some connection to the participating universities and human rights institutes.

Finding the Field

My ethnography has an unusual background as I, a young Finnish urban adult fascinated by human rights, originally enrolled in SCANET as a student. Such a background is clearly charged – for one thing, it will most likely be read by those it has been written about[40] – and consequently an explanation of origins is appropriate. When starting my doctorate research, I initially planned not to treat SCANET as a field site, but rather my orientation was more 'student-like': I looked forward to it as a context in which to carry out my research, engage in

[40] Brettel, Caroline B. (Ed.): When They Read What We Write: The Politics of Ethnography. Bergin & Garvey, Connecticut, 1993.

discussions and learn more of human rights. Further, my research proposal indicated plans to do fieldwork in a US-based human rights NGO, a plan that stayed with me for a considerable period. This desire was inspired by my experiences in the fall of 2000 as an NGO intern in Hyderabad, India, the rapidly growing capital of the province of Andhra Pradesh. At the time I was finishing my Master's degree in anthropology and had already commenced studies in international law, which had given me some, although limited background in human rights. This background was complemented by a keen interest in human rights and a plan originating from my youth to pursue a career in relation to them. I embarked on the internship with a desire to both learn more and to 'do good'. The NGO worked at the grassroots level with various slum development projects: it ran schools, offered vocational training to women, supervised two shelters for street children, and rehabilitated disabled children. Combined, these produced impressive results with meagre resources. One of my tasks was to find funding from Northern NGOs, a task I attempted with no success whatsoever. Despite my poor results, this experience awakened the desire to contrast and complement it by working on the other end of human rights NGOs; to move from the recipients to the donors. This appeared also anthropologically exciting, as little similar fieldwork had been done at the time.

This plan was, however, altered already during my first visit to SCANET in early 2002 where I presented my research proposal. The proposal was encompassed in desires to find fresh approaches to a stale and predictable discussion – namely the 'universalism-relativism' debate – and it utilized an approach of abstraction and logic: it demonstrated, through various examples not directly related to human rights, how phenomena are never simply good or 'white', but instead always acquire "shades of grey".[41] This analysis was expanded with a discussion on how this 'grey area' tinted all action, transforming their outcomes from unambiguous benefits into ambiguous consequences. I elaborated this conclusion with excerpts both from my anthropological background and my views on the work of the Indian NGO. One example became the role of religion. Although the organization was not openly religious, most of its employees were Christian, prayers opened each working day, words of prayer hung on office walls and

[41] Levi, Primo: The Drowned and the Saved. Summit Books, New York, 1986.

when I arrived at the organization, the organization's minister gave me specific Bible verses for my personal guidance. Religion affected likewise the organization's operations as the majority of target groups were Muslim, alike most slum dwellers in Hyderabad. Slum programs encouraged girls to attend school and women to participate in the workforce, both changes that removed them from the immediate family context. Christian employees also commonly expressed disapproval toward the lifestyle of Islamic slum dwellers strongly affected by religion. Subsequently Christian NGO workers encouraged lifestyle changes which induced cultural consequences.

This problematized the outcomes of these programs, and I had difficulties to accept them without reservations. An even more extreme case was that of a social worker who, working for the 'best interest of the child', considered it necessary and justified to remove a child from his parents and place him in a home for street children where he would receive an education as "*all the parents wanted him to do was to go out on the street and beg*". This concretized how abstract and seemingly unambiguous categories became complex when applied to reality – a finding that has serious consequences also on human rights norms. In my research plan I proceeded to search for truly 'white' actions, and was able to come up with only one: teaching parents to *boil the water* their children drink. This simple remedy could account for enormous benefits without costs that would transform it to grey. However, as soon as my enthusiasm for this discovery veined, I began to see its absurdity: there I was, a foreign 'expert' with years of academic education, thousands of kilometers away from home, and the best I could come up with was to guide parents to bring water to 100C! To make matters worse, I realized I was unable to do even that as I shared no common language with the slum dwellers; few of them spoke English, and I had no competence in the most common local languages of Hindi, Telugu or Urdu. Even had I known their language, I was in great doubt of my ability to convince my audience. After all, what did I, a foreigner from another world, know of their life? Would the message not be more efficient coming from a local volunteer?

From Irritation to Interest

When I presented my research proposal in SCANET, it was assigned a radically different ontological quality: instead of empirical data without other intrinsic attributes, it was considered controversial – instead of facts or description,[42] it was perceived as *arguments*. As will be discussed later, this finding was to become an important anthropological insight into the nature of human rights knowledge, but at the moment it remained merely perplexing. In the following period my participation in SCANET activities was marked by intense irritation and even antagonism. I was deeply frustrated with knowledge I considered, in light of my earlier anthropological training as well as my experiences in India, as insufficient and flawed. I made these sentiments evident through frequent comments introducing additional and alternative data with which I argued that the empirical foundations behind the theory on human rights were inadequate. My consistent argument became that the epistemological assumptions of 'the other', primarily non-Europeans and indigenous peoples as well as occasionally minorities, were as misguided as the assumptions made of 'us', the representatives of the liberal north. In this moment my PhD research was primarily motivated by the desire to 'translate' existing anthropological data for human rights actors. I attempted to make my research "relevant".[43] I later discovered I had not been alone in this, as a great number of anthropologists had similar goals: to provide specialized knowledge to complement human rights actors' outdated notions of cultural issues, and to act as "epistemological technicians" who would provide a "principled and theoretically informed empirical approach" to human rights.[44]

These efforts become, however, complicated as many anthropologists in the field encounter human rights activists, bureaucrats, victims and perpetrators "actually anticipating the anthropologist's descriptive, analytical, and critical practices",[45] sometimes inviting scholars in to study them.[46] Although my suggestion of treating SCANET as a field site was favourably received, it would be exaggerated to argue that I was invited in. Rather I discovered that anthropology as a discipline

---

[42] Latour, Bruno: Reassembling the Social: An Introduction to Actor-Network Theory. Oxford University Press, Oxford, 2005, 146.

[43] Jean-Klein & Riles: 'Introducing Discipline', *supra* note 27, 173–203.

[44] Cowan, Jane K.; Dembour, Marie-Bénédicte & Wilson, Richard A.: 'Introduction.' In *Culture and Rights* (Eds. Cowan, Jane K.; Dembour, Marie-Bénédicte & Wilson Richard A.). Cambridge University Press, Cambridge, 2001, 1–26; Jean-Klein & Riles: 'Introducing Discipline,' *supra* note 27, 181.

[45] Jean-Klein & Riles, *ibid.*, 184.

[46] Jean-Klein, Iris: 'Alternative Modernities, or Accountable Modernities? The Palestinian Movement(s) and Political (Audit) Tourism During the First Intifada.' In *12 Journal of Mediterrannean Studies 1*, 2002, 43–80.

was treated with considerable reservation, the primary reason being its dubious connection to 'relativism'. Consequently my attempts to act as an epistemological educator were unsuccessful, and SCANET provided an environment where the anthropologist was welcomed, above all, as a student. As my association with SCANET continued I found my orientation changing. Instead of wishing to persuade, I was aiming to understand – I was becoming interested in views that had earlier provoked irritation. This altered my view on how SCANET activities introduced human rights. Instead of wishing to prove its foundations erroneous, I wished to comprehend the logic behind it. Repeated questions became: what is the nature of the knowledge distributed in SCANET activities? Who produces it, and what are the mechanisms through which the necessary cultural acceleration is created for its dispersal?[47] These questions introduced the most significant insight of the current venture: instead of a novel, superficially conjured field site, the most organic site for examining them became the context that had generated them in the first place – SCANET.

Fieldwork in SCANET

Thus I began to study SCANET, to continue with the concepts of Jean Lave and Etienne Wenger, from the perspective of a *legitimate peripheral participant*,[48] a student. SCANET membership was a pleasant experience. Its activities were organized in attractive venues ranging from charming university towns to mountainous resorts, and by the standards of the Nordic academia, they were well funded. All participants, including students, enjoyed accommodated travel expenses and private hotel lodging in three or four star hotels; all meals were included, with numerous dinners organized in trendy restaurants. The general atmosphere in SCANET activities was lively and convivial, leading to new collegial relations, collaboration and even friendships. SCANET experts participated with enthusiasm, and many invested far greater personal time and energy than the mere call of duty required with little or no financial compensation. All events were diligently organized both before, during and after activities, and this applied to practical matters as well as recreational programs which included boat rides, mountain hikes and steam saunas. In formal SCANET activities great

[47] Urban: Metaculture, *supra* note 13.
[48] Lave & Wenger: Situated Learning, *supra* note 31.

dedication was invested to ensure extensive participation of experts from different areas of human rights research, including both 'mainstream' and 'critical' scholars. For this study decisive of SCANET become the central ontological assumptions about human rights held by many permanent experts: they are 'human rights believers'. To them human rights form absolute facts which receive their most authoritative articulations in UN human rights instruments. They view the autonomous liberal individual embedded at the core of the human rights discourse to be a universal phenomenon. They contemplate that even if societies exist today that do not take the autonomous individual as their primary organizing principle, improvement of the human condition requires such communities to change. In addition to being necessary, SCANET experts consider such change as possible. Prominent SCANET experts believe in tolerance and equality, and think that traditional customs often challenge the well-being of mankind. They view hierarchical societies to benefit dominant individuals at the expense of less powerful members and believe that great atrocities have in history been committed in the name of religions, particularly religious fundamentalism which insists that its ideology represents *the truth*. SCANET experts advocate religious freedom where all individuals may freely choose their religious beliefs, and see that this allows different religions and conceptions of truth to coexist peacefully. Simultaneously they are responsive to suggestions, forwarded for example by Boaventura de Sousa Santos, that human rights mark "the return [...] of the religious".[49] This was also acknowledged by a prominent SCANET expert who stated in one activity: "*I have no problem to accept that human rights form a secular religion*".

These conceptions differ from those guiding this study in the following manner: the autonomous individual is, instead of as a universal phenomenon, treated as a distinct formulation stemming from a particular cultural heritage.[50] Global societal change which starts with this conception of the individual as well as the ideal of absolute equality is difficult to realize as well as suspect in nature, as it establishes a hierarchy between different modes of societal organization in favour of liberal individualism. Whether such change would improve the human

[49] Sousa Santos, Boaventura de: 'Toward a Multicultural Conception of Human Rights.' In *18 Zeitschrift für Rechtssoziologie 1*, 1997, 2.

[50] Dumont, Louis: Essays on Individualism: Modern Ideology in Anthropological Perspective. The University of Chicago Press, Chicago, 1986.

condition as envisioned by SCANET experts is also questioned; certainly it would result in increasing global homogeneity. This study views religions and customs not as decisive causes of human suffering. Instead humans are construed as capable of finding contentment in circumstances that may be impossible for outsiders to comprehend. Great atrocities have undeniably been committed in the name of religions, but this study does not consider this outcome to vanish with retort to the human rights discourse. Numerous instances already exist that can in the future be interpreted as atrocities in the name of human rights. The human rights phenomenon also poses a danger of creating yet another "dictatorship of the virtuous" which have, in the words of Henry Kissinger, in the past led to "inquisitions and even witch-hunts".[51] In the human rights phenomenon this condition applies particularly to the continually increasing societal influence of human rights experts, who are often regarded as "globally virtuous", as has been phrased by David Kennedy.[52] Although this development is not feared to result in inquisitions, it is construed, through the conceptions of *noblesse oblige, the civilizing mission* and *colonial duty*, to reproduce global relationships of dependency and victimization which are responsible for much human suffering both today and in the past.

The most important difference in the ontological assumptions of this study and those of its informants relates to the conception *truth*: for SCANET experts human rights create *the truth* which is universal and absolute, whereas this study regards the human rights discourse as *one* articulation of a possible universal truth about the human condition. This difference is illuminated by Graph 1.

In these differences this study resonates with the approach of Faye Ginsburg among Pro-Life activists in an American community: being 'Pro Choice' and a self-confessed feminist, to Ginsburg the ideologies of the women she studied were "against their own interests".[53] Thus her project primarily studied a group whose views she did not share. Simultaneously this study holds a more intimate relation to its

---

[51] Kissinger, Henry: 'The Pitfalls of Universal Jurisdiction: Risking Judicial Tyranny.' In *80 Foreign Affairs 4*, 2001.

[52] Kennedy, David: The Dark Sides of Virtue: reassessing international humanitarianism. Princeton University Press, Princeton, 2004.

[53] Ginsburg, Faye: Contested Lives: The Abortion Debate in an American Community. Revised Edition. University of California Press, California, 1998, 166.

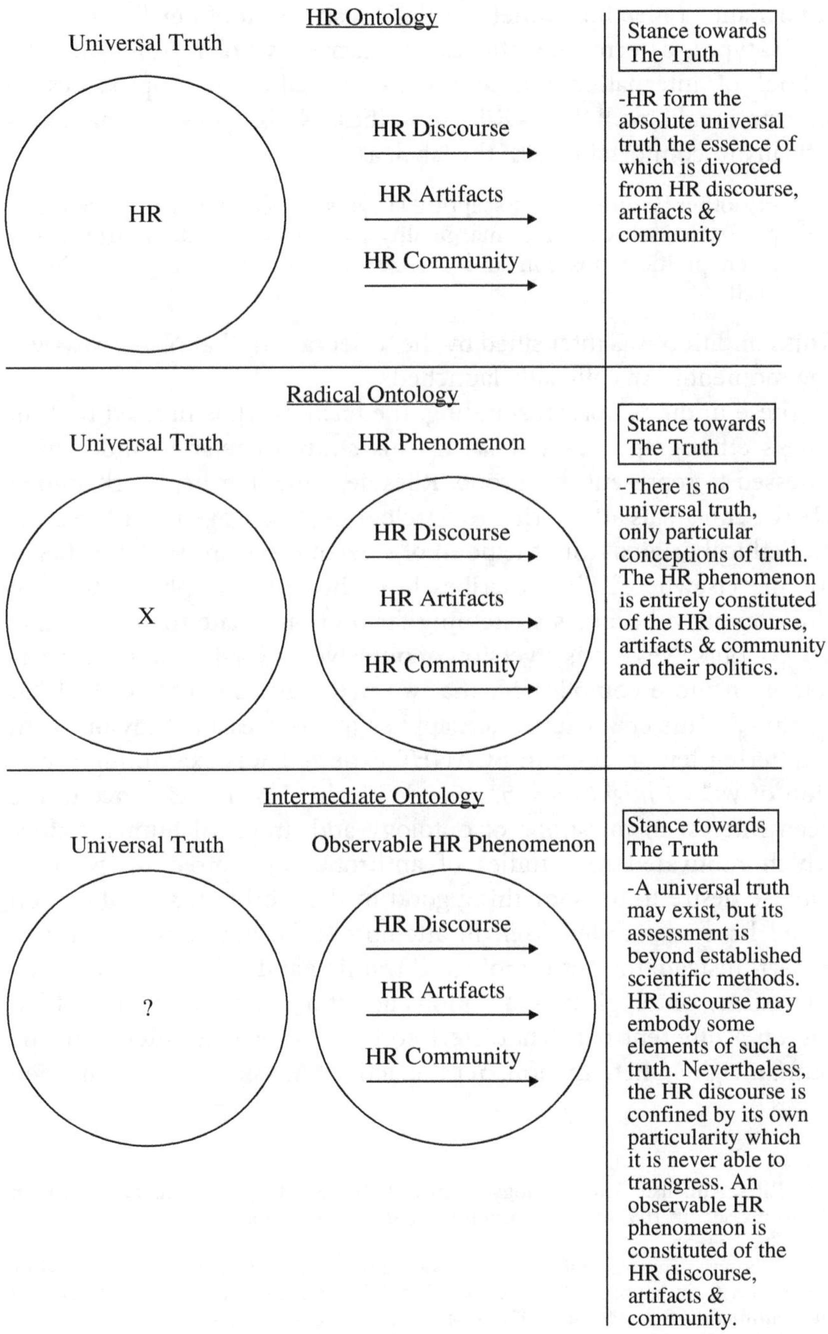

Graph 1: *Human Rights Ontology*

informants, reflecting Annelise Riles's description of her fieldwork of NAIL-types, a term she utilizes to describe scholars following the school of international legal theory termed 'New Approaches to International Law'.[54] Yet, as Riles describes, 'NAIL-types' are characteristically uncomfortable with the label, as

> [a]nother feature of these sceptical lawyers' subjectivity is a [...] carefully performed self-conscious marginality at arm's length distance from every given political position and associated group, including even NAIL itself.[55]

This condition was intensified by the "celebration" that NAIL was over the moment it was officially launched.[56]

These findings notwithstanding, the term NAIL is utilized both in Riles's ethnography as well as in this study to refer to individuals assessed to represent this group. Riles describes her fieldwork among NAIL scholars as attempting to "circle back, to engage my intellectual and ethical origins from the point of view of problems that now begin for me elsewhere". She describes how the "ethnographic subject in this condition becomes something far more intimate than an analog [...] of ourselves – it is a version of ourselves, a version, to make matters even more complicated, that we may have thought we had left behind".[57] This characterization applies to the present study but with a differing temporality: in SCANET experts I was examining a version of what *I might have become*. With this I make reference to the keen interest in questions of ontology and universal human nature which motivated my studies of anthropology. Paired up with an intense desire to do something good in the world, this combination could have manifested itself in attempts to become a human rights expert. Instead, my anthropological training and experiences in India altered my ontological assumptions about a universal truth, and led me on a different path characterized by an analytical interest in the human rights phenomenon. Yet the activist has not entirely vanished

[54] Riles, Annelise: 'Anthropology, Human Rights, and Legal Knowledge: Culture in the Iron Cage.' In *108 American Anthropologist 1*, 2006, 52–65.
[55] *Ibid.*, 54–55.
[56] Skouteris, Thomas: 'Fin de NAIL: New Approaches to International Law and Its Impact on Contemporary International Legal Scholarship.' In *10 Leiden Journal of International Law 3*, 1997, 415–420; Riles, *ibid.*
[57] Riles, *ibid.*, 54.

as the present venture echoes desires to 'do good' as is elaborated in its Conclusion.

Human Rights and Anthropology as Cultural Critique

One decisive factor affecting this study is collaboration with NAIL scholars which commenced already prior to my association with SCANET. Despite the differences in the ontologies of prominent NAIL scholars and this study – illustrated by Graph 1 – the sophistication with which they analyze international law, discussed also by Annelise Riles, provided inspiration as well as theoretical articulation for hypotheses I attempted to depict through empirical data. NAIL scholarship provided insight on how to approach the concept of rights ethnographically: instead of entities defined by their universal essence, to treat them as open-ended, indeterminate legal fictions that become material facts only as they are defined and applied through social processes. As this process is always political, the human rights phenomenon becomes a part of the struggles it attempts to redress.[58] NAIL scholars have demonstrated how the universal liberal project of human rights law ends up reproducing colonial discourses, cultural essentialism, and victim rhetoric.[59] They have criticized how protection of human rights problematizes international interventions

[58] Koskenniemi, Martti: From Apology to Utopia: The Structure of International Legal Argument. Lakimiesliiton Kustannus, Helsinki, 1989; Kennedy: Critique of Adjudication, *supra* note 25; Kennedy, Duncan: 'The Critique of Rights.' In *Left Legalism / Left Critique* (Eds. Brown, Wendy & Halley, Janet). Duke University Press, Durham & London, 2002, 178–228; Tushnet, Mark: 'An Essay on Rights.' In *62 Texas Law Review 8*, 1984, 1363–1403; Boyle, James: 'Ideals and Things: International Legal Scholarship and the Prison-House Language.' In *26 Harvard International Law Journal*, 1985, 327–359; Onuf, Nicholas: 'Do Rules Say What They Do? From Ordinary Language to International Law.' *26 Harvard International Law Journal 2*, 1985, 385–410; Alston, Philip: 'Making Space for New Human Rights: The Case of the Right to Development.' In *1 Harvard Human Rights Yearbook 3*, 1988, 3–40. These insights are founded on an extensive tradition of critique commenced by the famous statement of Bentham from his inquiry of the Declaration of Rights during the French Revolution, see Waldron, Jeremy (Ed.): 'Nonsense upon Stilts': Bentham, Burke and Marx on the Rights of Man. Oxford University Press, Oxford, 1987, 46–76. Another renown account is that of Karl Marx in the 'Jewish question.' See Waldron, 137–150.

[59] Anghie, Antony: Imperialism, Sovereignty and the Making of International Law. Cambridge University Press, Cambridge, 2005; Kapur, Ratna: Erotic Justice: Law and the New Politics of Postcolonialism. Glasshouse Press, London, 2005; Mutua: Human Rights, *supra* note 23.

and peace-keeping missions, overshadowing other mandates such as community-building,[60] as well as demonstrated how such concepts as 'universalism' end up forwarding particular interests.[61]

A venture focusing on the social processes accompanying the making of rights claims resonates with the approach of science studies investigating, instead of the outcomes, the processes through which scientific facts are discovered.[62] Such an approach also concurs with Mark Goodale's suggestion that novel anthropological engagement could stem, not from focus on the 'correctness' or truthfulness of universalistic human rights claims, but from the examination of the 'how' of human rights practices.[63] Studies of this description are increasing, but continually form a minority within the anthropological study of human rights. Although the relationship of human rights and anthropology has been amply recounted, an overview of its long and conflictual past, going back to the famous or infamous 1947 statement by the American Anthropological Association on the problems of the planned UDHR is useful.[64] This "engagement" by the – primarily American – anthropological community was followed by decades of

---

[60] Klabbers, Jan: 'Redemption Song? Human Rights Versus Community-building in East Timor.' In *16 Leiden Journal of International Law 2*, 2003, 367–376.

[61] Leino-Sandberg, Päivi: Particularity as Universality: The Politics of Human Rights in the European Union. The Erik Castrén Institute Research Reports 15, Helsinki, 2005.

[62] See Latour, Bruno: Science in Action. Harvard University Press, Cambridge, 1987; Latour: 'Scientific Objects and Legal Objectivity,' *supra* note 42, 88–93. Latour emphasizes how the false conception that the attempt of science studies is to 'relativize' scientific discoveries has led to enormous misunderstandings. He stresses that the goal of science studies has never been to present all truths as equally valid – an approach that Marianne Valverde has described as rendering it as more conservative than the Foucaultian post-modernism, in which the term 'science' can be utilized in the plural form to emphasize the particularity of Western science. See Latour, 88–98; Valverde, Mariane: Law's Dream of a Common Knowledge. Princeton University Press, Princeton, 2003, 5–9. Simultaneously some scholars have demonstrated how some scientific facts have been artificially constructed, 'made up' instead of being scientifically 'discovered', see Geison, Gerald L.: The Private Science of Louis Pasteur. Princeton University Press, Princeton, 1995.

[63] Goodale, Mark: 'Ethical Theory as Social Practice.' In *108 American Anthropologist 1*, 2006, 25–37.

[64] American Anthropological Association: 'Statement on Human Rights.' In *49 American Anthropologist 4*, 1947, 539–543; Steward, Julian H.: 'Comments on the Statement on Human Rights.' In *50 American Anthropologist 2*, 1948, 351–352; Washburn, Wilcomb E.: 'Cultural Relativism, Human Rights, and the AAA.' In *89 American Anthropologist 4*, 1987, 939–943; Goodale, Mark: 'Introduction to Anthropology and Human Rights in a New Key.' In *108 American Anthropologist 1*, 2006, 1–8.

"disengagement" with human rights issues which began to translate into "reengagement" only during the 1990s.[65] In this development the pieces by Terence Turner[66] and Ellen Messer[67] are commonly viewed as seminal, as well as the edited work by Richard Wilson from 1997.[68] In the new millennium these have been followed for example by the volumes edited by Jane Cowan, Marie-Bénédicte Dembour and Richard Wilson;[69] Bartholomew Dean and Jerome Levi;[70] Charles Zerner,[71] and Mark Goodale and Sally Engle Merry.[72] Since the 1990s human rights have become a focal topic with continually proliferating contributions, and the discipline's changed attitude was in 2001 characterized by Karen Engle as a transformation from "scepticism to embrace".[73]

The most enduring problematic between human rights and anthropology has been the 'universalism-relativism' debate.[74] To many human

[65] Goodale, *ibid.*

[66] Turner, Terence: 'Anthropology and Multiculturalism: What Is Anthropology That Multiculturalists Should Be Mindful of It?' In *8 Current Anthropology 4*, 1993, 411–429; Terence Turner: 'Human Rights, Human Difference: Anthropology's Contribution to an Emancipatory Cultural Politics.' In *52 Journal of Anthropological Research 3*, 1997, 273–291; Nagengast, Carole & Turner, Terence: 'Introduction: Universal Human Rights versus Cultural Relativism.' In *53 Journal of Anthropological Research 3*, 1997, 269–273.

[67] Messer, Ellen: 'Anthropology and Human Rights.' In *22 Annual Review of Anthropology*, 1993, 221-249; Messer, Ellen: 'Pluralist Approaches to Human Rights.' In *53 Journal of Anthropological Research 3*, 1997, 293–317.

[68] Wilson, Richard (Ed.): Human Rights, Culture and Context: Anthropological Perspectives. Pluto Press, London, 1997.

[69] Cowan et al.: 'Introduction,' *supra* note 44, 1–26.

[70] Bartholomew, Dean & Levi, Jerome M. (Eds.): At the Risk of Being Heard: Identity, Indigenous Rights, and Postcolonial States. The University of Michigan Press, Ann Arbor, 2003.

[71] Zerner, Charles (Ed.): Culture and the Question of Rights. Duke University Press, Durham, 2003.

[72] Goodale, Mark & Merry, Sally Engle (Eds.): The Practice of Human Rights: Tracking Law Between the Global and the Local. Cambridge University Press, Cambridge, 2007.

[73] Engle, Karen: 'From Skepticism to Embrace: Human Rights and the American Anthropological Association from 1947–1999.' In *23 Human Rights Quarterly 3*, 2001, 536–559. As an example, see the changed attitude of the American Anthropological Association. In 1995 the Association founded a Human Rights Committee aiming to "stimulate informed involvement in the human rights among professional anthropologists through publications, panels and network building", as well as to "gather information on selected, anthropologically relevant, cases of human rights abuse and to propose action in the name of the AAA." In 1999 the Association also issued a new statement on Human Rights. See AAA: Declaration on Anthropology and Human Rights, http://www.aaanet.org/committees/cfhr/index.htm (2.12.2003).

[74] Renteln, Alison Dundes: International Human Rights: Universalism Versus Relativism. Sage Publications, Newbury Park, Delhi and London, 1990.

rights scholars the debate signifies that anthropologists are 'against' human rights, and consequently anthropological insights have been effectively marginalised. Perhaps as a reaction many anthropologists have abandoned relativist caution, and in efforts to preserve 'their' native peoples began utilizing the human rights discourse as if entailing a predefined and essential significance. This approach can be described as 'rights to culture'.[75] Yet it has been criticized for essentializing culture and introducing it as "discrete, clearly bounded and internally homogenous, with relatively fixed meanings and values".[76] Another approach focussing on the relationship of rights and culture, less prevalent in anthropological scholarship but common in 'mainstream' writings on human rights, is one that sees culture as depriving individuals of their rights. The problem of this approach is that it politicises the notion of tradition[77] as well as ignores other influential factors such as poverty.[78]

To continue with the rhetoric of rights and culture – even though for example to Jane Cowan scholarship is past it[79] – the third prospective approach, for example called for by Mark Goodale, focuses on how human rights practices and transnational expert communities create 'cultures' of their own through distinct knowledge practices, ontologies and membership criteria. This approach generates exciting scholarship, including the works by Michael Herzfeld;[80] Yves Dezalay and

[75] Samson, Colin: 'Rights as the reward for simulated cultural sameness: the Innu in the Canadian colonial context.' In *Culture and Rights, supra* note 44, 226–248; Fried, Gorson: 'Writing for Their Lives: Bentian Dayak Authors and Indonesian Development Discourse.' In *Culture and the Question of Rights, supra* note 71, 142–183; McIntosh, Ian S.: 'Reconciling Personal and Impersonal Worlds: Aboriginal Struggles for Self-Determination.' In *At the Risk of Being Heard, supra* note 70, 293–323.

[76] Cowan et al.: 'Introduction,' *supra* note 44, 3; Sieder, Rachel & Witchell, Jessica: 'Advancing indigenous claims through the law: reflections on the Guatemalan peace process.' In *Culture and Rights, supra* note 44, 201–225; Bartholomew & Levi: At the Risk of Being Heard, *supra* note 70.

[77] Stephen, Lynn: 'Indigenous Autonomy in Mexico.' In *At the Risk of Being Heard, supra* note 70, 191–216.

[78] Montgomery, Heather: 'Imposing rights? A case study of child prostitution in Thailand.' In *Culture and Rights, supra* note 44, 80–101.

[79] Cowan, Jane: 'Culture and Rights after Culture and Rights.' In *108 American Anthropologist 1*, 2006, 9–24.

[80] Herzfeld, Michael: The Social Production of Indifference: Exploring the Symbolic Roots of Western Bureaucracy. The University of Chicago Press, Chicago, 1992.

Bryant Garth;[81] Kim Fortun;[82] Annelise Riles,[83] AnnJannette Rosga;[84] Peter Redfield;[85] Sally Engle Merry;[86] as well as Aihwa Ong and Stephen Collier.[87] Yet by vast majority anthropologists continually explore human rights practices in isolated and distant 'local' contexts, leading Richard Wilson to wish that more anthropologists would venture out "into the sites of production of international human rights laws and norms".[88] This study addresses Wilson's wish by focusing on a site where human rights knowledge is both produced as well as disseminated by influential Northern human rights experts to a future generation of prospective experts. In addition, this study hopes to contribute to numerous ongoing debates including the ethnographic and sociological study of law; particularly the emerging tradition of Finnish empirical socio-legal analysis, which is seen to lack.[89] A contribution is also made to scholarship on human rights education, which has so far been accompanied by little empiria on how human rights education realizes hopes of emancipation.[90] This study wishes to continue earlier collaboration with NAIL scholars particularly by pairing theoretical

---

[81] Dezalay, Yves & Garth, Bryant G.: Dealing in Virtue: International Commercial Arbitration and the Construction of a Transnational Legal Order. The University of Chicago Press, Chicago, 1996.

[82] Fortun, Kim: Advocacy after Bhopal: Environmentalism, Disaster, New Global Orders. The University of Chicago Press, Chicago, 2001.

[83] Riles: 'Anthropology, Human Rights, and Legal Knowledge,' *supra* note 54; Riles, Annelise: Documents: Artifacts of Modern Knowledge. The University of Michigan Press, Ann Arbor, 2006; Riles: Network Inside Out, *supra* note 37; Riles, Annelise: 'Encountering Amateurism: John Henry Wigmore and the Uses of American Formalism.' In *Rethinking the Masters of Comparative Law* (Ed. Riles, Annelise). Hart Publishing, Oxford, 2001.

[84] Rosga, AnnJanette: 'The Traffic in Children: The Funding of Translation and the Translation of Funding.' In *28 Political and Legal Anthropology Review 2*, 2005, 258–281.

[85] Redfield, Peter: 'Doctors, Borders, and Life in Crisis.' In *20 Cultural Anthropology 2*, 2005, 328–361.

[86] Merry: Human Rights & Gender Violence, *supra* note 30.

[87] Ong, Aihwa & Collier, Stephen J. (Eds): Global Assemblages: Technology, Politics, and Ethics as Anthropological Problems. Blackwell Publishing, Oxford, 2005.

[88] Wilson, Richard: 'Tyrannosaurus Lex: The Anthropology of Human Rights and Transnational Law.' In *The Practice of Human Rights, supra* note 72, 342–369, 366.

[89] Haavisto, Vuola: Court Work in Transition: An Activity-Theoretical Study of Changing Work Practices in a Finnish District Court. Yliopistopaino, Helsinki, 2002; Ervasti, Kaius: Tuomioistuimet ja oikeuslaitos tutkimuksen kohteena: lähestymistavan valinta, www.comi.fi/tiedostot/seminaari_2007_02_26_ervasti.pdf. (5.6.2007).

[90] Andreopoulos, George J. & Claude, Richard Pierre (Eds.): Human Rights Education for the Twenty-First Century. Pennsylvania University Press, Pennsylvania, 1997.

constructions and analysis of legal documents with empirical data on human rights in action. With this combination this study hopes to contribute to the vast body of human rights scholarship, much of which emphasizes empirical description or legal analysis over theoretical debate.

Faye Ginsburg mentions how the success of her ethnography on the Pro-Life advocates was determined by approaches and methods that allowed her to remain unbiased and to represent the integrity of both positions of the abortion debate as, she states, "[i]t is not my place or task in this book to take a partisan position".[91] Such an approach resonates with the 'traditional' understanding of anthropology as offering unbiased description of different contexts without active engagement; an approach also seen as difficult if not impossible to realize. Even more importantly, such an approach fails to transform anthropology into cultural critique, as has been famously phrased by Marcus and Fischer.[92] This study has sought to provide transparent and systematic description of discussed issues, but it also aims for a more engaged position: to demonstrate through ethnographic data how human rights in action contradict the abstract human rights discourse, and thus to criticize notions which insist on separating the two levels – abstraction and action – from each other.

If a venture is to succeed in contributing to such diverse debates, it needs to be accessible to highly differing audiences. Accessibility forms a paramount challenge for the numerous recent sophisticated ethnographies, as many of them remain open only to selected highly specialized scholars. Thomas Hyllend Eriksen characterizes failure to communicate to contribute to the intellectual exclusion of anthropologists in particular, hijacking them from a "pivotal societal role as political analysts".[93] To avoid this outcome, he advocates that more

[91] Ginsburg: Contested Lives, *supra* note 53. Incidentally she ended up so successful that her anthropological audience construed her to have forsaken her own political beliefs and 'gone native'. It was even suggested that her data – transcripts of life story interviews – simply were not true. Ginsburg calls this 'the case of mistaken identity'. See Ginsburg, Faye: 'The Case of Mistaken Identity: Problems in Representing Women on the Rights.' In *When They Read What We Write: The Politics of Ethnography* (Ed. Brettell, Caroline, B.). Bergin & Garvey, Connecticut, 1993, 163–176.

[92] Marcus, George E. & Fischer, Michael M.: Anthropology as Cultural Critique: An Experimental Moment in the Human Sciences. Second Edition. University of Chicago Press, Chicago, 1999.

[93] Eriksen, Thomas Hyllend: 'Between universalism and relativism: a critique of the UNESCO concept of culture.' In *Culture and Rights, supra* note 44, 127–148, 145.

anthropologists 'translate' their data to wider audiences. This study takes these concerns seriously, which is reflected primarily in its reliance on numerous graphs and tables. This produces a relatively formalistic description of SCANET activities. Particularly the use of quantified data requires elaboration, as it, although no stranger to ethnographic description, is often criticized today. For the present venture quantified data has been utilized for two primary reasons. In primary phases of research, statistics offered the required analytic distance between myself and my informants who, although distinguished by their ontological assumptions, by objective standards bore close similarity to myself. The inclusion of tables in the finalized version stems from another reason, namely the high knowledge status assigned to quantified data by the numerous groups with which this study wishes to correspond. When earlier versions of this study were read by scholars of various disciplines, practically all made some comment on the tables – many complimenting their inclusion and hoping to see more of them. Iris Jean-Klein and Annelise Riles have reminded that, in collaboration with other disciplines and wider audiences, anthropologists should not surrender their own ground for other disciplines and interest groups who are often more powerful.[94] Quantified data enjoys an undisputedly high status in the discussions this study wishes to address, and thus it has been utilized to support non-quantified analysis.

Finding Approaches

This study has two levels. The general level explores the human rights phenomenon particularly in the Finnish context, and the specific level focuses on SCANET educational activities. SCANET educational activities are examined from two perspectives: through participant observation and the analysis of documents distributed by SCANET. Analyzed documents include background papers provided by expert, papers produced by students for SCANET activities, statements of purpose by SCANET and its funder, and membership profiles. Jointly these amounted to thousands of pages as will be elaborated in Chapter 4. Participant observation was conducted in six educational activities which lasted from three to seven days and were organized between early 2002 and summer 2005. In terms of fieldwork this project has numerous noteworthy elements. First, due to SCANET activities'

[94] Jean-Klein & Riles: 'Introducing Discipline,' *supra* note 27.

periodic nature, fieldwork was carried out in short and intensive periods, and followed by lengthy gaps during which the only continued signs of SCANET's existence were occasional e-mails sent by its coordinator. This condition challenges comprehensive ethnographic description, but it also entails possibilities: field-data can be analyzed in between events, and analysis accompanied by continued reading. Thus these repeated instances of 'going into' and 'coming back' from the field clarified my research hypothesis and offered later fieldwork periods greater focus.

The second noteworthy element became that each analyzed activity occurred in a different location. This introduced the possibility to consider fieldwork either as *deterritorialized*, as has been done by Sally Engle Merry in her study of how women's human rights were adopted and articulated in different global localities,[95] or as *multi-sited*, as has been described by George Marcus.[96] Both formulations are suited to describe the human right expert community of practice, yet they simultaneously misdirect attention by strengthening the gap often construed to exist between such 'global' phenomena as that of human rights and different 'local' phenomena. Instead of adopting terminology that emphasizes difference, this study prefers to highlight the continuity that these 'global' activities introduce through shared ideologies and knowledge practices. Even as localities change, the overarching notions – in SCANET ontological assumptions on the nature of human rights, conceptions of knowledge, learning and expertise – remain unchanged, and thus conjoin to form one large entity suitable for study. From this perspective 'global' phenomena resemble different 'local' phenomena.

Material from SCANET was complemented by some participant observation in various human rights seminars and hearings particularly at the Finnish Foreign Ministry, as well as UN treaty body proceedings. Primary additional data was formed by the numerous documents produced and circulated by different human rights domains. These include material both from the UN and the Finnish policy makers including, among others, Finland's 2004 Human Rights Report. To investigate the role of the human rights discourse in the Finnish political discourse, I examined how the discourse was utilized

[95] Merry: Human Rights & Gender Violence, *supra* note 30.
[96] Marcus, George E.: 'Ethnography In/Of The World System: The Emergence of Multi-Sited Ethnography.' In *24 Annual Review of Anthropology*, 1995, 95–117.

by Finland's Foreign Minister in his speeches between 1999 and 2006. To understand how an issue becomes translated into a human rights issue I explored the rhetoric strategies utilized in efforts to articulate the concerns of sexual minorities as human rights issues particularly in the debates accompanying the drafting of the 2004 report. In addition I recorded instances, primarily between 2004 to 2006, where human rights were talked of in the Finnish media. I also explored online English-language chatrooms to analyze how the human rights discourse was utilized; how it was circulated, by whom, and in what kind of quantities.

These contemporary developments were contextualized by an analysis of the early phases of the human rights phenomenon. I examined how the American civil liberties movement had developed between 1900 and 1945, and examined events between 1940 and 1945 that eventually led to the drafting of the UDHR. In order to understand how the human rights phenomenon had expanded in the decades following the adoption of the UDHR, I inspected the founding years of different human rights NGOs, institutes, journals, as well as investigated when principal human rights instruments had been created. To understand Finland's role in the global human rights phenomenon, as well as to comprehend the role of the human rights discourse in Finland, I overviewed Finnish historical events as well as political developments. This investigation sketches the context that has given rise to SCANET, and outlines the temporality with which the human rights phenomenon has expanded. It also illustrated mechanisms of expansion as well as explained the current ideological position of human rights in Finland. These issues are so numerous and vast that no single venture can address all of them in depth. This study makes no claims that all of the discussed issues are offered exhaustive treatment. Instead it highlights general patterns and indicates avenues in need of further research. Simultaneously, such a broad approach has been vital for an understanding of SCANET activities: as the human rights phenomenon is multifaceted and complex, in order to address any specific area in it, a researcher must hold broad awareness of the abundant elements that are related to each other.

Division of Chapters

The book is divided into five chapters. Chapter 2 examines through the concepts of *centre* and *periphery* how the human rights phenomenon has expanded in the Finnish society. It explores how, through the political turmoil of past decades, the human rights discourse has acquired a central position in the Finnish society, and it further discusses how this development reflects Finland's position in international collaboration. Chapter 2 continues by discussing the expansion of the human rights discourse, and concludes by outlining expansionary strategies in the case of 'LGBT- rights'. Chapter 3 discusses how expansion of the human rights discourse has transformed the concept of human rights into 'free-floating' signifiers, and continues by examining – through the introduction of SCANET, the Scandinavian Network of Human Rights Expert – how this development has given rise to the experts' influential systemic agency, as well as assigned the human right experts' community of practice a favourable societal position in contemporary Finland. Through exploration of SCANET membership criteria, the chapter offers a profile of expertise, as well as explores the temporality with which the human rights expert community has emerged. The chapter concludes by investigating SCANET as a part of the global elite of transnational activist networks. Chapter 4 focuses on SCANET educational activities, which are contextualized with exploration of the recent global proliferation of human rights educational programs as well as the UN Decade of Human Rights Education of 1995-2004. Primary in this chapter become the patterns of flow that SCANET activities institute as well as the conceptions of knowledge, learning and expertise they embody. This inquiry departs from the notion that human rights education should be emancipatory in its outcomes, and observes how this ideal is reflected in SCANET activities. Simultaneously the chapter explores whether a formal educational context such as SCANET offers a successful medium for reproducing the human rights expert community of practice by investigating central expert knowledge practices. This analysis relies primarily on the proceedings accompanying the submission of China's first state report to the Committee on Economic, Social and Cultural Rights.

Chapter 5 moves focus to the complex relationship of human rights and law through the controversial project of legalization. It explores the 'passionate engagement' and controversy over expertise that this project awakens between SCANET and NAIL scholars, and examines how the relationship of human rights and law is embodied in SCANET activities. The chapter concludes by focussing on the *creative space* of human rights experts. This refers to a domain that emerges when, instead of being considered as 'ready', human rights knowledge is construed by SCANET experts as incomplete and in need of being 'opened up'. This inquiry explores what sources of knowledge are relied on in such instances, as well as what kind of consequences the creative space induces. Chapter 6 investigates the geographic origin and gender of both SCANET experts and students, and connects them to global and local structures of inequality and oppression. The book concludes by discussing whether, based on its analysis of SCANET, human rights in action realize the promises of the abstract discourse by altering oppressive structures.

CHAPTER TWO

EMERGENCE OF THE HUMAN RIGHTS PHENOMENON IN FINLAND

> *Gone With the Wind*
> *...I sail because I love sailing, not because I love the sea. This is because it is possible to love the sea also from dry land. Actually those staying ashore treat the ocean better than those sailing in the waters, as they pollute it less. When I discovered how common it is among boaters to empty their septic tanks into the ocean, I got furious ... Nowadays it is more common to wonder why a small boat cannot empty its waste into the ocean, as many cargo and passenger ships do so too. Good question, but one has to start from somewhere. And this is not a question of rights, but of obligations. It is not a human right to pollute the ocean.*
>
> *Bettina Sågbom*[1]

The above excerpt originates from the monthly column of a celebrated journalist in one of Finland's foremost women's magazines. The passage is noteworthy due to its ingenious use of the human rights discourse as something suitable to decide whether boaters are allowed to dirty the already damaged Baltic Sea. However, for present purposes even more important is that the discourse is used in the first place. This illustrates the societal and ideological position that human rights enjoy in today's Finland: they form a popularised discourse utilised by a wide spectrum of actors to address everyday matters. The present chapter examines how the human rights phenomenon has evolved both in Finland and internationally since the UDHR was adopted. By connecting this analysis to post-World War II era political developments, this chapter observes how the human rights discourse has moved from the *periphery* of the Finnish society to its *centre*. Simultaneously Finland has transformed from a peripheral into a central actor in the global human rights phenomenon. Finnish scholars, practitioners and civil society participants concur that existing textual sources fail to provide a comprehensive account of the discussed events. Thus this chapter

[1] MeNaiset, 6.7.2006, 77; original in Finnish, translation by author.

relies, in addition to textual sources, on interviews, correspondence and numerous discussions.[2]

The concepts *centre* and *periphery* are familiar from the world-systems analysis of Emmanuel Wallerstein, who has utilized them to describe structural positions in a world economy.[3] Ulf Hannerz has expanded the concepts to the flow of meanings,[4] which is also the principal significance in which they are utilized here. The concepts are treated further as entailing cultural attributes by borrowing from Sally Engle Merry's analysis of the human rights regime. Merry characterizes transnational consensus building as something that occurs in a social space – a *centre* – where actors from all parts of the world come together.[5] This space has its own norms, values and cultural practices; it is an English-speaking, largely secular, universalistic, law-governed culture organized around the formal equality of nations as well as their economic and political inequality.[6] The term *periphery* refers to the opposite: non-English speaking, religion-oriented local cultures which are characterized by traditional customs and social structures. Following both the analysis of Merry and Hannerz, the *centre* of the human rights phenomenon is construed as being 'de-territorialized'.[7] Consequently, in addition to emerging in such concrete locations as UN offices in Geneva and New York, *centre*s may emerge in any place that becomes the site of transnational human rights activity. Particularly during the first decades of the post-World War II era the processes directing Finland's policy making resembled a *periphery*: for example the Lutheran church inserted significance over many areas of public policy making. By contrast during the past decades policy making has increasingly, particularly in international issues, acquired cultural characteristics of the *centre*: it occurs primarily in English in close collaboration with the de-territorialized transnational social space of international consensus-building.

[2] Many thanks to Juhani Kortteinen, Martin Scheinin, Tuomas Ojanen, Klaus Törnudd, Mikael Hidén, Matti Pellonpää, Holger Rotkirch and Kristiina Kouros. For an introduction into the historical origins of human rights in Finland, see Törnudd, Klaus: Finland and the International Norms of Human Rights. Martinus Nijhoff Publishers, Dordrecht, 1986, 13–18.

[3] Wallerstein, Immanuel: The Essential Wallerstein. The New Press, New York, 2000.

[4] Hannerz, Ulf: Cultural Complexity: Studies in the Social Organization of Meaning. Columbia University Press, New York, 1992.

[5] Merry, Sally Engle: Human Rights & Gender Violence: Translating International Law into Local Justice. The University of Chicago Press, Chicago, 2006, 37.

[6] *Ibid.*

[7] *Ibid.*

The Discourse and the Dawning Human Rights Phenomenon

Commentators have characterized that "the rise and rise of human rights"[8] since the adoption of the UDHR has led to "the age of rights".[9] This chapter investigates how this development is reflected in the Finnish context by examining three elements of the human rights phenomenon: the human rights discourse, the community and artifacts (Graph 2). This study considers the contemporary human rights phenomenon to have commenced with the adoption of the UDHR in 1948. The human rights discourse is viewed to originate from the Age of Enlightenment and the natural rights theory articulated by such 17th and 18th century figures as John Locke and Immanuel Kant.[10] The natural rights theory is further seen as having transformed into a distinct and societally prestigious discourse primarily in the late 19th and early 20th century. This development is construed as having created a

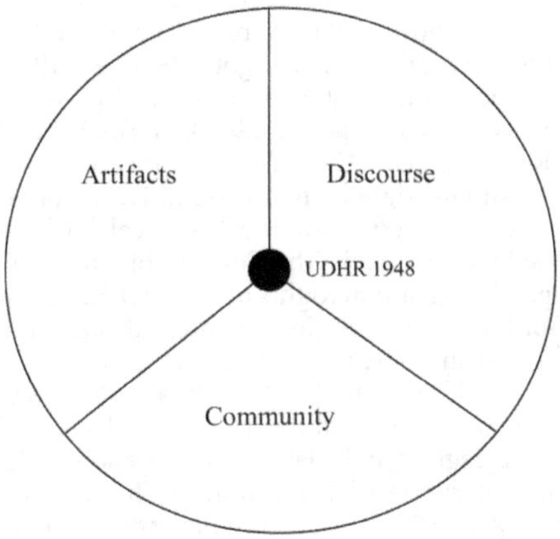

Graph 2: *Human Rights Phenomenon*

---

[8] Sellars, Kirsten: The Rise and Rise of Human Rights. Sutton Publishing, Phoenix Mills, 2002.

[9] Henkin, Louis: The Age of Rights. Columbia University Press, New York, 1990.

[10] See for example Locke, John: Two Treatises of Government. Awnsham and John Churchill, Black Swan [1689]. Reproduced at http://www.lonang.com/exlibris/locke/loc-001a.htm (12.1.2007); Kant, Immanuel: 'The Idea of a Universal History with a Cosmopolitan Purpose.' In *Kant, Immanuel: Political Writings* (Ed. Reiss, Hans). Second enlarged edition. Cambridge University Press, Cambridge, 41–53, 1991 [1784]. For an introduction to natural rights theories, see Tuck, Richard: Natural Rights Theories: Their Origin and Development. Cambridge University Press, Cambridge, 1979.

budding human rights community, many members of whom advocated in the 1940s for the adoption of the UDHR.[11]

Scholars differ greatly in their treatment of events leading up to the adoption of the UDHR. Most common narratives emphasize revulsion provoked by the Holocaust,[12] and associate the emergence of the human rights discourse with the founding conference of the United Nations in San Francisco in spring 1945.[13] Such narratives often emphasize the contributions of key individuals including Eleanor Roosevelt, René Cassin and John Humphrey.[14] However, many researchers view these narratives as problematic. Mark Mazover notes

---

[11] For an introduction of the human rights phenomenon, see among others Macfarlane, L. J.: The Theory and Practice of Human Rights. Maurice Temple Smith, London, 1985; Helminen, Marjut & Lång, K. J. (Eds.): Kansainväliset ihmisoikeudet. Lakimiesliiton kustannus, Helsinki, 1987; Steiner, Henry J. & Alston, Philip: International Human Rights in Context: Law, Politics, Morals. Second Edition. Oxford University Press, Oxford, 2000; Ignatieff, Michael: Human Rights as Politics and Idolatry. Princeton University Press, Princeton, 2001; Freeman, Michael: Human Rights: An interdisciplinary approach. Polity Press, Cambridge, 2002; Nowak, Manfred: Introduction to the International Human Rights Regime. Brill Academic Publisher, Leiden, 2003; Donnelly, Jack: Universal Human Rights in Theory & Practice. Second Edition. Cornell University Press, *supra* Ithaca, 2003; Marks, Susan & Clapham, Andrew: International Human Rights Lexicon. Oxford University Press, Oxford, 2005; Mahoney, Jack: The Challenge of Human Rights: Their Origin, Development, and Significance. Blackwell Publishing, Malden, 2007. For the historical background of the human rights phenomenon, see Donnelly, Jack: The Concept of Human Rights. Croom Helm, London, 1985; Galtung, Johan: Human Rights in Another Key. Polity Press, Cambridge, 1994; Lauren, Paul Gordon: The Evolution of International Human Rights: Visions Seen. University of Pennsylvania Press, Philadelphia, 1998; Arat, Zehra F. Kabasakal: 'Forging A Global Culture of Human Rights: Origins and Prospects of the International Bill of Rights.' In *28 Human Rights Quarterly 2*, 2006, 16–437. For an introduction outlining the human rights regime in the late 1990s, see Hanski, Raija & Suksi, Markku: An Introduction to the International Protection of Human Rights. Second edition. Åbo Akademi University, Åbo, 1997; Isa, Felipe Gómez & Feyter, Koen de: International Protection of Human Rights: Achievements and Challenges. University of Deusto, Bilbao, 2006.

[12] Powers, Samantha: A Problem from Hell: American and the Age of Genocide. Harper Perennial, New York, 2003; Freeman: Human Rights, *supra* note 11; Glendon, Mary Ann: 'The Forgotten Crucible: The Latin American Influence on the Universal Human Rights Ideal.' In *16 Harvard Human Rights Journal*, Spring 2003, 27–39.

[13] Alfredsson, Gudmundur & Eide, Asbjorn: 'Introduction.' In *The Universal Declaration of Human Rights: A Common Standard of Achievement* (Eds. Alfredsson, Gudmundur & Eide, Asbjorn). Kluwer Law International, The Hague, 1999, 5–16; Morsink, Johannes: The Universal Declaration of Human Rights: Origins, Drafting & Intent. University of Pennsylvania Press, Philadelphia, 1999; Glendon: 'The Forgotten Crucible', *supra* note 12; Waltz, Susan: 'Universalizing Human Rights: The Role of Small States in the Construction of the Universal Declaration of Human Rights.' In *23 Human Rights Quarterly 1*, 2001, 44–72.

[14] Glendon, Mary Ann: A World Made New: Eleanor Roosevelt and the Universal Declaration of Human Rights. Random House, New York, 2001; Lauren: The Evolution

that Nazi atrocities were far less central to perceptions of the war in 1945 than they are today.[15] The 'visionary individual' narrative overlooks state power and ignores other individuals who propagated the cause earlier, such as the émigré Russian lawyer Andre Mandelstam,[16] H.G. Wells,[17] or Hersch Lauterpacht.[18] It overlooks the numerous coalitions that had formed around the human rights discourse at the turn of the 20th century particularly in Europe, among them the famous Ligue francaise pour la défense des droits de l'homme et du citoyen.[19] Scholars also criticize the general tone of narratives outlining the origins of the human rights phenomenon, which isolates political and legislative developments from their wider context.[20]

This study wishes to highlight one factor often missing from narratives emphasizing European actors behind the UDHR:[21] the

---

of International Human Rights, *supra* note 11; Korey, William: NGOs and the Universal Declaration of Human Rights: 'A Curious Grapevine'. St. Martin's Press, New York, 1998.

[15] Mazover, Mark: 'The Strange Triumph of Human Rights, 1933–1950.' In *47 The Historical Journal 2*, 2004, 379–398, 381. Mazover's discussion provides one reflection of a significant discussion among historians of the interpretation of historic events; see Skinner, Quentin: Visions of Politics. Volume I: Regarding Method. University of Cambridge, Cambridge, 2002; Palonen, Kari: A Struggle with Time: A Conceptual History of "Politics" as an Activity. Lit Verlag, Münster, 2006; see also Tuori, Kaius: Ancient Roman Lawyers and Modern Legal Ideals. University of Helsinki, Helsinki, 2006.

[16] Mandestam's efforts are discussed by Mazover: 'The Strange Triumph of Human Rights', *supra* note 15, 381.

[17] Wells, H. G.: The Rights of Man or What are We Fighting For? Penguin Books, Harmondsworth, 1940.

[18] Lauterpacht, Hersh: An International Bill of the Rights of Man. Columbia University Press, New York, 1945.

[19] The Ligue was founded in France in 1898 and prior to World War I enjoyed a huge membership, between 200 000 and 300 000 people. It promoted the founding of similar organizations elsewhere in Europe, although not in the UK, and the French colonial possessions. National Ligues were founded in Belgium and Greece the same year, and in Germany and Austria some decades later. In 1922, the International Federation of Human Rights Leagues was founded. See Wiseberg, Laurie S. & Scoble, Harry M.: 'The International League for Human Rights: The Strategy of a Human Rights NGO.' In *7 Georgia Journal of International and Comparative Law*, 1977, 292–293. For discussion on other European initiatives, see Simpson, A. W. Brian: Human Rights and the End of Empire: Britain and the Genesis of the European Convention. Oxford University Press, Oxford, 2001; Petman, Jarna: 'Human Rights, Democracy, and the Left.' In *2 Unbound Harvard Journal of the Legal Left*, 2006 Spring, 63–90; L'Institut de Droit International: 'Déclaration des Droits Internationaux de l'Homme.' In *36 Annuaire de l'Institute de Droit International: Session de New York*, 1929, 110–112.

[20] Mazover: 'The Strange Triumph of Human Rights', *supra* note 15, 397.

[21] See for example Petman: 'Human Rights, Democracy, and the Left', *supra* note 19.

importance of American influence. Different American documents are commonly discussed as the most significant predecessors for the UDHR, a matter elaborated in Chapter 3, and American NGOs were decisive in the efforts to include a mention of human rights in the UN Charter, whereas for example the Ligue francaise was effectively destroyed during World War II.[22] Individuals born and educated in North America held key positions in the drafting of the UDHR both through formal channels, namely membership in the drafting committee, and through informal channels, primarily through the 42 American NGOs that enjoyed observer status during the drafting process; no NGOs from other countries enjoyed a similar status.[23] Many prestigious internationalist groups lobbying for the UDHR exerted significant influence in the White House during the Roosevelt administration. These groups still recalled the disappointment over US refusal to join the League of Nations, and viewed strong US involvement in the new world organization as their key goal.[24] Many regarded human rights as a paramount element of the UN charter, and numerous sources suggest that the US delegation only came to favour their inclusion as a

---

[22] The Ligue's members were dispersed and many emigrated to the US where it was reorganized and renamed the International League for the Rights of Man. Korey recognizes the League as one of the only NGOs focussing on human rights during the drafting of the UDHR. It included as members Eleanor Roosevelt and Charles Malik, future chair of the Drafting Committee. See Wiseberg & Scoble: 'The International League for Human Rights,' *supra* note 19, 292–293; Korey: NGOs and the Universal Declaration of Human Rights,' *supra* note 14, 99–100. For an account on the emigration of European intellectuals during World War II, see Krohn, Claus-Dieter: Intellectuals in Exile: Refugee Scholars and the New School for Social Research. The University of Massachusetts Press, Massachusetts, 1993.

[23] Korey: NGOs and the Universal Declaration of Human Rights, *supra* note 14, 29; 35–39. Annelise Riles discusses how this is still characteristic due to "the leadership of U.S. trained lawyers (of various nationalities) in the building of key institutions of the postwar international legal regime". Riles, Annelise: 'Anthropology, Human Rights, and Legal Knowledge: Culture in the Iron Cage.' In *108 American Anthropologist 1*, 2006, 52–65, 59.

[24] Johnstone, Andrew E.: Clark Eichelberger, Internationalism and the State, 1941–1948. Ph.D., University of Birmingham, Birmingham, 2006, 133–164; Josephson, Harold: James Shotwell and the Rise of Internationalism in America. Feirleigh Dickinson University Press, Rutherford, 1975; Cooper, John Milton Jr.: Breaking the Heart of the World: Woodrow Wilson and the Fight for the League of Nations. Cambridge University Press, Cambridge, 2001; Eichelberger, Clark M.: Organizing for Peace: A Personal History of the Founding of the United Nations. Harper & Row Publishers, New York, 1977, 268–272; Korey: NGOs and the Universal Declaration of Human Rights, *supra* note 14, 29–50; Simpson: Human Rights and the End of Empire, *supra* note 19, 190–202.

consequence of these lobbying efforts. With the Soviet Union and Great Britain opposing references to human rights, US support became pivotal for the success of the evolving UN human rights regime.[25] The efforts of these internationalist groups reflected a more general development where, following decades of activism, the civil liberties movement had gained importance throughout the country including the US Supreme Court, and the American Bill of Rights was celebrated as the defining safeguard of individual liberties.[26] Thus the movement's international adherents wished to secure these same liberties on the international level through an 'International Bill of Rights', as the Declaration was commonly called during drafting.[27]

---

[25] Korey states: "What is especially striking, and generally not known, is that the historic breakthrough never would have taken place without the commitment, determination and pressure of a group of American nongovernmental organizations". Korey: NGOs and the Universal Declaration of Human Rights, *supra* note 14, 29, 35–39. A key moment in the input of American NGOs was May 2, 1945, which marked the deadline of amendments to the Dumbarton Oaks proposals, then entailing no reference to human rights. Interest groups sprung into action, persuading the US delegation to back up the matter, and leading to inclusion of human rights in the UN Charter. See Proskauer, Joseph M.: A Segment of My Times. Farrar, Straus and Company, New York, 1950, 219–227; Eichelberger.: Organizing for Peace, *supra* note 24, 268–272; Commission to Study the Organization of Peace: Petition to 'The Honorable Edward R. Stettinius, Jr.' March 31, 1945; Glendon: A World Made New, *supra* note 14, 17. For a more cautionary version of this origin, see Simpson: Human Rights and the End of Empire, *supra* note 19, 243–244; 251–253.

[26] Walker, Samuel: In Defence of American Liberties: A History of the ACLU. Second Edition. Southern Illinois University Press, Carbondale, 1999; Cottrell, Robert C.: Roger Nash Baldwin and the American Civil Liberties Union. Columbia University Press, New York, 2000; Murphy, Paul L.: World War I and the Origin of Civil Liberties in the United States. W. W. Norton & Company, New York, 1979; US Supreme Court: Members of the Supreme Court of the United States, http://www.supremecourtus.gov/about/members.pdf (23.9.2005). Central here was the 1925 Scopes 'Monkey' trial over the teaching of the Darwinian theory of evolution versus the Biblical story of creationism, a still ongoing controversy. See Scopes Trial: Case Number 5232, the State of Tennessee v. John Thomas Scopes; Larson, Edward J.: Summer for the Gods: The Scopes Trial and America's Continuing Debate over Science and Religion. Harvard University Press, Cambridge, 1997, 35; Marsden, George M.: Fundamentalism and American Culture. Oxford University Press, Oxford, 2006. The American civil liberties movement has a link to the drafting of the UDHR through the persona of Roger Baldwin, who is stated to have single-handedly re-organized the League for the Rights of Man in the US. See Cottrell: Roger Nash Baldwin and the American Civil Liberties Union, 169; Walker: In Defence of American Liberties, 67, 392.

[27] Roosevelt, Eleanor: The Autobiography of Eleanor Roosevelt. Da Capo Press Inc., New York. 1992 [1961], 314. Mary Ann Glendon mentions how as drafting progressed, the drafting committee slowly came to use the term *declaration* more often than *bill*. See Glendon: A World Made New, *supra* note 14, 66.

First Decades

Scholarship commonly portrays the developments following the Declaration's adoption in 1948 to mark a smooth and unchallenged triumph for the human rights phenomenon. Closer examination suggests that the first decades were overshadowed by the Cold War and labelled by uncertainty and slowness. The 1950s and the early 1960s were particularly challenging: drafting efforts for the Covenants on Civil and Political Rights (CCPR) as well as Economic, Social and Cultural Rights (CESCR) faced continual difficulties, and UN offices, including the Human Rights Commission, were charged of 'politicization' which caused inefficiency and coalition building.[28] Numerous powerful American NGOs turned away from UN bodies and began exerting impact on the American and other governments instead.[29] After a brief period of intense engagement the US resorted back to its earlier isolationist policies and increasingly remained outside the UN framework, which intensified American unilateralism. Combined these developments undermined the hopes for the new era of multilateral collaboration that had accompanied the organization's founding. Researchers have also assessed that the UN human rights framework was challenged by the adoption of the European Convention on Human Rights in 1950 as well as the founding of the European Court of Human Rights. The Court provided a supranational forum for individual petitions, which is something that in the UN context was much weaker.[30] This intensified European collaboration – an outcome to which disappointment over the prolonged treaty negotiations at the UN certainly contributed – and some commentators have assessed that this made the future of the UN's human rights regime uncertain.[31] For much of the period between 1945 and the early 1970s human rights remained "a "minority" interest"[32] in the UN. Dag Hammarskjöld, for example,

[28] Franck, Thomas M.: Nation Against Nation: What Happened to the U.N Dream and What the U.S. Can Do About It. Oxford University Press, New York, 1985, 94–116; Glendon: A World Made New, *supra* note 14, 208; Evans, Tony: US Hegemony and the Project of Universal Human Rights. MacMillan Press Ltd, Houndmills, Basingstoke, Hampshire and London, 1996, 86.

[29] Korey: NGOs and the Universal Declaration of Human Rights, *supra* note 14, 139.

[30] Glendon: A World Made New, *supra* note 14, 217.

[31] Simpson: Human Rights and the End of Empire, *supra* note 19, 511–542; Glendon: A World Made New, *supra* note 14, 200–202.

[32] Evans: US Hegemony and the Project of Universal Human Rights, *supra* note 28, 148.

is stated to have given them low priority when he became the organization's Secretary-General in 1953.[33] Global public attention was occupied by security concerns, the Warsaw Pact and its tanks, the energy crisis and nuclear disarmament, and the human rights phenomenon remained at the margins of international collaboration.[34]

In the mid-1960s and 1970s the scales began to tip as the "painfully slow" drafting efforts for the two Covenants started to bear fruit.[35] In 1966 the CCPR as well as CESCR were finally signed. It took yet another decade for the Covenants to enter into force, but in 1976 the 'International Bill of Rights' was finally completed.[36] In terms of ratifications the 1970s became decisive: whereas for example the CESCR was during the 1960s ratified by only 6 states, by the end of the 1970s the number had grown to 61.[37] After this start, other documents soon followed: the Convention on the Elimination of All Forms of Racial Discrimination (CERD) entered into force already in 1969; the Convention on the Elimination of All Forms of Discrimination against Women (CEDAW) in 1981; the Convention against Torture and Other Cruel, Inhuman or Degrading Treatment or Punishment (CAT) in 1987; and the Convention on the Rights of the Child (CRC) in 1990. As is illustrated by Table 1, after the 1970s treaty ratification received its second peak during the 1990s, a matter elaborated later.[38]

---

[33] Glendon: A World Made New, *supra* note 14, 208.

[34] Evans: US Hegemony and the Project of Universal Human Rights, *supra* note 28, 148; Franck: Nation Against Nation, *supra* note 28, 76–93.

[35] Glendon: A World Made New, *supra* note 14, 206.

[36] http://www.unhchr.ch/html/menu3/b/a_cescr.htm (4.4.2006); Working Groups 2006, http://www.unhchr.ch/html/menu2/2/chrwg.htm (27.4.2007); Evans: US Hegemony and the Project of Universal Human Rights, *supra* note 28, 91–95; Sellars: The Rise and Rise of Human Rights, *supra* note 8, 75–81; Craven, Matthew: The International Covenant on Economic, Social, and Cultural Rights: A Perspective on Its Development. Oxford University Press, New York, 1995; Henkin, Louis (Ed.): The Intenational Bill of Rights: The Covenant on Civil and Political Rights. Columbia University Press, New York, 1981.

[37] Office of the United Nations High Commissioner for Human Rights: Status of Ratifications of Principal Human Rights Treaties as of 09 June 2004, http://193.194.138.190/pdf/report.pdf (10.5.2005). In the 1960s the CESCR was ratified by Cyprus, Tunisia, Syria, Colombia, Equador and Costa Rica. Slow momentum can in part be ascribed to the necessity of bringing domestic legislation into conformity with the provisions of the Convention before ratifying it.

[38] Table 1 includes the treaties that are enlisted in the website of the UN Office of the High Commissioner for Human Rights as the 'Principal Human Rights Treaties' see *ibid*. This formulation is utilized later in this chapter to refer to these same documents. The years of Table 1 refer to entrance into force and the table excludes optional protocols. The list includes additionally the Convention on the Rights of Migrant Workers (CMW) ratified in 2003.

Table 1: UN Human Rights Instruments

Decade	Covenants	CESRC rat	Total CESRC rat
1940	UDHR 1948		
1950	(ECHR 1950)		
1960	CERD 1969	6	6
1970	CCPR 1976 CESCR 1976	55	61
1980	CEDAW 1981 CAT 1987	30	91
1990	CRC 1990	50	141
2000	CMW 2003	10	151

From 'Finlandization' to 'EU Model Pupil'

The relationship of Finland and the human rights phenomenon in the past decades remains a source of intense debate. This section introduces the different viewpoints of this discussion, and outlines how this study understands past developments in light of legislative developments, policy making, and the sentiments of the civil society. To summarize, this study sees Finland's attitude until the late 1980s as being marked by a certain internal and external distance due to its former external affairs' policy of *neutrality* as well as its relationship with the Soviet Union. Recent historical developments explain this circumstance.[39] The geographic area that today forms the state of Finland was ceded to Russia in 1809 as the consequence of the war of 1808–1809, after having been a part of Sweden for seven centuries. During the Russian rule Finland held the status of an autonomous Grand Duchy. At the turn of the 20th century a nationalistic sentiment emerged among the Finnish population – in part as a response to the harshening and assimilatory policies implemented by Russia – leading to desires for independence. The nationalistic sentiment was followed

[39] This section highlights key elements of Finnish history. For a more comprehensive introduction, see for example Klinge, Matti: A Brief History of Finland. Otava, Helsinki, 1987.

by political initiatives, and in 1917 Finland declared her independence. During the same year a civil war broke out in Finland between the 'Whites' and the 'Reds', the latter group supporting the establishing of a communist regime in Finland and gaining military support from Russia. The war left deep ideological tensions in the otherwise unified population, and it disturbed the relationship between Finland and Russia, as the involvement of the Russian military had been so extensive that a peace settlement was adopted between the two countries in 1920. For the next two decades, despite underlying tensions, peace prevailed over Finland. This changed at the dawn of World War II when the Soviet Union attacked Finland. First the Winter War of 1939–1940 followed, then the Continuation War of 1941–1945.[40]

Although Finland lost some of its territory, it maintained its independence and became a part of the small group of countries to border the Soviet Union but to remain outside the socialist regime after World War II. Finland's official post-war foreign policy was governed by the principle of *neutrality*, which intended to keep the country outside the bi-polar conflicts of the Cold War. However, it has since become commonly agreed upon that during the following decades the Soviet Union exerted a certain influence on both Finland's external affairs as well as its domestic climate. In external affairs this was most concretely embodied by the Agreement of Friendship, Cooperation, and Mutual Assistance concluded in 1948.[41] Particularly some international commentators but also increasingly Finnish scholars have argued that

[40] To avoid occupation, Finland allied itself with Germany, a matter that still causes discomfort for the Finnish population. See Polvinen, Tuomo: Between East and West: Finland in international politics, 1944–1947. University of Minnesota Press, Minneapolis, 1986. In standard school books, for example, the matter is devoted only fleeting and ambiguous attention. The wars created a great uniformity among the Finnish population as practically all families had members who participated in them.

[41] In the Agreement Finland agreed to defend its territory against military invasion, if required, with Soviet Union assistance, and not to allow its area to be utilized in military action against the Soviet Union. See Rasila, Viljo; Jutikkala, Eino & Kulha, Keijo K.: Suomen poliittinen historia 1905–1975. Werner Söderström, Porvoo, 1980; Blomstedt et al.: Suomen Historia, osa 8: Paasikiven aika, Kekkosen aika, taloudellinen kasvu ja yhteiskuntamurros, massakulttuurin maihinnousu, taistelut kulttuurista. Weilin Göös, Espoo, 1988; Saraviita, Ilkka: YYA-sopimus. Lakimiesliiton kustannus, Helsinki, 1989; Joutsamo, Kari: Puolueettomuus ja EY. Euro Consulting Oy, Turku, 1990. The nature and impact of the Agreement continue to generate discussion, as the Soviet Union and Finland held occasionally greatly differing interpretations of the topic.

on the one hand Western influences were in Finnish politics and public debates treated with reservation, on the other that the Finnish media treated the Soviet Union without criticism; the era is talked of as *Finlandization*.[42] However, the extent of Soviet influence continues to generate vivid discussion, and whereas some commentators claim that Soviet influence has been exaggerated, others construe that its full extent has yet to be established.[43]

This ongoing debate also impacts the manner in which Finland's participation in international collaboration is viewed. Whereas some commentators emphasize continuity in Finnish policy, others place a decisive qualitative shift in the late 1980s; this is the view followed in this study. According to this view Soviet influence remained predominant in Finnish foreign policy until the end of the 1980s, when the European political turmoil – led by the collapse of the Berlin Wall in 1989 and the crumbling of the socialist regime – induced rapid and profound changes. Many commentators construe these developments as marking a shift in Finland's foreign policy toward stronger political association with Western Europe, of which one reflection was membership in the Council of Europe. Whereas Finland had previously remained outside of the Council because of "reasons of (Eastern) foreign politics",[44] in 1989 Finland joined it as the last Western democracy – only months before the first former socialist state, Hungary. 1991 saw the end of the Agreement of Friendship, Cooperation, and Mutual Assistance, and in 1995 Finland joined the European Union following a favourable referendum. Other subtle yet significant

[42] See Vihavainen, Timo: Kansakunta rähmällään: suomettumisen lyhyt historia. Otava, Helsinki, 1991; Luoto, Jari: Ulkopolitiikka ja Ihmisoikeudet: Suomen kansainvälisen ihmisoikeuspolitiikan murroskausi 1985–1995. Gaudeamus, Helsinki, 1997. Finland, however, did participate in the collaboration between the Nordic countries – formed by Finland, Sweden, Norway, Denmark and Iceland – joining the Nordic Council in 1956. Finland also participated in the OECD as well as EFTA from the 1960s onwards, and became a full member in EFTA in 1986.

[43] For example in November 2007, the publication of a new book by Alpo Rusi – a former ambassador who had previously been accused of being a DDR spy, leading to tremendous media interest – was highly featured in all major Finnish newspapers as well as in principal news broadcasts; it was likewise accompanied by vivid debate. The book claimed that in the past, many central politicians in power today continually provided the Soviet Union with information about Finland's internal affairs. Rusi, Alpo: Vasemmalta ohi: – Kamppailu Suomen ulkopoliittisesta johtajuudesta rautaesiripun varjossa 1945–1990. Gummerus, Helsinki, 2007; MTV3 Netti: 'Rusi Rankkana,' 6.11.2007, http://www.mtv3.fi/uutiset/txt/kotimaa.shtml/arkistot/kotimaa/2007/11/578343 (8.11.2007).

[44] Luoto: Ulkopolitiikka ja Ihmisoikeudet, *supra* note 42, 63; translation by author.

changes in the general atmosphere of the Finnish society accompanied these political developments. Signs were visible particularly in the metropolitan area of Helsinki: numerous international chains opened their stores in the downtown area; the streets began to portray a more diverse mixture of different races, whereas the population had previously been almost uniformly Finnish; English and other foreign languages became a regular part of city life. In the late 1990s and the new millennium these cosmopolitan influences have become ever more evident as Finland has become an active participant in EU policies, being among the first nations to adopt the EURO as its national currency. Despite its formal policy of 'non-alignment' in military affairs, today politicians regularly discuss Finland's possibilities to join NATO.[45] In particular, the speeches of many politicians convey the impression that, in addition to Western Europe, there exists the desire to strengthen Finland's ideological proximity to the US while taking distance from Russia.[46]

These developments provide the background for exploring as well the role of the human rights discourse in the Finnish society as Finland's position in the international human rights phenomenon. Also both of these elements were until the early 1990s influenced by Finland's relationship with the Soviet Union.[47] The Soviet Union had conflicts with the new regime already at its dawn: during the planning for the UN the Soviet Union – echoed by Great Britain – opposed the inclusion of human rights references in the UN Charter.[48] During the drafting for the UDHR opposition channelled itself into ideological

---

[45] Finland's activeness in the EU as well as the pro-EU sentiment of many predominant Finnish politicians have lead some sardonic Finnish journalists to cite the country as the EU's 'model pupil'. The political enthusiasm – particularly right wing – toward both the EU and the US often appears to exceed that of the Finnish population. Consequently NATO membership remains unlikely due to lack of popular support.

[46] In the autumn of 2007 this was illustrated by the speech of Finland's Defence Minister during his official visit to the US: he stated – speaking, according to most leading Finnish politicians, without due consideration and consequently causing significant internal controversy – that Finland's greatest security challenge is today created by Russia. See Yle Uutiset: 'Häkämiehen Venäjä-kommentit puhuttavat,' 7.9.2007, http://www.yle.fi/uutiset/24h/id69201.html (29.10.2007).

[47] Luoto: Ulkopolitiikka ja Ihmisoikeudet, *supra* note 42, 63–65. Yet also this issue continues to generate controversy, as other commentators construe such an assessment to overemphasize the importance of Finland's refraining from ethical judgements regarding the human rights circumstances of the East Bloc countries.

[48] Mazover: 'The Strange Triumph of Human Rights,' *supra* note 15, 398; Proskauer: A Segment of My Times, *supra* note 25, 219–220; Korey: NGOs and the Universal Declaration of Human Rights, *supra* note 14, 33–34.

strife and heated exchanges between the West and the Soviet Bloc on the content of rights, among other things.[49] In the end these circumstances led to the "disappointing abstentions"[50] as the Soviet Bloc resigned to vote for the adoption of the UDHR.[51] During the Cold War the Soviet Union seized upon opportunities to highlight US racial policies via the human rights discourse[52] – a topic raised at the UN in 1947 by the National Association for the Advancement of Colored People (NAACP).[53] Later the Soviet Union took a leading role – along with the US – in efforts to stall the negotiations for the CCPR as well as CESCR.[54] Through their ongoing protest, the Soviets "gained themselves a reputation for obstruction",[55] and scholars have described them as, among other things, becoming notorious for their efforts to "silence the NGOs at the UN".[56]

---

[49] Sellars: The Rise and Rise of Human Rights, *supra* note 8, 67–85; Evans: US Hegemony and the Project of Universal Human Rights, *supra* note 28, 79–95; Evans, Tony: 'Power, hegemony and HR.' In *Human Rights Fifty Years on: A Reappraisal* (Ed. Evans, Tony). Manchester University Press, Manchester, 1998, 10; Korey: NGOs and the Universal Declaration of Human Rights, *supra* note 14, 46–50; Morsink: The Universal Declaration of Human Rights, *supra* note 13, 157–190; Glendon: A World Made New, *supra* note 14. This tension was summarized in candid fashion by Eleanor Roosevelt in her autobiography: 'Thus, over the years, in one capacity or another, I saw a great deal of the Russian delegates and not infrequently felt I saw and heard too much of them, because they were usually the centre of opposition to our ideas'. Roosevelt: The Autobiography of Eleanor Roosevelt, *supra* note 27, 311.

[50] Roosevelt *ibid*.

[51] UDHR, http://www.un.org/Overview/rights.html (4.4.2006). The only countries to abstain from voting in addition to the 6 countries of the Soviet bloc were South Africa and Saudi-Arabia, protesting against the articles related to religious freedom, marriage rights and racial equality. Honduras and Yemen were absent from the vote, whereas all the other 48 members states of the UN voted for the adoption of the Declaration.

[52] Glendon: A World Made New, *supra* note 14, 193–199.

[53] The NAACP issued a petition that focused on the 'alienable rights' of African Americans in the US. See Smythe, Hugh H.: 'The N. A. A. C. P. Protest to UN.' In *8 Phylon (1940–1956) 4*, 1947, 355–358; Mazover: 'The Strange Triumph of Human Rights,' *supra* note 15, 395; Adams, Francis & Sanders, Barry: Alienable Rights: The Exclusion of African Americans in a White Man's Land 1619–2000. Harper Collins Publishers, New York, 2003. The US retaliated by focussing on forced labour in the Soviet Union, calling it an institutionalized form of slavery. This charge was initially raised by Britain. See Sellars: The Rise and Rise of Human Rights, *supra* note 8, 67–75.

[54] Glendon: A World Made New, *supra* note 14, 195–199; Simpson: Human Rights and the End of Empire, *supra* note 19, 511–542; Sellars, *ibid*., 75–78.

[55] Sellars, *ibid*., 76.

[56] Korey: NGOs and the Universal Declaration of Human Rights, *supra* note 14, 77–94. Also the relationship of the US and the human rights regime was continually distraught, as the US treated human rights and human rights violations as something that existed abroad, notwithstanding its intense ongoing battle for the civil rights of

From the 1950s to the End of the Cold War

After becoming a member of the UN in 1955, Finland followed the momentum of the other Nordic countries – commonly construed as progressive regarding the human rights discourse[57] – for example ratifying the principal human rights treaties in the same pace with them in the 1970s and 1980s. These ratifications importantly included the optional protocols which entailed the provisions that subjected ratifying parties to the monitoring proceedings outlined by the treaty (Table 2).[58]

In the 1960s Finland worked actively in the Commission on the Status of Women, particularly through the personal contribution of Helvi Sipilä, who later became the first female Assistant Secretary General of the UN. Finland also contributed to the issue of discrimination and the protection of minority rights, particularly through the personal efforts of Voitto Saario. In 1975 Finland hosted the important Conference on Security and Co-operation in Europe (CSCE), which brought together government leaders from both the West and the Eastern Bloc. Particularly during the preparations for the Conference, human rights issues were thoroughly discussed.[59] By the 1980s Finland

African Americans. See Sellars: The Rise and Rise of Human Rights, *supra* note 8, 114–133; Adams & Sanders: Alienable Rights, *supra* note 53, 265–294. This policy of 'double standards' continues to arouse criticism along with the heavy reservations that accompany US ratifications of human rights treaties. See Chomsky, Noam: 'The United States and the challenge of relativity.' In *Human Rights Fifty Years on, supra* note 49, 24–56; Redgewell, Catherine: 'US reservations to human rights treaties: all for one and none for all?' In *United States Hegemony and the Foundations of International Law* (Eds. Byers, Michael & Nolte, Georg). Cambridge University Press, Cambridge, 2003, 392- 415; Glendon: A World Made New, *supra* note 14, 193–199; Sellars: The Rise and Rise of Human Rights, *supra* note 8, 75–85; Evans: US Hegemony and the Project of Universal Human Rights, *supra* note 28, 72–95.

[57] See for example Lauren: The Evolution of International Human Rights, *supra* note 11, 13, 46–47, 51, 79, 81, 107; as well as Pelkonen, Heli & Rosas, Allan (Eds.): Mänskliga rättigheter in Norden. Åbo Akademi, Åbo, 1983. Nordic countries acquired a high profile in the new UN, reflected in the nomination of Norwegian Trygve Lie as the first Secretary General, and Swedish Dag Hammarskjöld as the second. See Bring, Ove: 'Dag Hammarskjöld and the Issue of Humanitarian Intervention.' In *Nordic Cosmpololitanism: Essays in International Law for Martti Koskenniemi* (Eds. Petman, Jarna & Klabbers, Jan). Brill Academic Publishers, Leiden, 2003, 485–518. These high-profile positions were followed by others, establishing a tradition of Nordic individuals in important posts in UN organs.

[58] High Commissioner, *supra* note 37.

[59] Bloed, Arie (Ed.): The Conference on Security and Cooperation in Europe: Analysis and Basic Documents, 1972–1993. Dordrecht, Boston & London, 1993; Pentikäinen, Merja: Human Rights Commitments within the CSCE Process: Nature,

Table 2: Ratifications of Principal Human Rights Treaties by Nordic Countries

YEAR		Country
1940	1948 UDHR (Signed)	Sweden Norway Iceland Denmark
1950	1955 Member of the UN	Finland
1960	1969 CERD	Iceland
1970	1970 CERD	Finland
	1970 CERD	Norway
	1972 CERD	Denmark
	1972 CERD	Sweden
	1976 CESCR	Denmark
	1976 CESCR	Finland
	1976 CESCR	Norway
	1976 CESCR	Sweden
	1976 CCPR	Denmark
	1976 CCPR	Finland
	1976 CCPR	Norway
	1976 CCPR	Sweden
	1979 CESCR	Iceland
	1979 CCPR	Iceland
1980	1981 CEDAW	Norway
	1982 CEDAW	Sweden
	1983 CEDAW	Denmark
	1985 CEDAW	Iceland
	1986 CEDAW	Finland
	1987 CAT	Denmark
	1987 CAT	Norway
	1987 CAT	Sweden
	1989 CAT	Finland
1990	1990 CRC	Sweden
	1991 CRC	Denmark
	1991 CRC	Finland
	1991 CRC	Norway
	1992 CRC	Iceland
	1996 CAT	Iceland

had established itself as an integral participant in the international human rights phenomenon, with a well-established record of membership in UN human rights treaty bodies as well as the Commission on Human Rights.[60] Finland received favourable feedback in its commitment to human rights, and in one evaluation from 1983 it was given the highest rating – together with only Denmark and New Zealand – in an effort at a worldwide comparison dealing only with civil and political rights.[61]

Despite these factors, Finland's participation has been simultaneously assessed as being impacted by Soviet influence. In his analysis on the relationship of Finnish foreign policy and human rights Jari Luoto notes that, although Finland's policy of neutrality led to reticence in all matters that fell within the domestic sphere of other states, this was most visible regarding questions that related to the Soviet Union.[62] A prominent SCANET expert describes how Finland "during the Cold War ... stood with [its] "mittens in the air" when we should have taken a stand". In the 1960s and 1970s the status of the human rights discourse within the Finnish society remained controversial, as the era was marked by deep ideological division. On the one end of the spectrum were the student groups which held close ties to Western Europe, yet exerted limited societal influence. These groups established for example the Finnish branch of Amnesty International in 1974.[63] On the other were the more influential left-wing groups from social democrats to communists – the group taistolaiset obtaining the highest profile[64] – which harboured close sympathies to the Soviet Union. Most of

Contents and Application in Finland. Advisory Board for International Human Rights Affairs No. 3, 1994. The Final Act led to the adoption of Charter 77 signed by prominent Czech intellectuals, which has since gained an important role for the human rights movement in European socialist countries. The Helsinki Final Act also led to the founding of the Helsinki Watch in 1978, later transforming into the prominent US-based Human Rights Watch. See Human Rights Watch: About HRW, http://www.hrw.org/about/whoweare.html (16.5.2006).

[60] Törnudd: Finland and the International Norms of Human Rights, *supra* note 2, 22–28; 276–285.

[61] *Ibid.*, 287, quoting Humana, Charles: World Human Rights Guide. Hutchinson & Co., London, 1983, 24–26, 184–185.

[62] Luoto: Ulkopolitiikka ja Ihmisoikeudet, *supra* note 42, 60–65.

[63] Amnesty's operations in Finland began in an informal manner in 1964, with the Finnish department founded in 1967. However, at that time it did not achieve national following. Thus a new board was selected in 1974, starting a new era reflected by growing membership numbers. See Amnesty International: 'Report 2006: Finland,' http://web.amnesty.org/report2006/fin-summary-eng (30.4.2007).

[64] Relander, Jukka: 'Ulkoinen totuus ja sisäinen kokemus taistolaisessa opiskelijaliikkeessä.' In *Tieteessä Tapahtuu*, 4/1997.

these groups viewed the human rights discourse as anti-Soviet propaganda perpetrated by the US, and consequently opposed any reference to it. Thus, despite treaty ratifications, at the beginning of the 1980s Finland held greater ideological distance to the human rights regime than the other Nordic countries which increased their development aid, and made direct connections to human rights through such programs as the "human rights based approach to development". By contrast, commentators construed as late as in the mid-1990s that this approach had not been sufficiently prevalent in Finland, and instead human rights were connected to development projects only in the new millennium.[65]

In the other Nordic countries human rights policies were accompanied by increasing discussions about human rights, also focussing on the countries' internal conditions. By contrast, a participant in the civil society remembers feeling that human rights were continually an unsuitable topic of internal political discussion in Finland. Thus, for example, the first doctoral dissertation focussing explicitly on human rights issues appeared in Finland as late as 1984.[66] It was only with the new winds of Glasnost that public attitudes began to alter.[67] In 1990, following Finland's membership in the Council of Europe, Finland ratified the European Convention on Human Rights.[68] Ratification was preceded by discussion on how the Finnish legal system complied with Convention requirements. Particular concern was raised by the length of service for conscripts who do not enter into public military service, the status of conscientious objectors, the personnel records held by the

---

[65] See for example Luoto, Jari: 'Suomi varovainen ihmisoikeussaralla.' In *Kumppani*, 10.3.1996, http://www.kepa.fi/kumppani/513/?searchterm=ihmisoikeudet%20kehitysyhteisty%C3%B6 (5.11.2007); Seppänen, Samuli: 'Possibilities and Challenges of the Human Rights-Based Approach to Development.' The Erik Castrén Institute Research Reports 17/2005, Helsinki, 2005.

[66] Pellonpää, Matti: Expulsion in International Law: A Study in International Aliens Law and Human Rights with Special Reference to Finland. Suomalainen tiedeakatemia, Helsinki, 1984.

[67] Some commentators mention as a seminal event for the new era the 1986 publication of Klaus Törnudd's 'Finland and the International Norms of Human Rights' see *supra* note 2. As Törnudd was at the time working at the Finnish Foreign Ministry, the book is in retrospect viewed as a semi-official discussion opener; yet Törnudd himself views such an assessment as dramatic exaggeration.

[68] European Court of Human Rights: Ratification of the European Convention on Human Rights, http://www.echr.coe.int/ECHR/EN/Header/Basic+Texts/Basic+Texts/Dates+of+ratification+of+the+European+Convention+on+Human+Rights+and+Additional+Protocols/ (14.6.2007).

police as well as certain matters relating to foreigners.[69] However, it has been pointed out how in many other respects Finnish legislation was already in conformity with the Convention due to earlier internal legal developments. By contrast, in the other Nordic countries similar incorporation occurred only greatly after the ratification of 1950.[70] That the 1990s introduced a qualitative shift in Finland's participation in the international human rights regime is also reflected in the personal experiences of human rights experts. A scholar enjoying a prominent expert status in SCANET sees that the time marked Finland's increasing activeness in UN contexts. She associates this changed policy with a specific meeting of the Human Rights Commission in spring 1990 when, during the preparatory meetings, the country's representative simply asked that Finland bring up certain considerations relating to the internal affairs of different states, ones that it would previously not have highlighted in its policy of *neutrality*.

Finland's intensified engagement at the end of the Cold War reflects the general development of the human rights phenomenon, which had continued its expansion in the 1980s. By the time the core content of the human rights discourse as articulated by the UDHR was reaffirmed at the Vienna World Conference on Human Rights in 1993,[71] the human rights discourse had already established itself as the primary discourse of international diplomacy and cooperation. However, for human rights to develop into the global phenomenon they would become in the new millennium, a seminal event was still required: the end of the Cold War. As has been repeatedly noted, only this elevated human rights into ideological trumps, making them the moral backbone of the new world order and bringing "the end of

[69] Pellonpää, Matti: 'Euroopan neuvoston ihmisoikeussopimus Suomen näkökulmasta,' Oikeusministeriön lainvalmisteluosaston julkaisu 21, Helsinki, 1988, 313–316; Tervo, Jouni: 'Pintaremontti riittää.' In *Helsingin Sanomat, Kuukausiliite* 11/1988, 36–38; Scheinin, Martin: Aseistakieltäytymisoikeus, Hakapaino Oy, Helsinki, 1988. The status of Finnish conscientious objectors continues to provoke occasional controversy.

[70] The Nordic countries have also been reserved over European Court jurisdiction: the first unfavourable rulings against Sweden by the European Court awakened great upset, escalating to discussions on whether the country should resign from the entire Convention. Many thanks to Matti Pellonpää for discussion on this point. See also Ervo, Laura: 'Förhållandet mellan Europadomstolen och nationella domstolar – findländska perspektiv.' In *JFT 4/2006*, 411–422. Of relevance here is also the 1995 Finnish constitutional reform, discussed on page 53.

[71] Vienna Declaration. Adopted on 25 June 1993. A/Conf. 157/23, http://www.ohchr.org/english/law/vienna.htm (21.12.2005).

history".[72] In their rush to join the liberal world, new post-socialist states hurried to participate in the human rights regime as it signified the abandonment of old ideologies in favour of the one embedded in the human rights discourse. This rush is reflected in the ratifications of the CESCR: in the 1990s it was ratified by the Former Yugoslav Republic of Macedonia, Turkmenistan, Uzbekistan, Slovakia, Slovenia, Moldova, Georgia, Czech republic, Croatia, Bosnia & Herzegovina and Armenia, as well as all the Baltic countries.[73] By the end of the 1990s the Covenant had 50 new ratifications, which made the decade almost as active in ratifications as the 1970s.[74] In terms of ratified treaties, former socialist states have rapidly become some of the most active participants in the human rights phenomenon: two have ratified all principal 12 human rights treaties – a record held by only three other states – and a supplementary eight have ratified all but one.[75]

In Finland at the beginning of the 1990s, the internal position of the human rights discourse was still in a flux and had not yet permeated Finnish law, nor was it viewed as the sole discourse on rights. This is reflected by the introduction to Finnish constitutional law by Mikael Hidén and Ilkka Saraviita published in 1994, a volume used as a text book in Finnish law faculties: in its discussion on the background and origins of "certain inalienable rights", the book uses the formulation "which can be named e.g. human rights or fundamental rights".[76] The reference to fundamental rights introduces an alternative discourse of *perusoikeudet*, which is more indigenous to the Finnish legal culture as well as holds a significantly longer pedigree. This is highlighted by examining a book by Mikael Hidén on constitutional rights from 1971: it makes no reference to human rights, discussing instead the origins of fundamental rights as deriving from old laws from the 18th century, when Finland was a part of Sweden. In discussion of the hierarchy of

[72] Fukuyama, Francis: The End of History and the Last Man. Harper Perennial, New York, 1993.

[73] Of these ratifications, six are successions continuing former treaty relations from the Soviet era.

[74] High Commissioner, *supra* note 37. Other ratified countries included such diverse states as Thailand, Liechtenstein, Burkina Faso, Brasil, Israel and Switzerland. In 2000 the wave slowed down, with 10 ratifications from geographically dispersed areas, the most noteworthy ratification coming from China.

[75] High Commissioner, *supra* note 37. In this discussion, the Optional Protocol for the Convention against Torture and Other Cruel, Inhuman or Degrading Treatment or Punishment (CAT) is excluded; the document has only been ratified by Madagascar.

[76] Hidén, Mikael & Saraviita, Ilkka: Valtiosääntöoikeuden pääpiirteet. 6th, revised edition. Lakimiesliiton kustannus, Helsinki, 1994, 272; translation by author.

legal norms, no reference is made to international human rights treaties, nor is the UDHR mentioned.[77] The same findings apply to an introduction to Finnish public law from 1982, which makes no mention of the human rights discourse.[78]

In the Finnish context the two discourses, that of human rights (*ihmisoikeudet*) and 'fundamental rights' (*perusoikeudet*), have further traditionally been substantively distinguished from each other: the latter has referred to the rights of Finnish citizens listed in the Finnish constitution, the former to rights deriving "from treaties of international law that bind Finland, or through other arrangements".[79] In the aforementioned textbook from 1994, the relationship of Finnish fundamental rights and human rights is defined as follows: "Although by no means identical to each other, in many central substantive questions the contents of fundamental rights and human rights norms correspond to each other".[80] This distinction has been radically altered by the fundamental rights reform of 1995, which has been characterized as ending their separation from human rights. Veli-Pekka Viljanen discusses how human rights and fundamental rights have become mutually *complementary* instead of competing orders; how the substantive differences between the two have been effectively annulled. He further notes how Finnish courts and officials have been active in promoting human rights, as well as how human rights have entered into the Finnish culture of rights through *pervasion*, a process also characterized as constitutionalization.[81] Combined, these developments have been called to end the closed Finnish legal culture.[82]

---

[77] Hidén, Mikael: Perusoikeudet Hallitusmuodon II luvussa. Suomalaisen Lakimiesyhdistyksen vuosikirja I, Helsinki, 1971.

[78] Merikoski, Veli & Vilkkonen, Eero: Suomen julkisoikeus pääpiirteittäin. Suomalaisen Lakimiesyhdistyksen julkaisuja, WSOY, Juva, 1982.

[79] Scheinin: Aseistakieltäytymisoikeus, *supra* note 69, 1; Scheinin, Martin: Ihmisoikeudet Suomen oikeudessa. Suomalainen Lakimiesyhdistys, Jyväskylä, 1991; Ojanen, Tuomas: Perusoikeudet ja ihmisoikeudet Suomessa. Forum Iuris, Helsinki, 2003; Ojanen, Tuomas & Haapea, Arto (Eds.): EU-oikeuden perusteita. Edita, Helsinki, 2006.

[80] Hidén & Saraviita: Valtiosääntöoikeuden pääpiirteet, *supra* note 76, 273; translation by author.

[81] Scheinin, Martin: 'Finland.' In *International Human Rights Norms in the Nordic and Baltic Countries* (Ed. Scheinin, Martin). Martinus Nijhoff Publishers, The Hague, 1996, 257–294.

[82] Viljanen, Veli-Pekka: 'Perusoikeusuudistus ja kansainväliset ihmisoikeussopimukset.' In *Lakimies 5–6*, 1996, 788–815.

Table 3: Human Rights mentioned in Finland's Foreign Affairs Minister's Speeches

Year	Speeches	HR mentioned	%
1999	8	1	13%
2000	17	3	18%
2001	17	6	35%
2002	26	13	50%
2003	23	16	70%
2004	27	23	85%
2005	32	15	47%
2006	12	8	67%
Total	162	85	52%

The Human Rights Discourse in the New Millennium

In the new millennium the human rights discourse has stabilized its position at the centre of Finland's foreign policy and political rhetoric. This is illustrated by the speeches of the country's Foreign Minister Erkki Tuomioja between the period 1999–2006:[83] whereas in 1999 human rights were mentioned in only one in eight and in 2000 one in five speeches, by the year 2006 the frequency was two speeches out of three (Table 3).

On the level of policy-making, a few examples illustrate the centrality of the human rights discourse. The Foreign Affairs Ministry's report on human rights from 2000 mentions the increased centrality of human rights as an explicit goal for foreign and security policy;[84] an emphasis repeated by Finland's 2004 Human Rights Report.[85] These

[83] Erkki Tuomioja became Foreign Minister in February 2000, following the election of the former Foreign Minister Tarja Halonen as president. In 1999 Tuomioja was the Minister of Commerce and Industry.

[84] See Human Rights Report (2000). Ihmisoikeudet ja Suomen ulkopolitiikka. Ulkoasianministeriön julkaisuja 9/2000.

[85] Foreign Affairs Ministry: 'Foreign Minister Tuomioja on International Human Rights Day: Finland committed to the rights of minorities,' 10.12.2004, http://formin.finland.fi/public/default.aspx?contentid=62930&nodeid=15630&contentlan=2&culture=en-US (29.8.2006). The 2004 report was celebrated as the first of its kind. Although similar reports were published in 1998 and in 2000, the 2004 report was greatly more expansive and featured domestic elements, contrary to earlier ones; yet the main emphasis has remained on external affairs. The report follows the model of Sweden, where similar reports have been drafted for decades. See Mänskliga rättigheter i Sverige (2001), Http://www.riksdagen.se/shopping/R_ShowItem____5715.aspx (2.10.2006).

developments find their origins in the mid-1990s, when a more general shift occurred in Finnish foreign policy from the former emphasis on disarmament to human rights; some commentators assign this development particularly to Finland's current President and then Foreign Minister Tarja Halonen. Emphasis on human rights has produced also different collaborational ventures between ministries, the civil society and international actors. These include the program funded by national ministries, the EU and the Ford foundation, and organized by the International Helsinki Federation for Human Rights in 2000, which calls itself "the broadest and most comprehensive program of human rights monitoring and advocacy in the history of the organization".[86] Human rights and their advancement were likewise highlighted by the new Finnish Government Programme of 2007, which mentions that the Finnish government actively promotes the global advancement of human rights.[87] The centrality of the human rights discourse in Finnish policy-making is reflected also in the educational reforms of the new millennium. In the governmental decree on education from 2002, "respect of life and human rights" was mentioned as forming the foundation for high school education.[88] In 2003, the primacy of human rights was highlighted by the online magazine of the Finnish Ministry of Education, likewise emphasizing how human rights form the foundational values of the new educational curriculum. According to Finland's 2004 human rights report human rights education should in the future begin in primary school, and ethical discussions in schools should be founded on the UDHR. The report discusses how in the new millennium human rights education has been directed toward the functionaries of foreign affairs as well as others in leadership positions in the government.[89] Finally, the educational plan by the Ministry of Education for the years 2006–2008 from 2007 characterizes human rights as "foundational values" for education.[90]

[86] International Helsinki Federation for Human Rights. Report 2001 (Events of 2000), http://www.ihf-hr.org/documents/doc_summary.php?sec_id=3&d_id=1783 (20.1.2010)

[87] Government Programme 2007, http://www.valtioneuvosto.fi/hallitus/hallitusohjelma/en.jsp. 2007 (5.11.2007).

[88] Valtioneuvoston asetus lukiokoulutuksen yleisistä valtakunnallisista tavoitteista ja tuntijaosta, 955/2002, 14.11.2002, http://www.finlex.fi/fi/laki/ajantasa/2002/20020955 (3.6.2007).

[89] Human Rights Report (2004). Valtioneuvoston selonteko Suomen ihmisoikeuspolitiikasta.

[90] Ministry of Education: 'Opetusministeriön ja opetushallituksen välinen tulosopimus vuosille 2006–2008,' http://www.oph.fi/info/netra/tulossopimus_2006_2008

To summarize these developments, from Finland's 1955 membership in the UN to the educational policy of 2007, the human rights discourse has moved from the *periphery* to the *centre* of Finnish policy making. Finland's relationship to the human rights phenomenon – measured in terms of its participation in the UN and European human rights regimes, its activeness in commenting on the internal human rights records of other countries, its alignment of public policy with human rights, as well as the activeness of its civil society – no longer differs from the other Nordic countries. Instead, the Nordic countries are jointly regarded as the global leaders of the human rights phenomenon and they belong to the group of 41 states that have ratified all but one of the 12 principal human rights treaties.[91] They are active in the UN diplomatic and political community, with numerous of their citizens in high positions in different UN human rights bodies, and they provide substantial funding for the High Commissioner for Human Rights. Finland's high status in the human rights phenomenon was reflected in its election to the newly formed Human Right Council in May 2006. Some evidence further suggests that Finnish citizens have become more active in the European human rights regime than some of their Nordic counterparts: Finland leads, along with Sweden, the number of complaints made to the European Court.[92] Whereas in Denmark and Norway it is constantly debated whether the powers of the European Court are too expansive, such a debate has seized in Finland and the Court is instead seen as a regular part of the Finnish legal system.[93] Finland's high international profile is likewise repeated

.pdf (3.6.2007). These developments gain context from international developments discussed in Chapter 4.

[91] High Commissioner, *supra* note 37. For all the Nordic countries the absent treaty is the same as for most Western European states, namely the Convention on the Protection of the Rights of All Migrant Workers and Members of their Families (CMW). The position of migrants in the Nordic countries has aroused some criticism, reflected for example in the 2006 Amnesty International report noting how Sweden has deported foreigners. See Amnesty International: 'Partners in Crime: Europe's role in US renditions,' 14.6.2006, http://web.amnesty.org/library/index/ENGEUR010082006 (24.8.2006). In 2004 and 2005 concern was raised over Sweden's actions to ban torture in the form of exporting suspected terrorists. See Amnesty International: 'Sweden: Concerns over the treatment of deported Egyptians,' 28.5.2004, http://web.amnesty.org/library/index/engeur420012004 (11.9.2006); Human Rights Watch: 'Sweden Violated Torture Ban with U.S. Help,' 20.5.2005, http://hrw.org/english/docs/2005/05/20/sweden10991.htm (28.8.2006). However, such criticism is usually presented against the backdrop of the special responsibilities of Nordic countries as world leaders in human rights affairs.

[92] Ervo: 'Förhållandet mellan Europadomstolen och nationella domstolar,' *supra* note 70, 417.

[93] *Ibid.*

in treaty body proceedings, which provides increasing motivation for participation: Sally Engle Merry mentions a Finnish delegate noting, of the CEDAW Committee proceedings, how "it is good for the government ministers to come to the hearings to hear the questions and the praise the experts give to countries such as her own that have made notable progress toward gender equality." This provides valuable feedback about "Finland's place and image in the world as a leader in women's human rights".[94] Although in the new millennium the human rights phenomenon has met its greatest challenge since World War II, namely the war against terrorism initiated by the US as a response to the terrorist attacks of 11 September 2001,[95] in the Finnish context this has not induced severe challenges. Instead, the human rights phenomenon appears to continually strengthen its ideological position.

Thematic and Substantive Expansion

Expansion has been the most salient element of the global human rights phenomenon. In the UN human rights regime, this is reflected in the continuous proliferation of new human rights instruments which expand the scope of the human rights discourse by introducing new rights and circumstances to it: in 2004 the website for the Office of the High Commissioner for Human Rights enlisted a total of 109 documents under the heading "International Human Rights Instruments", including both legally binding and non-binding documents such as Declarations, Optional Protocols, Principles, Recommendations, Guidelines and Codes of Conduct; and an additional nine working groups working on new documents (Table 4).[96]

---

[94] Merry: Human Rights & Gender Violence, *supra* note 5, 85.

[95] For three central scholarly contributions on the effects of the war on terrorism, see 'Agora: Military Commissions.' In *96 American Journal of International Law 2*, 2002, 320–364; 'Symposium: 'A War against Terrorism': What Role for International Law? US and European Perspectives.' In *14 European Journal of International Law 2*, 2003, 209–379; and 'Symposium: Lovtiltak mot terror.' In *Mennesker & Rettigheter: Nordisk Tidsskrift for Menneskerettigheter 2*, 2002. On the impact of the US hegemonic position on the foundations of international law, see Byers, Michael & Nolte, Georg (Eds.): United States Hegemony and the Foundations of International Law. Cambridge University Press, Cambridge, 2003.

[96] High Commissioner, *supra* note 37; Working Groups, *supra* note 36. The information on the website is a few years old, as no update has been made on the Convention on the Rights of Persons with Disabilities, nor does the website enlist any of the Declarations adopted after the year 2000, for example the Declaration

Table 4: UN Human Rights Instruments

	1940	1950	1960	1970	1980	1990	2000
Signed Covenants	2	7	7	2	2	1	1
In Force	2	4	5	5	2	1	1
Declarations	1	1	6	8	5	5	4+1
Total of Decade	5	12	18	15	9	7	6+1
Total of All	5	17	35	50	59	66	72+1

Thematic expansion is illustrated by the transformation of 'women's rights' into 'women's human rights'. This development started in the 1980s – the Convention on the Elimination of all Forms of Violence Against Women (CEDAW) entered into force in 1981[97] – and gained enormous momentum in the 1990s. Today the link between the two has become commonplace, and talk of women's rights appears old-fashioned.[98] This thematic shift has been accompanied by substantive expansion which has enlarged the significance of key concepts. Sally

of Commitment on HIV/AIDS from 2001, http://www.un.org/ga/aids/coverage/FinalDeclarationHIVAIDS.html (25.9.2006).

[97] High Commissioner, *supra* note 37.

[98] Hilary Clinton's speech at the Beijing Conference in 1995 is often mentioned as a key moment. See Cook, Rebecca J. (Ed.): Human Rights of Women: National and International Perspectives. University of Pennsylvania Press, Philadelphia, 1994, 20; Keck, Margaret E. & Sikkink, Kathryn: Activists beyond Borders: Advocacy Networks in International Politics. Cornell University Press, Ithaca, 1998; Peterson, V. Spike & Parisi, Laura: 'Are women human? It's not an academic question.' In *Human Rights Fifty Years on: A Reappraisal, supra* note 49, 132–160; Pentikäinen, Merja: 'The Right to Speak for the Women's Cause: May also Women Participate? The Case of the Holy See in the UN.' In *Nordic Cosmpololitanism: Essays in International Law for Martti Koskenniemi, supra* note 57, 141–154; Marks & Clapham: International Human Rights Lexicon, *supra* note 11, 411–428; Tyler, Patrick E.: 'Hillary Clinton, In China, Details Abuse of Women,' in *The New York Times*, 6.6.1995, Section A, 1; Riles, Annelise: 'Rights Inside Out: The Uses of Genre in the Women's Human Rights Campaign.' In *15 Leiden Journal of International Law 2*, 2002, 285–303. This development has led to the establishing of such organizations as 'Women's Human Rights Net,' see http://www.whrnet.org/ (17.5.2006), and formulations such as 'Global Women's Human Rights' in the speeches of George and Laura W. Bush, see The White House: President, Mrs. Bush Marks Progress in Global Women's Human Rights, 12.3.2004, http://www.whitehouse.gov/news/releases/2004/03/20040312-5.html (17.5.2006). For an overview on the relationship of the UN and women, see Pietilä, Hilkka: Naiset ja YK: vuosikymmenen menestystarina, 2005, http://www.minna.fi/minna/artikkelit/ykpietila.html (11.9.2006).

Engle Merry describes how the meaning of 'violence against women' has expanded from the original meaning – men's violence against their partners in the form of rape, assault, and murder – to include "female genital mutilation/cutting, gender-based violence by police and military forces in armed conflict as well as in everyday life, violence against refugee women and asylum seekers, trafficking and prostitution, sexual harassment, forced pregnancy, forced abortion, forced sterilization, female foeticide and infanticide, early and forced marriage, honor killings, and widowhood violations".[99] Similar examples are abundant. Today indigenous and minority rights are increasingly formulated as 'human rights to culture'; a trend that started with full vigour in the 1990s.[100] The same decade saw environmental law become increasingly articulated in the human rights discourse through arguments that nature should be protected in order to preserve the best environment for human beings.[101] This development has continued in the new millennium.[102] These years have also seen the human rights discourse

---

[99] Merry: Human Rights & Gender Violence, *supra* note 5, 21, 59–60.

[100] Margalit, Avishai & Halbertal, Moshe: 'Liberalism and the Right to Culture.' In *71 Social Research 3*, 2004, 529–548; Cowan, Jane K.; Dembour, Marie-Bénédicte & Wilson, Richard A.: 'Introduction.' In *Culture and Rights* (Eds. Cowan, Jane K. et al.). Cambridge University Press, Cambridge, 2001, 1–26; Samson, Colin: 'Rights as the reward for simulated cultural sameness: the Innu in the Canadian colonial context.' In *Culture and Rights, ibid*, 226–248; Fried, Gorson: 'Writing for Their Lives: Bentian Dayak Authors and Indonesian Development Discourse.' In *Culture and the Question of Rights* (Ed. Zerner, Charles). Duke University Press, Durham, 2003, 142–183; McIntosh, Ian S.: 'Reconciling Personal and Impersonal Worlds: Aboriginal Struggles for Self-Determination.' In *At the Risk of Being Heard: Identity, Indigenous Rights, and Postcolonial States* (Eds. Dean, Bartholomew & Levi, Jerome M.). The University of Michigan Press, Ann Arbor, 2003, 293–323; Sieder, Rachel & Witchell, Jessica: 'Advancing indigenous claims through the law: reflections on the Guatemalan peace process.' In *Culture and Rights, ibid.*, 201–225; Halme, Miia: 'Between Culture and Rights – beyond Relativism?' In *28 Polar: The Political and Legal Anthropology Review 2*, 2005, 307–315. These claims can be linked to the trend of using the concept of culture to back up claims for differential treatment, a wave that began with full vigour in the 1980s and has today raised the concept as perhaps the biggest buzzword of minority and indigenous rights. As Jane Cohen, Richard Wilson and Marie-Bénédicte Dembour note, the time for this is curious, as the same years saw criticism increase towards the concept in anthropology. See Cowan et al: 'Introduction.' In *Culture and Rights*, 3.

[101] Sakamoto, Hyakudai: 'The Genome, Artificial Evolution & Human Rights.' In *Protection of the Human Genome and Scientific Responsibility* (Eds. Okamoto, Michio; Fujiki, Norio & Macer Darryl R.J.). Eubios Ethics Institute, 1996, 30–31; Boyle, Alan & Anderson, Michael (Eds.): Human Rights Approaches to Environmental Protection. Clarendon Press, Oxford, 1996.

[102] See Kolari: Tuula: The Right to a Decent Environment with Special Reference to Indigenous Peoples. Juridica Lapponica 31, Sevenprint Ltd., Rovaniemi, 2004.

utilized in issues of labour law,[103] the WTO, and trade law – the last discussion giving rise to the curious phrase 'the human rights of companies'.[104] In 2006 the Human Rights Quarterly introduced one of the most surprising academic invocations to date, talking of "the emerging human right to tobacco control".[105]

This thematic expansion of academic invocations has been accompanied by a steady increase of academic journals focussing on human rights, as is illustrated by an overview of English-language journals.[106] This investigation reproduces the temporality observed regarding treaty ratification: the start was slow and few concrete developments occurred in the first decades after the UDHR was adopted. In the 1960s the only English-language human rights journal was the Columbia Human Rights Law Review founded in 1967. In the 1970s two additional journals were founded, of which most important was the Human Rights Quarterly founded in 1979. Although a few more publications emerged in the 1980s, it was only in the 1990s that real proliferation commenced, with a total of 12 new journals appearing during the decade.[107] The pace intensified in the first years of the new millennium, as by 2005 12 new journals had appeared after the year 2000 (Table 5). When the entire period after 1948 is examined, the decade between 1995 and 2005 appears particularly active: whereas prior to 1995,

---

[103] Marceau, Gabrielle: 'The WTO Dispute Settlement and Human Rights.' In *13 European Journal of International Law 4*, 2002, 753–814.

[104] The core themes of this discussion were summarized by a debate-inciting article by Ernst-Ulrich Petersman in which he discusses how the functioning of the WTO must increasingly take human rights reflections seriously. See Petersman, Ernst-Ulrich: 'Human Rights and the Law of the World Trade Organization.' In *37 Journal of World Trade 2*, 2003, 241–281. See also Thomas, Caroline: 'International financial institutions and social and economic human rights: an exploration.' In *Human Rights Fifty Years on, supra* note 98, 161–185.

[105] Dresler, Carolyn & Marks, Stephen: 'The Emerging Human Right to Tobacco Control.' In *28 Human Rights Quarterly 3*, 2006, 599–651.

[106] Table 5 aims to cover most principal English-language human rights journals located online through various means. A helpful source list of journals is supported by the Washington and Lee Law School, http://lawlib.wlu.edu/LJ/index.aspx?country=All%20Countries&subject=Human+Rights%2c+Civil+Rights (25.8.2006). Information on founding year as well as publisher are derived from journal home sites, found primarily through google.com.

[107] The 1970s saw the publications of several pivotal human rights books, of which one example is the book by Ronald Dworkin in 1977, see Dworkin, Ronald: Taking Rights Seriously. Harvard University Press, Cambridge, 1977. The book commenced the development of a positivist system of rights, allowing lawyers to make sense of the emerging human rights regime; a German equivalent is Robert Alexy's *Theorie der Grundrechte* from 1985; Alexy, Robert: Theorie der Grundrechte. Suhrkamp, Baden-Baden, 1985.

Table 5: Human Rights Journals

YEAR	Name	Publisher	Total
1960	1967 Columbia Human Rights Law Review	U of Columbia	**1**
1970	1971 Israel Yearbook on Human Rights	Brill	**2**
	1979 Human Rights Quarterly (formerly Universal Human Rights)	John Hopkins U	
1980	1982 The Netherlands Quarterly of Human Rights	Intersentia (2002–)	**5**
	1982 The Nordic Journal of Human Rights	U of Oslo	
	1985 South African Journal on Human Rights	U of the Witwatersrand	
	1988 Harvard Human Rights Journal	U of Harvard	
	1988 Harvard Human Rights Yearbook	U of Harvard	
1990	1993 The East African Journal of Peace and Human R	University of Makerere	**12**
	1993 Int Journal of Minority & Group Rights	Brill	
	1993 Int Journal of Children's Rights	Brill	
	1994 The Buffalo Human Rights Law Review	U of Buffalo	
	1994 The Human Rights Brief	C for HR & Humanit. Law	
	1994 Australian Journal of Human Rights	U of New South Wales	
	1996 International Journal of Human Rights	Routledge	
	1996 The European Human Rights Law Review	Sweet and Maxwell	
	1996 Human Rights Magazine	Amer. Bar Association	
	1997 Mediterranean Journal of Human Rights	University of Malta	

(*Continued*)

Table 5 (*Contd.*)

YEAR	Name	Publisher	Total
	1997 Indiana International Human Rights Law Bulletin	Indiana U	
	1999 Yale Human Rights and Development Law Journal	U of Yale	
2000	2000 BMC International Health and Human Rights	U of Helsinki	**12**
	2000 Human Rights & Human Welfare	U of Denver	
	2000 Asia Pacific Journal of Human Rights and the Law	Martinus Nijhoff	
	2000 Asia Rights	Asian Civic Rights Net	
	2001 The Human Rights Law Review	U of Nottingham	
	2001 African Human Rights Law Journal	U of Pretoria	
	2001 Journal of Human Rights	Routledge	
	2002 Journal of Human Rights	U of Connecticut	
	2003 Journal of International Human Rights	Northwestern U	
	2003 Muslim World Journal of Human Rights	Berkeley U (e-version)	
	2005 Intercultural Human Rights Law Review	U of St Thomas	
	2005 Human Rights Law Commentary (online)	U of Nottingham	
TOTAL			**32**

only 13 human rights journals and periodicals existed, during the following decade 17 new journals were established, bringing the total number to 30.

Outside the academia, as is expected, the human rights discourse has seen even greater expansion. The issue of women's human rights has expanded into the question of the "human right to wear a jilbab";[108]

[108] Appleton, Josie: 'There's no human right to wear a jilbab.' In *Spiked-liberties*, 21.3.2006, http://www.spiked-online.com/articles/0000000CAFD5.htm (19.5.2006).

the claim of 'human right to family' has been utilized to defend desires to marry one's former father-in-law.[109] A disabled Danish man has argued for the existence of a " "human right" to a sex life".[110] Online chatrooms talk of the "human right to a nuclear free world";[111] they discuss the "human right to renewable energy"[112] and ask how far this right extends – "Free speech as a human right yes, free TV as a human right no".[113] What about the "human right to a nice hot cup of tea?"[114] San Francisco's mayor Gavin Newson – undoubtedly tongue-in-cheek – utilized the human rights discourse to describe Wi-Fi, a new technology, as " "a basic human right" – sort of like gay marriage, but for nerds".[115] An online abortion debate asks: "[i]f a human is crossbred with dog, shouldn't the outcome of that not have human rights?"[116] In Spain and Austria activists attempt to secure human rights to the great apes;[117] and in the UK an activist utilizes the human rights discourse to

---

[109] Gibb, Frances: 'Woman wins right to wed father-in-law.' In *The Sunday Times*, 14.9.2005, http://www.timesonline.co.uk/article/0,,2–1779188,00.html (19.5.2006).

[110] Taipei Times: 'Disabled man fights for "human right" to a sex life,' 2.1.2006, http://www.taipeitimes.com/News/world/archives/2006/01/02/2003287074 (19.5.2006). In concordance with social service guidelines from 2001, the man attempted to get social services to offer financial support to bring prostitutes to his flat, prostitution being legal in the country. When his plea was refused, the man initiated legal proceedings against the state, arguing that the decision violated his human right to a sex life.

[111] Maguire, Mairead Corrigan: 'The Human Right to a Nuclear Free World' In *Counterpunch*, 1.3.2006, http://www.counterpunch.org/maguire03012006.html (19.5.2006).

[112] Renewable Energy Access: '"The Human Right to Renewable Energy" Means "Energy Independence for All",' 5.12.2005, http://www.renewableenergyaccess.com/rea/news/story?id=40096 (19.5.2006).

[113] World Changing: 'Renewable Energy as a Human Right,' http://www.worldchanging.com/archives/003822.html (19.5.2006).

[114] *Ibid.*

[115] Orlowski, Andrew: 'Google wins SF wireless gig.' In *The Register*, 6.4.2006, http://www.theregister.co.uk/2006/04/06/google_sf_muni_wifi/ (19.5.2006).

[116] Internet Infidels Discussion Board: 'Using Ockams Razor In An Abortion Debate?' http://www.iidb.org/vbb/archive/index.php/t-130793.html (19.5.2006).

[117] The Spain Herald: 'Socialists: Give apes human rights,' 25.4.2006, http://www.spainherald.com/3438.html (19.5.2006); Great Ape Project 2006, http://www.greatapeproject.org/ (19.5.2006); Ahtiainen, Ilkka: 'Simpanssille haetaan ihmisoikeuksia Itävallassa.' In *Helsingin Sanomat*, 3.4.2007. Many thanks to Varro Vooglaid for this quote. Discussions on what constitute a human being have their scholarly equivalents, stemming from advances in gene technologies. These developments bring new vigour to abortion debates. In law, compelling are questions related to how the social is constituted and persons and things made in legal processes. See Pottage, Alain & Mundy, Martha (Eds.): Law, Anthropology, and the Constitution of the Social: Making Persons and Things. Cambridge University Press, Cambridge. 2004.

advocate for the right of sheep to remain homosexual.[118] The expansion of the human rights discourse appears infinite, and has – quite justifiably – started to awaken serious concern. This is reflected by the following newspaper article on the consequences of the UK 1998 Human Rights Act which has been followed by an avalanche of different, competing and conflicting human rights claims. The article notes how

> Afghan hijackers and ranting mullahs had a human right not to be deported. A Nigerian visitor had a human right to a National Health Service heart transplant. A released killer had a human right not to have his parole terms enforced. The dying had a human right to euthanasia and the living a human right to reject a cancer-carrying embryo… Rights are cited against sexual harassment, personal offence, noisy neighbours, landscape views and the wheelchair navigation of a spiral staircase.

The article concludes by noting that

> A tribunal actually bothered to hear, at public expense, a teacher claiming that a "farting chair" infringed her human right to avoid embarrassment. A silly law is an invitation to silliness.[119]

Expanse of the Finnish Discourse

Expansion has characterized the human rights discourse also in Finland, yet similar critical accounts as the one cited above have been scarce. Examination of a hearing organized in October 2003 in association with preparations for Finland's 2004 Human Rights Report illustrates expansion.[120] In addition to government representatives, the hearing featured NGO representatives, bureaucrats and scholars, and its exchanges exemplify instances where the human rights discourse is transformed into a part of wider social and political currents as well as ongoing political debate. This was particularly visible in the interventions of parliament members, which came to reflect the wider concerns of their political parties.[121] Discussion opened with a comment from a

---

[118] Hamilo, Marko: 'Julkilesbo tennistähti: lampailla oikeus homouteen.' In *Helsingin Sanomat*, 20.3.2007.

[119] Jenkins, Simon: 'Basic freedoms are being lost in the human rights circus.' In *The Sunday Times*, 14.5.2006, http://www.timesonline.co.uk/article/0,,2088–2179499,00.html (19.5.2006).

[120] Human Rights Report (2004), *supra* note 89.

[121] In total, parliament members representing left and right-wing parties made five comments each, while the parliament member representing the centre party made three comments.

left-wing party member who expressed concern over the weakening of the health care system as well as regional inequality in Finland. Particularly the first of these concerns is traditional for the Finnish left. A right-wing party member opened her intervention by emphasizing the benefits of globalization and trade, and continued by enforcing the importance of education to ensure Finland's success at international competition – again traditional right-wing views. The right-wing party member continued to address the criticism Finland had received on the speedy manner refugee applications were handled, stating that this criticism was unwarranted as the Finnish practice was good. Next spoke a centre party representative who likewise highlighted domestic issues. He focussed on children, mentioning explicitly the position of children taken into custody. This area had also aroused international criticism toward Finland. He then mentioned children's mental healthcare in Finland. In 2003 this topic was subject to intense controversy at the Finnish Parliament due to plans to cut back on public funds allocated to it.[122]

For the present analysis these comments gain significance from the manner they stemmed directly from ongoing internal political debates and utilized the hearing as a medium for expanding the human rights discourse to address them. Simultaneously the comments expanded the human rights discourse to areas which are not mentioned in Finland's human rights treaty obligations or the eventual 2004 Report, for the preparation of which the hearing was organized. It appears unlikely that the commenting politicians even expected or were particularly interested in whether their comments would find a place within Finland's official human rights discourse. Rather, the hearing formed one additional forum within the Finnish political life in which the representatives could pursue their agendas. This tendency was likewise visible in many of the later interventions by NGOs, most conspicuously the intervention of a representative focussing on the position of children in Finland. She opened her intervention with an explicitly polemic comment, stating that "as I get paid for provoking, I shall do so now as well". After this, the representative outlined a list of concerns, most of which had remote or no connection with international

[122] The topic had received both intensive media attention and initiatives from parliament members, and in the end the plans were cancelled. 'Kela kiintiöi psykoterapiavarat,' 18.12.2003, http://www.verkkouutiset.fi/arkistojuttu.php?id=46356&hakusanat=Hoitosuhde (29.10.2007).

human rights norms and were instead directly linked to local politics. She mentioned, for example, how a Finnish city had cut back on its educational budget by 3%, and emphasized how this jeopardized the right of the area's children to equal education.

The Human Rights Discourse and 'LGBT-rights'

The hearing also provided an example of an instance where the expanse of the discourse was challenged due to the controversial nature of issues that were attempted to be incorporated into it, namely the rights of sexual minorities or LGBT-rights: lesbian, gay, bisexual and transsexual rights. Despite repeated attempts to mainstream the issue as a part of the Finnish human rights discourse and policy-making, its position has remained marginal. To fully grasp the Finnish developments as well as the rhetorical tools utilized in these initiatives, a glance into international developments is useful. Although occasional arguments suggest a much longer background,[123] the first initiatives on LGBT-rights in an international forum are most clearly associable with the late 1970s.[124] In the new millennium orchestrated efforts have been made for the adoption of a UN resolution on the matter, first in 2002 at the UN General Assembly, where attention was drawn to the lack of elaboration by an intergovernmental body of the concepts 'sexual minority' or 'sexual orientation'.[125] The following year saw the most prominent initiative to date: the resolution proposed by the Brazilian delegation of the UN Human Rights Commission to prohibit discrimination based on sexual orientation.[126] The resolution was discussed in

---

[123] Sanders, Douglas: 'Human Rights and Sexual Orientation in International Law.' In *25 International Journal of Public Administration 1*, 2002, 13–44.

[124] In 1978 the International Lesbian and Gay Association was founded in 1981 (see http://www.ilga.org/ (27.11.2006)), and the first case, Dudgeon v. United Kingdom, was adjudicated at the European Court of Human Rights, affirming the protection of lesbian and gay rights by noting that a law criminalizing consensual homosexual conduct in Northern Ireland violated the Convention. For this case as well as a summary of jurisprudence on sexual orientation and gender identity, see Human Rights Watch: Resource Library for International Jurisprudence on Sexual Orientation and Gender Identity, http://hrw.org/lgbt/jurisprudence.htm (22.1.2007). However, this remained the only favourable ruling of the 1980s, and in 1986 Klaus Törnudd stated 'there are no United Nations norms specifically concerned with the human rights of homosexuals'; Törnudd: Finland and the International Norms of Human Rights, *supra* note 2, 269. The 1990s were characterized by positive rulings particularly at the European Court of Human Rights, a development continuing in the new millennium.

[125] See discussion on these developments at Choike.org, http://www.choike.org/2009/eng/informes/854.html (6.11.2009).

[126] *Ibid.*

sessions in 2003 and 2004, but it proved too controversial for adoption. It has since been dropped from the Commission's agenda, and it appears unlikely that the Human Rights Council will bring it up in the near future.[127] Consequently lobbying efforts have altered their form. Spring 2007 saw the publication of the 'Yogyakarta Principles' on the application of international human rights law in relation to sexual orientation and gender identity.[128] Their publication was the result of a high-profile meeting including leading human rights scholars and UN experts, and they were introduced, for example, in an unofficial lunch meeting of the Fall 2007 session of the Human Rights Committee, where treaty members were encouraged to consider how the principles could be applicable to the Committee's work.

Finnish developments reflect the international momentum, as the issue was first raised by a Finnish interest group at an international forum in 1979. Then the NGO for sexual equality, SETA, made a formal complaint to the Human Rights Committee claiming that a provision of the Finnish Penal Code relating to public encouragement to "indecent behaviour between persons of the same sex" violated free speech.[129] Since then systematic attempts have been made to incorporate sexual orientation under the human rights discourse, particularly under provisions related to equality and non-discrimination, yet with limited success. For example in the 2000 Human Rights Report, whereas the rights of the disabled were discussed on three pages,[130] those of sexual minorities were mentioned in one paragraph under the rubric of minority rights.[131] Also, analysis of Finland's Foreign Minister's speeches in the period of 1999–2003 demonstrates that he made no references to the issue. In the 2004 Report sexual minorities were mentioned in the chapter discussing discrimination. The adjacent text referred to the 2002 UN General Assembly Third Committee meeting, where Finland supported the proposed resolution containing the term

---

[127] Redding, Jeffrey A.: 'Human Rights and Homo-Sectuality: The International Politics of Sexuality, Religion and Law.' In *4 Northwestern Journal of International Human Rights 3, 2006*, 436–492; Marks & Clapham: International Human Rights Lexicon, *supra* note 11, 327–343.

[128] Yogyakarta Principles: 'Principles on the International Human Rights Law in Relation to Sexual Orientation and Gender Identity,' March 2007, http://www.yogyakartaprinciples.org/ (6.11.2009).

[129] Törnudd: Finland and the International Norms of Human Rights, *supra* note 2, 269–270.

[130] Human Rights Report (2000), *supra* note 84, 121–123.

[131] *Ibid.*, 93.

sexual orientation. The 2004 Report also mentions that Finland actively supports the initiative of Brazil to have a resolution dealing with sexual orientation approved in the UN Human Rights Commission, nowadays Council. Finally, the Report emphasizes that Finland will highlight the rights of sexual and gender minorities in other contexts as an essential human rights question that has remained without sufficient attention.[132] Yet the space allotted to the issue of 'LGBT-rights' remains brief – one paragraph in the 130-page entity.[133]

This outcome was far more limited than the one desired by Finnish interest groups. The extensive intervention made by an NGO representative on sexual minorities in the discussed hearing of 2003 illustrates this. The representative started with a general reference to the position of sexual minorities, mentioning violence against transsexuals, particularly women. After that, he highlighted the problems of intrasex people and the question of adoption by same sex couples; and continued by discussing the practices of the Lutheran church, which were described as discriminatory against homosexual employees. The representative then addressed the problems of transsexuals, emphasizing how the demographic profiles of government records continued to hold information of previous gender after sex-change operations; this was seen as a violation of the protection of information. Finally the intervention drew attention to the corrective surgeries performed usually on newborns or young intrasex children, meaning children who are born with identifiers of both sexes. These comments entail important elements requiring closer attention. To begin with the references to homosexual employees of the Lutheran church, they illustrate instances where the human rights discourse is utilized to address controversial domestic political topics which have otherwise occasionally failed to gain wider societal attention. That these issues were articulated through the human rights discourse can be connected to the hope that this might invest them with greater legitimacy and lead to general acceptance. The same applies to the comment relating to the position of homosexual church employees. This topic had at the time received considerable media attention, but its progress remained uncertain. An even more controversial topic was that of adoption by same-sex couples. The issue had been discussed by the Parliament on numerous

[132] Human Rights Report (2004), *supra* note 89, 103.
[133] *Ibid.*, 102.

occasions, so far without agreement. Yet future success of legislative initiatives on the issue appears likely.

When examining the rhetorical strategies utilized in these initiatives, international lobbying efforts include arguments that they 'already exist' in the current human rights instruments. This approach surfaced particularly after the Brazil proposal was rejected, with views commenting that the setback was not as severe as initially feared. According to this argument, since the rights being advocated for are all effectively covered by the existing documents, the role of any potential new document is primarily to *unify* existing discourses.[134] This strategy is visible also in the Finnish context. The interventions of the representative of an NGO focussing on sexual minorities demonstrate how acceptance for the controversial topic of LGBT-rights is attempted by connecting it to issues already enjoying a more clearly defined status within the Finnish human rights discourse. Here illustrative are the comments where the NGO representative described the corrective surgery commonly performed on intrasex children as "intrasex genital mutilation". This terminology connected this issue to another one holding a central profile in the human rights discourse, namely female genital mutilation, also called FGM. FGM was at the time invested with considerable political attention in Finland, and it was mentioned repeatedly in the 2003 hearing, among others by the Foreign Minister who opened the event. By equating these two practices with each other the NGO representative sought to position the cause of transsexual children more favourably due to the common disapproval bestowed upon female genital mutilation. The representative equated the position of intrasex children also with the disabled, a group whose concerns likewise hold a more recognized position in the human rights discourse, as is reflected by the 2006 adoption of the Convention on the Rights of Persons with Disabilities.[135] He clarified this equation by noting: "It is not an entirely marginal group I am talking about: there are more intrasex children born annually than those with Down syndrome."

The intervention of the NGO representative included an additional rhetorical strategy, one where the position of sexual minorities was

[134] WHRNet, *supra* note 98.

[135] United Nations Convention on the Rights of Persons with Disabilities. Adopted on 27 August 2006, http://www.un.org/disabilities/convention/conventionfull.shtml (6.11.2009).

approached through extension of existing categories. This applies particularly to the conception of discrimination. In the hearing he phrased the group that might potentially face discrimination as being constituted of the "disabled, homosexual, religious minority". Examination of the NGO representative's speeches and writings from the following years suggest that this connection was no isolated instance, but rather part of a systematic strategy to expand the category of discrimination in the human rights discourse by equating the socially and politically controversial topic of sexual orientation with that of more readily acceptable minorities.[136] Combined interventions on behalf of sexual minorities appear to have produced some, although modest results. To evaluate the position of sexual minorities in the Finnish political human rights discourse, the 91 analysed speeches by Finland's Foreign Minister show that prior to 2004 they entailed no references to sexual minorities. Instead the group facing discrimination emerges as being constituted of women, children, ethnic groups and indigenous peoples, minorities and to a more marginal extent, disabled people. Although the Foreign Minister referred explicitly to these other groups as he opened the hearing in 2003, sexual minorities were not mentioned. The year 2004 demonstrates a differing pattern as sexual minorities are mentioned on four occasions. Yet, for example, one of these mentions differs considerably from those of the NGO representative: the Foreign Minister phrased the matter as "people with disability within minority groups, and sexual minorities within immigrant groups". The 2004 Report focusses exclusively on the position of sexual minorities. Thus all the other comments of the hearing are left outside it and the Report makes no reference, for example, to the more contested issue of right of adoption by same sex couples. In the sector on "Discrimination", referring to Article 6 of the Finnish Constitution, sexual minorities are not explicitly mentioned as the text entails, in addition to enlisting the groups conventionally associated under this category in the human rights discourse, instead the phrase "other

[136] For example in an article from a left wing magazine from 2003 he discusses the group facing discrimination as being constituted by 'gay, transvestite, immigrant, hearing impaired, Muslim'. In 2005 he equated in two speeches the position of sexual minorities to other groups facing discrimination such as gender, age, ethnic background, disability, and conviction; and an article from 2006 makes the same reference by associating discrimination on the basis of 'homosexuality, transgender, ethnicity, age, disability'.

Table 6: 'Rights of', Total 1999–2006

	minority	ethnic/ indig-enous	women	children	disabled	sexual minority	total
1999	-	-	-	-	-	-	-
2000	2	2	2	1	1	-	8
2001	1	3	3	1	-	-	8
2002	-	-	4	1	-	-	5
2003	4	4	6	6	3	-	23
2004	4	7	8	5	3	4	31
2005	1	-	1	-	-	-	2
2006	-	-	3	2	-	-	5
Total	**12**	**16**	**27**	**16**	**7**	**4**	**82**
%	15%	20%	33%	20%	9%	5%	100%

matter relating to a person".[137] The Foreign Minister did not mention sexual minorities in any of the examined speeches to the Parliament upon presenting the report,[138] nor has he mentioned the topic in any speech after 2004 (Table 6). Combined this indicates that despite systematic lobbying efforts, the position of sexual minorities has not established itself as an integral part of the Finnish political human rights discourse.

From the Periphery to the Centre

To summarize this analysis on the discussions around Finland's 2004 Human Rights Report, two primary observations emerge of the human rights discourse in Finland and the processes contributing to its expansion. First, these discussions demonstrate how in practical situations the human rights discourse transforms into a venue for discussing local social and political issues which at times may be greatly distant from the abstract provisions of international human rights instruments. Second, the success with which different interests become

[137] Human Rights Report (2004), *supra* note 89, 102.

[138] Foreign Affairs Ministry: 'Ulkoasiainministeri Tuomioja valtioneuvoston ihmisoikeuspoliittisesta selonteosta,' 31.3.2004, http://formin.finland.fi/public/default.aspx?contentid=61378&nodeid=15631&contentlan=1&culture=fi-FI (28.9.2006).

accepted as a part of the discourse depends greatly on their wider social and political acceptance. Consequently, although controversial issues might benefit greatly from being accepted into the discourse, their controversial nature renders their wider societal recognition as human rights issues significantly difficult. To conclude, a few general conclusions can be drawn of the position of the human rights discourse among the Finnish population. Today most Finns are familiar with the discourse and view it with great favour. This has been reflected, for example, in rapidly growing membership numbers for the Finnish Amnesty International in the new millennium: in the years between 2003 and 2007 the number has tripled, jumping from 10 000 to over 30 000. Examination of membership profiles suggests that the group reflects primarily the same demography as the group leading the statistics in separating from the Lutheran church as they are primarily young urban adults. Expansionary development has been likewise visible for example for UNICEF when explored in terms of people making regular monthly donations to the organization: whereas in 2000 this group included only some hundreds of individuals, by 2006 the figure had exceeded 40 000. In addition to membership and financial donations, particularly many young Finns participate readily in such human rights initiatives as signing online Amnesty petitions. The human rights discourse is becoming increasingly prevalent for addressing a great range of issues, as was reflected in the opening quotation of this chapter. Three additional examples demonstrate how the discourse is utilized in surprising and innovative contexts by laymen. A Finnish book on sleeping disorders describes how sleep and sleeping, through being constitutive to a good life, become human rights.[139] A representative of the council of the City of Helsinki utilizes the functioning of libraries as essentially human rights work.[140] Finally, the food pages of Finland's largest newspaper utilize the human rights discourse as follows:

> To the hunters of wild greens [edible plants that grow in nature] spring is what autumn is to those picking mushrooms [...]We acquire our food far too easily, which [...] harms us in many, invisible ways [...] We are drowning in food, evidenced in increasing food wastage, increased production rates and obesity [...] People could search for their food, find it,

---

[139] Hyyppä, Markku T. & Kronholm, Erkki: Uni ja vire. Kansaneläkelaitos, Turku. 1998, 192.

[140] Tiia Aarnipuu speaking in the City Council of Helsinki, 1.2.2006, http://www.aarnipuu.net/puheenvuoroja.htm (30.8.3006).

pick it up, carry it home and prepare it [...] People not only have a right to enjoy their food, but also to the pleasure brought by its finding [...] I am talking of a topic that in my opinion should belong to human rights.
Vivi-Ann Sjögren.[141]

[141] Helsingin Sanomien kuukausiliite 5/2006, 95–99. Original in Finnish, translation by author.

CHAPTER THREE

THE SCANDINAVIAN NETWORK OF HUMAN RIGHTS EXPERTS

Two high school acquaintances run into each other after ten years. They briefly exchange news of their lives. One has had two children, the other is working on a PhD. The first one asks what the PhD is about, the other answers "human rights". Before the other has time to elaborate, the first one exclaims: "It's nice to know that at least some of us are doing something good".

This exchange occurred to me when I was about two years into my research. It stuck with me due to its distinct and unambiguously positive conception of my work; an unlikely notion had I told my classmate that I was pursuing my earlier research on the relationship of the Miccosukee Indians and the State of Florida. The above instance was not an isolated one, either. When discussing my topic with friends working in diverse fields, as well as with strangers, I observed how the very reference to 'human rights' was received as entailing noble aspirations to improve the world. Whereas this rendered me occasionally uneasy – I felt I was operating under a false banner due to my more complex analytical approach to the human rights phenomenon – it communicated to me that people identified as (aspiring) human rights experts are received as kind-hearted and well-intentioned individuals. These sentiments directed my ethnographic gaze to the favourable societal position enjoyed by human rights experts in Finland. This position is illustrated by the tone utilized to describe human rights experts in the Finnish media, a matter explored through two featured articles from a prominent newspaper and a magazine following the nomination of a human rights expert to a high-status international position.[1] The articles highlight the expert's persona by emphasizing

[1] Nousiainen, Anu: 'Aina pienten puolella.' In *Helsingin Sanomat*, 4.9.2005, D3; Riitta Kylänpää: 'Hän.' In *Suomen Kuvalehti*, 19.8.2005, 52–56. The original language of the articles is Finnish and all quotes are translations by the author. The following dictionary has been consulted for translation of individual terms: Hurma, Raija; Malin, Riitta-Leena & Syväoja, Olli: Finnish-English General Dictionary. WSOY, Helsinki, 1984.

two characteristics: on the one hand kindness, on the other, toughness. The first characteristic emerges from expressions describing the expert as agreeable and good-humoured. The articles mention how "she laughs gently – at herself" and how she upon being greeted is "visibly in a good mood even though the day appears to have been a busy one"; they describe how she "states kindly" and talks "without raising her voice". The articles emphasize that "self-indulgence is not a part of [her] style" and that "she is not one of those who greatly crave to dress in a business suit". Both articles discuss the expert's family ties, which are cultivated and privileged. They also include detail connecting the expert to her wider context. This description emphasizes imagery of nature and everyday artifacts. They outline how in the interview setting "the surface of the river is moss-green, the oaks old and great" and mention how "a gust of wind strokes across the table and raw apples fall from the tree". They note how the expert "sniffs the south-west wind" while sitting "under the apple trees". Both articles mention the expert making and drinking coffee, one of them enclosing detail on the type of cup used – "an old fashioned porcelain cup" – the other on the quality of the coffee made by the expert – "good, strong coffee". They mention that the expert enjoys entertaining guests and describe the dishes she is planning to offer them.

This image is contrasted with the one where the expert "howls", "scolds", and "does not get along with others at any cost". The expert is known "as a snappish discussant" who does not leave it "unclear what her opinion is". She is described as "so to speak, to have balls" which "stops her knees from trembling" in difficult situations. As reasons for such strongly contrasting personal characteristics the articles mention the expert's commitment to her beliefs, which are "always on the side of the weak against the strong" and for the defence of which she is willing to engage in strong disagreements. Both articles mention her desire to improve the world through her work for the defence of human rights which she characterizes as "work for building a global societal peace". Both articles highlight how the expert's commitment to her values has a long pedigree, as she "already in primary school brought home the most ragged and dirty school mates and gave them her books". They emphasize her role as a pioneer who concerned herself with human rights also during an era "when human rights were not in fashion". The articles discuss how her commitment has guided her career, leading first to involvement in domestic policy-making and human rights education. From this her engagement has globalized, as she now travels over 120 days a year, meeting people from all parts of the world. This leads to tremendously long working hours. She mentions being "used to 14–16 hour days", a condition for which her new engagement, added on top of her existing commitments, contributes. To summarize the lay conception of a human rights expert emerging from these two articles, she is portrayed as a kindhearted yet courageous person; a visionary and a pioneer willing to make great temporal investments in her attempts to improve the world even while facing opposition or personal unpopularity.

The conception of human rights experts is strongly contrasted by the tone used particularly in Finnish tabloid newspapers to describe Lutheran ministers, whose actions are today regularly featured in headlines and front pages. To illustrate this with a few examples, four recurring themes can be identified. One of them relates to ministers' violent behaviour, resulting for example in June 2007 in the headline by the tabloid paper Iltalehti "The police were summoned – a confirmation camp disrupted", with the article telling how "the children ran to escape the enraged minister".[2] In 2005 headlines focussed particularly on the actions of 'the Beating Minister' (*hakkaajapappi*) referring to a minister convicted of physical assault.[3] The second recurring theme is formed by ministers who appear in their workplaces intoxicated by alcohol; for example in April 2007 Iltalehti reported how a minister was fired for drinking.[4] The third, and perhaps the most enduring source for headlines, is the still ongoing controversy over the position of female ministers. Although the Finnish Lutheran church approved the right of women to serve as ministers in 1988, conservative male ministers continue to hold the option to refrain from working in the same service with female ministers.

---

[2] This instance also generated an online debate with participants commenting for example: 'is it any surprise that my child and I don't belong to the church'. Both the link to the article as well as the discussion are available at KeskusteluSuomi 24, http://keskustelu.suomi24.fi/show.fcgi?category=1000000000000003&conference=1500000000000012&posting=22000000027187631 (7.11.2007); the Iltalehti website offers direct links only to its recent issues.

[3] Kivioja, Pasi: 'Kolmen vuosikymmenen skandaalit,' speech held at Julkinen yksityinen -seminaari, 23.8.2007, skandaali.files.wordpress.com/2007/08/julkyks.ppt (7.11.2007).

[4] Reference to article available at Plaza 2007: 'Lyhyestä virsi kaunis, sanoi Iltalehti, kun pappi erotettiin juopottelun takia,' 27.4.2007, http://plaza.fi/ajassa/polttopisteessa/iltalehden-varoittava-esimerkki-typeryydesta (7.11.2007).

This option is commonly frowned upon by the press, and for example in May 2007, Iltalehti featured the headline "Female minister chased from the church" to describe an instance where a male minister refused to work with a female minister.[5] The fourth, and perhaps the most frequent source of headlines, is formed by issues of morality and sexuality. In 2005 this was most visible in the numerous headlines utilizing the expression 'The Cheating Bishop' (*pettäjäpiispa*) to discuss an instance where the marriage of a bishop was dissolved due to an extramarital affair.[6]

These four themes have raised particularly the personal lives of Lutheran ministers as a genre of the new 'scandals' reported on and sought after by the Finnish tabloid media.[7] Simultaneously instances where church-related headlines in mainstream media are positive remain scarce.[8] Although this applies to most headlines dwelling on disasters and scandal, the above examples demonstrate how in the media Lutheran ministers fail to occupy a position of spiritual leadership and moral integrity, which contributes to a vacuum of public role models. Although it is overstated to claim that this position has been filled by human rights experts, media portrayals suggest that today public conceptions view these experts, in addition to being people knowledgeable about human rights, as morally righteous individuals who provide leadership for others. Importantly, such descriptions entail nothing inevitable. Scholarship offers contrasting portrayals

---

[5] Article available at the discussion forum Blogspot: 'Naispappi ajettiin kirkosta,' 3.5.2007, http://rankinen.blogspot.com/2007/03/naispappi-ajettiin-kirkosta.html (7.11.2007).

[6] Kivioja: 'Kolmen vuosikymmenen skandaalit', *supra* note 3. This element is, of course, not restricted to the Finnish Lutheran Church, as particularly the Catholic Church is a recurring source of similar headlines. Consequently, for example in October 2007, Iltalehti reported of a new Vatican sex scandal where a priest in a high position had made sexual advances toward a young man. See Iltalehti: 'Seksiskandaali Vatikaanissa: Pappi lähenteli nuorta miestä,' 16.10.2007, http://www.iltalehti.fi/ulkomaat/200710156719442_ul.shtml (7.11.2007).

[7] Kivioja: 'Kolmen vuosikymmenen skandaalit,' *supra* note 3.

[8] One exception was formed by the autumn 2007 headlines relating to the actions of one parish to assist an asylum seeker whose application had been rejected by the Finnish immigration officials. This instance was part of a larger campaign by the Lutheran church to actively assist asylum seekers. See Kirkko turvapaikkana, http://www.ekumenia.fi/kirkot_ja_maahanmuuttajat/kirkko_turvapaikkana/ (7.11.2007). Another important instance was provided by the November 2007 shooting incident in a Finnish school, after which the church was highlighted as a place of sanctuary by most of Finnish press.

where human rights experts are depicted, instead of world reformers, above all as bureaucrats characterized by their distinct knowledge practices.[9] The research of Daniel Goldstein provides yet another contrast: while exploring public conceptions of human rights advocates in Bolivia, he noted that although the political elites celebrate the human rights discourse, increasing inequality and civil unrest have left public sentiments more divided. Thus "[i]t is widely believed in the barrios of [the Bolivian town of] Cochabamba that human rights advocates defend the delinquents, positioning them as enemies of law-abiding citizens".[10]

The Systemic Agency of Human Rights Experts

Despite positive connotations bestowed upon human rights experts in Finland as well as the frequent use of the concept 'human rights expert' to denote individuals working with human rights, the concept's content has received little systematic attention: who human rights experts are, what they do, and how they acquire their status, among other things. Finnish media invocations suggest the concept to be rather fluid and utilized about individuals with highly diverse backgrounds. This finding reflects the membership criteria of UN treaty bodies. Although members are required to be 'experts', no exhaustive definition is offered on what renders an individual as such.[11] To approach the issue more analytically, the concept 'community of practice' becomes useful.

The concept is utilized by Jean Lave and Etienne Wenger to describe learning processes, and although they offer no exhaustive definition, they characterize it as a "set of relations among persons, activity, and world over time and in relation with other tangential and

[9] See for example Riles, Annelise: The Network Inside Out. The University of Michigan Press, Ann Arbor, 2001.

[10] Goldstein, Daniel M.: 'Human rights as culprit, human rights as victim: rights and security in the state of exception.' In *The Practice of Human Rights: Tracking Law Between the Global and the Local* (Eds. Goodale, Mark & Merry, Sally Engle). Cambridge University Press, Cambridge, 2007, 49-77.

[11] See for example Human Rights Committee: Members, http://www.ohchr.org/english/bodies/hrc/members.htm (31.3.2006); also Craven, Matthew: The International Covenant on Economic, Social, and Cultural Rights: A Perspective on Its Development. Oxford University Press, New York, 1995.

overlapping communities of practice".[12] This study construes the community of practice of human rights experts as formed of individuals who have both training and professional experience in human rights issues and gain all or part of their income from human rights work: consultative positions, research and teaching, NGO work and UN positions, among others. The community is viewed as being relatively new, as professional positions have emerged only recently; in the past UN treaty bodies, for example, were populated by senior officials who were often charged of representing political government interests and lacking human rights expertise.[13] Professional human rights experts began to emerge in significant numbers only in the 1980s and particularly in the 1990s. This temporality reflects the findings of Yves Dezalay and Bryant Garth on the community of practice of international arbitration lawyers.[14]

To acquire precision, the profile of human rights expertise is explored through the members of the Scandinavian Network of Human Rights Experts, SCANET. Before that, the significance of human rights expert positions needs to be addressed. Why does it matter who is called a human rights expert? What kind of authority do experts exert in the human rights phenomenon? This study connects answers to these questions to the continual expanse of the human rights phenomenon illustrated by Graph 3. The graph enlists the adoption of new artifacts, as well as overviews how the discourse and the community utilizing the human rights discourse to articulate their claims have enlarged. The graph connects this process further to the concepts of *centre* and *periphery*, as the phenomenon moves continually to novel and often distant domains.

[12] Lave, Jean & Wenger, Etienne: Situated Learning: Legitimate Peripheral Participation. Cambridge University Press, Cambridge, 1991, 98. Membership in communities of practice includes knowledge of 'who is involved; what they do; what everyday life is like; how masters talk, walk, work, and generally conduct their lives; how people who are not part of the community of practice interact with it', see Lave & Wenger, 95.

[13] Craven: The International Covenant on Economic, Social, and Cultural Rights, *supra* note 11, 45. Little scholarship is available on such facets of UN work. Here the primary source has been an interview with a predominant SCANET expert and former treaty body member.

[14] Dezalay, Yves & Garth, Bryant G.: Dealing in Virtue: International Commercial Arbitration and the Construction of a Transnational Legal Order. The University of Chicago Press, Chicago, 1996.

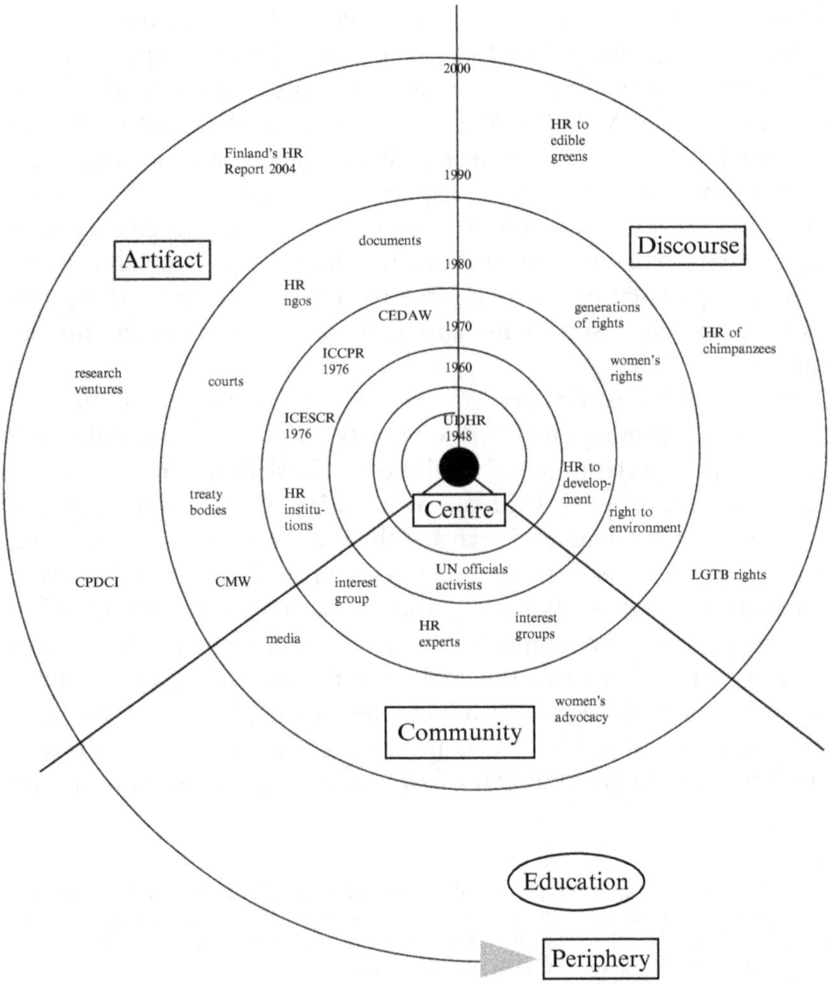

Graph 3: *Expansion of the Human Rights Phenomenon*

Expansion has a complex momentum which moves on the one hand from the centre to the periphery, on the other from the periphery to the centre as different actors seek recognition for their claims at the centre for example in artifacts. Continual expansion is commonly regarded as a positive development, yet it entails a decisive risk: the more the human rights discourse expands, the more the concept of human rights acquires characteristics of a free-floating signifier to be filled with any meanings the speaker wishes.[15] This development is reflected in instances where the discourse is utilized to support mutually contradictory claims, such as anti-homosexual initiatives. For example in August 2006 a Polish politician argued against public gay parades by stating: "[t]hey bring deprivation to public places and through this violate the human rights of other citizens".[16] Possibilities to utilize the human rights discourse to forward any given claims pose sombre challenges for the human rights phenomenon and undermine the potency of the discourse to function as 'trumps' by forwarding 'factoid'[17] statements about the desired state of the human condition.

Human rights experts occupy a pivotal position to prevent this outcome from becoming a reality. Their position finds elaboration through the concept of systemic agency utilized by Marshall Sahlins to describe the contributions of individuals in historic events. Sahlins explains how through the structural relays of the society authority is conveyed to particular persons.[18] This characterization illustrates the authority of human rights experts, who through their structural empowerment within the human rights phenomenon enjoy a systemic agency that assigns them power to adjudicate the content of the human rights discourse. Simultaneously this agency produces the inherent structure of experts and laymen discussed by Ulf Hannerz in relation to the flow of meaning. Expertise leads a situation where laymen submit elements of their

[15] The term floating or empty signifiers has a long pedigree originating from the writings of Claude Lévi-Strauss in the 1950s, moving to the works of Jacques Lacan and Roland Barthes. For summaries of its utilization, see Mehlman, Jeffrey: 'The "Floating Signifier": From Lévi-Strauss to Lacan.' In *Yale French Studies 48*, 1972, 10–37. Ernesto Laclau has discussed the role of 'empty signifiers' in politics, see Laclau, Ernesto: Emancipation(s). Verso, London, 1996.

[16] Kause, Pilvikki: 'Puolalainen ääripuolue lähti ristiretkelle homoja vastaan.' In *Helsingin Sanomat*, 10.8.2006, B3. Many thanks to Taina Tuori for this quotation. The recent anti-homosexual activities of Poland and other former communist countries have invoked intense concern from interest groups working to improve the position of sexual minorities, see LiveJournal: 'How many Polish people does it take to celebrate pride?,' 12.6.2006, http://mikeijames.livejournal.com/1385073.html (28.8.2006); Kitlinski, Tomaz; Leskowics, Pawel & Lockard, Joe: 'Poland's transition: From Communism to Fundamentalist Hetero – Sex,' http://bad.eserver.org/issues/2005/72/kitlinskileszkowiczlockard.html (11.9.2006).

[17] Kennedy, Duncan: 'The Critique of Rights.' In *Left Legalism / Left Critique* (Eds. Brown, Wendy & Halley, Janet). Duke University Press, Durham & London, 2002, 178–228.

[18] Sahlins, Marshall: Apologies to Thucydides: Understanding History as Culture and Vice Versa. The University of Chicago Press, Chicago, 2004, 155–156.

autonomy; they are transformed into 'clients'.[19] The functioning of expert systemic agency is illustrated by Bruno Latour's description on the social construction of scientific facts. Latour describes how

> The "average man who happens to hit the truth", naively postulated by Galileo, will have no chance to win over the thousands of articles, referees, supporters and granting bodies who oppose his claim.[20]

This applies likewise to the human rights phenomenon, where the claims of the average man – be they for the human right to renewable energy, edible greens or the degradatory effects of homosexual parades – fail to gain recognition for the issue as a human right in international treaty making, human rights research or political rhetoric, as was demonstrated by the issue of LGBT-rights. In order for an individual to make successful claims for laymen that a given issue forms part of the human rights discourse, access is required to the "thousands of articles, referees, supporters and granting bodies" of the human rights phenomenon.

Here individuals hold highly differing positions: while average men have limited access to and competence with these domains, they are readily available for human rights experts. The distinction between experts and laymen is also often reinforced by human rights experts themselves, who emphasize how laymen have only a vague understanding of what human rights *really* are.[21] The asymmetry of knowledge relations between experts and laymen assigns human rights experts significant structural authority as intermediaries. The term derives from the analysis of Sally Engle Merry, who describes as its central component the ability to translate the abstract human rights discourse into concrete meanings in particular circumstances (Graph 4).[22]

---

[19] Hannerz, Ulf: Cultural Complexity: Studies in the Social Organization of Meaning. Columbia University Press, New York, 1992, 119.

[20] Latour, Bruno: Science in Action. Harvard University Press, Cambridge, 1987, 44.

[21] This was illustrated by a 2006 commentary in Finland's largest newspaper by leading human rights NGO representatives who emphasized how, although the concept of human rights is commonly known by the Finnish population, the exact content of human rights remains unclear. Kouros, Kristiina; Johansson, Frank & Laukko, Helena: 'Ihmisoikeudet tunnetaan heikosti.' In *Helsingin Sanomat*, 10.12.2006, C6.

[22] Merry, Sally Engle: Human Rights & Gender Violence: Translating International Law into Local Justice. The University of Chicago, Chicago, 2006, 41; Merry associates three dimensions in this process: framing, program appropriation and definition of target population. She offers an example on defining the target population through the concept of domestic violence. In the US it refers to actions between romantic partners, in China also to actions within households. See Merry, 136–137.

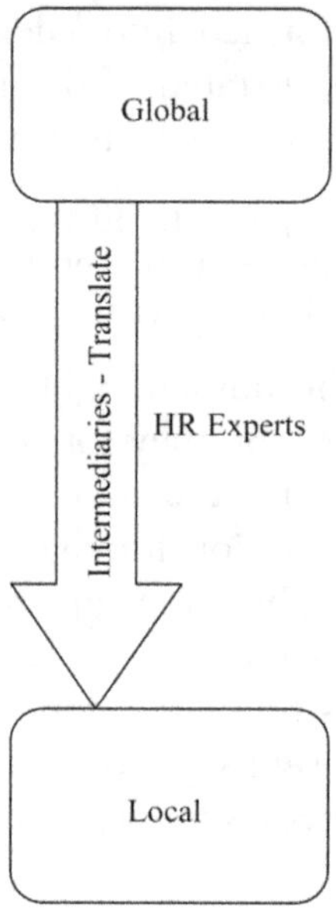

Graph 4: *Human Rights Experts as Intermediaries*

Examples from the Finnish context demonstrate how this position has gained increasing influence: human rights experts are called upon by interest groups for the disabled peoples to translate abstract provisions of international human rights instruments to correspond to their specific concerns[23] and experts are cited as authorities by free-thinkers who advocate for the separation of the state and church,[24] as well as by Christian politicians who support their continued alliance.[25] As the influence of the human rights discourse has grown, also the systemic agency of human rights experts has gained greater impact. This has led

[23] Dialogi: 'Lisääntymisoikeus on kiistaton,' http://www.stakes.fi/dialogi/06/d206/44.htm (19.5.2006).The article argued that children are too often removed from their disabled parents and placed into foster care, and that instead the rights of parents to care for their children should be assigned greater importance. This concern finds no direct articulation from existing international covenants and thus the interviewed expert acted as an intermediary translating provisions of existing treaties to support these claims.

[24] Vapaa-ajattelijat: 'Viite: 34/041/1998 Lausuntopyyntönne uskonnonvapauskomitean mietinnöstä (06.04.2001),' http://www.vapaa-ajattelijat.fi/kannanottoja/komitea_lopullinen.html (2.6.2007).

[25] Eduskunta: Täysistunnon pöytäkirja PTK 8/2006 vp, http://www.parliament.fi/faktatmp/utatmp/akxtmp/ptk_8_2006_ke_p_3.shtml (3.6.2007).

to increasing instances where knowledge relations mesh with power relations since through their systemic agency experts wield significant societal power, as has been discussed by David Kennedy in regards to international humanitarian efforts.[26] In the Finnish context, through their multiplying consultative positions, human rights experts continually have greater influence on how the society should be developed, which invests them likewise with significant societal power.

Simultaneously the systemic agency of human rights expert is vicarious in nature: human rights experts become particularly powerful arbiters of truth in instances where no direct consequences fall on people's everyday lives. In other words, their authority is most influential in abstract circumstances which pose no direct challenges to existing societal structures. This is illustrated by the following instance relating to an ongoing controversy in Northern Finland between reindeer herders and forestry workers. Behind the controversy are disagreements over land rights as well as conceptions of sustainable forest cultivation. The disagreement led into the submission of two complaints to the UN Human Rights Committee. One side complained that the forest works violate traditional rights to practice Sami reindeer herding, the other argued that to stop foresting violates the forestry workers' human right to their livelihood. Both sides consulted known human rights experts in the matter.[27] For the present purposes relevant becomes the tone in which the controversy and the statements of a participating human rights expert were described in a Finnish news broadcast.[28] The journalist sided with the perspective of forestry workers and perceived the controversy as posing a threat to their livelihood. This interpretation assigned the actions of the human rights expert with real life consequences on a group of individuals with whom he sympathized.

The journalist responded to this condition with confrontational undertones. Upon asking the expert why a UN body had been involved, the reporter commented: *"and why then should some body in Geneva rule our internal affairs*?" The expert responded by stating that along

[26] Kennedy, David: The Dark Sides of Virtue: reassessing international humanitarianism. Princeton University Press, Princeton, 2004.

[27] Foreign Affairs Ministry: 'Nellimin metsähakkuut keskeytetään,' Tiedote 358/2005, 16.11.2005, http://www.valtioneuvosto.fi/vn/liston/base.lsp?r=97998&k=fi&old=376 (18.11.2005); Tahkolahti, Jaakko: 'Inarin mestäkiista kaipaa sovittelijaa.' In *Helsingin Sanomat*, 11.12.2005, A5.

[28] News at Finland's MTV 3 on November 16, 2005.

the same lines one could ask why any country should abide by human rights norms. After all, as the UN rarely sends armed forces or imposes embargos, the most probable consequence of non-compliance is unfavourable publicity. The journalist appeared unconvinced by this response and concluded the segment by noting, in a bewildered tone: "*tomorrow an embargo will begin here: machinery will not operate and hundreds of men face losing their job*." This account illustrates how the systemic agency of human rights experts entails vicarious elements and becomes challenged when faced with undesired consequences. When parties stand to benefit, human rights experts are readily invited in as intermediaries, and their systemic agency recognized and respected. The possibility of undesirable immediate consequences alters this status: instead of being welcomed, systemic agency faces suspicion and challenge. In the disagreement over forestry the expert's translation of abstract treaties threatened to delimit the capacity of participating interest groups, and thus the systemic agency of the expert, as well as the UN human rights regime, was contested.

SCANET and the Emergence of the Community of Practice

The high authority enjoyed by the community of practice of human rights experts in the Finnish context renders it paramount to examine who are the individuals belonging to it. This matter is explored by investigating what kind of social capital, a concept utilized by Yves Dezalay and Bryant Garth in their analysis of the transnational community of arbitration lawyers,[29] membership in the Scandinavian Network of Human Rights Experts (SCANET) requires. This section examines factors of inclusion and exclusion, which lays the foundation for inspecting how the community is socially constructed. SCANET is a loose coalition of human rights experts in the Nordic and Scandinavian region including Finland, Sweden, Norway, Denmark and Iceland. It was officially founded in 2002, and it is exemplary of the communities of practice that have emerged within the human rights phenomenon particularly in the new millennium. SCANET members include an executive board, a board of administration, senior researchers, doctorate candidates as well as a part-time coordinator attending to practical matters. Membership in SCANET is varied. On the one

[29] Dezalay & Garth: Dealing in Virtue, *supra* note 14.

hand qualifying individuals may themselves request inclusion into the SCANET website, on the other, they may be included by the administrator as a consequence of involvement in, for example, a joint research venture. Also practical affiliation to SCANET alternates, and whereas some participate actively in its operations and probably view SCANET as a significant community, others frequent its activities scarcely and assign membership minor importance. Since its inception, SCANET membership numbers have continually grown: whereas in 2004 the number of senior researchers included in its website was 31 and in 2005 39, in November 2007 it was 51. The majority of this increase stems from the 25 doctorate degrees awarded during SCANET's existence and listed on its website, transforming previous doctorate candidates into senior researchers. Simultaneously also the number of new doctorate candidates has increased, primarily through new doctorate schools that have been aligned to SCANET in the different Nordic countries. The growth of SCANET membership numbers exemplifies the general expanse of the Nordic community of practice of human rights experts that has occurred particularly during the new millennium.

The SCANET website mentions as the primary aim of its operations to enhance already existing Nordic cooperation in human rights research and training while simultaneously strengthening its efficiency and quality. To reach these goals, SCANET operates by three primary functions: organizing events, distributing mobility grants and updating an e-mail list. The e-mail list functions primarily to provide information about upcoming events and career options, and it averages between one to two messages per week. Although all SCANET members have the possibility to distribute messages, their majority is sent by the SCANET coordinator who maintains the list. Thus the list does not function, for example, as a general discussion forum on ongoing human rights issues. Mobility grants originate from SCANET's general funder and provide funding for participating in SCANET activities as well as conducting research stays in different Nordic human rights institutions. The most important of SCANET functions are the activities it organizes, the number of which was 31 by February 2005 since the launching of SCANET in 2002, and 53 by November 2007. These activities vary in nature, and they include policy-oriented events such as expert meetings discussing current human rights issues, and more academic seminars and conferences, both organized in collaboration with Nordic human rights institutes, universities or different UN bodies. In the subsequent analysis attention is directed to the educational activities organized by SCANET, which intend to help participating students in their ongoing PhD research. In addition to permanent SCANET members – primarily senior researchers and doctorate candidates – educational activities include visiting experts who originate mostly from Europe or North America and represent well-known universities, UN bodies and human rights institutes among others.

SCANET origins are twofold. As was mentioned, it was officially founded in 2002 when it was awarded a funding period by a large public Scandinavian academic funder assigned the pseudonym 'ScaFund'. In addition to SCANET, ScaFund provides funding for numerous networks which are similar in their organization and operate in different scholarly fields in the Scandinavian and Nordic region. In 2006, when SCANET's first funding period ended, it was awarded with another period with a slightly modified research plan, yet with the same collaborational domains. The importance of collaborational relations is of fundamental importance for investigating SCANET, particularly its 'unofficial' narrative of origin. This narrative has significantly longer roots, and goes back to the 1980s, when collaboration between Scandinavian and Nordic human rights experts began to ensue. Consequently, instead of being something dramatically new, SCANET can be approached as another reification of these earlier collaborative relations. This is reflected in the statement of a prominent SCANET expert:

> It is difficult to put an exact starting point for SCANET … it is primarily a question of new names and forms depending on the funding that is currently available. The funding proposals and outlines have in recent years favoured the formation of these kinds of academic networks through the Nordic region, and thus it is natural that this is the form SCANET took.

Although collaborational patterns have distinct importance in SCANET operations, its operations embody also the specific requirements set forth by ScaFund, relating primarily to equal geographic representation to ensure genuine Nordic collaboration. Consequently both SCANET general organization as well as its individual activities need to meet distinct participant quotas from each of the participating countries. SCANET activities have been successful in meeting these quotas, yet closer examination demonstrates how, both in the number of events and the people participating in them, some of its formal

Finnish participants have acquired a more active role whereas others remain more passive. Consequently, despite attempts at equal geographic representation, actual SCANET activities show in their content as well as their structure and organizing venues, strong correlation with the active input of interested parties. Thus for example in 2005, half of the activities enlisted in the SCANET website were planned and carried out by one of the numerous participating domains.

SCANET Profile of Expertise

The unofficial SCANET narrative of origins has outlined how collaborational relations come to hold implicit importance over the definition of who is included in its community of practice. Explicit elements of expertise emerging both from the member profiles of SCANET senior researchers and its organizing rationale form four criteria. First, as a rule with only few exceptions, all SCANET experts have a PhD, which creates a strong correlation between SCANET expert status and high university education. Second, following guidelines laid forth by ScaFund, all permanent SCANET members need to have some association to the Nordic geographic area, a matter elaborated in Chapter 6. Third, in terms of professional background, by far the most common experience derives from research, with three fourths of SCANET experts mentioning it in their CVs. The other prevalent background is formed by law, which is mentioned by two thirds of experts; the relationship of human rights and law is more generally discussed in Chapter 5. The fourth criterion becomes that for SCANET experts, prior experience at the UN and different domestic governments is much more common than experience in different NGOs.[30] These four criteria offer a distinct characterization of the SCANET profile of expertise: it is occupied primarily by legal academics who have experience in research and different UN functions as well as their respective governments (Table 7). To place these findings in context as well as to provide the emergence of the community of practice of human rights experts with a temporality, these different elements are next considered individually.

[30] Table 7 includes examination of expert CVs that have been available at the SCANET website in February 2005. Thus the number of expert backgrounds examined is 21, whereas the total number of types of experiences is 70, as experts commonly mention more than one of these categories in their profiles.

Table 7: SCANET Expert Backgrounds (n = 21)

PROFESSIONAL		% (n = 70)	% (n = 21)
ACADEMIC	16	23%	76%
GOVERNMENT	5	7%	24%
UN	7	10%	33%
NGO	3	4%	14%
LAW	14	20%	67%
OTHER	25	36%	119%
TOTAL	70	100%	333%

Research Career Options

The emergence of research as a viable career option for aspiring human rights experts reflects the discussed SCANET narrative of origins by going back to the early 1980s when the different human rights institutes were founded in the Nordic countries. In 1983 the Norwegian Chr. Michelsen Institute (founded in 1978) commenced its human rights program,[31] followed by the founding of the Raoul Wallenberg Institute of Human Rights and Humanitarian Law in Sweden in 1984.[32] In 1986 the Institute for Human Rights was founded in Finland,[33] and in 1987 the Norwegian Institute for Human Rights was founded in Norway.[34] Increasing research interest was reflected in the founding of the Nordic Journal of Human Rights in 1982,[35] and the same years saw

[31] Chr. Michelsen Insitute, http://www.cmi.no/ (23.9.2005).

[32] The Raoul Wallenberg Institute of Human Rights and Humanitarian Law, http://www.rwi.lu.se/institute/aboutrwi.shtml (16.5.2006); Training Courses in Sweden, http://www.rwi.lu.se/coop/itp/overview.shtml (10.10.2007).

[33] Åbo Akademi Institute for Human Rights, http://www.abo.fi/instut/imr/ (16.5.2006 and 12.11.2007).

[34] Norwegian Centre for Human Rights, http://www.humanrights.uio.no/english/ (16.5.2006). Iceland has followed a different path, as the Icelandic Human Rights Centre was only established in 1994, see Icelandic Human Rights Centre, http://www.humanrights.is/english/about-us/history-and-mandate/ (21.12.2005). These are not the only human rights institutes of these countries, as Denmark has the Danish Institute for Human Rights, for which a founding year is unavailable, see The Danish Institute for Human Rights, http://www.humanrights.dk/frontpage/ (16.5.2006). Finland also has, for example, the Finnish League for Human Rights and the Erik Castrén Institute of International Law, founded in 1998. It is occasionally difficult to draw a distinction between a human rights NGO and an Institute – for example, many institutes are members of the International Coalition of NGOs.

[35] Mennesker & Rettigheter: Nordic Journal of Human Rights, http://www.humanrights.uio.no/forskning/publ/mr/ (2.11.2006).

for example in Finland the first PhDs focussing on human rights issues. Today the personnel of the Nordic human rights institutes ranges from a few individuals to some dozens. All the institutes engage in human rights research as well as organize events such as different expert meetings and academic conferences. Some of these institutes enjoy the status of national human rights institute, something encouraged by the Paris Principles of 1993, which provides them with certain steady funding.[36] The institutes that do not enjoy this status rely on more varied funding through a combination of academic projects and more policy-oriented work such as consulting statements and expert reports. Today, despite concerns related to employment security, career advancement or low wage standards, research has established itself as a viable career option for aspiring and current human rights experts. This development has been actively encouraged by a policy shift visible in Finland which seeks to increase the number of doctorate degrees obtained annually.[37] As desires exist simultaneously to lower the average age in which PhDs are acquired – a doctorate is increasingly viewed as a researcher's 'driving licence', a maturation into a professional research career, whereas it used to be the culmination of one's research career – also funding has been available for human rights research through, among others, the Finnish Graduate School in Human Rights Research. In addition to research positions, the human rights institutes offer career options in managerial positions, including heads of research ventures. As is elaborated in Chapter 4, research careers provide in addition increasing opportunities for teaching through the growing number of educational programs and courses on human rights.

Government and UN Career Paths

Table 7 demonstrated how prior experience in the government was another central component of SCANET expert profiles. To explore

[36] The 'Paris Principles' were adopted in 1993 and they outline the status of national institutions for the promotion and protection of human rights, see Office of the High Commissioner for Human Rights: Fact Sheet No. 19, National Institutions for the Promotion and Protecion of Human Rights, http://193.194.138.190/html/menu6/2/fs19.htm (17.5.2006).

[37] Ministry of Education: 'Toimenpideohjelma tutkijankoulutuksen ja tutkijanuran kehittämiseksi vuosille 2007–2011' http://www.minedu.fi/OPM/Julkaisut/2007/Toimenpideohjelma_tutkijankoulutuksen_kehittxmiseksi.html (6.5.2007); 'Opetusministeriön ja opetushallituksen välinen tulosopimus vuosille 2006-2008,' http://www.oph.fi/info/netra/tulossopimus_2006_2008.pdf (3.6.2007).

the temporality of this career option as it has emerged in Finland, the Unit for Human Rights Policy, which is a part of the Political Department of Finland's Foreign Ministry, was founded in the mid-1990s. At first it employed around half a dozen individuals, which has since grown to about a dozen; the number was doubled for Finland's EU Presidency in 2006. However, although the employees of the Department work on a wide range of human rights issues, according to the SCANET conception of expertise they, like other government functionaries, are not seen primarily as experts, as their views and actions are instead treated as reflecting 'politics'; a characterization familiar from human rights literature. In the SCANET conception of expertise, greatly more prestigious is involvement in the different UN expert positions such as membership in a treaty body. Exploration of SCANET expert backgrounds demonstrates how these experiences are mentioned by one of three SCANET experts (Table 7). Also here the emergence of professional positions is relatively recent, as the Human Rights Committee monitoring the compliance of the CCPR was founded in 1977,[38] and the Committee on Economic, Social and Cultural Rights monitoring the CESCR was established by ECOSOC in 1988.[39]

To explore the functioning of treaty bodies briefly, today there exist seven treaty bodies monitoring the most important human rights treaties. For all treaties except the CESCR, treaty bodies have been formed according to the treaty provisions they monitor. Treaty bodies commonly convene between one and three times a year in Geneva or New York in sessions continuing from three to six weeks. Participants in these meetings include treaty body members, research assistants, representatives of state parties, and members of domestic and international NGOs who represent the civil society, as well as other observers; they also include interpreters and different UN personnel attending to practical matters, among others. The existence of treaty bodies stems

---

[38] Nowak, Manfred: 'The International Covenant on Civil and Political Rights.' In *International Protection of Human Rights: Achievements and Challenges* (Eds. Isa, Felipe Gómez & Feyter, Koen de). University of Deusto, Bilbao, 2006, 148; McGoldrick, Dominic: The Human Rights Committee: Its Role in the Development of the International Covenant on Civil and Political Rights. Oxford University Press, Oxford, 1994.

[39] Craven: The International Covenant on Economic, Social, and Cultural Rights, *supra* note 11, 39.

from the responsibility of state parties to produce reports on their compliance with treaty provisions at the intervals specified by the treaty. The treaty body then reviews these reports as well as possible additional material from other domains such as NGOs, and produces a statement where it compliments and reproaches state parties according to their conduct. In the absence of formal courts, treaty bodies are commonly considered the most important implementation mechanisms of human rights treaties. Yet the legal status of both the documents they produce as well as the bodies themselves is somewhat ambiguous.[40] In the proceedings, treaty body members hold a paramount role in examining the state reports beforehand as well as participating in their submission by state parties in the treaty body sessions.

Today treaty bodies increasingly include individuals construed as human rights experts instead of government representatives. This is also reflected in their composition: their members are increasingly academics, primarily professors, as well as acting judges, as is demonstrated by Tables 8 and 9.[41] The tables demonstrate how legal background and experience again emerge as significant, with 15 of 18 members of the Human Rights Committee listing prior professional legal experience. Noteworthy concerning treaty bodies are the scarce mentions of NGO experience found in biographic profiles: such experience is mentioned by only one member of the Committee on Economic, Social and Cultural Rights and three members of the Human Rights Committee.

[40] See discussion among others at UN Treaty Bodies, http://www.ohchr.org/english/bodies/treaty/index.htm (15.3.2006); Craven: The International Covenant on Economic, Social, and Cultural Rights, *supra* note 11; McGoldrick: The Human Rights Committee, *supra* note 38; Alston, Philip & Crawford, James: Human Rights Reform in the 21th Century. Cambridge University Press, Massachusetts, 2000; Merry: Human Rights & Gender Violence, *supra* note 22; Nowak: 'The International Covenant on Civil and Political Rights.' In *International Protection of Human Rights: Achievements and Challenges, supra* note 38, 137–154; O'Flaherty, Michael: 'The Concluding Observations of United Nations Human Rights Treaty Bodies.' In *6 Human Rights Law Review 1*, 2006, 27–52.

[41] Each treaty body has its own guidelines for selecting members. The homepage for the CESCR mentions that 'The Committee on Economic, Social and Cultural Rights is composed of 18 'independent experts' who are persons of 'high moral character and recognized competence in the field of human rights'. Members are elected for a term of four years by State parties. See Committee on Economic, Social and Cultural Rights: Members, http://www.ohchr.org/english/bodies/cescr/members.htm (21.12.2005 and 31.3.2006).

Table 8: Committee on Economic, Social and Cultural Rights (n = 17)

PROFESSIONAL		% (n = 53)	% (n = 17)
ACADEMIC	8	15%	47%
GOVERNMENT	14	26%	82%
UN	15	28%	88%
NGO	1	2%	6%
LAW	8	15%	47%
OTHER	7 (UN)	13%	41%
TOTAL	53	100%	312%

Table 9: Human Rights Committee (n = 18)

PROFESSIONAL		% (n = 84)	% (n = 18)
ACADEMIC	12	14%	67%
GOVERNMENT	17	20%	94%
UN	24	29%	133%
NGO	3	4%	17%
LAW	15	18%	83%
OTHER	13	15%	72%
TOTAL	84	100%	467%

This is again contrasted with the high frequencies with which members mention professional experience both from the government and the UN. These findings suggest that despite the high status assigned to NGOs in the human rights phenomenon, in practice there is surprisingly limited mobility between such positions as treaty body membership and NGOs.[42]

[42] It has been pointed out that despite not mentioning it in their profiles, many treaty body members do in fact have NGO experience which they have not highlighted in the concise treaty body webpages. Many thanks to Michael O'Flaherty for discussion on this point. Although this is likely accurate, absence of references nevertheless indicates that NGO experience does not enjoy an equally high status with the other professional engagements consistently mentioned by treaty body members.

In SCANET association with UN human rights bodies is construed as highly influential, as is elaborated in Chapter 4. In addition to being prestigious, SCANET experts characterize UN positions as professionally satisfying, which is reflected in the following profile by a former treaty body member:

> *The expert was elected for the Committee on Economic, Social and Cultural Rights in January 1995, where her term continued until December 2002. When elected, she was in her forties and clearly younger than the delegates in general, who are often in their 60s and 70s. She had been involved in international human rights work already for a decade, having been nominated for the first consultative position in the late 1980s. Back then she was still working on her PhD, which she describes as "critical human rights research focussing on national shortcomings": a thesis she completed in the early 1990s. She describes her work in the Committee as a "highly fascinating experience", and views a UN treaty body as the "professionally most satisfying position for a human rights expert", as it allowed her to treat "hundreds if not thousands of genuinely interesting problems which have a processually transforming impact."*

Human Rights NGOs

Both SCANET and treaty body member profiles have demonstrated how NGO experience is held by a small minority of members; only one in eight SCANET members mentioned previous experience among them (Table 7). Despite this outcome, it remains impossible to discuss the community of practice of human rights experts without reference to NGOs, as they are commonly construed as being in the *centre* of advancing the human rights phenomenon. For instance, William Korey notes how

> NGOs [...] would take on the challenge of transforming the words of the Declaration from a standard into reality; it was they who would assume the function of implementing the demands of international morality.[43]

[43] Korey, William: NGOs and the Universal Declaration of Human Rights: 'A Curious Grapevine'. St. Martin's Press, New York, 1998, 2. Korey borrows the title of his book from Eleanor Roosevelt, whom he quotes as calling NGOs the "curious grapevine" that would spread the message of the UDHR, see Korey, ix. Although few agreed-upon definitions exist for NGOs, a useful starting point for the present purposes is Keck and Sikkink's characterization of transnational activist networks as "motivated by values rather than by material concerns or professional norms", see Keck, Margaret E. & Sikkink, Kathryn: Activists beyond Borders: Advocacy Networks in International Politics. Cornell University Press, Ithaca, 1998, 2. For an analysis of the legal role of NGOs in international law, see Lindblom, Anna-Karin: Non-Governmental

Subsequently NGO positions will be briefly reviewed to appreciate the temporality with which the community of practice of human rights experts has evolved. Also here the developments are significantly recent: when the drafting of the UDHR took place, there were very few NGOs exclusively focussing on human rights, and "[n]ot until the fifties, sixties and seventies would there be created the prominent international human rights NGOs with which the contemporary world is familiar".[44] A salient event was the founding of the UK-based Amnesty International in 1961.[45] This was followed by the establishing of the Minority Rights Group International in 1965 and the predominant Human Rights Watch in 1978, as the result of the Helsinki Final Act of 1977 (Table 10).[46] In the 1970s NGOs started to proliferate, a development that has continued in the following decades. In addition to increasing in numbers, human rights NGOs have grown in their membership and their mandates. For example, between 1987–2002 the Human Rights Watch is stated to have tripled in size, with greatly expanding geographic reach and numerous special projects devoted to refugees, children's rights, academic freedom, international justice, AIDS, LGBT-rights, and the human rights of multinational corporations.[47] The same applies to Amnesty International, which has expanded its mandate significantly in recent years.[48]

Also in terms of NGOs, Nordic countries reflect the overall pulse of the human rights phenomenon, with the 1970s and 1980s becoming

---

Organisations in International Law. Cambridge University Press, Cambridge, 2005. For discussion on the role of NGOs in the human rights phenomenon, see Brett, Rachel: 'Non-Governmental Action in the Field of Human Rights.' In *An Introduction to the International Protection of Human Rights* (Eds. Hanski, Raija & Suksi, Markku). Åbo Akademi University, Åbo, 1997, 399–413.

[44] Korey: NGOs and the Universal Declaration of Human Rights, *supra* note 43, 3; 53.

[45] Amnesty International: 'AI's First 40 years,' http://web.amnesty.org/pages/aboutai-timeline-1960s-eng (16.5.2006); Power, Jonathan: Like Water on Stone: The Story of Amnesty International. Northeastern University Press, Darthmouth, 2001.

[46] Minority Rights Group International, http://www.minorityrights.org/ (24.8.2006); Human Rights Watch: About HRW, http://www.hrw.org/about/whoweare.html (16.5.2006); Keck & Sikkink: Activists beyond Borders, *supra* note 43, 89–97; LSE: Profile of Kenneth Roth, executive director of Human Rights Watch, http://www.lse.ac.uk/collections/pressAndInformationOffice/newsAndEvents/archives/2000-2002/Human_Rights_Symposium.htm (30.7.2002).

[47] LSE, *ibid*.

[48] Power: Like Water on Stone, *supra* note 45.

Table 10: Human Rights NGOs[49]

YEAR	NGOs & HR Centres		COUNTRY
-1940	1787	Anti-Slavery International	UK
	1898	Ligue des droits de l'homme et du citoyen	France
	1898	Ligue des droits de l'homme	Belgium
	1898	Ligue Hellenique des droits de l'homme	Greece
	1914	Internationale Liga Fur Menschenrechte	Germany
	1937	Liga Argentina por los derechos del hombre	Argentina
1940	1942	International League for the Rights of Man	US
1950	1952	International Commission of Jurists	Switzerland
1960	1961	Amnesty International	UK
	1965	Minority Rights Group International	UK
1970	1971	Médécins Sans Frontiers	France
	1975	Associacion por derechos humanos	Spain
	1976	Irish Council for Civil Liberties	Ireland
	1976	Ass.permanente de lost derechos humanos de Bolivia	Bolivia
	1977	Association for the Prevention of Torture	Switzerland (Geneva, ind)
	1978	Lawyer's Committee for Human Rights	US
	1978	Human Rights Watch (– Helsinki Watch)	US
	1978	International Helsinki Federation for Human Rights	Austria
	1979	Finnish League for Human Rights	Finland
	1979	Association Marocaine des droits humains	Marocco
	1979	Com. permanente por la defensa de los der. humanos	Colombia

[49] Table 10 covers central international human rights NGOs up to the end of the 1970s and a selection of others, primarily the members of the Fédération Internationale des Ligues des Droits de l'Homme. It also includes the major human rights NGOs identified by Raija Hanski and Markku Suksi, see Hanski, Raija & Suksi, Markku:

decisive. The Finnish chapter of Amnesty International was founded in 1974, and for example the Finnish League for Human Rights in 1979.[50] In the 1990s, following the shift in Finnish foreign policy to link development issues more tightly to human rights issues, collaboration between human rights NGOs and the government intensified, which was reflected in the founding of the Finnish NGO foundation for human rights in 1999. Previously similar foundations had been established in Norway in 1988, and in Sweden in 1991.[51] In Finland human rights NGOs are also invited to different hearings such as the already discussed hearing from 2003, organized as a background for the Human Rights Report of 2004. The new millennium has further witnessed rapidly growing membership numbers. Chapter 2 mentioned how the Finnish Amnesty has grown, and the same development applies to Denmark, where Amnesty membership numbers have grown in the new millennium from under 15 000 to over 80 000. In Sweden and Norway membership numbers are likewise around 50 000. Simultaneously NGO work has emerged as a viable career option for present and aspiring human rights experts as professional positions, although still modest in numbers, have proliferated in the new millennium: in 2003 the Finnish Amnesty had 11 full-time staff members, and in 2007 it had 21. Annelise Riles discusses how in Fiji the sums handled by NGOs were substantial, and consequently they were able to pay employees salaries that made activist work a lucrative and respected career entered into by the foreign-educated elite.[52] Although in the Finnish context revenues handled by NGOs are certainly more modest, these positions still provide for additional

---

An Introduction to the International Protection of Human Rights. Second edition. Åbo Akademi University, Åbo, 1997. Information on year of founding as well as country are derived from the websites of the organizations. For a more comprehensive list of references for useful NGO sites, see bibliography.

[50] Finnish League for Human Rights, http://www.ihmisoikeusliitto.fi/tausta/introduction (24.8.2006). The League pursues the work of the League for Human Rights established in 1935. Here the pattern seems similar to the already discussed Fédération des Ligues des Droits de l'Homme: that the operations of the League were interrupted with World War II, and picked up again as the human rights movement started to gain momentum.

[51] The Finnish NGO foundation for human rights, http://www.kios.fi/index.jsp (31.8.2006).The foundation was established by 11 human rights NGOs, including Amnesty International, Finnchurchaid and the Finnish UN Association.

[52] Riles: The Network Inside Out, *supra* note 9, 36, 47, 126. Riles mentions how "[t]he cost of attending the Beijing Conference, for example, equated the yearly salary of the average full-time worker in the capital city. A single project to produce several issues of a newsletter – a task requiring several weeks of work – could procure

professional positions for members of the community of rights experts.

Yet, NGO employees remain largely excluded from the SCANET expert community of practice. Three factors can be identified as contributing to this. The first relates to the guidelines set forth by ScaFund, which emphasize the formation of academic networks. Thus, reflecting these requirements, SCANET has ended up including primarily academics. However, whereas this may explain the profile of permanent SCANET members, it fails to clarify why NGO representatives are not included in SCANET activities as visiting experts. This outcome likely stems from the existing professional collaborational relations of permanent SCANET experts, most of which have been formed among academics. Consequently these relations are reflected in who is invited to SCANET activities as an expert.

This appears likely, considering for example the World Social Forum, a global coalition of NGOs, which gathers tens of thousands of people to its meetings: its newsletter, in addition to providing media for discussions on diverse ideologies and searching for alternatives for the current world order organized on the basis of neo-liberal economics, also highlights human rights, which are called a vital component in the realization of the new world order.[53] Despite such common substance and the ample visitors that both domains entail, no collaboration has emerged between them for example regarding the World Social Forum's meeting, which was organized in Helsinki in 2007.[54] Whereas this outcome could result from the different techniques utilized by the two entities – the World Social Forum in Finland incorporates more radical NGOs relating to animal rights, among others, that favour modes of activism foreign to SCANET experts – the relationship has more likely simply not emerged. SCANET has its origins in the Nordic human rights work with particular emphasis on the UN; the Social Forum has its origins in Brazil. The third plausible answer for lack of collaboration between SCANET and NGOs stems from the conception of expertise held by permanent SCANET members. Instead of holding substantive expertise on human rights, NGO representatives are commonly viewed

funding at a rate that exceeded the yearly starting salary for a university-educated civil servant", see Riles, 36.

[53] Sosiaalifoorumi. Hämeen paino Oy, Forssa, 2007.

[54] Importantly, both the Finnish chapter of Amnesty International as well as the Finnish League of Human Rights were also absent, demonstrating how also the NGO realm has expanded, see *ibid*.

as activists advocating for specific interests. Thus the competence that they hold fails to translate to what SCANET experts construe as human rights *knowledge*, and consequently they are not construed as experts in a manner similar to researchers or UN functionaries.

SCANET as Characteristic Human Rights Community

This chapter has outlined the emergence of the community of practice of human rights experts, focussed on the systemic agency of experts as well as explored the conception of expertise that has emerged from the profile of permanent SCANET members. The remaining section expands this analysis by observing how collaborational relations impact the *substance* of human rights knowledge in SCANET activities: what kind of issues are included in them, what is excluded. After that, SCANET is examined as a characteristic community of practice of the human rights phenomenon, with attention invested on the selection of English as its operational language. This analysis is set in context by exploring the position of English in the Finnish society. The chapter concludes by observing how SCANET comes to embody the global elite, and how this elitism also characterizes the international human rights phenomenon.

'International Relations on the Abstract Level'

This chapter has outlined how, due to the vicarious nature of human rights expertise, its systemic agency is most potent in abstract circumstances that pose no direct challenges to existing societal structures. Perhaps consequently, human rights are often treated as something that exist in external affairs instead of the domestic context. This distinction resonates with the discussed separation between fundamental or constitutional rights and human rights that characterized the Finnish legal culture prior to the fundamental rights reform of 1995. The conception of human rights as existing in external affairs is reflected in SCANET operations through topics selected and excluded as targets of research. An issue that has been left outside SCANET is exemplified by the topic of violence against women, a topic assigned high profile in the field of women's human rights and repeatedly discussed by the CEDAW treaty body. Examination of Finland's Foreign Minister's speeches indicates that in Finland, on the level of political rhetoric, women's rights are also generally highlighted, and women

Table 11: 'Rights of', Total 1999–2006

	minority	ethnic/ indig- enous	women	children	disabled	sexual minority	total
1999	-	-	-	-	-	-	-
2000	2	2	2	1	1	-	8
2001	1	3	3	1	-	-	8
2002	-	-	4	1	-	-	5
2003	4	4	6	6	3	-	23
2004	4	7	8	5	3	4	31
2005	1	-	1	-	-	-	2
2006	-	-	3	2	-	-	5
Total	12	16	27	16	7	4	82
%	15%	20%	33%	20%	9%	5%	100%

emerge as the most often mentioned group for the protection of whom human rights are intended; of all the specific groups the Minister mentions, women account for one third (Table 11).

Violence against women, which in the Finnish context translates in particular as domestic violence, forms a serious problem in the country and has received increasing domestic emphasis, for example from the Finnish Amnesty International through the campaign *Joku Raja* ('Some Limit').[55] The campaign highlighted the prevalence of domestic violence in Finland, and quotes a study according to which two in five women have faced physical or sexual violence or been threatened by it since turning 15. What is striking is that half of the acts and threats of violence come from a former spouse. Patterns of Finnish domestic violence are gender-specific, as nine times out of ten the perpetrator is a man and the target a woman.[56] In May 2006, Finland's largest newspaper reported how an Amnesty International representative described Finland's situation as "scandalous". She accused the Finnish government for having failed to grant the issue sufficient attention, and

[55] Amnesty International: 'Joku raja!' http://www.amnesty.fi/jokuraja/svaw.htm (10.11.2005).

[56] *Ibid.*; Lahti, Minna: Domesticated Violence: The power of the ordinary in everyday Finland. University of Helsinki, Helsinki, 2001.

emphasized the position held by Finland and the other Nordic countries as models for those states where human rights enjoy significantly weaker status. Consequently, as a northern democracy and a member of the EU, Finland holds special responsibilities to provide an example.[57] The Finnish chapter of Amnesty raised the topic again in March 2007 on Women's day under the Finnish parliamentary elections, emphasizing that statistics suggest no change in the matter since 1997, and urging the government to highlight the issue in the new parliament program.[58]

Despite such high attention invested to the issue, it has not been highlighted by SCANET: in the observed activities no expert lectures or student presentations focussed on it. Also, the SCANET website enlisted no activities focussing on the topic. Why is this so? A prominent SCANET expert described how no systematic reasons exist for this, and instead connected the matter to existing research practices by stating:

> Human rights consciousness is relatively new, and this question has traditionally fallen into the scope of criminal law. Thus no tradition exists for research in this topic. It is entirely possible that it might have arisen, but that has not happened in SCANET. Strong traditions exist for this topic in the area of women's studies as well as criminal law. It is a question of division of labour which has been rather arbitrarily formed based on the persons who are involved in such ventures.

The expert emphasized that absence does not suggest that the topic is belittled. Instead she mentioned how its exclusion is also a question of financing.[59] Examination of SCANET activities demonstrates also a more general exclusion, namely critical discussions on the participating Nordic countries' own human rights issues, which were likewise

---

[57] Sipilä, Annamari: 'Amnesty moittii Suomea naisiin kohdistuvasta väkivallasta.' In *Helsingin Sanomat*, 24.5.2006, B2; Amnesty International: 'Report 2006: Finland,' http://web.amnesty.org/report2006/fin-summary-eng (30.4.2007). Gilmore's comments ignited discussion on the newspaper's online chatrooms. While some praised Amnesty for bringing attention to the matter, others were more sceptical, questioning the integrity of the research utilized by Amnesty. Some comments demonstrate the vicarious nature of human rights: one commentator states that the credibility of Amnesty suffers when the organization places Finnish citizens in the same category as victims of dictatorships, urging Amnesty to "focus on the essential and more blatant violations", see Helsingin Sanomat: 'Jospa ketään ei lyötäisi – keskustelua verkossa,' 27.5.2006, C7.

[58] Amnesty International, http://www.jokuraja.fi/ (8.3.2007).

[59] After this discussion, a known expert in women's studies has joined SCANET.

the topic of very few lectures and presentations in the observed activities. This area has emerged as the source of significant human rights discussions in Norway and Denmark among others. Why has this not occurred in SCANET? The international reputation of the Nordic countries suggests that great atrocities do not occur in their scope, as their human rights record is exemplary. Does the absence of discussion stem from absence of human rights concerns and violations in these countries? A prominent SCANET expert refutes this view, stating that:

> I wouldn't say that no breaches occur. Rather SCANET holds an orientation toward international law, and consequently the tradition for the analysis of national legal systems is perhaps customarily a matter of different branches of law.

In Finland such branches include, for example, constitutional law, which has a strong tradition of fundamental rights. The expert notes that her own university has not been particularly strong in the various branches of domestic law, which may have contributed to the lack of collaboration. However, she is not comfortable with the view that in SCANET, human rights focus primarily on the 'other', not on the self. Instead she phrases the relationship as follows: "*[h]uman rights research is concerned with international relations on the abstract level, which applies equally to the self*", of which concrete examples are offered by discrimination and racism. Yet, whether due to lack of collaboration or issues of financing, in practice the human rights issues explored in SCANET activities focus largely on the 'other', either in the form of European collaboration or for example African human rights issues, with such critical internal issues as domestic violence invested scarce attention. The topics addressed by SCANET highlight the importance of collaborative patterns in shaping what kind of issues become construed as human rights issues. As collaborational patterns have not emerged between SCANET experts and scholars focussing on the issue of violence against women, this issue has ended up being excluded from the SCANET activities, and human rights have instead become defined as something applying to the self particularly on the abstract level.

Navigating between Centre and Periphery with English

To locate SCANET in relation to the centre and periphery of the human rights phenomenon, it can be seen to occupy an *intermediate* position: it is explicitly connected to the Nordic region which, although a periphery in terms of geography, has in terms of activeness acquired a more central position. SCANET also holds numerous personal connections to the centre, as many of its permanent and visiting experts are associated for example with UN treaty bodies. For the present purposes the defining feature of SCANET status becomes the selection of English as the language of both its formal and informal operations. As a rule, all documents produced by SCANET are in English, be they doctoral dissertations, articles or other background material provided for lectures. English is the only language used in lectures and presentations, as well as introductions and welcome speeches. In informal contexts English is utilized with less consistency, as it is the native tongue of few permanent members. Instead, in discussion with each other, members sharing the same language will utilize for example Finnish, Swedish, Norwegian and Estonian. Whereas particularly Swedish and Norwegian are mutually intelligible, the other languages are not, and thus the selection of other languages than English ends up separating participants from each other, limiting their possibilities to converse. Aware of this consequence, for example during dinners organized by SCANET, participants, who are frequently quite randomly seated, will commonly utilize English.

English has been the central language of the global human rights phenomenon since its origins. This is illustrated by the documents most commonly mentioned as the precedents of the UDHR, namely the British Magna Carta of 1215, the British Bill of Rights of 1689, the American Declaration of Independence of 1776 and the Bill of Rights of 1789, the French Déclaration des droits de l'homme et du citoyen of 1789, the Four Freedoms speech by Franklin Delano Roosevelt of 1941, and, a lesser known yet highly influential document, the Statement of Essential Human Rights of the American Law Institute of 1945.[60]

[60] This document is highlighted by both scholars and participants of the drafting process. Johannes Morsink quotes John Humphrey stating, as he prepared the first draft of the UDHR subsequently extensively revised by Rene Cassin, as "the best of the texts from which I worked", see Morsink, Johannes: The Universal Declaration of Human Rights: Origins, Drafting & Intent. University of Pennsylvania Press, Philadelphia, 1999, 6; The American Law Institute Seventy-fifth Anniversary 1923–1998. The American Law Institute, Philadelphia & Pennsylvania, 1998, 23, 132–137, 267, 269–270. For discussion on the document's origins and significance, see Commission to Study the Organization of Peace: Petition to 'The Honorable Edward R. Stettinius, Jr,' March 31, 1945; Proskauer, Joseph M.: A Segment of My Times. Farrar, Straus and Company, New York, 1950, 221–224; Eichelberger, Clark M.: Organizing for Peace: A Personal History of the Founding of the United Nations. Harper & Row Publishers, New York, 1977, 270–272; and Glendon, Mary Ann: 'The Forgotten

Of these documents, the original language of the Magna Carta is Latin and the Déclaration des droits de l'homme et du citoyen French, while all other documents are in English.[61] The impact of these English documents is clearly reflected in the wording of the UDHR: it holds affinity particularly to the Statement of Essential Human Rights through the phrase of "Everyone has the right", an expansionistic phrasing not prevalent in the other documents.

This phrase is also prevalent in the French version of the UDHR, which is embedded in the singular structure "tout individu /chacun ... a le droit" – a direct translation of the expression "everyone has" and an uncommon expression for the Déclaration of 1789 embedded in plural forms and more varied verbal structures.[62] In the drafting of the UDHR English soon established itself as the primary working language. The negotiations – carried out primarily on US soil[63] – were conducted in English by North Americans or people who had commonly been educated there, as was discussed in Chapter 2. Mary Ann Glendon notes how the French René Cassin was disappointed to discover upon his arrival that there was "no European" among the drafters and that the main common language of the commissioners was English, a language in which he had limited competence.[64] Also the first version of the UDHR prepared by John Humphrey was in English.[65]

Crucible: The Latin American Influence on the Universal Human Rights Ideal.' In *16 Harvard Human Rights Journal*, Spring 2003, 32. The Statement, further, has a strong American emphasis: a copy of the US Bill of Rights is included as an appendix for the Statement, with discussion on the similarities and differences of the two documents, see The American Law Institute, 290–292.

[61] Scholars make occasional mention of the 'Panama proposal', which in fact is the same document as the Statement of Essential Rights. This is an outcome resulting from the participation of Panama's former President in its drafting, see The American Law Institute, *ibid.*, 269.

[62] The French Déclaration des droits de l'homme et du citoyen also makes more extensive reference to 'duties', a feature Mary Ann Glendon assigns to the European and American rights discourses already in the 18th century. See Glendon, Mary Ann: Rights Talk: The Impoverishment of Political Discourse. The Free Press, New York, 1991, 11. This formulation was central in the Statement of Essential Human Rights, but not in the UDHR, which entails only one mention of duties in Article 29.

[63] Roosevelt, Eleanor: The Autobiography of Eleanor Roosevelt. Da Capo Press Inc., New York, 1992 [1961].

[64] Glendon, Mary Ann: A World Made New: Eleanor Roosevelt and the Universal Declaration of Human Rights. Random House, New York, 2001, 49.

[65] Glendon quotes Humphrey commenting on the subsequent drafting work by René Cassin; Humphrey comments: 'In many cases ... Cassin merely prepared a new French version of the official United Nations translation, and when this was translated back into English the result seemed further removed from the original than it really was', see *ibid.*, 65.

The continued centrality of English in the human rights phenomenon is exemplified by Merry's discussion on UN treaty negotiations. She notes how, although meetings have simultaneous translation into the six official UN languages, draft treaty texts as well as suggested alternative wordings are presented in English. Thus a person who has not mastered the language "would have a great deal of difficulty assessing the implications and innuendos of different phrases and sentences".[66] The choice of language is not always voluntary. For example, NGO caucuses are typically held in English in UN contexts only because NGOs cannot afford translators. Thus shortage of resources reproduces the privileged position of the powerful English-speaking actors also in the NGO community.[67] Annelise Riles describes the same occurrence, noting how newsletters among the Fijian NGOs she studied were almost always in English, although it was the mother tongue of few network participants. English as the language of the colonial and postcolonial bureaucracy has emerged as the *lingua franca* of contemporary multiculturalism in Fiji, and it holds "strong connotations of specialization, professionalization, and elite education".[68] The prevalence of English was visible in the presentation of the State Report of China to the Committee on Economic, Social and Cultural Rights discussed in Chapter 4. Although simultaneous translation was available in the official UN languages, English dominated the discussion, and for example treaty body members posed questions solely in English. The prevalence of English was reproduced in the proceedings accompanying the submission of Costa Rica's fifth state report to the Human Rights Committee in October 2007: during the oral proceedings numerous treaty body members mentioned how they had been unable to read the additional information provided by the state, as it was in Spanish.

---

[66] Merry: Human Rights & Gender Violence, *supra* note 22, 44.

[67] This practice, nevertheless, has its consequences, as Merry mentions how at Beijing Plus Five, some Spanish-speaking representatives complained about feeling excluded. This sentiment can perhaps be contemplated as significant for the emergence of the World Social Forum utilizing French and Portanhol as primary languages. Merry notes how in those discussions most active participants came from countries where English is the language of the educated class; "thus it tended to trace the boundaries of the former British Empire and its settler states", see *ibid.*

[68] Riles: The Network Inside Out, *supra* note 9, 126. Riles notes how "The English of network communications, whether oral or written, was replete with acronyms, nominalisation, and document titles strung together as if to form a network of their own. Focal points referred to this language as a "technical vocabulary," and they enjoyed using it," see Riles, 126.

English in the Finnish Society

Finland has two official languages: Finnish, the language of the majority, and Swedish, the language of the 6% minority.[69] Despite its official status, the position of Swedish has commonly been construed as problematic by parts of the Finnish-speaking population. During the Swedish rule and up to the awakening national sentiment of the late 19th century, Swedish was the primary language of the upper classes, although the Swedish-speaking community also included members from different domains of the society such as farmers, fishermen and peasants. Consequently many Finns still denote some of the group's members cynically as '*svenskatalande bättre folk*, 'Swedish-speaking better folk'. The language continues to be a mandatory subject in Finnish-language schools, a status that awakens negative sentiments among some Finnish-speakers. Yet, despite reserved attitudes, historically Swedish has undisputedly been, and continues to be, the most influential language in the country after Finnish: for example public offices are required to offer services in both languages, and street signs include the two languages.[70]

Russian, on the other hand, has never achieved a prevalent position due to the ambivalent attitudes awakened by the Russian rule. Consequently it has never occupied a distinct status in public policy-making or arisen as the favourite language studied at schools – despite Soviet sympathies harboured by youth groups in the 1970s and the fact that today Russians form the largest group of foreigners in Finland, with around 50 000 members, making Russian the most common foreign language spoken in the country. Instead the foreign language enjoying the highest influence, besides Swedish, has traditionally been German, the influence of which has been decisive particularly through the Lutheran Church. German influences have impacted Finnish legal culture and literature,[71] and for example the productions of German

[69] Finnish belongs to the Finno-Ugric language family, and its closest relative is Estonian. Finnish is also related to Hungarian, although more distantly. While Finnish is mutually intelligible with Estonian to a degree, its relationship with Hungarian is most evident in the languages' grammar. Finnish is not related to the Scandinavian languages, nor, thus, to the Indo-European language family.

[70] Finland's national poet Johan Ludvig Runeberg, wrote in Swedish; it is also the original language of the Finnish national anthem.

[71] Merikoski, Veli & Vilkkonen, Eero: Suomen julkisoikeus pääpiirteittäin. Suomalaisen Lakimiesyhdistyksen julkaisuja. WSOY, Juva, 1982.

composers are strongly emphasized in the training of classical musicians. In the past, Swedish and German were the languages most commonly studied in schools, and until the 1970s they formed the foreign languages in which the Finnish population had the best competence.[72]

It was only in the 1970s that English became a compulsory language in Finnish schools.[73] Despite the increasing influence of Anglo-American youth culture and although English was increasingly studied at schools, it had in the past decades remained a minority language. However, in the 1970s a rapid change started, as English soon overshadowed other languages in popularity – a development to which increasing subtitled English-language TV programs certainly contributed.[74] By the 1980s and 1990s English had become established as the language in which the Finnish youth held both the greatest interest as well as competence. Today fluent knowledge of English has become a practical prerequisite for numerous university degrees relying on English textbooks. It increasingly dominates the Finnish scientific community, which has awakened worry relating to the future of Finnish as a viable academic and professional language.[75] Competence in English has come to mark a generational gap, as few members of the older age segments, primarily born before the 1950s, have full command of it; of the members of the older age segments knowing the language, many belong to the socio-economic elites. Outside these groups, many members of older generations regard the

[72] Also French, the traditional language of international collaboration, was studied, but its position in Finland was more marginal.

[73] Leppänen, Sirpa & Nikula, Tarja: 'Diverse uses of English in Finnish society: Discourse-pragmatic insights into media, educational and business contexts.' In *26 Multilingua 4*, 2007, 333-380.

[74] American programs have occasionally aroused stark criticism, as is discussed by Iiris Ruoho regarding the reactions awakened by *Peyton Place* in the early 1970s, and *Dallas* in the early 1980s, see Ruoho, Iiris: 'Double Standards in Evaluating Television: "Peyton Place" and "Dallas" in the Finnish television culture.' In *Inescapable Horizon: Culture and Context* (Eds. Leppänen, Sirpa & Kuortti, Joel). University of Jyväskylä, Jyväskylä, 2000. Today English-language programs form the majority of Finnish TV programs, and subtitled TV has remained one of the most effective English instructors in Finland.

[75] For example Suomen antropologi: Journal of the Finnish Anthropological Society, a peer-reviewed quarterly, made a policy decision to limit its content to English contributions at the expense of Finnish and Swedish in 2007, thus breaking a tradition of three decades. English publications in international journals enjoy a significantly higher status in assessing academic achievement than Finnish ones.

frequent use of English with occasional resentment, seeing it as elitist and exclusionary.[76] This generational gap is reflected in scholarship, as is illustrated by contributions discussing fundamental rights and human rights from the 1970s, 1980s and 1990s. An introduction to Finnish fundamental rights, published in 1971 by Mikael Hidén, concludes with an English summary,[77] but includes no English references in its bibliography. Instead, most references are in Finnish with a few in Swedish. An introduction to Finnish public law from 1982 by Veli Merikoski and Eero Vilkkonen has no English references nor summary, instead its sources are in Finnish.[78] By contrast, the article published in 1996 by Veli-Pekka Viljanen, discussing the Finnish constitutional reform of 1995 and international human rights norms, features mostly English sources with only a minority in Finnish.[79]

English vs. Skandinavisk

In SCANET operations the selection of English is conspicuous due to the strong emphasis set forth by ScaFund that the networks funded by it embody Nordic collaboration. This collaboration has a long and well-established record, reflected for example in the already mentioned Nordic Council. Importantly, this collaboration has been marked with a distinct language, namely 'Skandinavisk'.[80] Although Skandinavisk has been slowly losing importance, its position has remained solid enough to cause the first occasions in which English was utilized instead of Swedish in the meeting of the prime ministers of Finland and Sweden to be commented on in the front page news of Finland's

[76] Leppänen & Nikula: 'Diverse uses of English in Finnish society, *supra* note 73; Ranta, Elina: International English – a Future Possibility in the Finnish EFL Classroom? Master's Thesis, University of Tampere, 2004, http://www.uta.fi/laitokset/kielet/engf/research/elfa/research_er.pdf (10.6.2007), 33–36.

[77] Hidén, Mikael: Perusoikeudet Hallitusmuodon II luvussa. Suomalaisen Lakimiesyhdistuksen vuosikirja I, Helsinki, 1971, 109–117.

[78] Merikoski & Vilkkonen: Suomen julkisoikeus pääpiirteittäin, *supra* note 71.

[79] Viljanen, Veli-Pekka: 'Perusoikeusuudistus ja kansainväliset ihmisoikeussopimukset.' In *Lakimies 5-6*, 1996, 788–815.

[80] Swedish, Norwegian and Danish belong to the same branch of the Indo-European language family, and are mutually intelligible to a degree. Although 'Skandinavisk' does not exist as an official language, the term is used of a modified version of each language, in which the more difficult or differentiated expressions are omitted in favour of mutual intelligibility. Of the five Nordic languages, Icelandic and Finnish fall outside this common group. Unlike Finnish, Icelandic is related to the other Scandinavian languages, but due to its isolation is different from Swedish, Norwegian and Danish.

largest newspaper.[81] Thus the language policy of SCANET in utilizing English can be seen as forming an exception to a pattern commonly found in Nordic collaboration. SCANET language policy also contrasts with the practices of some other networks funded by ScaFund.[82] In one of them English and Skandinavisk were used alternately, with both background papers and lectures occurring in the two languages. In the other, all background papers were produced in English but the language of verbal exchanges was Skandinavisk. This practice has sometimes resulted in confusion, as Skandinavisk spoken with radically differing dialects is difficult to comprehend. Yet the utilization of Skandinavisk has been a cherished element, concretizing the special Nordic element of the network. This is reflected in the regretful tenor utilized by one of their members to describe a future network event which would for the first time feature English as its official language; the member wondered if this was the beginning of the end for Skandinavisk, and whether English would take over entirely.

Although Nordic academic collaboration in the human rights field has a long tradition of utilizing English, reflected for example in numerous English collaborative publications, the field includes domains that emphasize Skandinavisk. This is reflected in the submission guidelines for the Nordic Journal of Human Rights.[83] The guidelines state that "[t]he bulk of submissions accepted must be written in one of the three main Scandinavian languages (Danish, Norwegian or Swedish)". They continue by stating that "[a]uthors who are fluent in [them] should, as a rule, write their contributions in one of these three languages". Of English submissions the guidelines note that "to a certain extent, the editorial staff may consider contributions written in English, primarily by those authors who are not fluent in one of the three principal Scandinavian languages". However, for authors wishing to write in English, yet fluent in one of the Scandinavian languages, the guidelines emphasize that they "must secure the approval of the editorial staff beforehand." Finally, the guidelines mention that the editorial staff

[81] Blåfield, Antti: 'Pienen pieni uutinen.' In *Helsingin Sanomat*, 19.10.2006, A2. Pressure for the spread of English usage in the Scandinavian countries is nevertheless high, demonstrated by a column by the Vice President of the European Law Student's Association in 'Legally prepared, the Magazine for Nordic Law Students' titled 'English is no longer a skill – it is a must'. See Lindholm, Ida: 'English is a Must.' In *Legally prepared: The Magazine for Nordic Law Students 1*, 2005, 63.

[82] Many thanks to Jarna Petman and Kaius Tuori for discussion on this point.

[83] Also the journal's full title emphasizes Skandinavisk, as it is Mennesker & Rettigheter: Nordic Journal of Human Rights.

> Reserves the right to refuse publication of English submissions if the total number of English contributions in any one edition of the Nordic periodical exceeds a reasonable maximum.[84]

Viewed against these observations, SCANET selection of English as the only language of operations becomes noteworthy. How can this policy be understood?

Analysing the practice from the perspective of the prevalence of English at the *centre* of the human rights phenomenon, the use of English in SCANET reflects desires to strengthen SCANET's connection to the *centre*: that it would render SCANET activities accessible to a wider audience and thereby increase their status. Whereas the selection of Skandinavisk strengthens the geographic particularity of activities, the use of English, due to its *lingua franca* status, assigns them qualities of embodying the universal that thus transgresses the narrow particularity of the Scandinavian context. Universal emphasis is vital for the human rights phenomenon, as only through impressions of representing the conceptions of universal mankind instead of the particular views of a distinct group do its norms become legitimate instead of cultural imposition. Consequently, the use of English in SCANET contributes to the conception that the knowledge disseminated in its scope enjoys, due to its direct link to the universal, higher legitimacy than knowledge that would merely represent the Nordic region. Nevertheless, this selection entails distinct consequences which require closer examination. Utilization of English rather than Skandinavisk renders the network inclusionary and open to people outside the Nordic region. Simultaneously the use of English entails exclusionary elements, as was mentioned earlier in relation to UN operations. Regarding SCANET, the use of English imposes on them the self-evident criteria that they are only accessible to those with sufficient English skills to both understand and produce written and spoken material in the language. Such skills have become increasingly common in the Finnish context, yet very few Finns hold competence in English equivalent to that of a native speaker. Thus the use of English creates asymmetry between participants, as native speakers enjoy higher status in SCANET operations due to their superior possibilities for sophisticated and accurate self-presentation. This was evident in

[84] Nordic Journal of Human Rights: 'Guidelines for Authors': Submissions to Mennesker & Rettigheter: Nordic Journal of Human Rights,' http://www.humanrights.uio.no/forskning/publ/mr/guidelines.html (2.11.2006).

SCANET activities which included individuals assigned student status from e.g. the Baltic countries, for whom fluent contributions in English posed a tremendous challenge. This linguistic limitation effectively excluded their potential contributions, as they failed to find intelligible articulations for their message.

Selection of English effects the basis on which visiting experts are invited in: by majority, they are either native English speakers or hold equivalent skills. Thus fluent command of English became a significant factor in determining who gains access to the SCANET community of practice. Consequently for example members of the already referred-to World Social Forum would likely be excluded, as its languages are French and Portanhol, a mixture of Portuguese and Spanish.[85] SCANET activities do not entail the possibility to include individuals not fluent in English, and thus also its human rights knowledge comes to reflect the viewpoints of individuals who fill this criterion, as debates across languages remain impossible. The selection of English in SCANET contributes to the development where the language dominates the small Nordic languages, and thus jeopardizes the future status of these other languages as viable academic languages. It strengthens the prevalent position of English over the other global languages such as Chinese, Hindu or Spanish, and from this perspective, action inside the human rights phenomenon contributes to rather than challenges the current global unequal power structures.

Embodying the Global Elite

Exploration of SCANET funding patterns demonstrates how it acquires elements of the elitist transnational practices characteristic to the *centre* of the human rights phenomenon, in which individuals traverse with ease the boundaries of time, space and particularity. SCANET activities were held in constantly changing venues from attractive university towns to resorts in the middle of mountains and the ocean. Due to ScaFund funding, all participant travel costs were covered by SCANET, including overseas air fares for visiting experts. Activity participants, including those assigned student status, stayed in private rooms in three or four star hotels, and in addition to breakfast and lunch, dinners were provided for nightly in trendy restaurants. These elements exceed the general standards of Nordic research funding, as

[85] Sosiaalifoorumi, *supra* note 53, 2.

researchers commonly enjoy, for example, more modest accommodation in association with seminars. That the SCANET standards were exceptional was noted by numerous participating students, who commented how they could not have participated in the activities without SCANET support, as their host domains lacked the funds to send them. The high standard of SCANET operations was also noted by a visiting expert, a professor and a UN treaty body member, and thus a member of what has been accused as forming "a privileged and corrupted global elite" of UN officials.[86] Following a dinner organized at a particularly successful location, the expert observed how well and generously everything was organized. She further commented how in the UN context dinners are never paid for.

Compared to general academic funding in Finland, characterized by low wages and poor predictability, the funding received by SCANET can be seen as one sign of the favourable societal position of human rights in the Nordic countries. However, as has been mentioned, SCANET is only one of numerous academic networks enjoying similar funding from ScaFund. Thus its generous level cannot be interpreted to stem exclusively from favourable social sentiments over the substance of its operations. Instead the ample funding transforms SCANET into one embodiment of the public wealth held by the Nordic countries, which in this instance results into possibilities to create transnational networks of scholars. These described elements assign SCANET characteristics of elitism. Importantly, this feature can effectively exclude individuals from participation if they fail to possess the material means that allow access. This is concretized by the following personal account. As has been mentioned, one of SCANET's constitutive elements is the e-mail list sustained by its coordinator. In addition to distributing information and background reading,[87] the list functions as a site for event registration through downloadable forms. These forms imposed certain technical requirements on the part of potential participants, namely access to the Internet and software of sufficient quality. Due to the rapid changes in software, this condition entailed

[86] Hancock, Graham: Lords of Poverty: the power, prestige, and corruption of the international aid business. The Atlantic Monthly Press, New York, 1989.

[87] The list served as the primary source of information about SCANET courses, including background material sent by experts and student papers which were expected to be printed out; only in exceptional circumstances were paper copies provided in SCANET activities. Combined, these could result in significant numbers of pages. For example, in one activity the number for student papers alone was 455 pages.

more difficulties than first appears plausible. In spring 2004 I attempted an unsuccessful registration from my work station at the University of Helsinki. The University is one of world leaders among (public) universities in using computerised and Internet-based services in its operations, and great effort is invested into offering up-to-date equipment to personnel. However, developments in the computer field outweigh the resources of the University, and most personnel end up using faculties which lagged behind in development. This applied to my work computer, manufactured in 1998, which was unable to download the prescribed SCANET file to allow signing up for an activity. At the end I sent a hard copy of the form through regular mail. The letter reached its destination only after registration had closed, and left me outside the event. Thus the shortcomings of the software available to me excluded me from participation in that particular SCANET activity.

As transnational coalitions rely increasingly on online communication this personal experience has wider relevance, as it exemplifies how only the global elites having either sufficient public or private funds at their disposal will be able to fully participate in its communities. The elitist nature of the contemporary human rights phenomenon has been noted by numerous scholars.[88] What is less frequently observed is how elitism is visible in the origins of the human rights phenomenon, for example, in the backgrounds of the American activists who lobbied for the adoption of the UDHR. The profile of Roger Baldwin, the long-time leader of the American Civil Liberties Union (ACLU) and the founder of the International League for the Rights of Man, is illustrative: he came from a wealthy background, and his ancestors included Mayflower Pilgrims as well as a general in George Washington's army. In his youth Baldwin attended "the inevitable Harvard" in the same class as Franklin Delano Roosevelt, and later in life married heiress Evelyn Preston, a well-educated Standard Oil heiress whose family was close to the Roosevelts.[89] Although money was "probably the closest thing to sin [Baldwin] could imagine"[90] and he believed that "people should work for other than wages", insisting on paying wages that

[88] For example Mutua, Makau: Human Rights: A Political & Cultural Critique. University of Pennsylvania Press, Philadelphia, 2002.

[89] Cottrell, Robert C.: Roger Nash Baldwin and the American Civil Liberties Union. Columbia University Press, New York, 2000, 237–254.

[90] Walker, Samuel: In Defence of American Liberties: A History of the ACLU. Second Edition. Southern Illinois University Press, Carbondale, 1999, 70.

"starved staff"[91], in reality the ACLU, like many liberal and radical causes, "depended on inherited wealth".[92] Other participants in lobbying and drafting efforts portray similar backgrounds, reflecting particularly the Ivy League elite. In addition to Baldwin, Harvard graduates related to the early phases of the human rights phenomenon included Charles Malik of the drafting committee, who held a PhD from Harvard, as well as Warren Seavey and Barton Leach, both of whom were key figures behind the American Law Institute's (ALI) Statement of Essential Human Rights. Lobbying and drafting efforts include numerous University of Columbia graduates such as Noel Dowling, who participated in the ALI Statement,[93] and the Columbia University history professor James Shotwell, called by William Korey one of the central lobbyists behind the UDHR.[94] Of the drafters, both P.C. Chang of China and Carlos P. Romulo of the Philippines, identified by many commentators as some of the most active participants in the drafting for the UDHR, were graduates of Columbia.[95]

The elitist background of key lobbyists and drafters for the UDHR is, of course, far from surprising: considering the high profile of the drafting of the UN Charter as well as the UDHR, it is only natural that individuals participating in them would reflect the backgrounds of the other participants in high-level international diplomatic initiatives likewise belonging to national elites. However, the elitist backgrounds of key individuals do pose a challenge to notions according to which the human rights phenomenon was the result of momentum emerging from the 'common people' around the world. Most of these common people likely had no awareness of a concept called human rights in 1945, nor would the common people have possessed the means to mobilize for the lobbying of such notions had they been familiar with them. In addition, 'the common people' lacked required cultural capital, as for example English, the language utilized in the drafting process, was far less commonly known outside the elites

[91] Cottrell, Robert C.: Roger Nash Baldwin and the American Civil Liberties Union, *supra* note 89, 302.

[92] Walker, Samuel: The Rights Revolution: Rights and Community in Modern America. Oxford University Press, New York, 1998, 70.

[93] The American Law Institute, *supra* note 60, 137.

[94] Korey: NGOs and the Universal Declaration of Human Rights, *supra* note 43, 31–32.

[95] Biography of Peng-Chun Chang, http://www.udhr.org/history/Biographies/biopcc.htm 23.5.2003; Biography of Carlos P. Romulo, http://www.bookrags.com/biography-carlos-p-romulo/index.html (27.2.2006).

at the time. Sally Engle Merry has discussed how the UN framework can still today be characterized as being formed by a transnational elite,[96] and this chapter demonstrates how such an intermediary domain as SCANET acquires elements of elitism. This challenges the egalitarian potential of the human rights phenomenon. Although local human rights communities have proliferated in recent decades, whether through fluent command of English or sophisticated software, full participation in characteristic transnational human rights communities conversing between people across diverse localities and languages remains open only to the global elites.

[96] Merry, Sally Engle: 'Anthropology and Activism: Researching Human Rights across Porous Boundaries.' In *28 Political and Legal Anthropology Review 2*, 2005, 240–258.

CHAPTER FOUR

TRAINING FOR EXPERTISE

Sender: SCANET

Subject: SCANET training course, June 5–10, 2004

> *Dear all,*
> *The 2004 SCANET training course in human rights research will be organized between 5 and 10 June, 2004. The course will feature lectures by permanent SCANET and international visiting experts. Participating doctorate candidates will hold presentations related to their ongoing PhD work. For this, they are expected to submit a 15-page paper prior to the activity. The presentations will be commented on by participating experts. Application deadline: 15 February, 2004. Course information and application forms can be downloaded from http://www.humanrights.edu/SCANET/courses.htm. A limited number of mobility scholarships are available for doctorate candidates from the Nordic and the Baltic countries.*
>
> *Best wishes, the SCANET coordinator*

The above message exemplifies e-mails sent at regular intervals by the SCANET coordinator to SCANET members. The messages reminded participants, dispersed around the Nordic area and engaged in research at their respective institutions, of SCANET's existence in the months between activities, and started a series of events which would culminate in the activity itself. Following the message, doctorate candidates fill in their application forms and work on their papers to be submitted by specific deadlines. Experts invited in to lecture send out background reading and prepare their lectures. Participants make travel arrangements followed by applications for mobility scholarships. The SCANET coordinator continues organization to ensure that all details are attended to at the activity venue. When the event dawns, participants convene at the prescribed location, out-of-town participants, usually a hefty majority, travelling by plane or train. After connecting flights and taxi rides, they arrive at the joint accommodation assigned to activity participants. As the venue usually holds no visible signs of the activity, participants attempt to shed nagging suspicions of having remembered the hotel – or the country, for that matter – incorrectly, passing an inquiry to the receptionist concerning rooms for SCANET activity participants.

Participants feel a sense of relief as the receptionist responds with a room key and an information package provided by the SCANET coordinator. Still seeing no signs of other SCANET members, participants check into their rooms and examine at what time they are to arrive at the activity venue. When returning to the lobby, they spot others carrying similar information packages. Closer examination reveals the group to include some familiar, some unknown faces. Small groups of lively discussion emerge, accompanied by a few individuals remaining outside them. As the starting time for the activity nears, a plan is organized to move jointly to its site. The brisk walk is accompanied by continued exchanges and a dawning sentiment of SCANET's real-life existence; it begins to emerge as an entity capable of generating a genuine sense of membership. Soon the participants reach the university building serving as the activity headquarters for the following week. Located at the centre of a charismatic university town, the building welcomes visitors with old-time academic charm. Upon entering the activity room, it appears small, as it is filled with people engaged in lively discussion while enjoying coffee and sandwiches provided by SCANET. Some participants are colleagues at their home universities, some have got to know each other in previous SCANET activities; many are meeting for the first time. A definite excitement is in the air and people appear pleased to make each others' acquaintance.

Soon the room is called to order and the activity announced to begin. The brief opening speech is followed by the familiar round of introductions by all participants. Sitting in the full seminar room with thirty or so people, SCANET's existence is palpable: for the next week it will be the community to which members would hold their greatest affiliation. As the activity program is once again fully packed, SCANET will, in fact, come to occupy most of its participants' waking hours. In the mornings, participants listen to lectures, in the afternoons, to student presentations. In between they have a common lunch break, followed by a joint dinner in the evenings that usually lasts at least until nine. If not followed by other social activities – going for drinks or having a sauna organized by SCANET among others – before bed participants read the numerous papers distributed to accompany lectures, as well as the background papers for the following day's student presentations.

For the first days virtually everyone participates in the program. By day three, participant numbers drop by three or four as people need to return back home; a few participants skip a session or two. By the second-to-last day more people leave, and by the time the activity concludes, the number of participants renders the event's closing into a pale shadow of its robust opening just a few short days before. The remaining participants make their way back to the airport, jumping on planes to take them to their diverse destinations. Soon all signs of SCANET's existence are again annulled. A few months later the post delivers an envelope to the participants' home universities containing the activity diploma and a group photo. Looking at the picture, many faces appear unfamiliar and names are forgotten. Participants place the envelope among their SCANET files and return to the responsibilities of their everyday academic life. SCANET fades back into its virtual existence, waiting to be revived by the next e-mail informing of future activities.

Decade of Human Rights Education

The years 1995 to 2004 marked the UN Decade of Human Rights Education.[1] Scholars have characterized the decade as the logical outcome of emphasis placed on education already in the UDHR and since reified in numerous documents such as the UN World Conference of Human Rights.[2] The same decade demonstrates significant proliferation of educational programs on human rights. A search of both an online LLM-program guide as well as Google offers information of only five human rights LLM-programs established prior to 1995. Two of them were founded in the US and three in the UK, with the University

[1] High Commissioner: United Nations Decade for Human Rights Education (1995–2004), http://www.unhchr.ch/html/menu6/1/edudec.htm (6.5.2007).

[2] Andreopoulos, George J.: 'Human Rights Education in the Post-Cold War Context.' In *Human Rights Education for the Twenty-First Century* (Eds. Andreopoulos, George J. & Claude, Richard Pierre). Pennsylvania University Press, Pennsylvania, 1997, 9–20; Baxi, Upendra: 'Human Rights Education: The Promise for the Third Millennium?' In *Human Rights Education for the Twenty-First Century*, 142–154; Vienna Declaration, Adopted on 25 June 1993. A/Conf. 157/23, http://www.ohchr.org/english/law/vienna.htm (21.12.2005).

of Essex advertizing its human rights LLM, founded in 1983, as the world's first.[3] By 2006 the number of human rights programs had grown to over 120.[4] In addition to national programs, the decade between 1995–2004 saw the establishment of numerous international programs. Of these the most significant in the European context was the European Master's Programme in Human Rights and Democratisation, a predominantly EU-funded collaboration of 39 European universities, which was launched in 1997 and runs in Venice.[5] In 2000 this program was followed by the European Regional Master's in Democracy and Human Rights in South-East Europe.[6] From the perspective of the universities master's programs offer a competitive advantage by attracting students. They further provide universities with substantial revenue: for example in spring 2007 the fee for the Master's Programme in International Human Rights Law at Oxford University was over 20 000 euros.[7]

In addition to higher education, numerous initiatives exist to introduce human rights education to all levels of schooling.[8] As was discussed in Chapter 2, this emphasis has been strongly featured in Finnish educational policy. Although the temporality with which educational programs have expanded coincides with the UN decade, the decade appears unlikely to provide the sole reason for this proliferation – for example critical commentator Graham Hancock argues that the "calendar events" favoured by the UN have been unable to induce "the slightest difference to the state of the world we live in".[9] Thus two

[3] University of Essex: Human Rights Centre, http://www2.essex.ac.uk/human_rights_centre/ (25.9.2006).

[4] The LLM guides consulted are available at http://www.llm-guide.com/university/562 (18.9.2006) and http://www.humanrightstools.org/masters.htm. Where not available from other sources, funding year has been requested directly from the program coordinators. The list makes no claims for being exhaustive.

[5] European Master's Programme in Human Rights and Democratisation, http://www.emahumanrights.org/index.php?option=com_content&task=view&id=12&Itemid=26 (18.9.2006).

[6] European Regional Master in Democracy and Human Rights in South-East Europe, http://137.204.115.130/activities/education/details-education.php?id=16&noindex=1 (18.9.2006).

[7] University of Oxford: Master's Degree in International Human Rights Law, http://international.conted.ox.ac.uk/mastersdegreeininternationalhumanrightslaw.php (30.4.2007).

[8] Andreopoulos, George J. & Claude, Richard Pierre (Eds.): 'Preface.' In *Human Rights Education for the Twenty-First Century, supra* note 2, xix–xxii.

[9] Hancock, Graham: Lords of Poverty: the power, prestige, and corruption of the international aid business. The Atlantic Monthly Press, New York, 1989, 100–101.

additional sources can be identified as having contributed to this development. First, the temporality of proliferation coincides among others with the establishing of human rights journals. Jointly with the other trends discussed in Chapter 2, the decade between 1995 and 2004 appears as particularly significant for the general expansion of the human rights phenomenon. Second, of the discussed 120 LLM programs, almost half have emerged in the UK. This development can in turn be connected to the adoption of the UK's Human Rights Act in 1998.

Human rights educational programs are connected also to another already discussed feature of the human rights phenomenon, namely the selection of English as their operational language. This applies particularly to joint ventures. The Mediterranean Master's in Human Rights and Democratisation – a program founded in 2000 in collaboration with the University of Malta, Bethlehem University, University of Jordan, University of Cyprus, Arab Institute for Human Rights, Istanbul University, Tel-Aviv University, Cairo Institute for Human Rights Studies, and the Foundation for Human and Humanitarian Rights in Beirut – mentions that while good working knowledge of French is "highly desirable", good command of English is "essential".[10] The LLM program in Human Rights and Democratisation in Africa – a joint program of the Centre for Human Rights at the University of Pretoria, the American University in Cairo, the Catholic University of Central Africa in Cameroon, Universidade Equardo Mondlane of Mozambique, the University of Ghana, Makerere University of Uganda, and the University of the Western Cape of South Africa founded in 2000 and mentioned as the only program of its kind in Africa – has likewise selected English as its language of instruction.[11] Also the European Master's program utilizes English as its primary language.[12]

---

[10] Mediterranean Master's in Human Rights and Democratisation, http://home.um.edu.mt/laws/entrance/introduction.html (18.9.2006).

[11] Human Rights and Democratisation in Africa, http://www.chr.up.ac.za/academic_pro/llm1/llm1.html (18.8.2006).

[12] Likewise, for example, the LLM in Human Rights offered by the University of Hong Kong since 1999 and advertized as 'the only Master's programme of its kind in Asia' utilizes English, see University of Hong Kong: LLM in Human Rights, http://www.hku.hk/ccpl/human_rights/index.html (18.9.2006). Links are, however, found to Spanish and French programs, yet the numbers are more moderate, as this search located 12 Spanish, and 24 French programs. Of the latter, only 13 explicitly mention the concept 'droits de l'homme' in their course curriculum. See DerechosNet: Spanish LLM programs, http://www.derechos.net/links/esp/edu/uni.html (19.9.2006); Centre

The Nordic region has numerous programs focussing on human rights reflecting both the above discussed temporality and utilizing English as their working language. The Raoul Wallenberg Institute of Human Rights and Humanitarian Law offers three different English Master's programs focussing on human rights,[13] and the University of Oslo, in association with the Norwegian Centre for Human Rights, offers an English-language Master's of Philosophy in the Theory and Practice of Human Rights, launched in 2001.[14] In Finland, the Åbo Institute for Human Rights introduced its English-language Master's degree program in international human rights law in 2006.[15] In 2002 the Finnish Research School in Human Rights Research was started, followed by its second 4-year term commenced in 2006. Although its official language is not English, in practice English has acquired a predominant position. In general PhD programs have proliferated more moderately, and the searched LLM guide enlists only three programs, of which two were in Spain. The third was the PhD program founded in the Netherlands in 1995 and continued until 2005.[16] This program can in many respects be held as a model for both the Finnish Research School as well as SCANET educational activities.[17]

Mary Robinson, former UN High Commissioner for Human Rights, has stated that human rights education is the highest priority of the human rights phenomenon, as education is fundamental in empowering individuals to defend their rights and those of others.[18] The authors of the substantial volume on human rights education edited by George J. Andreopoulos and Richard Pierre Claude – a book published with

de recherces et d'études sur les droits de l'Homme et le droit humanitaire, http://www.credho.org/enseignts/deadess.htm (6.5.2007).

[13] The Raoul Wallenberg Institute of Human Rights and Humanitarian Law, http://www.rwi.lu.se/institute/aboutrwi.shtml (16.5.2006).

[14] University of Oslo: Human Rights Master of Philosophy in the Theory and Practice of Human Rights, http://www.llm-guide.com/university/463/university-of-oslo-norwegian-centre-for-human-rights (19.9.2006).

[15] Åbo Akademi Institute for Human Rights, http://www.abo.fi/instut/imr/ (12.11.2007).

[16] KNAW: The School of Human Rights Research, http://www.uu.nl/uupublish/homerechtsgeleer/onderzoek/onderzoekscholen/rechtenvandemens/english/general/20817main.html (12.11.2007).

[17] No futher information on human rights PhD programs has been available through general online searches.

[18] Toivanen, Reetta; Mahler, Claudia & Mihr, Anja: 'Teaching Human Rights in Europe and its role for minority movement.' In *Rights in Europe – A Fragmented Regime* (Ed. Brosig, Malte). Peter Lang Verlag, Berlin, 2006, 171.

the support of the Organizing Committee for the UN Decade – elaborate this statement. They emphasize that human rights education "offers hope for the future of our children and the destiny of humanity as a whole". They further view human rights education as essential to a "genuine process of global social change",[19] and highlight how it provides a unique strategy for the "building of a universal culture of human rights".[20] Viewed against such expectations, surprisingly little scholarship exists evaluating human rights programs: the teaching they offer and how the programs contribute to realize these emancipatory goals.

Garth Meintjes introduces guidelines to elaborate empowerment and discusses how emancipation is connected to central utilized pedagogies. He notes that human rights education is unique in its goal to induce societal change as conventional education socializes individuals into existing norms and thus reproduces the society. Consequently elites occasionally see human rights education as threatening.[21] Meintjes discusses different approaches to education, and contrasts empowerment, which increases people's mastery over their own lives, and "banking". He borrows the latter expression from Paulo Freire, who has defined it as a process in which "knowledge is a gift bestowed by those who consider themselves knowledgeable upon those whom they consider to know nothing". Banking is further governed by the assumption of "an absolute ignorance" of others, and it is "characteristic of the ideology of oppression".[22] Meintjes notes how, as students are treated "as receptacles to be filled with useful ideas and information", they are deprived of their own critical conscience and deceived "into believing that knowledge is an object to be received rather than a continuous process of inquiry and reflection"; students are subjected to the "violence of anti-dialogue". By contrast, empowered students become conscious of how they participate in the creation of knowledge as well as how they can conceptualize their experiences of reality. Thus, in order to challenge existing oppressive structures, human rights education needs to be "dynamic" instead of "static".[23]

[19] Koenig, Shulamith: 'Foreword.' In *Human Rights Education for the Twenty-First Century*, *supra* note 2, xiii.

[20] Andreopoulos & Claude: 'Preface,' *supra* note 8, xxii.

[21] Meintjes, Garth: 'Human Rights Education as Empowerment: Reflections on Pedagogy.' In *Human Rights Education for the Twenty-First Century*, *supra* note 2, 65.

[22] *Ibid.*, 66.

[23] *Ibid.*, 66–67.

These observations provide the backdrop for examining SCANET educational activities. This analysis continues with the concepts of Lave and Wenger, namely the *learning curriculum* and the *legitimate peripheral participant*. Lave and Wenger connect the concept of the *learning curriculum* to the reproduction of communities, and emphasize that learning is essentially situated activity. Thus, in addition to acquiring substantive facts, learning is understood to include the construction of identities as well as socialization to a new identity. The learning curriculum represents the perspective of learners – the 'newcomers' and the legitimate peripheral participants – who aspire to gain access into the community's social practices. This concept is contrasted by the *teaching curriculum*, which refers to the agenda of intentional instruction reflecting particularly what the community's 'old-timers' – its full members – construe relevant for newcomers.[24] According to Lave and Wenger the relationship of newcomers and old-timers entails an intrinsic tension: whereas the reproduction of communities requires new members to gain full access, this can on a personal level awaken resentment in old-timers as they may lose influence and status in the process.[25] As a consequence old-timers may be reluctant to offer newcomers thorough access to the all elements of full membership. This prevents newcomers from forming identities of mastery, and their legitimate peripheral status is transformed from an inclusionary and dynamic position into one of "unrelatedness or irrelevance".[26]

The SCANET community of practice can be seen to embody the second generation of Nordic human rights experts with the first, now retired generation of pioneers emerging in the 1980s. A prominent SCANET expert lists the pioneers in Norway to include the late Torkel Opsahl, Jan Helgessen, who is still continuing his work, and the retired Asbjorn Eide, who held a leading role. In Finland Allan Rosas became influential and started to recruit younger researchers, in Sweden Göran Melander's impact was central, and in Denmark key figures were above all Lars Adam Rehof and Mårten Kjaerum. For the previous two generations of Nordic experts, as formal educational programs did not exist, socializing and education occurred through informal training

[24] Lave, Jean & Wenger, Etienne: Situated Learning: Legitimate Peripheral Participation. Cambridge University Press, Cambridge, 1991, 36–37, 40–41, 53, 97, 116.

[25] *Ibid.*, 116.

[26] *Ibid.*, 101–104.

which could be characterized as apprenticeship.[27] This raises the question whether such a formal 'school' as SCANET is successful in reproducing the community of practice of human rights experts. Do SCANET activities render the community transparent, which allows students to develop expert identities, or leave expert practices opaque, thereby marking the status of legitimate peripheral participants by unrelatedness and irrelevance? In addition to these questions, the subsequent analysis explores SCANET activities from the perspective of empowerment. It asks whether the SCANET educational model provides students with increasing mastery over their own lives with which to challenge oppressive structures, or whether it is characterized by "banking", which socializes its students to the "violence of anti-dialogue".

Conceptions of Knowledge, Expertise and Learning

The SCANET website lists annually around a dozen activities in its name. These include seminars, training courses and expert meetings held at its participant universities. For the present inquiry focus is invested on the training courses organized by SCANET with funding provided by ScaFund. Each year commonly includes one week-long activity and one or two shorter, two to three day activities. The activity venues typically change and activities have been organized in different parts of the Nordic region. Due to their short duration as well as limited number, SCANET activities do not provide a comprehensive doctorate study curriculum. Instead they complement the training that participating candidates receive at their home institutions. Due to the high number of visitors in SCANET activities, they commonly expose doctorate candidates to a greater range of scholars and practitioners from the human rights field than their local settings. Following the emphasis placed on transnational collaboration in the human rights phenomenon, SCANET activities can thus be seen to hold a higher status than instruction occurring in distinct local settings. It could be questioned whether activities bearing numerous changing

[27] Due to its empirical focus on SCANET, this study does not offer a comprehensive analysis of the socialization processes of previous human rights expert generations, but rather provides mere glimpses. The concept of apprenticeship again follows that utilized by Lave and Wenger.

elements – venues, participants, topics – yield in the kind of unity that permits their examination as a distinguishable entity. Despite changing elements, SCANET activities entail numerous consistent features which form the basis of analytical commonality: they are organized by the SCANET coordinator and numerous prominent experts frequent practically all activities. Activity programs entail a distinct and consistent structure. The prevalence of common features has also been expressly emphasized by prominent experts who emphasize SCANET as forming a distinct 'school' of human rights research.

The following analysis focuses on three week-long activities and two shorter, two-three day events. In total these activities included 148 participants, of which 42 were experts and 106 students. A characteristic week-long activity featured around 30 students and eight experts, both permanent SCANET experts as well as visitors. Activity programs include formal and informal elements, and most participants are present in all organized program as parallel sessions are an exception. The subsequent analysis observes particularly, through examination of the SCANET *learning curriculum*, how the activities contribute to empowering their participants from oppressive structures; this inquiry is pursued in Chapter 6. The primary observation of the analysis is the 'school-likeness' of both the organizing of SCANET activities as well as their approach to learning. On the conceptual level this is reflected in the division of participants into 'faculty' and 'students'. These categories were instituted by SCANET organizers and prominent experts, who utilized them to introduce activity programs as well as to denote events, for example by announcing: "*tonight we will have a faculty meeting*". In SCANET activities these categories were visible both in the substantive contributions expected from these groups as well as in spatial arrangements for the activities. This study explores the significance of these categories by investigating how they are reflected in the qualities invested in the speech acts of different participants. *Speech act* is a term utilized by linguists, and paramount for the present purposes is how the nature and content of speech acts are construed to emanate from the syntactic and social context in which they are uttered, instead of from their grammar or formal content.[28] By focussing on speech acts, this analysis explores how in SCANET activities the nature invested in the speech acts of individuals assigned into different

[28] Hanks, William F.: Language and Communicative Practices. Westview Press, Colorado, 1996, 92–94.

categories reflects SCANET's internal hierarchy. This analysis also investigates what kind of conceptions of knowledge, expertise and learning this hierarchy reflects.

From Presentations to Knowledge through Comments

In SCANET activities both individuals assigned the status of faculty and student are expected to offer verbal contributions. These contributions are distinguished from each other through the terminology utilized by activity programs as well as prominent SCANET experts: whereas faculty are invited to hold 'lectures', students are invited to give 'presentations'. Presentations are expected to be based on ongoing PhD work and, as their background, to be accompanied by a paper ranging between 10–15 pages distributed to other participants in advance. Lectures are related to the activity's theme and reflect the research interests and background of the expert; during an activity each expert commonly holds between two to four lectures. Differences in terminology are reflected in the division of time accompanying these contributions: although both lectures and presentations are in general assigned an equal amount of time – commonly 45 minutes – in lectures the time is most often occupied by faculty monologue followed by brief discussion, in presentations it is divided between student monologue and discussion. Also the terms used for the speech acts of subsequent discussions differ from each other. In lectures, the discussions are characterized as consisting of 'questions' and 'answers', in presentations of 'comments' (Table 12).

As such, the above description may appear to merely reproduce a conventional division of academic labour where senior scholars lecture and assist younger ones through comments in their research. Yet it also contains elements that require closer attention. The first of these

Table 12: SCANET Speech Acts

	FACULTY	STUDENT
TYPE of SPEECH ACT	Lecture	Presentation
TOTAL TIME	45	45
TIME FOR SPEAKER	35–40	10–20
TIME FOR DISCUSSION	5–10	25–35
CONTENT OF DISCUSSION	Questions/Answers	Comments

is the direction and volume of flow: the division of time accompanying lectures and presentations establishes a pattern where flow moves, by a vast majority, from faculty to students. As Table 12 demonstrates, in their presentations students were assigned between 10 and 15 minutes for their personal contribution, with the majority of the remaining 45 minutes being consumed by the comments of two pre-assigned experts. The first commentator was encouraged by SCANET organizers to occupy around 20 minutes, the second around 10 minutes. After these comments, jointly lasting between 25 and 35 minutes, the presenting student was reserved up to five minutes to reflect on them. Commonly, scarcity of time prevented this from becoming a meaningful dialogue. Instead many students concluded their presentations by merely thanking the experts for their comments. This outcome contributed to the impression that students were encouraged to adopt the comments of experts without, at least, public reflection.

This division of time induced an outcome that also prevented the other venue participants from contributing to the discussion, despite having been required to read the papers. Often the activities included other students who were conducting research in fields similar to the presenting student, which could have provided them with distinct insight for comments. Importantly the same did not necessarily apply to all commenting experts: although SCANET organizers invested significant attention in matching presentations with commentators – students could in most instances wish for specific experts as commentators – the great diversity of student topics prevented all papers from finding corresponding expertise from faculty members. Yet the described pattern was upheld also in such instances, and the observed activities portrayed no examples where the expert chose to depart from this structure, such as instead inviting students conducting research in similar issues to contribute. This pattern introduced a circumstance where the other participants were expected to be present during the presentations, yet the division of time prevented them from offering contributions to the expert comments; their participation was reduced into that of a silent audience. Simultaneously the division of time communicated to them that the comments of experts were *knowledge* that could likewise benefit their own projects despite of themselves potentially holding greater speciality in their field.

The second noteworthy element relates to the ontological quality invested in lectures and presentations. This matter can be explored by focussing on the terminology utilized to describe the speech acts of the

Table 13: Summary

	Total	Students	% of total	Experts	% of total
Questions	44	36	82%	8	18%
Answers	56 (9 in answer+)	2 (1 in answer+)	4% (11% in answer+)	54 (8 in answer+)	96% (89% in answer+)
Comments	13	6	46%	7	54%
Total	113	44	39%	69	61%

discussions following lectures and presentations, namely questions, answers and comments. These terms are again ones utilized and encouraged systematically by prominent SCANET experts. In SCANET activities questions characteristically address specific points raised by lectures, and therefore in this analysis they are treated as instances where an individual seeks supplementary information. Answers, on the other hand, are construed as instances where an individual provides additional information. In SCANET activities they, like questions, commonly follow lectures. As can be expected, questions are mostly posed by students and answers offered by faculty (Table 13).[29] Students often participate actively in this pattern, as they may include direct questions to experts in their presentations; as a rule, experts include no similar questions to students in their lectures. Differing from these two categories of speech acts are comments, which commonly follow presentations. Comments focus on the merits and shortcomings of presentations. They also often include suggestions for supplementary reading or point to relevant human rights documents. Likewise, they stem mostly from experts. Students commonly participate in this pattern of flow, in many instances concluding their presentations by stating "*I look forward to the comments of the experts*." Yet as Table 13 demonstrates, also students are active in formulating their interventions to discussions following lectures as comments instead of questions. In such instances comments often stem from practical

[29] Table 13 is based on the analysis of five discussions following lectures, occurring in three sessions over two days in a week-long activity. The sessions were intended for all the participants of the SCANET activity and in addition to students, they were participated by two or three experts. Table 13 includes in addition a category of 'answer+' which signals more than one answer per question. This accounts for the greater number of answers than questions. This category is explored in Chapter 6.

experiences held by the student in the human rights phenomenon. This is exemplified by the intervention of a student who commented on an expert lecture on the rights of indigenous peoples. The student had participated in an indigenous delegation lobbying for the inclusion of particular provisions to the Declaration on the Rights of Indigenous Peoples in different UN contexts. He utilized this insight to complement the views forwarded by the expert in her lecture, thus offering additional knowledge. Activities feature additionally instances where experts ask questions. These are primarily directed to other experts but occasionally also to students. Yet, as Table 13 demonstrates, such instances are scarce and do not form a major diversion from the general observed patterns of flow.

To examine the conception of knowledge and expertise emerging from these patterns of flow, both the division of time as well as terms utilized to describe speech acts accompanying lectures and presentations differ from each other. The characterization of speech acts following lectures as questions and answers introduces lectures as domains entailing ready knowledge from which students can benefit by both listening to them as well as by asking questions to be answered by experts. Student presentations, on the other hand, emerge as raw data that is to be transformed into knowledge by listening to and adopting the comments forwarded by the pre-assigned experts. This pattern where flow moves, by majority, from faculty to students entails elements that construe knowledge as "an object to be received" rather than as something that evolves through a "continuous process of inquiry and reflection".[30] The lack of dialogue both between faculty and students as well as different members of the faculty in the above patterns introduces a distinct conception of expertise: it emerges as a domain of individual mastering of skill and knowledge instead of as the result of collective, interactive and collaborational activity by a community of practice.[31]

Structural Elements of Expertise

The observed patterns of flow introduce important structural elements to the systemic agency of human rights experts: only by being included

[30] Meintjes: 'Human Rights Education as Empowerment,' *supra* note 21, 66–67.

[31] See discussion of similar findings in Haavisto, Vuola: Court Work in Transition: An Activity-Theoretical Study of Changing Work Practices in a Finnish District Court. Yliopistopaino, Helsinki, 2002, 63–64.

in faculty will the information held by an individual be viewed to constitute *knowledge* which forms expertise in SCANET activities. The significance of structural elements is reinforced by inspection of faculty and student academic profiles. Instead of being clearly delineated from each other, significant overlap can be identified between them. This is illustrated by three features concluded to mark academic experience and expertise: a PhD, published articles and teaching experience at university level. Exploration of student profiles shows that these experiences are not solely the domain of faculty, as the category of students also includes individuals who fill one or all of these categories. Thus many students have published articles, they have teaching experience – in one SCANET activity this applied roughly to one third of participating students – and some already hold a PhD; for the latter reason they may have been enlisted in the category of senior researchers in the SCANET website.[32] Of faculty, although all its members have published significantly and hold extensive teaching experience, it importantly includes a few members not holding PhDs. The activities featured, for example, a prominent young scholar who was internationally merited, yet at the time of her visit she was finishing her PhD thesis. Another instance was that of an accomplished senior scholar who had a doctorate honoris causa but no PhD degree, as they were very rare in her generation. SCANET activities also included a few visiting experts who had experience in international organizations such as the UN instead of academic research, and for that reason did not hold a PhD. These exceptions enforce the empirical overlap between the two groups, demonstrated by Table 14 as well as Graphs 5 and 6.

The importance of these findings could be downplayed by arguing that although students hold academic experience, it does not necessarily translate into human rights expertise if these experiences derive from fields other than human rights. This argument is inapplicable to SCANET activities as, although many students are new to the human rights field, many hold prior knowledge and have for example published in the field. Although their area of competence is likely more restricted than that of scholars with longer experience, doctorate candidates have engaged significantly with their topics, which could be

[32] Information on student profiles stems from a combination of sources, including CVs available on the SCANET website and informal discussions in activities.

Table 14: Profiles of Expertise

	FACULTY	STUDENT
PHD	Most	Some
PUBLISHED ARTICLES	All	Some
TEACHING EXPERIENCE	All	Many

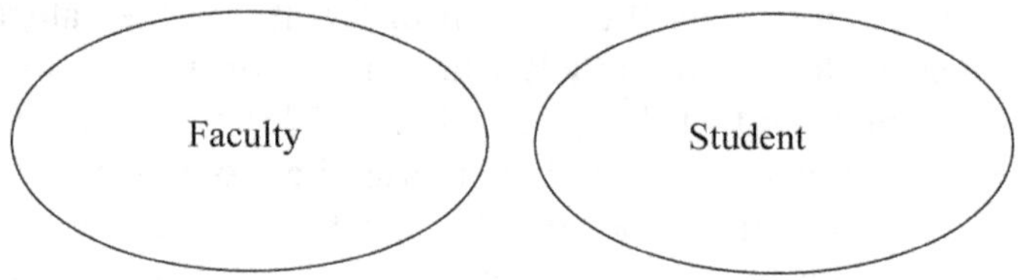

Graph 5: *Categories of Faculty and Students in SCANET Activities*

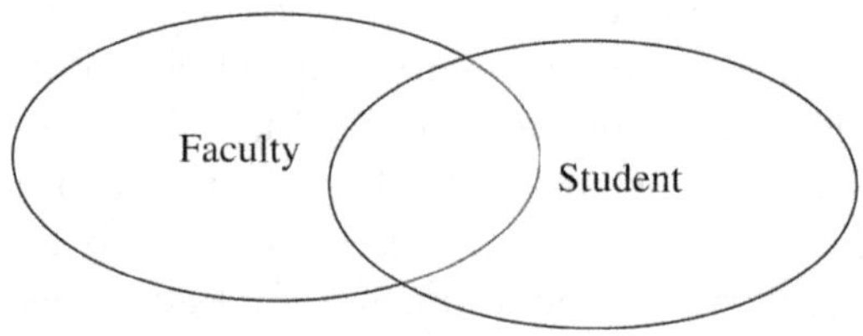

Graph 6: *SCANET Faculty and Students on the Basis of Academic Experience*

argued to have assigned them knowledge in their particular areas that translates into expertise. This possibility was not recognized in SCANET activities, which were instead organized on the basis of a structural division of participants into faculty and students also in the cases of individuals who were in the final stages of their PhD research; their presentations were treated according to the pattern of flow described above. The importance of structural elements regarding SCANET conceptions of expertise is reinforced by activity programs, which are organized into distinct sections of lectures and presentations. Faculty and students are distinguished from each other in seating patterns, of which two types are common: one where participants sit around a common table with faculty on the one end and students on the other, and another where participants are separated into speakers and audience (Graphs 7 and 8).

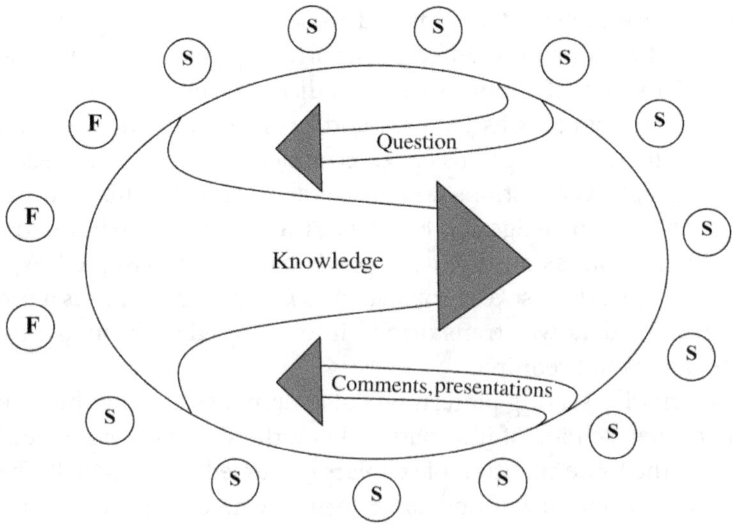

Graph 7: *SCANET Pattern of Flow 1*

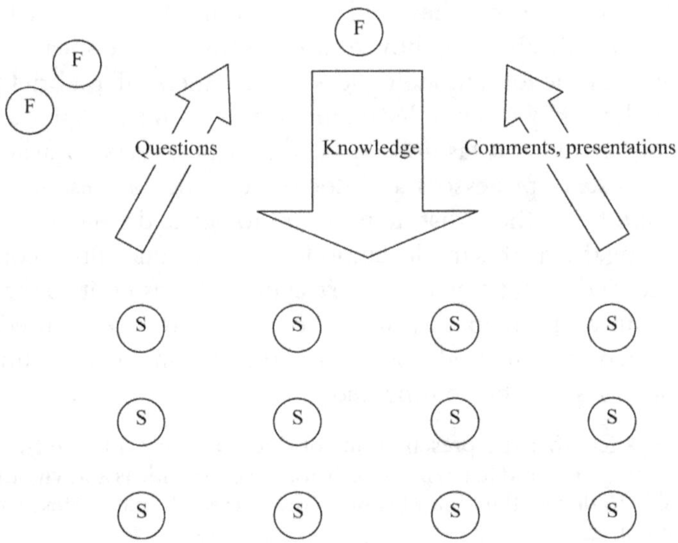

Graph 8: *SCANET Pattern of flow 2*

These distinctive seating arrangements were contrasted by a pattern that emerged in another SCANET event called, instead of a training course, an 'expert meeting'. In this activity no distinctions in seating patterns were established and instead all participants sat together. This activity's patterns of flow differed importantly from those discussed here: participant contributions were not distinguished from each other through such concepts as lectures and presentations, nor was their processing followed by pre-assigned commentators or such predetermined concepts as questions and answers. To connect this finding to conceptions of knowledge and expertise, these patterns give rise to the interpretation that as all the event participants were assigned expert status, all contributions were construed as *knowledge*, and thus a process where raw data was transformed into knowledge through expert comments was not required.

An alternative seating pattern was also demonstrated by the activities of another 'school' of international law, the seminars organized by the 'NAIL', the loose coalition of scholars discussed in Chapter 1. These seminars incorporate a round-table format where all participants sit together without regard for academic status. This seating pattern reflects conceptions of expertise and knowledge that likewise contrast with those of SCANET activities: NAIL events are commonly organized with 30-minute speeches held one after another, with each presenter individually choosing how to use the time. Some speakers will utilize the full time for a monologue whereas others offer a brief presentation followed by general discussion. Contributions are not organized in any systematic fashion based on such aspects as academic status, but instead professors and doctorate students present papers one after another without distinctive terminology to denote the speech acts following them. This model embodies a more Foucaultian conception of knowledge and expertise, portraying them as entities that can be located in all participants, instead of being invested in predetermined, structurally allotted positions.[33] This sentiment was summarized by a professor who commented:

> I always feel that the presentations of doctorate students are the most interesting ones and teach me a lot. They have fresh ideas and vigour, and are able to devote the kind of time to their research that professors only dream of.

Another professor emphasized how "*[m]any revolutions in the sciences were done by relative newcomers to their fields, for example Einstein and*

[33] See Foucault, Michel: The Archaelogy of Knowledge & The Discourse on Language. Pantheon Books, New York, 1972.

the theory of relativity". It should, however, be noted that this NAIL model represents above all an ideal, not one actually realized. Instead, in the NAIL activities doctorate candidates display respect, even intimidation toward established professors, commonly making them hesitant toward commenting on the professors' papers. Some senior scholars display indifference to this ideal of equal time division, extending their presentations well beyond their assigned 30-minute slot and consequently confusing the schedule. Despite formal debunking of status, NAIL circles portray significant celebration of its key scholars, who primarily hold influential positions in prestigious universities. These factors notwithstanding, the events led to an atmosphere where experimentation and novelty were cherished – sometimes with embarrassing results: in one NAIL event a story spread among junior scholars of an article recently published in a NAIL type journal. The article incorporated psychoanalysis, metasciences and what-not and was for a moment celebrated in NAIL circles. It was only later discovered that the article was a hoax made up with the intent to mock the NAIL approach to the conception of knowledge described here.

Exploring Conceptions of Learning

In SCANET activities the observed patterns of flow create circumstances in which doctorate candidates will, in the course of a week-long activity, be expected to listen to around 30 hours of lectures while they, in addition to participating in the discussions following lectures, offer a contribution between ten to fifteen minutes through their presentations. As lectures and presentations are practically the only two modes of contributions that SCANET activities entail, doctorate candidates do not engage in such practices as examining state reports, for example processing from the perspective of the different parties – a practice suggested by Rita Maran as one option for how human rights could be taught at the university level.[34] Why are such practices absent and the SCANET activity curriculum structured around these two observed models?

One possible answer is the conception of learning held by the prominent SCANET experts in charge of structuring activities: as the activities are limited in duration, they can entail only elements construed to

[34] Maran, Rita: 'Teaching Human Rights in the Universities.' In *Human Rights Education for the Twenty-First Century, supra* note 2, 204.

allow most effective learning, namely the discussed structure of lectures and presentations. This assigns SCANET activities with elements that Vaula Haavisto has characterized as the command-and-control mode, where learning is construed as the adoption of necessary information 'poured' by authorities to those who are to receive it.[35] Lave and Wenger have characterized this process as the internalization of knowledge.[36] The patterns of flow observed in SCANET activities entail also elements of the already mentioned 'banking' education which portrays knowledge as "a gift bestowed by those who consider themselves knowledgeable upon those whom they consider to know nothing".[37] These conceptions of learning have met serious criticism in past decades. Lave and Wenger note how the idea of learning as internalization leaves the "nature of the learner, of the world, and of their relations unexplored" as well as establishes a sharp dichotomy between 'inside' and 'outside' knowledge. It suggests "that knowledge is largely cerebral, and takes the individual as the non-problematic unit of analysis", and construes learning too easily as an unproblematic process of "absorbing the given, as a matter of transmission and assimilation".[38]

As was discussed, Meintjes emphasizes such conceptions to be particularly ill-suited for human rights education, as they subject the assumed recipients of knowledge to the "violence of anti-dialogue". This makes the outcome of the learning process static, instead of empowering students to become conscious of their own participation in the creation of knowledge. Also, this model of learning fails to convince students of their critical ability to conceptualize their experiences of reality, which would assist them to challenge existing oppressive structures.[39] Although it is exaggerated to characterize SCANET activities to embody anti-dialogue violence, as the discussions do encourage some exchanges, their question-answer format as well as the hierarchy of participants suggests that learning in SCANET includes static elements. Importantly, this model was occasionally discussed and questioned by students in informal exchanges, but never explicitly addressed by experts during the formal SCANET activities.

---

[35] Haavisto: Court Work in Transition, *supra* note 31, 54.
[36] Lave & Wenger: Situated Learning, *supra* note 24, 47.
[37] Meintjes: 'Human Rights Education as Empowerment,' *supra* note 21, 66.
[38] Lave & Wenger: Situated Learning, *supra* note 24, 47.
[39] Meintjes: 'Human Rights Education as Empowerment,' *supra* note 21, 66–67.

Pierre Bourdieu has argued in his seminal study of the Kabyle household how tacit understandings of social relations, worldviews and structural principles are largely acquired through everyday practices.[40] Although an educational activity differs in significant ways from a household, Bourdieu's analysis entails integral aspects for the present context. The practices of SCANET activities – organization of program, utilized terminology, seating arrangements and patterns of flow – socialize participants assigned student status into a conception that knowledge is a ready object that can be passed from the individuals who possess it to those who lack it. SCANET activities further convey a conception of expertise as the mastering of knowledge by individuals enjoying the structurally allotted position as members of SCANET faculty. Finally, they introduce learning as a process where knowledge is 'poured in' by knowledgeable individuals to those lacking it. These findings gain importance from two additional elements. The first of them is that SCANET activities are directed toward doctorate candidates, thus individuals working toward the highest university degree at a level where research is customarily expected to demonstrate independent inquiry as well as critical analysis. This assigns the engagement students have with their topics significantly different from that of, for example, first year undergraduates for whom it could be argued necessary that they adopt general knowledge as well as central practices in their fields. Consequently questionable emerges whether such a 'school-like' approach to learning is suitable at such a high academic level; whether it is a model that most effectively encourages the formation of new identities of mastery in research.

The second element is that a PhD has in the Finnish context traditionally signalled the culmination of a research career. Thus doctorate candidates have included, in addition to recent post-graduates, university personnel well in their fifties who have commonly had extensive teaching commitments. Consequently the status of doctorate candidates has been mixed as, in addition to being 'students', they have been considered as researchers and experts. Educational policy in Finland has since the mid-1990s sought to lower the average age for obtaining a PhD, and simultaneously, particularly through the establishment of numerous research schools funded by the Finnish Ministry of

[40] Bourdieu, Pierre: Outline of a Theory of Practice. Cambridge University Press, Cambridge, 2007 [1972].

Education as well as the Finnish Academy, policy guidelines have sought to identify doctorate candidates more clearly as 'doctorate students' in formal contexts. These initiatives have met consistent opposition for example from the central association of Finnish researchers, which construes the term 'student' to belittle the actual experience of researchers working on their PhDs, and simultaneously to convey the wrong impression of their level of professional experience to potential employers outside the university. Instead the research association supports that doctorate candidates be called 'researchers'. Whereas official terminology appears to shift toward the uniform use of 'students', the position of doctorate candidates within Finnish academic circles continues to be in flux. Against this background the unequivocal denoting of doctorate candidates as students in SCANET becomes conspicuous and departs from the general practices embedded in Finnish academic life. This gives rise to the following question: how can this conception be understood; what kind of domains emerge as its possible sources? The following section explores this matter from three perspectives: SCANET patterns of flow as reflecting conceptions of expertise embedded in the functioning of courts; SCANET activities as reflecting the educational experiences of its faculty; and conception of expertise and learning as reflections of the ontological qualities assigned to human rights knowledge.

Legal Context and Patterns of Flow

The SCANET conception of expertise finds commonality with the analysis by Vaula Haavisto on the patterns of flow and conceptions of expertise embedded in Finnish court proceedings before and after the court reform of 1993.[41] This finding gains relevance particularly from the manner SCANET activities are interpreted as part of ongoing efforts to increase the legality of the human rights phenomenon, an element elaborated in Chapter 5. Haavisto's analysis demonstrates similarity particularly between SCANET activities and pre-reform proceedings, which were likewise largely constituted of monologues emanating from legal experts. Haavisto concludes that judges occupied particularly influential roles in mediating and directing patterns of flow.[42] This was also demonstrated by seating patterns portraying

[41] Haavisto: Court Work in Transition, *supra* note 31.
[42] *Ibid.*, 10, 120.

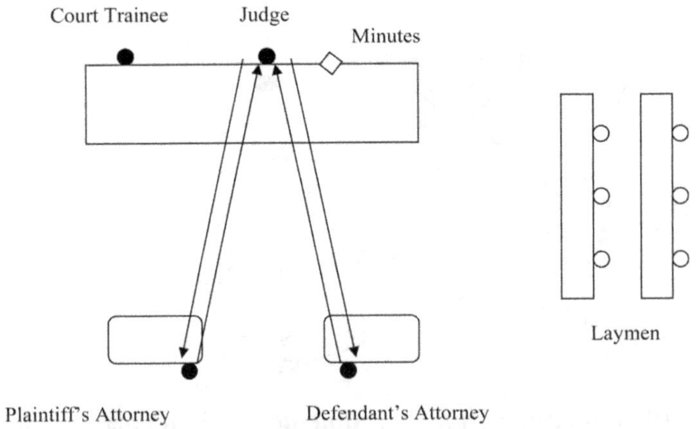

Graph 9: *Physical Setting and Interactive Relations in the 1990 Construction*

physical distance between the different trial parties – attorneys, the judge and laymen – as well as interactive relations (Graph 9).[43]

These elements assigned judges a structural position of authority and expertise comparable to that of SCANET faculty. As is demonstrated by Graphs 7 and 8, the patterns of flow from the two contexts resemble each other. In addition, parallels exist in the manner the position of a judge and human rights experts are described. Haavisto discusses how the work of judges has traditionally represented "the most individual and independent expertise with minimal collaboration", with court trials forming the "nucleus of judicature and the area in which judicial expertise appears in its purest form".[44] Similar characteristics were outlined by a prominent SCANET expert who described her work in a UN treaty body: she emphasized how in her tasks she acted alone on the basis of her individual expertise, not, for example, as the representative of her government. As is elaborated in Chapter 5, in the description of treaty body work their 'court-likeness' is further emphasized. This suggests desires to characterize the work of individual human rights experts with the same attributes that Haavisto uses to describe the work of judges: as independent experts relying on minimal collaboration with external domains.

---

[43] *Ibid.*, 123, 124. These same pages feature also original versions of Graphs 9 and 10. Warm thanks to Vaula Haavisto for permission to reproduce these figures here.

[44] *Ibid.*, 65.

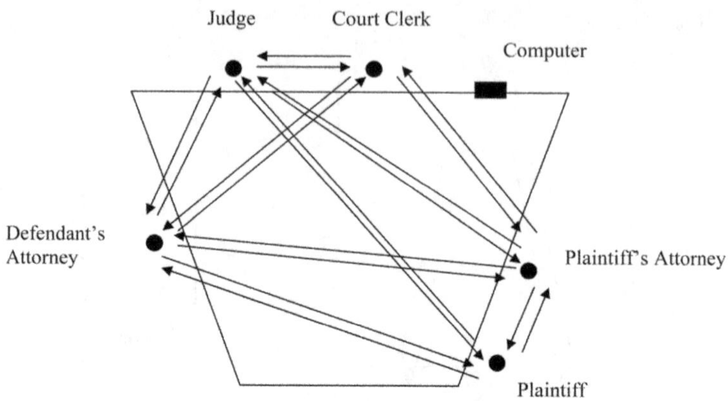

Graph 10: *Physical Setting and Interactive Relations in the 1997 Construction Dispute*

However, Haavisto found significant differences in conceptions of expertise and patterns of flow after the 1993 reform: patterns were more reciprocal, creating a diversified profile of expertise as located both in legal experts as well as in lay experiences.[45] Instead of formal monologue, proceedings were more embedded in exchanges and informal dialogue.[46] In seating patterns physical distance had been replaced by greater intimacy and more direct interaction (Graph 10).[47]

These elements create patterns of flow that bear similarity to the NAIL events (Graph 11). Haavisto discusses how the post-reform model introduced possibilities to treat court proceedings as instances of mutual learning as well as gave rise to alternative dispute resolution models.[48] In SCANET activities such changes were not observable, as the patterns remained uniform in all examined events with one exception: the last activity entailed parallel sessions for the student presentations. Yet, despite of greater time available for each paper, the described patterns of flow, with two pre-assigned commentators, remained unchanged. Why have SCANET patterns of flow remained unmodified? One possible reason is the strong tradition of legalism, which Haavisto suggests forms a Finnish cultural characteristic.[49]

[45] *Ibid.*, 10, 120.
[46] *Ibid.*, 123, 286.
[47] *Ibid.*, 123–124.
[48] *Ibid.*, 301. See also Roberts, Simon & Palmer, Michael: Dispute Processes: ADR and the Primary Forms of Decision-Making. Cambridge University Press, Cambridge, 1998.
[49] Haavisto: Court Work in Transition, *supra* note 31, 67.

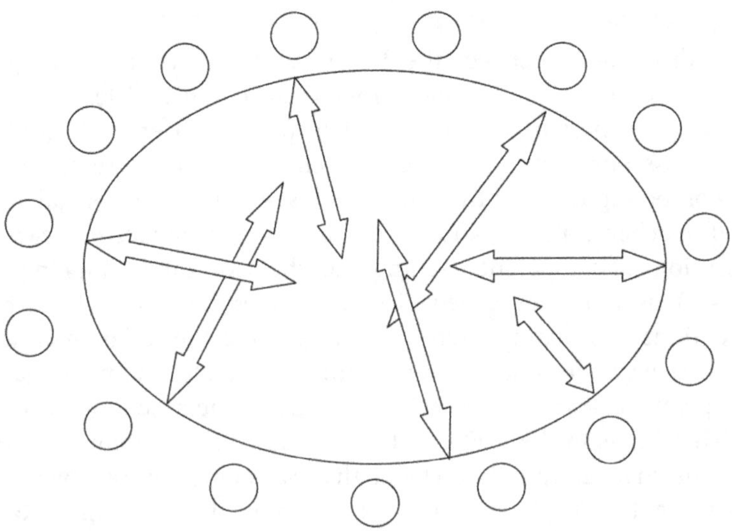

Graph 11: *NAIL Pattern of Flow (Ideal)*

Another possible source is the increasing specialization or fragmentation of international law,[50] a process scholars have analyzed to describe international law already in the 1980s.[51] Thus, as the field of international law has become increasingly complex and professional practices have grown continually more diverse, changes in one area of the law – in this case domestic Finnish law – are likely not passed on to other areas, which instead continue to follow the practices that have emerged in their own field over the past decades.

Filtering of Educational Experiences

Another plausible source for the learning conception of SCANET activities – their 'school-likeness' – stems from the past educational experiences of SCANET faculty members. These experience form what Martyn Denscombe describes the "hidden pedagogy" of teaching.[52]

[50] Koskenniemi, Martti: Fragmentation of International Law: Difficulties Arising from the Diversification and Expansion of International Law. Report of the Study Group of the International Law Commission. Hakapaino, Helsinki, 2007.

[51] Alston, Philip: 'Making Space for New Human Rights: The Case of the Right to Development.' In *1 Harvard Human Rights Yearbook 3*, 1988, 3–40.

[52] Denscombe, Martyn: 'The "Hidden Pedagogy" and Its Implications for Teacher Training.' In 3 *British Journal of Sociology of Education 3*, 1982, 249–265.

In his analysis of the professional practices of teachers, Denscombe notes a discrepancy between the theories and practices of teaching. He locates it to the implicit conceptions of teaching and learning that classroom teachers have kept from their own experiences as students in the classroom setting. These implicit conceptions are so potent, Denscombe argues, that they filter themselves through formal 'theoretical' teacher training, and have even greater impact on teachers' conceptions of competent teaching than their formal training in pedagogics. Denscombe's argument also illuminates the observed SCANET conceptions of learning. Here decisive emerge the learning conceptions that were dominant when prominent faculty members gained their primary learning experiences during their school years. In Finnish schools in the 1960s and 1970s learning was commonly seen as the internalization of knowledge that was being 'poured' by a commanding authority. In her analysis of school work, Pauliina Rainio notes that, although this model is today commonly undesirable, it remains the predominant model in Western countries.[53]

In addition to school experiences, two further domains can be identified as having contributed to the hidden pedagogy of SCANET experts. The first of these are experiences in legal education: a realm of education that Duncan Kennedy has characterized as being organized around an implicit model of hierarchy.[54] Another possible source are the educational experiences that SCANET experts have had through apprenticeships from different UN contexts which have likewise reflected distinct hierarchies based on professional status.[55] These hierarchies are illustrated by two examples from UN treaty body proceedings of the relationship between treaty body members and their research assistants, who are often doctorate students.[56] The first is from an informal lunch meeting during a Human Rights Committee session. The meeting included four treaty body members as well as three

[53] Rainio, Pauliina: Tietotyön malli koulun kehittämisessä: Muutoksen esteet, edellytykset ja mahdollisuudet opettajien puheessa. Helsingin yliopisto, Helsinki, 2002.

[54] Kennedy, Duncan: 'Legal Education as Training for Hierarchy.' In *The Politics of Law: A Progressive Critique* (Ed. Kairys, David). Revised Edition. Pantheon Books, New York, 1990, 38–58.

[55] Hancock: Lords of Poverty, *supra* note 9, 37–41.

[56] In this study contacts with UN domains have remained limited, as its primary ethnographic focus has been invested in SCANET activities. Thus these examples aim to illustrate relevant elements through examples rather than to offer comprehensive ethnographic description.

members of different NGOs working on the topic. In addition, present were three research assistants and an NGO representative who was taking notes.

During the meeting treaty body members and NGO representatives sat around a table located in the centre of the room while the research assistants and the person taking notes sat by the walls in seats provided for observers. The hour-long meeting was commenced by the presentation of an NGO member, and followed by discussion in which treaty body members as well as NGO representatives participated, while the research assistants remained a silent audience. The general atmosphere indicated that it would have been both highly irregular as well as unwelcome for them to intervene in the discussion. The second example stems from another lunch, this time accompanying a session of the Committee on Economic, Social and Cultural Rights. Six individuals participated in the lunch, and they were all seated at a common table. Of the participants, four were treaty body members while two, both PhD candidates, held assistant status. Lunch discussion demonstrated that instead of being equals, the participants held highly distinct status: the treaty body members addressed exclusively each other (by their first names) while the assistants were not addressed and sat in silence through the lunch listening to the discussion. Throughout the dinner they were in no manner welcomed to join in the discussion. The difference in the status of the two groups was reinforced at the end of the lunch, when treaty body members considered it natural to ask the assistants to clear their plates and fetch them coffee.

Importantly, although both of the described events involved informal events organized around treaty body proceedings, they demonstrate the substantive differences assigned to the status of treaty body members and assistants. The hierarchy between these groups is, of course, much more prevalent in formal treaty body proceedings, where it would be unacceptable for individuals not allotted distinct status to offer contributions. As was noted, the present generation of SCANET experts have often been trained into the community of practice of human rights experts through apprenticeships of different kinds. Thus they have probably entered the community as research assistants or other individuals with a legitimate peripheral position. These experiences have led to the internalization of hierarchies, and consequently, as the individuals today hold the position of full members in the community of practice as SCANET experts, these hierarchies are reflected in SCANET activities. The significance of the implicit pedagogy formed by these socialization experiences holds undisputedly even greater weight in a context such as SCANET where, differing from school teachers, the individuals acting as teachers do not, as a general rule, hold formal training in pedagogics; none of the examined expert CVs mention such experience.[57] Consequently it can be assessed that the conceptions of learning held by SCANET experts reflect importantly their conceptions of what forms good teaching.

"You Are Being Tempted by Relativism"

The third factor explaining the conceptions of learning, expertise and knowledge described above relates to how prominent SCANET experts view human rights knowledge. Here decisive are instances where students are encouraged to avoid critical queries. This is illustrated by an exchange that followed a student presentation which explored how the concept of human rights was treated in the European Court of Human Rights. The discussion following the presentation became unusually intense. Paramount for the present analysis is the tone in which both the presentation and paper were received: faculty comments suggested that they considered them to 'challenge' the universality of human rights; they were seen as potentially hostile to the general mission of advancing human rights. These sentiments were summarized by an expert who, after growing visibly aggravated, commented that the student was being "tempted by relativism". This exchange is compelling for numerous reasons. It utilizes the concept of relativism as entailing a certain, predefined essence that can 'tempt' or 'seduce' students. The term relativism is, of course, familiar from the six decades of 'universalism-relativism' debate which had as its first official marker the 1947 statement by the American Anthropological Association.[58] Today 'relativism' is increasingly utilized by liberal multiculturalist scholars in a manner similar to that of the SCANET expert, as something the 'temptation' of which should be 'avoided'.[59] Yet, as has been marked by Clifford Geertz, the meaning of the concept has largely

---

[57] Even if some experts do have such training, the fact that it is not highlighted demonstrates that it is not decisive for membership in SCANET faculty.

[58] American Anthropological Association: 'Statement on Human Rights.' In *49 American Anthropologist 4*, 1947, 539–543.

[59] Benhabib, Seyla: The Claims of Culture: Equality and Diversity in the Global Era. Princeton University Press, Princeton, 2002, 29; Freeman, Michael: Human Rights: An interdisciplinary approach. Polity Press, Cambridge, 2002, 9.

remained confused. He notes how it is today associated with such "moral and intellectual consequences" as "subjectivism, nihilism, incoherence, Machiavellianism, ethical idiocy, esthetic blindness, and so on".[60] In SCANET, the presentation was also accompanied by high emotional charge; instead of being a calm and rational exchange it was characterized by passion and intensity.[61] Thus, instead of fact or description,[62] the presentation and the research it was founded on were politicised and perceived as *arguments*. This suggests that both the paper and the presentation touched upon matters that instead of 'stale' or 'cold' objects were still 'warm'.[63]

To explore this exchange as reflecting a distinct conception of human rights knowledge, it formed an instance where both the student holding the presentation as well as those participants who were present in the session were communicated by SCANET faculty that the paper led to unappreciated outcomes. As it challenged the unbiased operation of a primary institution regarded to advance the realization of human rights, it resulted in conclusions that should be avoided. Geertz notes how this has become a principle function of the concept of relativism: it is used to "scare[s] us away from certain ways of thinking and toward others".[64] In a different context, the same paper as well as the presenting student were characterized by a prominent SCANET expert as belonging to a different 'school' of thought from SCANET. This suggested that both the paper's approach as well as its conclusions stemmed rather from adherence to this external entity – a 'school' of thought – rather than from its data. The significance of this statement on the assumptions made of human rights knowledge is clarified by another instance from SCANET activities where discussion turned to the drafting of the UDHR. As was mentioned, the topic remains the source of ongoing research and has in recent years been met with numerous contributions.[65] In this scholarship researchers have invested

---

60 Geertz, Clifford: 'Anti Anti-Relativism.' In *86 American Anthropologist 2*, 1984, 263.

61 Latour, Bruno: 'Scientific Objects and Legal Objectivity.' In *Law, Anthropology, and the Constitution of the Social: Making Persons and Things* (Eds. Alain Pottage & Martha Mundy). Cambridge University Press, Cambridge, 2004, 73–114.

62 *Ibid.*, 146.

63 See discussion on this transformation in Latour, Bruno: Science in Action. Harvard University Press, Cambridge, 1987.

64 Geertz: 'Anti Anti-Relativism,' *supra* note 60, 263.

65 Lauren, Paul Gordon: The Evolution of International Human Rights: Visions Seen. University of Pennsylvania Press, Philadelphia, 1998; Morsink, Johannes: The

distinct attention on exploring the Western influences of the drafting process: while some scholars perceive their impact exaggerated,[66] others acknowledge this legacy, yet construe that the global spread of the human rights phenomenon has made it insignificant.[67] In SCANET discussions a third approach emerged, namely one that saw these influences as irrelevant. This is illustrated by the following statement made by a visiting expert during a discussion accompanying a presentation:

> I don't really see why it is relevant where the human rights discourse emerged. So what if it is of Western origin? That doesn't mean that it is not universal. That kind of an argument does not make sense. By the same logic you could argue that the theory of relativity or electricity are Western creations merely because they were invented in the West.

This statement equates human rights knowledge with the findings of 'hard' sciences, to phenomena that exist as objective facts. Assessed from the perspective of scientific methods, this equation entails a problem of logics: whereas the existence of electricity or the accuracy of the theory of relativity can be verified with empirical experimentation, the same is impossible for human rights. Thus it is impossible to establish through empirical experimentation whether a given claim is a human right by its essence or not.[68] Instead, as was demonstrated with the case

---

Universal Declaration of Human Rights: Origins, Drafting & Intent. University of Pennsylvania Press, Philadelphia, 1999; Glendon, Mary Ann: A World Made New: Eleanor Roosevelt and the Universal Declaration of Human Rights. Random House, New York, 2001.

[66] Waltz, Susan: 'Universalizing Human Rights: The Role of Small States in the Construction of the Universal Declaration of Human Rights.' In *23 Human Rights Quarterly 1,* 2001, 44–72; Glendon, Mary Ann: 'The Forgotten Crucible: The Latin American Influence on the Universal Human Rights Ideal.' In *16 Harvard Human Rights Journal,* Spring 2003, 27–39.

[67] Alfredsson, Gudmundur & Eide, Asbjorn: 'Introduction.' In *The Universal Declaration of Human Rights: A Common Standard of Achievement*, (Eds. Alfredsson, Gudmundur & Eide, Asbjorn). Kluwer Law International, The Hague, 1999, 11.

[68] This equation of human rights with scientific facts finds an interesting parallel in the already mentioned ongoing controversy over whether the Darwinian theory of evolution and the Biblical story of creationism should be taught at US schools. For the present discussion what emerges as significant is how the proponents of creationism are increasingly forwarding their arguments through the rhetoric of science, both in criticism toward the theory of evolution as 'myth' based on 'icons' and by introducing the theory of intelligent design, see Wells, Jonathan: Icons of Evolution: Science or Myth? Why Much of What We Teach About Evolution is Wrong. Regnery Publishing Inc., Washington D.C., 2002; ABCNEWS: '1925 Monkey Trial Still With Us.' 23.7.2000, http://abcnews.go.com/sections/us/DailyNews/scopestrial000723.html (24.9.2003). Both attempts have, however, faced serious challenge; Wells's scholarship has received severe criticism and the teaching of the theory of intelligent design has been accused

of LGBT-rights, whether a claim is recognized as a human right or not is guided by the social processes defining the claim's acceptability. An approach equating human rights to scientific facts denies the importance of such social processes, and instead construes human rights as something that merely *exist*. Such a characterization induces significant consequences on the conception of human rights knowledge: as human rights are portrayed as something with an undisputed absolute existence which, further, cannot be verified by empirical observation, human rights are transformed into articles of faith; a secular religion.

The conception of human rights as forming a secular religion has been discussed extensively in scholarship, and it is also visible in the manner scholars of different human rights 'schools' view each other. Thus for example a prominent NAIL scholar stated – in a passionately engaged tone explored in the next chapter – how she has "*no patience for the human rights believers*". Another critical scholar described a human rights educational program as forming a "*human rights church*". The characterization of human rights as articles of faith was accepted also by a prominent SCANET expert who, upon being asked how she felt about such such a view, stated that she has no trouble accepting that human rights create a secular religion. In other contexts she has expanded this characterization by describing certain human rights as "sacred", reflecting the commonly cited characterization of Michael Perry.[69] This conception of human rights knowledge as an article of faith induces important consequences to the SCANET conception of learning: if knowledge is construed as a ready object, learning becomes a process where this object is passed from knowledgeable individuals to those lacking knowledge – from faculty to students. Instead of vigorous questioning and analysis, learning acquires elements of internalisation.

Knowledge Practices

The second half of this chapter explores SCANET activities from the perspective of reproducing the community of practice of human rights experts. It investigates whether they render the community

of violating the constitutional separation of church and State, see MSNBC. 'Judge rules against "intelligent design", http://www.msnbc.msn.com/id/10545387/ (2.1.2006).

[69] Perry, Michael: The Idea of Human Rights: Four Inquiries. Oxford University Press, Oxford, 1998.

transparent, thus allowing its legitimate peripheral participants to gain full membership, or whether they leave elements of its content opaque. By focussing on the knowledge practices of the community of experts, this section inspects whether students learn to process documents in a characteristic manner; it also assesses whether students have access to the implicit knowledge held by experts. The chapter commences by exploring whether SCANET activities teach its students to speak like experts. Greg Urban has identified a discourse and its circulation as central factors in the creation of a community.[70] A distinct discourse inaccessible to outsiders strengthens the impression of the community as an expert one, as is often noted of medical specialists. Sarat and Felstiner discuss how access to a specific language is constitutive of expert positions in divorce court proceedings, sometimes to the great resentment of lay participants.[71] Command of a distinct discourse is also pivotal for membership in the community of practice of human rights experts. This is illustrated by the vigour and dedication invested in efforts to find 'appropriate' terminology for various human rights documents.[72] Appropriate discourse is central in the process through which an issue is construed as a human rights issue instead of a lay experience,[73] and a distinct vocabulary has been characterized as constitutive in the politics of universalism integral to the community of practice of human rights experts.[74]

In the process where laymen become human rights experts – are transformed from outsiders into legitimate insiders in the community of practice of human rights experts – "learning how to talk (and to be silent)" as full participants is decisive.[75] The previous analysis of SCANET conceptions of learning has demonstrated how its activities offer ample opportunities for students to learn *from* the talk of experts.

---

[70] Urban, Greg: Metaculture: How Culture Moves through the World. University of Minnesota Press, Minneapolis, 2001, 95.

[71] Sarat, Austin & Felstiner, William L. F.: Divorce Lawyers and Their Clients: Power & Meaning in the Legal Process. Oxford University Press, Oxford, 1995, 26.

[72] Merry, Sally Engle: Human Rights & Gender Violence: Translating International Law into Local Justice. The University of Chicago, Chicago, 2006; Riles, Annelise: Documents: Artifacts of Modern Knowledge. The University of Michigan Press, Ann Arbor, 2006.

[73] Brenneis, Don: 'Reforming Promise.' In *Documents*, *ibid.*, 41–70.

[74] See discussion of this transformation in Kennedy, David: The Dark Sides of Virtue: reassessing international humanitarianism. Princeton University Press, Princeton, 2004.

[75] Lave & Wenger: Situated Learning, *supra* note 24, 105.

Yet, to qualify as full members, according to Lave and Wenger, they need to learn *to* talk as experts.[76] This section utilizes a notion of speech as including also written texts produced by students. In this it follows the concept utilized by Anna Maria Viljanen in her study of psychiatric statements to determine the accused's mental state in court proceedings. Yet in her analysis she relied solely on written statements, although many of her informants would have been easily available for interviews. She explains this choice by stating that in her context the analysed documents constitute the informants' 'speech' for the courts, and thus the actual speech acts delivered in person become superfluous.[77] In the attempt to explore whether SCANET students gain the ability to express themselves in the expert discourse of human rights through SCANET activities, this study has a more comprehensive approach, including in the concept of speech also actual verbal exchanges.

Learning to Talk like Experts

In beginning this analysis, focus is directed to the skill SCANET students demonstrate in utilizing the human rights discourse in the papers they prepare as background material for their presentations. Sally Engle Merry has outlined distinctive characteristics of this discourse by describing her first experience of a UN human rights treaty body meeting as a 'newcomer': '

> I was overwhelmed by all the acronyms – UNDP, WFP, WHO, UNIFEM, CEDAW, CRC, ICCPR, and many more – and the catch phrases, such as gender mainstreaming, capacity building, best practices, gender focal points, and political will, that I heard all around me. Everyone else seemed to know what was going on … and what all those letters stood for.[78]

Annelise Riles describes similar experiences in her research of Fijian NGO workers, mentioning:

> Although speakers often expressed a desire to communicate with outsiders, they peppered their presentations with acronyms and references to particular documents or conferences and therefore spoke in terms that

---

[76] *Ibid.*, 109.

[77] Viljanen, Anna Maria: Psychiatry and culture. A study of forensic psychiatric argumentation. University of Helsinki, Helsinki, 1994.

[78] Merry: Human Rights & Gender Violence, *supra* note 72, 36.

> were both too general and too specific for anyone but a seasoned participant to follow.[79]

In the course of SCANET activities students participate in a high number of lectures as well as are expected to read a significant amount of material assigned by faculty members as background reading for lectures. Both of these elements include the characteristics described by Merry: they entail frequent references to documents, utilize ample acronyms and expressions that Merry describes as "catch phrases", and feature numerous references to different human rights domains.

These patterns are illustrated by one randomly selected 22-page expert paper submitted as background reading for one SCANET training course. The paper includes mentions of 10 different types of committees. Of these, seven are explicitly named, while the paper includes a general reference of the Committee of Experts. Of institutions and organizations, the text mentions the European Court of Human Rights and the International Labour Organization, and of international legal instruments the European Convention on Human Rights and the European Convention for the Prevention of Torture and Inhuman or Degrading Treatment or Punishment. The term Covenant is repeatedly used, also in the formulation "Covenant and the protocols thereto". In addition, the text includes the expressions "human rights treaty body", "Paris Principles", "UN Standard Minimum Rules for the Treatment of Prisoners", as well as "quasi-judicial procedure", "High Contracting Parties", "Concluding Observations", "Individual Observation", "General Comments", "Final View", "Individual complaint" and "Standard Minimum Rules and Final View" (all capital lettering in the original).

To conclude what kind of learning this exposure induces – whether it translates to student competence of the expert discourse of human rights – student papers are compared to the randomly selected SCANET expert paper. To gain greater precision for analysis, only the use of acronyms in these papers is scrutinized. That acronyms create perhaps the most integral element of the expert discourse on human rights – as well as that of international law – is well reflected in Merry's writing: although she starts out by noting how their frequent use by 'insiders' enforced her outside status, in her analysis of treaty body proceedings

[79] Riles, Annelise: The Network Inside Out. The University of Michigan Press, Ann Arbor, 2006, 52.

Table 15: Acronyms in SCANET student papers

	STUDENT	FACULTY
N	15	1
USING ACRONYMS	73% (=11/15)	1
NO ACRONYMS	27% (=4/15)	-
AVERAGE of acronyms PER PAPER using acronyms	44	78
Average number of pages per paper	15	22
AVERAGE of acronyms PER PAGE (STUDENT N =11)	2.9	3.5

she ends up reproducing their high frequency.[80] The centrality of acronymous was also reflected in faculty comments accompanying SCANET student papers. Even in instances where their use was clearly exaggerated – one paper featured over 250 acronymous in under 20 pages – there were no instances where experts commented on the matter, encouraging restraint.

To examine how SCANET students have generally been socialized into this element of the human rights expert discourse, a randomly selected sample of 15 papers out of a total of 29 papers prepared for one SCANET training course have been examined. Text lengths varied between 5 and 22 pages per document; the total number was 200 pages. In this analysis, only the main text is analysed, while footnotes and bibliography are left unexamined. This inspection shows three in four student papers utilizing acronyms with frequencies that correspond to those of the expert paper, suggesting that a high portion of students have learned how to utilize this element of the expert discourse of human rights (Table 15). Student papers also demonstrate competence in the expert discourse by the diverse types of acronyms utilized. In addition to such conventional acronyms as the UN and UDHR, they include for example the acronyms DK, TRNC, MRT, FRY, EU-ACP, AU, AOU, DRC and ASEAN countries. In addition, the papers produce more unconventional formulations such as MS, WG, IGC, GSP, GSP and NHRI. Other non-standard acronyms include POW and GWT (Appendix). Both of these tendencies – the high frequency of acronyms as well as their invocation to unconvential domains – can be

[80] Merry: Human Rights & Gender Violence, *supra* note 72.

interpreted as signalling that students have internalized the prevalence of acronyms in translating an issue from an everyday one into a human rights issue. Through their papers students thus present their message in a discourse recognizable to insiders of the human rights phenomenon, while it is simultaneously difficult for outsiders to access.

So far this examination has focussed on written texts. However, full membership in communities of practice includes the ability to *speak* in the expert discourse. This is emphasized by Maija Gerlander, Lena Levander and Saara Repo-Kaarento, who in their guide directed for university teachers to improve seminars highlight verbal skills as a constitutive element in the socialization of students as members of a scientific community.[81] For the community of practice of human rights experts these skills include such things as the ability to give interviews, hold lectures and act as intermediaries. Gerlander, Levander and Repo-Kaarento mention, as pedagogical alternatives that introduce students to these skills, the organization of student presentations through a format where other students are assigned as commentators or opponents. Such practices encourage students to translate their competence into the relevant expert discourse in concrete verbal exchanges.[82] As has been demonstrated, the SCANET learning curriculum offers students limited opportunities for acquiring such skills, as for example opponent practices are not utilized. The most important element enabling students to practice speaking in the expert discourse is formed by their presentations. Yet, as each student holds only one presentation in each activity, these opportunities remain limited. SCANET activities entail neither direct instruction or feedback on how to hold a successful presentation. In addition to presentations, students rehearse formulating their verbal exchanges in the expert discourse in the discussions following lectures. Possibilities for such instances are, however, scarce, and thus students are primarily incorporated into the activities as a silent audience, limiting their possibilities to learn to talk as experts.

Knowledge Practices in Processing Documents

In addition to competence in the expert discourse of human rights, human rights experts share knowledge practices that students need

[81] Gerlander, Maija; Levander, Lena M. & Repo-Kaarento, Saara: Säpinää seminaareihin: Opas seminaarityöskentelyn kehittämiseen. University of Helsinki, Helsinki, 2006.

[82] *Ibid.*

to learn in order to gain full membership of this community of practice. This section explores those knowledge practices, aiming to discover how SCANET activities socialize students in them. Focus is directed to two aspects: processing documents and utilizing research resources in SCANET activities. Both of these practices are approached through glimpses aiming to exemplify characteristic expert practices. Documents – "artifacts of modern knowledge" – occupy a distinct position in contemporary societies, leadings scholars to view their analysis as increasingly decisive for understanding modern expert knowledge practices.[83] For the human rights phenomenon, the primary observation becomes abundance. Whether acting as UN treaty body members, professors or consultants, human rights experts are continually showered with documents. Combined, these amount to tremendous quantities of documents, a fact which was illustrated by a visiting SCANET expert – in a discussion about propositions to introduce new documents for the inspection of treaty body members – by stating:

> This all sounds very exciting, but one cannot but wonder how this concurs with the existing workload of treaty body members who already receive daily on our desks a stack of papers this high [holds hands 40 centimetres apart].

Subsequently treaty body members are in the course of their duties faced with state reports varying in length from below a hundred to several hundred pages, 'shadow' reports from domestic and international NGOs among others, general comments and concluding observations as well as their drafts, committee memos, background papers and e-mails. These are accompanied by documents deriving from their other responsibilities as professors and institute leaders including funding applications, evaluation reports, travel bills, annual reports, consultative statements, recommendations, student papers, articles for peer review, as well as their own writings such as articles and manuscripts in the process of being completed.

In addition to abundance, the processing of documents becomes challenging as they form only part of the responsibilities of human

---

[83] Riles, Annelise: 'Anthropology, Human Rights, and Legal Knowledge: Culture in the Iron Cage.' In *108 American Anthropologist 1*, 2006, 52–65; Riles, Annelise: '[Deadlines]: Removing the Brackets on Politics in Bureaucratic and Anthropological Analysis.' In *Documents, supra* note 72, 71–92.

rights experts. In addition, experts participate for example in treaty body proceedings and meetings of different kinds, attend seminars, hold lectures, participate in different kinds of negotiations, travel; as has been mentioned, a prominent expert may travel for up to 120 days a year.[84] Combined, these tasks create circumstances in which time is of the essence. This imposes distinct conditions on the processing of documents. To evaluate human rights expert knowledge practices – to explore what kind of attention they can allow documents while 'staying on top of things' – an experiment is conducted with the State Report of Norway submitted to the Committee on Economic, Social and Cultural Rights on 6 July, 2004, and discussed on 3 May during the 34th Session of the Committee on 25 April to 13 May, 2005.[85] The purpose of this section is to illuminate general factors; a comprehensive analysis of knowledge practice would require more numerous experiments with different readers. Also, this section does not suggest that human rights experts treat all documents identically, making no alterations to their knowledge practices regarding the documents they are processing. Let us assume that a human rights expert has daily on average two hours at her disposal for work-related documents. Let us translate the estimated 40 centimetres of paper described by a SCANET visiting expert to 1000 pages. If all these documents are to be read in the allotted two hours, this translates to reading 8 pages a minute or one page in slightly over 10 seconds. What kind of reading can be given to the 85-page report by Norway in that time? What kind of characteristics emerge as compelling in the document, and what kind of personal qualities can be associated with a successful human rights expert on the basis of this experiment?[86]

---

[84] Many human rights experts consider travelling time well suited for processing documents, not separating these two responsibilities from each other.

[85] State Report of Norway, 2004, http://www.ohchr.org/english/bodies/cescr/cescrs34.htm (26.4.2006).

[86] Yet other treaty body members construe this quantity exaggerated, pointing out that this may instead refer to the amount of documents treaty body members receive during an entire session. Many thanks to Michael O'Flaherty for discussion on this point. Instead of exact quantities, the figure attempts to illustrate a general pattern of abundance. In their processing of documents, treaty body members naturally draw distinctions between different types of documents. They also receive State Reports six months prior to the session, allowing for processing time prior to it. Thus the attempt here is again to illustrate knowledge practices through an experiment instead of providing an accurate representation of their processing.

The State Report of Norway

To gain an appreciation of the nature of the document at hand, brief description of the composition and the aesthetic of a State Report is useful. Its front page contains the distinctive markers of the UN as well as the name of the respective agency in bold as well as also, the number, date and language of the document. The middle section of the page is reserved for the name of the document in the following form:

IMPLEMENTATION OF THE INTERNATIONAL COVENANT ON ECONOMIC, SOCIAL AND CULTURAL RIGHTS

Fourth periodic reports [sic] **submitted by States parties under articles 16 and 17 of the Covenant**

Addendum

This is followed by the name of the State Party, as well as the document date. The first page is completed with various footnotes holding additional information such as the following: "The third periodic report concerning rights covered by articles 6 to 9 (E/1994/104/Add.3) was processed by the Committee on Economic, Social and Cultural rights in 1995 (E/C.12/1995/SR.34 and 36–37; E/C.12/1995/13)".[87] The actual text is divided into two parts: A and B. In addition, the text is divided into paragraphs which connect the document in its aesthetics to legal texts. Page two holds a table of contents divided into "Articles", and in addition to offering page numbers, it enlists paragraph numbers. Page three commences the actual text, which is frequently interrupted by paragraph numbers and subheadings. Combined, these make the text light and easy to access. The text itself is broken into tidbits of a maximum of ten lines. Relevant treaty articles are highlighted by bold and placed at the centre. In addition, the document contains numerous lists outlining the initiatives taken to meet the treaty's requirements. In these contexts language is short and understandable, 'commonsensical'. For example:

[87] State Report of Norway, *supra* note 85.

> 201. Based on food consumption trends, the Norwegian authorities seek to promote:
>
> - breastfeeding of infants
> - increased consumption of vegetables, fruit, berries and potatoes
> - increased consumption of fish… (page 33)

These statements create a strong contrast to the expert jargon commonly associated with legal documents, making the document easily accessible to vast audiences. The document also contains percentages, such as the following from page 55:

> 33. As of December 2002, the following percentages of two-year-olds (born in 2000) had been immunised against:
>
> Pertussis: 92%
> Diphtheria: 93%
> Tetanus: 93% …

The document concludes with a list of appendices, in this instance featuring 34 additional documents ranging from handbooks such as the 2001 "Handbook in Human Rights Assessment", and various tables such as the 2002 "Table, Regional differences in employment", to different reports, judgements and brochures, such as the "Brochure, Mental Health Services in Norway" (page 84–85).

This experiment highlights speed: in order to accomplish the task in the allotted time, the material needs to be processed rapidly, with emphasis placed on a general impression. Scarcity of time limits the reader's possibilities to weigh the reliability of data presented in the state report itself or in the documents listed as its sources. This also applies to data presented in statistical form. Simultaneously this segment demonstrates the need for more specialized knowledge, as in order to be meaningful, it is necessary to know, for example, what the diseases enlisted above are. Yet these findings assign primacy in the overall assessment on the document's outlook. To evaluate the quality of the data contained in the report, what emerges as integral is how well or poorly the document corresponds with the familiar aesthetic of such documents. In addition, what becomes compelling is how the report utilizes the expert human rights discourse; whether it articulates its message through the appropriate terminology, acronyms and reference to relevant documents. In verifying the document's reliability, scarcity of time prevents in-depth analysis, placing emphasis instead on the previous knowledge held by the domain delivering it. These elements give rise to knowledge practices emphasizing the rapid formation of general impressions. This was also summarized by a visiting SCANET expert, a treaty body member, who described her processing of documents by stating: "*I go through text very quickly – I just glance through it and am able to form a general impression on it. In fact, I can read any book in a day*". Such a reading allows the processing of material primarily from the perspective of existing frameworks of knowledge. Its primary focus becomes invested on the extent to which material concurs with or differs from the existing framework of human rights knowledge, as scarcity of time and abundance of material do not permit the kind of focus that imposes radical challenges to underlying ontological assumptions.

SCANET Student Knowledge Practices

When beginning the inspection of how the SCANET learning curriculum socializes students into the above described processing of documents, the first observation is that activity programs are tremendously long. The following sample of one SCANET activity program illustrates this:

DAY 0: WEEKEND 4pm leave house, 6pm flight, 8pm arrive, 9pm arrive at hotel
DAY 1: 8am breakfast, 9–12am opening, lectures, 12–1 pm lunch, 1–6 pm presentations, 7–10 pm dinner
DAY 2: 9–12am lectures, 12–1pm lunch, 1–6pm presentations, 7–10pm dinner
DAY 3: 9–12am lectures, 12–1 pm lunch, 1–6pm presentations, 7–10pm dinner
DAY 4: RECREATION – 9–12am working groups, 12–11pm lunch, 1–5pm workshop of expert presentations, 6–10pm sauna & dinner
DAY 5: 9–12am lectures, 12–1pm lunch, 1–6pm presentations, 7–10pm dinner
DAY 6: WEEKEND 9–12 lectures, 12–1pm lunch, 1–4pm presentations, 4pm closing
DAY +: WEEKEND leave hotel at 8am, flight 9.30am, arrive 11.30am, home 1pm

This demonstrates that SCANET activities likewise make great demands on the time of students, allowing few possibilities for competing engagements for their duration. This conveys an accurate representation of the temporal requirements ensuing from expert positions, characterized by long days and numerous responsibilities. SCANET activities socialize students also to the abundance of documents faced by human rights experts. As was mentioned, for each activity students are required to process two types of documents: student papers and background reading for expert lectures. In the examined SCANET activity, the number of student papers was 29,[88] and their length ranged between 6 to 44 pages, with an average of 16 pages. This brings the total number of pages to 455. Background papers were provided by six lecturers, who each assigned on average three articles of 30 pages, bringing the total to 540 pages. Combined, this results in 1000 pages of text for one SCANET activity.[89] As students likewise have numerous competing assignments in their home universities related to their ongoing PhD work, they will likewise have to learn to process these documents with efficiency. This suggests that SCANET activities are successful in socializing students into expert knowledge practices where documents need to be processed with great speed, focussing attention particularly on the general impression created by the document as well as how it utilizes the expert discourse of human rights.

Utilizing Research Resources

SCANET activities introduce another significant knowledge practice of experts which did not become transparent to students, namely the capacity to utilize research resources during SCANET activities. This practice is exemplified by instances where a discussion embodied controversy or questions on how certain issues, such as the rights of indigenous peoples, were addressed in existing human rights instruments. In general SCANET experts portray an impressive command of the content of existing instruments. Yet as documents continually proliferate, no individual can know all of them by heart. Instead in certain instances SCANET experts will reproduce a text through their laptop, allowing them to make authoritative contributions to ongoing discussions. This exemplifies another key element of human rights expert knowledge practices: the ability to derive relevant information with speed and efficiency. In SCANET activities this practice occurred through a medium that was not available to SCANET students. As a

[88] The total number of student participants in the course was 32, with 3 failing to submit papers.

[89] These 1000 pages were expected to be printed by participating students, as hard copies were available only in exceptions. Going back to the discussion of Chapter 3 on SCANET as part of a global elite: this mundane feature offers another example of this, as such significant quantities of printing would not be available for example to the NGO workers I worked with in India in autumn 2000.

general rule, SCANET activities do not overtly recommend students to utilize their laptops during activities. It is also not commonly advertized that activity venues offer ready access to the internet. Consequently SCANET activities contained no instances where students were explicitly encouraged to experiment with this aspect of expert knowledge practices, for example through sessions where students would receive direct training on how to derive documents from relevant sources. This element of expert practices was not reproduced in SCANET activities but instead left implicit. Ability to utilize research resources became a factor emphasizing the distinction between the categories of expert and student, and from this perspective left elements of the community of practice of human rights experts opaque.

Gaining Access to Implicit Expert Knowledge

This section concludes by exploring the implicit knowledge embedded in human rights expert practices, asking whether SCANET activities render it available to participating students. Implicit knowledge can be described as the "space between" official and unofficial knowledge.[90] It resonates with what Sarat and Felstiner call "private knowledge" – intimate knowledge of the subtle details of the functioning of the legal process not available even to well-educated and well-read clients.[91] The notion of implicit knowledge also applies to the transnational space of human rights activism, which Sally Engle Merry has described as having its own values and culture.[92] This section explores one element of this culture, examining how text functions as an ambiguous source of knowledge through description on the proceedings accompanying the submission of the state report of China. Numerous scholars have demonstrated the vigour that goes into the making of international treaties and other international human rights documents. However, research has simultaneously suggested that after documents are produced, their wording often ceases to be the target of scrutiny as significance is invested, in addition to what the documents actually say, to the fact that they exist and that they are processed. Annelise Riles has explored this element through circulation of documents among Fijian NGO workers through the analogy of circulation of ritual mats.[93] This section

[90] Riles: The Network Inside Out, *supra* note 79, 22.
[91] Sarat & Felstiner: Divorce Lawyers and Their Clients, *supra* note 71, 101–102.
[92] Merry: Human Rights & Gender Violence, *supra* note 72.
[93] Riles: The Network Inside Out, *supra* note 79.

focusses on the low knowledge status assigned to text in the submission of China's state report, and inspects ceremonial aspects of treaty body proceedings. Finally, it asks how SCANET activities render these elements transparent to students.

It was lunchtime for the treaty body members who were convened in Geneva for the 34th session of the Committee on Economic, Social and Cultural Rights in April 2005. The day was an exciting one, as it was the first time China was submitting its state report; the electricity generated by the event was palpable both in the cafeteria as well as the remainder of the vast conference building. By lunchtime China's presentation had progressed to day two and was nearing its end. After lunch, the floor would be open for questions, and the event was naturally the main topic of discussion for the four treaty body members present. During lunch various comments were made on the attitude of the Chinese delegation toward the proceedings. Treaty body members noted with delight how pleasant the head of the delegation had been; the fact that he had opened his presentation with a joke about "communist explanations" was recounted on three occasions. However, this appreciation for his playfulness did not translate to a lack of criticism as it was observed that *"the leader's voice changes when he shifts from English to Chinese"*. This comment indicated that he was perhaps not as benevolent in his own tongue as his pleasant demeanor in English suggested. Various comments were also made on the Chinese delegation as a whole, with one treaty body member asking why China had brought such a large delegation to the meeting: *"it was, after all, a developing country."* The tone of this comment – made by a treaty body member originally from Serbia – made it obvious that such a large size was seen as inappropriate, as it presented a sign of carelessness on the part of the Chinese government. Being a developing country with limited financial resources, instead of spending money on such a large delegation, the comment insinuated that the money would have been more wisely spent on addressing the various developmental difficulties the state was facing. The comment appeared to entail, in addition, a second level, namely disapproval toward the flamboyance with which China had made its entry into treaty body proceedings. Instead of portraying itself as a developing nation coming in front of the treaty body with a humble and earnest attitude, the inappropriately large delegation was interpreted as a sign of arrogance from a malignant communist state still aspiring to portray the image of a superpower.

The Chinese delegation was indeed large, occupying four centre tables in the large conference room. In total it included, in addition to members directly related to the report's presentation, a member who appeared to be documenting the proceedings by vigorous writing, as well as a few women who were present primarily as companions. The proceedings incited excitement in Chinese participants, demonstrated by the numerous photographs taken by junior delegation members in them. During lunch, treaty body members observed that *"there are two kinds of Chinese* [in the delegation]: *those who are under 40 are Western and modern, those over 40 or 50 are traditional and hierarchical"*. The comment's tone indicated approval toward the younger generation and welcomed this change. With all these participants the delegation had an impressive presence, conveying the scorned image that this was a superpower – after all, one of the five permanent members of the Security Council – not a random developing state. This sentiment was evidenced during the question period which commenced after lunch. Although questions opened with customary diplomatic politesses on how nice it was that China was participating in these proceedings, after the introductions their tone altered; questions became direct and intrusive. The first treaty body members raised the issue of abortions – *"are there forceful abortions and how do Chinese officials treat them?"* The second question likewise addressed abortion, expanding it to pregnancy more generally, as well as to the issue of homelessness. The third question focussed again on abortion. Then a question addressed domestic violence and the position of women in Chinese society. Questions on illiteracy and access to education ensued, as well as inquiries into the freedom of press and teaching religion at schools.

Combined, these questions give rise to two observations. First, their tone was sharp, almost confrontational – far beyond the standard level of diplomatic parlance embedded in mutual politeness, introducing a greatly adversarial aspect into the proceedings. This experience differs greatly from that of Sally Engle Merry, who describes how, although some questions were pointed, the tone of treaty body expert comments and questions was unfailingly courteous, and criticism was rarely explicit. The experts Merry talked with emphasized that their goal was to be constructive as well as to offer criticism. However, also in her experience a difference existed between the public and private realm, as in private discussions experts commented on their frustration on a certain country's report. These views were, nevertheless, not raised in the public hearings.[94] Second, all asked questions related to matters

[94] Merry: Human Rights & Gender Violence, *supra* note 72, 85.

already covered in the State Report. Thus it was difficult to comprehend why they were asked, as they had already been addressed by China in the report. Presenting questions – in an adversarial tone – on topics for which answers were already provided for indicated disapproval and disbelief toward the accuracy of the data included in the document, and the questions indicated that the material of the State Report could be not treated as knowledge. The low knowledge status assigned to the material included in the State Report was illuminated by treaty body members who, during lunch discussion, commented that they "*do not wish to speak to the leaders* [of the Chinese delegation], *but to those who do not speak English.*"[95] It was construed evident that knowledge was not to be obtained from the representatives of State, but rather from the common people. As the state report had inevitably been constructed by the State, it was given low status as a source of knowledge. This conclusion was supported by the statement of another treaty body member, who noted that he is not really waiting for the State report drafted by the Chinese authorities but rather for the shadow-reports filed by various NGOs, who were considered to have access to what "*really happens*".

The questions posed to China were primarily answered by the same delegation head who had delighted the audience with his opening joke. His responses confirmed that, indeed, he was no mere showman but instead a highly skilled diplomat and politician. His demeanour was not in the slightest shaken or offended by the adversarial tone of questions. Instead he replied to them as if the treaty body members had never seen the State Report, often reading text directly from the Report itself. His responses alternated between Chinese and English, which had not been the case during his earlier presentation, held consistently in English. The shifting of languages created the image that it stemmed not from limitations in language skills, but from something else – namely from efforts to distance answers from original questions, making replies only available through the words of interpreters.[96] The tone of his responses was energetic, even aggressive. Through the words of

[95] During lunch no indication was made that the present treaty body members had competence in Chinese; the biographies of treaty body members suggests the same. Subsequently such discussions would have required interpreters.

[96] As is customary in UN meetings, the proceedings were being simultaneously translated into five languages: English, French, German, Spanish and Chinese, and most participants listened to presentations via headphones in the words of the translators.

the English translator he declared: "*We do not allow people to live on the streets. There is no homelessness in China.*" He then went to complement his response, referring to a Housing Act by reading the precise text of the Act from the State Report in front of him. To return the discussion to the status of knowledge and the ways in which knowledge is produced in the human rights field – to the 'spaces between' officially 'existent' and 'nonexistent' sources – the status given to the above document and exchange requires closer attention. Officially documents such as state reports are valued as primary sources of knowledge in the proceedings of numerous human rights bodies. Yet, 'unofficially', their pivotal element becomes the way the vocal exchange accompanying the submission of state reports creates a ceremony of *dialogue* between different parties. The rhetoric of *dialogue* is pervasive in the human rights discourse and is commonly used to explain benefits of a particular instrument among others. As an example, the website for the Delegation of the European Commission states on its relations to China: "Constructive dialogue remains the Union's preferred channel for working to improve the human rights situation in China".[97] 2001 was also named the UN Year of Dialogue Among Civilizations 2001.[98]

The ceremonial nature of vocal exchanges is demonstrated by the answers, which often relied on the precise wording of the document for the elaboration of which the question was asked in the first place. In this context the Chinese representative answered questions on the State Report with the exact wording included in the document, providing no additional knowledge. The low knowledge status of the answers appears previously known to those asking questions, rendering the motivation for these questions to stem not from the desire to gain knowledge but from aspirations to engage in dialogue. Thus in this instance the treaty body proceedings acquired strong ceremonial characteristics, as little new knowledge was exchanged in them. Instead most of what was brought up in the discussion was already known to the participants before hand. The ceremonial nature of dialogue appeared further to be known to both the Chinese delegation as well as treaty body members. The Chinese delegation head answered

---

[97] Human Rights Dialogue, http://www.eu-in-china.com/euch_poli3.htm (15.6.2006).

[98] UN: Year of Dialogue Among Civilizations, 2001, http://www.un.org/Dialogue/ (15.6.2006). No empirical studies have been available on the rhetoric of 'dialogue', yet the practices surrounding the term's invocation suggest strong emphasis on the ceremonial elements of collaboration.

questions with a readiness that suggested great awareness of the charges the delegation would face in the question period, thus encouraging them to prepare answers beforehand. Lunch discussions among treaty body members suggested that they were also well aware of the answers to be provided by the Chinese delegation, and thus expected no new information to emerge. During the proceedings, the ceremonial nature emerged as both known and accepted to at least some participants, highlighted by the practice of individual treaty body members to leave the conference room before their questions were answered. These elements render the described treaty body proceeding as ill-suited to be described as "a cyclical process of the repetitive exchange of information between the parties", "resulting in the adjustment of expectations and preferences".[99] Instead it emerges as a ceremonial event in which, instead of the transformation of new knowledge, what emerged as primary was the engagement of different parties in a joint dialogue. This outcome imposes a supplementary requirement on successful members of the community of practice of human rights experts: in addition to keen interest and engagement in the substantive elements of human rights, they need to have tremendous bureaucratic stamina, translating into patience and endurance in the face of abundant committee meetings and proceedings among others, following commonly established procedures. Only these qualities allow the kind of participation and space that eventually translates into 'dialogue'.

As the afternoon wore on, the session's ceremonial characteristics gained even more emphasis. After the momentary vigour of lunch accompanied by stimulating social exchanges, a general sense of inertia started to overwhelm the atmosphere. This was visible from the faces of delegate and treaty body members as well as observers dispersed around the sides and back of the conference room: people started to fall deeper into their seats and many rested their eyes due to the exhaustion of the long day. Numerous individuals had focussed their attention on their laptops and were checking e-mails accumulated during the day's proceedings. Participant numbers in the conference room started to decrease as people sneaked out of the room to convene in the panoramic cafeteria of the lobby. In front of the view of lush green parks, mountains (would Mont Blanc be visible today?) and the city of Geneva bathing in a gorgeous sunset, greetings were given to long-lost acquaintances, and little groups engaged in lively chat

[99] Haavisto: Court Work in Transition, *supra* note 31, 301; see also Roberts & Palmer: Dispute Processes, *supra* note 48, 70.

started to form around the tables spread apart. Soon drinks would be ordered, and the mood would be set for dinner.

Implicit Knowledge in SCANET activities

This analysis concludes by exploring how SCANET activities socialize students into such implicit knowledge of the community of practice of human rights experts: the low knowledge status of some documents as well as the importance of ceremonial aspects of formal activities. As was noted, SCANET activities introduce significant quantities of text to its participants, encouraging them to adopt the fast processing of documents already discussed. Processing of student papers by assigned faculty commentators also entails elements that could be construed to have assigned them low knowledge status. Although many commentators invested great energy into reading and commenting on papers, for others this was not the case. Some experts commented that they had not received the papers beforehand, but were instead offered them as they arrived to the SCANET activity. Others had, probably due to numerous competing engagements, not read them yet prior to the activity, noting instead, for example at dinnertime, that they still needed to read the papers they were to comment on the following day. During presentations similar differences were visible. Whereas many commentators forwarded comments explicitly on the basis of the specific student papers, referring to distinct passages of text, others maintained their comments on a more general level, commenting on broad themes instead of the specific content of distinct papers. The latter practice gave rise to the conception that the source of comments was not formed primarily by the student paper, but rather by general developments in the human rights field raised by the presentation. This finding can be connected to the ambiguous status of documents in treaty body proceedings, where, instead of being sources of knowledge, their primary function becomes their existence. Another element that can be construed to socialize SCANET students into this implicit knowledge practice relates to the abundance of documents handed out during activities: as was noted by numerous participants during activities, their quantity was construed as too great, and therefore it become impossible to digest them all.

To explore whether SCANET activities socialize their students into the bureaucratic stamina of successful experts, the ceremonial elements of SCANET activities will be considered. This analysis is facilitated by the primary observation of activities, namely their high quantity. As was demonstrated by the excerpt from SCANET activity program, days are significantly long and fully-packed. This renders it greatly challenging for participants to remain active and alert for their entire duration. This assigns SCANET activities similar elements as those described at the treaty body proceedings: particularly as the program wore on, people would lose concentration, fall deeper into their seats, send and read text messages by cell phone; some experts would glance at e-mails from laptops. Yet notably few participants were absent from activities. Experts, including those not holding lectures at the time, participated in the sessions with high frequency, and with a few exceptions, also student participation remained exceedingly high throughout activities. Particularly during lectures many students appeared to engage in active note taking and listen attentively to the experts. To characterize these events as primarily ceremonial appears misguided, as they were instead often instances where students actively sought information from lecturing experts. Instead such a characterization finds more resonance with student presentations. Touching upon issues that were frequently remote from the interests of other students, and followed by a division of time that offered practically no possibilities for audience contributions in many instances assigned student presentations qualities of ceremony. Instead of being instances of mutual learning, occasionally the primary element of presentations became the fact that they were held. To connect these findings to the observations of treaty body proceedings, these instances become moments when SCANET students are socialized into the bureaucratic stamina of successful human rights experts.

Characteristics of Peripheral Participation in SCANET

The previous chapter has analysed SCANET activities from perspectives that have produced at times a formalistic and critical description of observed practices, particularly of the identified learning curriculum. In discussions during activities many students portrayed genuine enthusiasm toward SCANET activities, stating how much they appreciated the opportunity to follow lectures by its well-established and knowledgeable experts. Many students participated in more than one SCANET activity, and since participation was voluntary, had they not been satisfied with earlier experiences, no requirements existed for them to return. High student satisfaction was also visible in the feedback forms requested after each event which, according to the

SCANET coordinator, contained predominantly positive evaluations. However, SCANET activities also included students who expressed dissatisfaction with its learning curriculum. Common sources of complaint were the scarcity of time for individual presentations, the absence of in-depth discussions on them, and the limited possibilities for audience participation. Many of those expressing complaints were advanced doctorate candidates holding, for example, teaching experience from their host institutions. Their criticism can be perceived as being directed primarily against the described SCANET structural conception of expertise, and thus to resonate with the present analysis. Importantly, no comments were encountered that formulated the SCANET learning curriculum as particularly ill-suited for a context teaching human rights due to its disempowering characteristics. Instead critical student views often reflect allegiance to different 'schools' of human rights thought. These 'schools' have been described both in the previous chapter as well as in the Introduction through Graph 1, outlining their differences in the ontological assumptions invested in human rights. Different ontological assumptions hold direct relevance for conceptions of learning. If human rights are approached as entailing a predefined, absolute and universal essence, a natural learning process becomes to adopt knowledge about this essence from experts. If such an essence is questioned and human rights are construed as the product of social processes and politics, a conception of learning as adopting ready knowledge becomes irrelevant. As was mentioned, differences in ontological assumptions have also impacted the present venture, contributing to its critical exploration of the observed learning curriculum.

The observations of the ceremonial nature of events are, of course, not restricted to SCANET activities or treaty body proceedings but instead can be held to reflect, to some extent, most organized events. For this study these findings gain relevance from the question of how SCANET activities socialize their legitimate peripheral participants into the community of practice of human rights experts. This analysis has demonstrated that, whereas numerous of its practices do become accessible to students, the community also entails elements for which insight is not acquired through such formal educational contexts as SCANET activities. This resonates with the division of 'abstract' and 'concrete' knowledge discussed by Lave and Wenger:[100] while SCANET

[100] Lave & Wenger: Situated Learning, *supra* note 24, 104.

activities offer its legitimate peripheral participants 'abstract' knowledge on human rights, its students remain without access to such 'concrete' knowledge as that embedded in the practices of, for example, UN treaty bodies. William Hanks discusses how a training program that consists of instructional settings separated from actual performance "would tend to split the learner's ability to manage the learning situation apart from his ability to perform the skill". Such circumstances raise the possibility of training actors who "become experts as a learner – that is, who become masters at managing the learning situation – but who never actually learn the performance skills themselves".[101] SCANET activities hold elements of this characterization. Again this finding is not restricted to SCANET, as Lave and Wenger discuss how learning how to 'do' school appropriately may be a major part of what school teaches. Thus, while SCANET students learn through their participation to meet the requirements set forth by faculty in terms of presentation – for example, they learn bureaucratic stamina, but not how this is relevant in such UN contexts as treaty body proceedings – this element assigns their legitimate peripheral participatory status 'irrelevance' to the ongoing activities.

To explore whether SCANET functions as a successful venue for reproducing the community of Nordic human rights experts, two features can be identified. On the one hand SCANET conveys its students necessary information on expert positions which can later transform into experimentation with them, and possibly also full membership in the community of practice. However, this process appears impossible solely through participation in SCANET activities without any further socialization into the community for example through apprenticeships as SCANET activities leave elements of the community of experts opaque. This is illustrated by the capacity in which the *centre* of the human rights phenomenon becomes construed in SCANET activities: instead of being a domain of which extensive knowledge is offered or to which students are introduced through concrete practices, it comes to function as a referential other utilized to increase expert status. This is observable particularly regarding association with different UN domains, which are commonly mentioned in SCANET activities both by the experts themselves as well as others during activities. Experts

[101] Hanks, William F.: Foreword. In *Situated Learning, supra* note 24, 21. Original quote in the singular; transformed into the plural by author.

may highlight their associations in discussions in SCANET activities, particularly in instances of disagreement or confusion. Thus an expert may emphasize her association to a UN treaty body by noting of a document drafted by it: "*I am the author of General Comment 4 which states..*" Other experts may seek for authoritative interpretation on the content of treaty articles from experts who hold membership in treaty bodies. Association to the centre was also brought up in an instance in which uncertainty prevailed over the precise arrival time of a visiting expert. When the expert finally arrived, she explained her tardiness by stating: "*I just arrived from Geneva, where I was attending a meeting for a UN working group on the draft convention on indigenous rights*". Exchanges among students likewise suggest that association with the centre increases the authority invested in experts. This sentiment was reflected in the statement of a student who, before a lecture held by a treaty body member, characterized her as a "*very important person*". Constitutive for the present analysis is that these references emphasize association with the centre while simultaneously leaving its content and practices unclear. The "black box" of expertise is not transformed into a "glass box".[102] These findings assign SCANET activities an additional characteristic: instead of functioning solely as a domain for reproducing the community of practice of Nordic human rights expert, they become a context in which expert positions are created for the present generation of SCANET faculty members.

The final element to be considered relates to the question whether SCANET activities can be seen to empower its legitimate peripheral participants so that they, following the analysis of Meintjes, challenge existing oppressive structures.[103] Lave and Wenger approach this issue from the quality of legitimate peripheral participation, noting how "[a]s a place in which one moves toward more-intensive participation, peripherality is an empowering position. As a place in which one is kept from participating more fully [...] it is a disempowering position".[104] From this perspective the predetermined patterns of flow as well as elements emphasizing the expert status of present faculty members assign the status of students in SCANET elements of a disempowering position. Exploration of interactive patterns demon-

102 Lave & Wenger: Situated Learning, *supra* note 24, 101–102.
103 Meintjes: 'Human Rights Education as Empowerment,' *supra* note 21, 66–67.
104 Lave & Wenger: Situated Learning, *supra* note 24, 36.

strated that, instead of encouraging individuals assigned student status to experiment and gain more experience in the role of experts, the separation of the two categories delimits student participation in SCANET activities sometimes to a level below their actual substantive competence. Instead of socializing its legitimate peripheral participants into consciousness of their own empowering potential to challenge existing structures, SCANET activities entail elements which socialize its students into a clear and predetermined hierarchy where expertise is located in only some individuals. Chapter 6 connects this finding to existing societal structures in the global and Nordic level, exploring what kind of consequences this socializing process induces for the emancipatory potential of human rights education.

CHAPTER FIVE

FROM TRANSLATION TO ADVOCATION THROUGH LAW

As the previous chapter sought to understand the SCANET teaching curriculum, it identified previous legal educational experiences of SCANET experts as one possible source of influence. This chapter continues to explore the relationship of human rights and law by examining both general developments as well as detailed instances of SCANET activities. The discussion commences with an overview of how this relationship was embodied in the drafting of the UDHR, and moves to describe general processes through which human rights are legalized particularly in the UN context. This analysis is followed by an introduction into the controversy that the process of legalization awakens in different 'schools' of human rights thought. The chapter then explores how legal emphasis is visible in the community of practice of human rights experts, and compares the observed SCANET expert profile to that identifiable in central UN human rights treaty bodies. This analysis is again connected to the drafting of the UDHR with an aim to understand how expert profiles have changed over the past decades.

The latter part of the chapter explores some practical consequences that legal emphasis has in SCANET educational activities. It examines how SCANET experts contribute to the process of legalization as they teach human rights, and explores how the experts aid in the general expansion of the human rights discourse through arguments of legitimacy. This analysis revisits and elaborates the discussion commenced in Chapter 2 on the systemic agency of human rights experts. It investigates how in SCANET activities experts enlarge their role from intermediaries, who merely translate the abstract human rights discourse, to passionately engaged activists through their *creative space*. This concept refers to the sources of knowledge and the ontological assumptions of a dignified human existence that SCANET experts rely on as they argue that new concerns need to be included into the body of human rights knowledge.

Human Rights and Law

The relationship of human rights and law is a significant, yet an often overlooked feature of the contemporary human rights phenomenon. To begin, a few words is needed on what the law is understood to mean for the present analysis. The concept of law has received extensive attention from socio-legal scholars who have demonstrated how, as an empirical phenomenon, it is multi-dimensional and entails extensive cultural elements as well as those of voluntary compliance.[1] Discussions on the topic have long roots in legal anthropology, and they include numerous efforts to offer a comprehensive definition of universal "law-stuff" that could be applicable cross-culturally.[2] These attempts have been accompanied with ample correspondents from legal philosophers, with some of the most influential accounts emanating from H.L.A. Hart and Hans Kelsen.[3]

Yet these debates remain without finalized answers, and instead of pursuing them further, this analysis focuses on the conception of law that has been interpreted as characteristic of SCANET experts; a conception that is also present in much influential human rights scholarship. This conception views law through a formalistic lense as being defined by rules, legal documents, processes, institutions, implementation, enforcement and sanctions. Simultaneously – and slightly contradictorily – it includes an extensive interpretation of customary law, *jus cogens* and *obligatio erga omnes*. It further includes extensive reliance on 'soft law' documents as well as arguments of legitimacy. Law is construed as being clearly delineated from politics, as being 'good' whereas politics is 'bad'. Global improvement of the human condition is seen to require the submission of politics to international human rights law

[1] See for example Merry, Sally Engle: Getting Justice and Getting Even: Legal Consciousness Among Working-Class Americans. The University of Chicago Press, Chicago, 1990; Greenhouse, Carol J.; Yngvesson, Barbara & Engel, David M.: Law and Community in Three American Towns. Cornell University Press, Ithaca, 1994; Valverde, Mariana: Law's Dream of a Common Knowledge. Princeton University Press, Princeton, 2003.

[2] Llewellyn, Karl N. & Hoebel, Adamson E.: The Cheyenne Way: Conflict and Case Law in Primitive Jurisprudence. University of Oklahoma Press, Oklahoma, 1941, 20–27; Halme, Miia: 'The Network Inside Out in Perspective: A Review of the Development of Legal Anthropology.' In *Finnish Yearbook of International Law* (Ed. Petman, Jarna). Kluwer Law International, The Hague, 2002, 417–430.

[3] Hart, H. L. A.: The Concept of Law. Second edition. Clarendon Press, Oxford, 1994 [1961]; Kelsen, Hans: Introduction to the Problems of Legal Theory (Translation of *Reine Rechtsteorie*). Clarendon Press, Oxford, 1994 [1934].

which thus evolves, through the 'domestic analogy', to resemble national legal systems. At present the greatest Achilles heel of the current framework of international human rights law is seen as being formed by its lack of enforcement, a condition to be corrected through international criminal and human rights courts. Once so completed, international human rights law is seen as capable of properly ending the 'rule of might' that today dictates international collaboration. Also connected to this conception of the law is a view that the role of nation states and their sovereignty vis-à-vis international human rights law is diminishing.[4]

Law in the Drafting of the UDHR

When drafting for the UDHR began in 1946, it soon became evident that the achievement of a legally binding instrument was politically untenable. Scholarship describes how this 'lowered' ambitions as efforts were instead directed toward the adoption of a legally non-binding Declaration.[5] During drafting efforts discussions also emerged on whether law was the most suitable tool for regulating matters seen to hold human rights substance. Thus for example in the Drafting Committee's first session on 1 July 1947, the UK representative Lord Dukeston commented:

> It is through the international cooperating so established that the United Nations can most effectively assist the realization of the right of all persons to work, to educate, to social security and similar social and economic rights, which *cannot by their nature* be defined in the form of legal obligations for states in an instrument such as the International Bill of Rights.[6]

[4] For examples of these features, see Cassese, Antonio: International Law. Second Edition. Oxford University Press, Oxford, 2005; Meron, Theodor: The Humanization of International Law. Brill Academic Publishers, Leiden, 2006; Ferencz, Benjamin: An International Criminal Court: A Step Towards World Peace – A Documentary History and Analysis. Volume 1. Oceana Publications Inc., New York, 1980; Bassiouni, M. Cherif & Blakesley, Christopher L.: 'The Need for an International Criminal Court in the New International World Order.' In 25 *Vanderbilt Journal of Transnational Law*, 1992, 151–182; Scheinin, Martin: Toward a World Court of Human Rights, 2.11.2005, discussion forum for the Office of the High Commissioner for Human Rights, http://portal.ohchr.org/tbforum/mvnforum/viewthread?thread=981 (28.4.2006). For an analysis of debates surrounding the establishing of the International Criminal Court, see Halme, Miia: The Hidden 'Theory' of M. Cherif Bassiouni. LL.M Thesis, University of Helsinki, 2003.

[5] For discussion, see for example Glendon, Mary Ann: A World Made New: Eleanor Roosevelt and the Universal Declaration of Human Rights. Random House, New York, 2001.

[6] United Nations Economic and Social Council: Drafting Committee on an International Bill of Rights. First Session. Report of the Drafting Committee to the

Although the legal framework around human rights has since been well established, such claims have never entirely disappeared. A different yet equally compelling challenge for the relationship of human rights and law relates to the origins of human rights, to notions that in the *essential* significance human rights precede law. This view surfaces in instances where legal regulation is argued as having *not yet* progressed to a level where all human rights have been codified in legally binding instruments.

Such approaches are exemplified by narratives on the evolution of the human rights phenomenon: although a gap of three decades existed between the legally non-binding declaration and the legally binding treaties – the most important being ICCPR and ICESCR – during which many central issues recognized today as human rights were without legal articulation, no scholars argue that the rights included in the UDHR were not proper human rights during this period. Contrarily, for example Paul Lauren discusses human rights as existing also *prior* to the UDHR.[7] These notions assign human rights the dual character of rights claims discussed by Duncan Kennedy: they exist both "inside and outside the law"; they are "either rules or reasons for rules".[8] Kennedy illustrates this quality with the American Constitution. It outlines highly abstract principles such as 'freedom of speech' which is invoked to support practices not exclusively listed in any particular legal provisions. Yet, cases exist where Courts have wanted to protect 'outside' rights not explicitly articulated by the Constitution.[9] This duality leads to circumstances where rights 'straddle'; they are "legal rights embedded and formed by legal argumentative practice (legal rules)" as well as entities existing "prior to and outside such legal instruments as Constitutions, subsequently becoming assertions about how an outside right should be translated into law".[10]

Commission on Human Rights. E/CN/21, 1 July 1947, 27; italics added. It should be noted that Lord Dukeston's performance was both highly criticized and short-lived; thus the weight assigned to this statement should be kept modest. See Glendon, *ibid.*, 44–45.

[7] Lauren, Paul Gordon: The Evolution of International Human Rights: Visions Seen. University of Pennsylvania Press, Philadelphia, 1998.

[8] Kennedy, Duncan: 'The Critique of Rights,' In *Left Legalism / Left Critique* (Eds. Brown, Wendy & Halley, Janet). Duke University Press, Durham & London. 2002, 185.

[9] *Ibid.*, 186.

[10] *Ibid.*, 187.

Legalizing Human Rights

To explore how legalization occurs in the UN framework, the following elements can be highlighted. First, an issue becomes the topic of informal discussions, which are commonly accompanied by scholarly contributions and the creation of study groups and expert meetings producing such documents as committee reports, concluding observations or special reports.[11] SCANET activities exemplified this stage with an expert meeting in Spring 2005 which explored the possibility to utilize indicators to monitor the compliance of human rights treaties.[12] The documents produced in this stage vary in form and their status in international law is undefined. Should the findings of a working group gain sufficient support, additional meetings may ensue, and they will lead to more documents such as guidelines for action. This was also the outcome of the SCANET indicators meeting, which concluded by producing an unofficial document suggesting plans for subsequent meetings. If received favourably, other non-legally binding documents enjoying higher visibility and prestige, such as General Assembly Resolutions, may follow. This step may further be accompanied by the establishing of a drafting committee for a Draft Declaration, a legally non-binding document that is discussed, among others, by the Human Rights Council and the General Assembly.

Ideally these stages lead to the adoption of an official Declaration: still a legally non-binding, yet a high-profile document. This step was recently observable regarding the Draft United Nations Declaration on the Rights of Indigenous Peoples of 1994.[13] Work for the declaration commenced already in the 1980s, and the issue has since been highlighted by two UN International Decades of the World's Indigenous People: the first from 1995 to 2004, the second from 2005 to 2014.[14]

[11] Such working groups represent a standard feature of UN operations, with for example the website for the High Commissioner for Human Rights listing a total of 9 groups in this category in spring 2007, see High Commissioner: Working Groups, 2006, http://www.unhchr.ch/html/menu2/2/chrwg.htm (27.4.2007). This list is likely not exhaustive, as no additions were made to it between spring 2006 and 2007.

[12] Sano, Hans-Otto & Lindholt, Lone: Human Rights Indicators: Country data and methodology. Danish Institute of Human Rights, Copenhagen, 2000.

[13] High Commissioner for Human Rights. Draft United Nations Declaration on the Rights of Indigenous Peoples of 1994, http://www.unhchr.ch/huridocda/huridoca.nsf/(Symbol)/E.CN.4.SUB.2.RES.1994.45.En (28.4.2007).

[14] UN Permanent Forum on Indigenous Issues: Second International Decade of the World's Indigenous Peoples, 2004, http://www.un.org/esa/socdev/unpfii/en/second.html (28.4.2007).

In June 2006 the Human Rights Council adopted the Draft Declaration by a great majority,[15] which gave rise to high hopes that the Declaration would be adopted at the General Assembly, the final required step for its approval. Here bitter disappointment ensued: led by the concerns of Australia, Canada, New Zealand and the US that the Declaration would interfere in their internal affairs, its adoption was postponed.[16] This outcome was described as "outrage and dismay", and as an instance missing a "historic opportunity to fill a critical gap in international human rights protection".[17] It was further seen to reflect "domestic political agendas" over the "promotion and protection of human rights",[18] a statement reflecting the above described separation of human rights law and politics. On September 13, 2007 the General Assembly finally adopted the Declaration with an overwhelming majority: 143 states voted for its adoption with only the US, Canada, Australia and New Zealand voting against it.

Although the adoption of the Declaration was celebrated as a historic moment for indigenous people, the stark opposition of the states voting against it leaves the creation of a legally binding Convention highly uncertain in the future. The UN human rights system offers, nevertheless, ample examples where this end-point has been reached. The most central of these is the process through which many of the rights articulated by the UDHR have found their legal articulation in the ICCPR and the ICESCR. A more recent example is offered by the adoption of the Convention on the Rights of Persons with Disabilities in 2006, which followed the 1975 Declaration on the Rights of Disabled Persons.[19] Some argue that the explicit goal of legalization is not the

---

[15] Human Rights Council: Elections, 2006, http://www.un.org/ga/60/elect/hrc/ (19.3.2007).

[16] United Nations Special Rapporteur, Press Release: Statement by UN Special Rapporteur on the Rights of Indigenous Peoples, on the General Assembly's decision not to adopt the Declaration on the Rights of Indigenous Peoples, http://www.iwgia.org/graphics/Synkron-Library/Documents/Noticeboard/News/International/SRpressreleaseDDDecember2006.htm (28.4.2007); HRO Statement: UN Declaration on the Rights of Indigenous Peoples: Human rights organizations condemn efforts to block vital human rights instrument, 2006, http://www.iwgia.org/graphics/Synkron-Library/Documents/Noticeboard/News/International/NGOStatementonDeclarationNov302006.htm (28.4.2007).

[17] HRO Statement, *ibid.*

[18] *Ibid.*

[19] High Commissioner for Human Rights: Declaration on the Rights of Disabled Persons, GA Resolution 3447, 9 December 1975, http://www.unhchr.ch/html/menu3/b/72.htm (27.8.2006); United Nations Convention on the Rights of Persons with

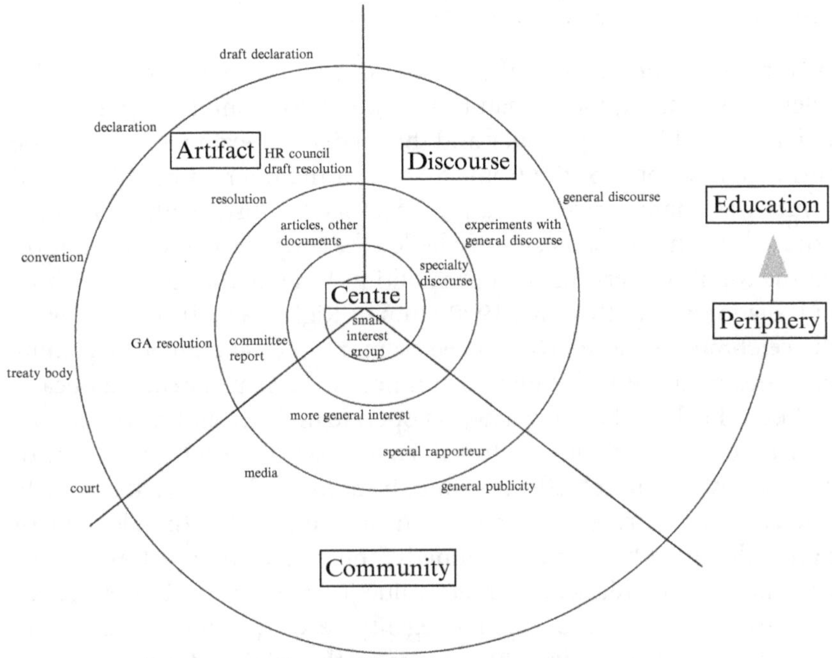

Graph 12: *The Process of Legalization*

adoption of new documents, but instead securing the rights in question the status of customary international law. Many also emphasize the importance of implementation mechanisms to "end the culture of impunity"[20] by establishing an international human rights court. This proposal was forwarded already during the drafting of the UDHR, when it nevertheless failed to receive decisive support.[21] The establishment of the International Criminal Court in 2002 was received as a significant step, yet initiatives for an international court of human rights are still ongoing.[22] The process of legalization is illustrated by Graph 12, which outlines how key events are located in terms of time.

Disabilities, 2006, http://www.un.org/disabilities/convention/conventionfull.shtml (6.11.2009).

[20] Akhavan, Payam: 'Beyond Impunity: Can International Criminal Justice Prevent Future Atrocities.' In *95 American Journal of International Law 1*, 2001, 7–31.

[21] Drafting Committee on an International Bill of Rights. First Session, *supra* note 6, 89, 91.

[22] Scheinin: Toward a World Court of Human Rights, *supra* note 4.

Controversy over Legalization

'Advances' in the process of legalization are commonly greeted with celebration among the human rights expert community of practice as well as the fields of diplomacy and the media. For example, in 2002 the entrance into force of the Rome Statute of the International Criminal Court was characterized as "a great victory for justice, and for world order"[23] and in 2006 satisfaction labelled the adoption of the Convention on the Rights of Persons with Disabilities.[24] Adam Tomkins notes how in the adoption of the UK's 1998 Human Rights Act "[n]owhere were the celebrations more pronounced or more intense than among communities of lawyers".[25] Philip Alston noted the same already a decade earlier as he described how lawyers operate in the front line of the battle where human rights are transformed from the exclusive realm of philosophy and moral reflection into the domain of law.[26] Jack Donnelly discusses the "virtues of legalization" and highlights the element of rights identified by Duncan Kennedy: their capacity to act as trumps which cannot be reduced to mere value judgements.[27] Mark Mazover discusses how efforts to upgrade legality become visible in narratives by human rights scholars which focus on the origins of human rights. He notes how "[l]ooking forward rather than back, these compendia of texts, with their scholarly apparatuses, commentaries, and bibliographies, are not neutral; they themselves form a part of the ongoing effort to assert the power of the law over politics".[28]

Legalization has also given rise to criticism. Saladin Meckled-Garcia and Basak Cali view human rights as originating from moral ideals, and emphasize that nothing dictates that they should primarily

[23] United Nations Information Centre: 'Rapid Entry into Force of International Criminal Court Statute "a great victory for justice, and for world order", Secretary-General Says.' http://www.unis.unvienna.org/unis/pressrels/2002/sgsm8201.html (27.8.2006).

[24] Convention on the Rights of Persons with Disabilities, *supra* note 19.

[25] Tomkins, Adam: 'Introduction: On Being Sceptical about Human Rights.' In *Sceptical Essays on Human Rights* (Eds. Ewing, K. D. & Tomkins, Adam). Oxford University Press, Oxford, 2001, 1–11, 1.

[26] Alston, Philip: 'Making Space for New Human Rights: The Case of the Right to Development.' In *1 Harvard Human Rights Yearbook 3*, 1988, 3–40.

[27] Donnelly, Jack: Universal Human Rights in Theory & Practice. Second Edition. Cornell University Press, Ithaca. 2003, 1; Kennedy: 'The Critique of Rights,' *supra* note 8, 185.

[28] Mazover, Mark: 'The Strange Triumph of Human Rights, 1933–1950.' In *47 The Historical Journal 2*, 2004, 379–398, 397.

be realized through law. They consider efforts to legalize human rights to expand the importance of law as means of social control.[29] A second source of criticism originates from the entanglement of legalized human rights with the instrumental rationalities of the law. Through it, what is compelling is no longer the search for the absolute 'truth' of a given situation but instead how it is depicted through the juridical process. This transformation is discussed by Austin Sarat and William Felstiner, who describe how during divorce proceedings, attention shifts – sometimes to the great displeasure of involved parties – from the search for an objective truth into the search for the legally relevant arguments which may bear more or less direct connection to issues of justice.[30] This outcome has been identified as applying to human rights, as the instrumentality of law subjects them to the structure where each claim becomes the topic of mutually competitive arguments, as has been discussed by Martti Koskenniemi.[31] Bruno Latour has explored this same condition in the French Conseil d'état,[32] and Duncan Kennedy discusses the personal discomfort the necessity to argue opposite claims caused him during an internship.[33]

Legalization has likewise become the source of controversy among different 'schools' of international lawyers. A central source of criticism by critical legal scholars is the reliance by human rights scholars on 'soft law' documents,[34] which is argued to result in "overly formal reliance on textual articulations which are anything but clear or binding".[35] Another consistent topic is the expansive significance given to the concepts of customary international law and obligatio *erga omnes*.[36]

---

[29] Meckled-Garcia, Saladin & Cali, Basak (Eds.): The Legalization of Human Rights. Routledge, London, 2006, 1.

[30] Sarat, Austin & Felstiner, William L. F.: Divorce Lawyers and Their Clients: Power & Meaning in the Legal Process. Oxford University Press, Oxford, 1995, 26, 104.

[31] Koskenniemi, Martti: The Gentle Civilizer of Nations: The Rise and Fall of International Law 1870–1960. Cambridge University Press, Cambridge, 2001; Koskenniemi, Martti: 'Human Rights, Politics and Love.' In *Mennesker & rettigheter 4*, 2001, 33–45.

[32] Latour, Bruno: 'Scientific Objects and Legal Objectivity.' In *Law, Anthropology, and the Constitution of the Social: Making Persons and Things* (Eds. Alain Pottage & Martha Mundy). Cambridge University Press, Cambridge, 2004, 73–114, 86–87.

[33] Kennedy: 'The Critique of Rights,' *supra* note 8, 193.

[34] Klabbers, Jan: 'The Redundancy of Soft Law.' In *65 Nordic Journal of International Law*, 1996, 167–182.

[35] Kennedy: 'The Critique of Rights,' *supra* note 8, 27.

[36] Klabbers, Jan: Review: The Concept of International Obligations Erga Omnes by Maurizio Ragazzi. Clarendon Press, Oxford. In The Finnish Yearbook of International Law VIII. Kluwer University Press, Leiden, 1997, 409–412.

David Kennedy summarizes this criticism by noting how this "degrades the legal skills of those involved, while encouraging them to believe that their projects are more legitimate precisely because they are presented in (sloppy) legal terms".[37] Attempting to locate the centre of the controversy, it emerges as one of expertise over technical legal skills. This is summarized by a NAIL scholar who described how her criticism is directed to "*the means, not the ends*" of human rights experts. Human right scholars respond to such charges likewise through arguments highlighting expertise. For example, a prominent SCANET expert noted of recent NAIL scholarship on human rights:

> I consider it superficial, lacking expertise; often a sentiment emerges that the people do not exactly know what they are writing about. It feels that they have not studied how human rights actors really operate.

The SCANET expert continued by emphasizing that the difference at stake is between expertise in international law and human rights, stating that "*to be an expert in the first does not mean that one is automatically also an expert in the field of human rights*". The notion of expertise was further present in the praise she forwarded for the work of one NAIL scholar by stating: "*I respect her juridical skills. Other critical voices rarely operate in the same manner.*"

Legal Profile of SCANET Expertise

According to official guidelines, listed among others in its website, SCANET offers doctoral candidates "a systematically built, scientifically ambitious, and multidisciplinary research education". In practice SCANET activities are predominated by the discipline of law. This is illustrated by SCANET experts´ professional experience, as was discussed in Chapter 3. Legal emphasis can be elaborated by exploring expert academic backgrounds from the SCANET website through six disciplinary categories: law, international relations, economics, humanities, languages and other. Humanities includes anthropology, sociology, history, Latin American studies, African & Asian studies and

[37] Kennedy, David: The Dark Sides of Virtue: reassessing international humanitarianism. Princeton University Press, Princeton, 2004, 27.

Table 16: SCANET Expert Educational Background (N of experts = 18)

DISCIPLINE		% (N = 19)	% (N = 18)
Law	11	58%	61%
IR/Pol Science	2	11%	11%
Economics	-	-	-
'Humanities'	6	32%	33%
Languages	-	-	-
Other	-	-	-
TOTAL	19	100%	105%

theology, the disciplines mentioned in the biographies, and languages includes English and French while expert profiles entail no references to formal education in other languages. Three in five SCANET experts list law as their primary academic background, compared to two in five assigned to all other disciplines (Table 16). The profiles of experts participating in SCANET activities strengthen this emphasis. Of the experts present in four SCANET activities occurring over 22 seminar days – the total number of experts was 29, of which half were visiting, half permanent SCANET faculty members – four in five had a background in law, compared to one fourth in all other disciplines (Table 17).

Table 17: SCANET Experts in SCANET Activities (N of experts = 29)

DISCIPLINE		% (N = 30)	% (N = 29)
Law	23	77%	79%
IR/Pol Science	3	10%	10%
Economics	-	-	-
'Humanities'	3	10%	10%
Languages	-	-	-
Other	1 (konstvetenskap)	3%	3%
TOTAL	30	100%	103%

Table 18: Committee on Economic, Social and Cultural Rights

FIELD		% (N of disciplines = 33)	% (N of experts = 17)
Law	14	42%	83%
IR	6	18%	35%
Economics	4	12%	24%
'Humanities'	4	12%	24%
Languages	3	9%	18%
Other	2	6%	12%
TOTAL	33	100%	194%

UN Treaty Body Member Profiles

This finding is replicated by the profiles of two human rights treaty bodies, of which information has been available on the treaty body websites.[38] The Committee on Economic, Social and Cultural Rights has 17 experts who mention 33 different disciplines in their biographic profiles. This suggests that an average treaty body member holds an educational background in two disciplines (Table 18). Background in law rises as predominant, as it is mentioned in 14 treaty body member profiles. The next common disciplines are international relations and economics, which, combined, were mentioned in 10 profiles, and humanities and languages, combined mentioned in 7 profiles. The profiles of the Human Rights Committee members reproduce these patterns, although with even greater emphasis on law: it is mentioned in 17 of 18 profiles (Table 19). International relations is again the second most prevalent discipline, this time mentioned in 11 profiles, and humanities the third most common group, receiving mentions in 6 profiles. In other bodies such as the Committee on the Elimination on All Forms of Discrimination Against Women, legal emphasis is less central as expert backgrounds are more varied.[39] Yet the scarcity of lawyers among Committee members forms a common cause of

[38] Committee on Economic, Social and Cultural Rights: Members, 2006, http://www.ohchr.org/english/bodies/cescr/members.htm (21.12.2005 and 31.3.2006); Human Rights Committee: Members, 2006, http://www.ohchr.org/english/bodies/hrc/members.htm (31.3.2006).

[39] Merry, Sally Engle: Human Rights & Gender Violence: Translating International Law into Local Justice. The University of Chicago Press, Chicago, 2006.

Table 19: Human Rights Committee

FIELD		% (N of Disciplines = 36)	% (N of experts = 18)
Law	17	47%	94%
IR/Pol Science	11	31%	61%
Economics	2	6%	11%
'Humanities'	6	17%	33%
Languages	0	0%	0%
Other	0	0%	0%
TOTAL	36	100%	200%

complaint for the few lawyers, who feel that members without legal education lack skill to draft the Committee's 'legal' documents, leaving this task with them. The legal scholars also complain that members without legal education lack the kind of objectivity and distance which legal education provides, instead getting too emotionally involved in the issues discussed.[40]

Legal Background and the UDHR

The emphasis of legal background was visible, although to a lesser extent, in the drafting of the UDHR: drafters included legal scholars such as René Cassin and John Humphrey, and key lobbyists for example Judge Joseph Proskauer.[41] Yet Cassin has pointed out how he was disappointed to note that most of the drafters had no legal training.[42] This applied as well to Eleanor Roosevelt, Charles Malik as P. Cheng who, alongside Cassin and Humphrey, are commonly mentioned as the most influential members of the Drafting Committee.[43] In the following decades, probably largely due to the advances in legally binding documents, this outcome changed and the community of practice of human rights experts gained legal emphasis. Michael Freeman describes how in the 1970s nearly all academic work on human rights

[40] Many thanks to Jan Klabbers for discussion on this point.

[41] Proskauer, Joseph M.: A Segment of My Times. Farrar, Straus and Company, New York, 1950; Korey, William: NGOs and the Universal Declaration of Human Rights: 'A Curious Grapevine'. St. Martin's Press, New York, 1998, 33.

[42] Cassin, René: La pensée et l'action. F. Lalou, Boulogne-sur-Seine, 1972, 105–106; discussed in Glendon,: A World Made New, *supra* note 5, 48.

[43] Glendon, *ibid.*, 59, 210–21.

was done by international lawyers. This trend continued in the 1980s, when particularly work originating from social scientists was notably absent.[44] This was the case for anthropologists, for whom the period was marked by "disengagement".[45] Anthony Woodiwiss notes how today the political concept of human rights is increasingly occupied by communities of lawyers in the level of regional human rights jurisdictions as well as the UN bodies, viewing this development as troublesome.[46]

Consequences of Legal Emphasis in SCANET Activities

What kind of consequences does legal emphasis induce in such contexts as SCANET educational activities? Here the first observation becomes the asymmetry of expert and student profiles. Whereas SCANET experts are predominantly legal scholars, SCANET students hold varied backgrounds, including international relations, theology, linguistics, anthropology and sociology among others. Due to the SCANET learning curriculum, this discrepancy establishes a hierarchy between these disciplines: it forms a pattern where knowledge flows from legal scholars to a multidisciplinary audience. By contrast, the activities entail few instances where knowledge flows from experts of other disciplines to law scholars; as was mentioned, the contributions of students are primarily treated as raw data and thus not assigned equal status as entailing knowledge. This construes human rights knowledge primarily as the domain of legal scholars, a conception that was explicitly encouraged by SCANET experts in both private discussions and general activities. In a private exchange a prominent expert responded to the question on how she viewed research such as my own – then embedded in the critical tradition of epistemological architecture discussed in Chapter 1 – stating:

---

[44] Freeman, Michael: 'Putting Law in its Place.' In *The Legalization of Human Rights, supra* note 29, 49–64, 52.

[45] Goodale, Mark: 'Introduction to Anthropology and Human Rights in a New Key.' In *108 American Anthropologist 1*, 2006, 1–8. Freeman notes a survey that in the 1980s found the same to apply to university courses on human rights, a trend that has, however, slightly altered today: of the human rights programs observed in Chapter 4, only an ample third were LLM, and thus law degree programs, while the rest were commonly MA programs. Freeman, *ibid.*

[46] Woodiwiss, Anthony: 'The law cannot be enough: Human rights and the limits of legalism.' In *The Legalization of Human Rights, supra* note 29, 32–48, 32.

> I think it addresses a relevant point, but that point has already been addressed. In this approach the questions come from extra-legal sources, but we inside the legal field are capable of answering them.

As the expert distinguished between intra- and extra-legal sources, she depicted human rights knowledge as falling exclusively within the field of law, as forming a 'closed' system which had ceased to be open for contributions from other disciplines. The same has been noted by Philip Alston as he criticizes the habit of human rights scholars to quote either each other, human rights documents or other 'internal' human rights domains without engaging in extensive discussions with 'external' domains.[47]

This impression was reinforced in the response an expert gave to a student question in one SCANET activity relating to the substance of human rights in cross-cultural settings. The expert held the question to be off-target and focussing on substance matter ill-suited for the present context as it stemmed from an extra-legal source. In her answer the expert defined human rights as fundamentally legal entities and reinforced the implicit hierarchy of legal and other scholars, stating how the latter were welcome to contribute to the work of human rights experts, but that this contribution should remain external, as the substance of human rights was not primarily their concern. These examples depict an image of SCANET activities as dominated by legal experts whereas the insights of non-legal participants, 'laymen', are marginalised. This resembles the analysis of Austin Sarat and William Felstiner of the relationship of divorce lawyers and their clients which is characterized by professional dominance and lay passivity.[48] It also resonates with Vaula Haavisto's description of the expertise of Finnish judges which she describes, particularly prior to the 1993 court reform, as "self-competent, self-contained within one individual not needing further refinement by other professionals".[49] After the reform, conception of expertise had altered as clients' contributions in the hearings acquired a subject-like position, which guides legal professionals to construct cases as more collaborative and dialogical.[50] In SCANET

[47] Alston: 'Making Space for New Human Rights,' *supra* note 26, 11–13.
[48] Sarat & Felstiner: Divorce Lawyers and Their Clients,' *supra* note 30, 19–20.
[49] Haavisto, Vuola: Court Work in Transition: An Activity-Theoretical Study of Changing Work Practices in a Finnish District Court. Yliopistopaino, Helsinki, 2002, 67.
[50] *Ibid.*, 300.

activities a similar transformation is not observable and patterns of flow are continually governed by legal knowledge. This in turn impacts the kind of issues that are construed as relevant, as well as the manner they are framed. Both of these factors are determined by the framework of law, which favours certain kinds of conceptions at the expense of others.

Expanse through Legality

This section moves discussion to a detailed analysis of how legalization is embodied by the SCANET learning curriculum through focus on three elements: the presentation of documents, the definition of treaty bodies, and the characterization of the personal authority of human rights experts. In the presentation of documents constitutive is emphasis placed on the legal aesthetic of the already mentioned 'soft law' documents,[51] which Sally Engle Merry has also called 'lawlike'.[52] Examples of such texts include committee reports and Platform for Actions -type documents. In SCANET activities such documents are commonly discussed by emphasizing the aesthetic characteristics that they derive from more 'legal' instruments such as conventions. This presentational model applied particularly to certain prominent experts who frequented SCANET activities regularly and included ample references to documents in their lectures; for other experts this feature was less central. In practice this model means the following: an expert projects a document onto the overhead and proceeds to discuss it through paragraphs, for example *"As is stated by Article 4, paragraph 3 of General Comment 6."* This approach emphasizes the legal nature of the document, conveying the impression that its juridical status corresponds to that of a treaty. Thus the presentational mode equates such documents to treaty texts as well as assigns them the status as clarifiers and specifiers of existing documents; they become domains that continue the text of human rights treaties. Here a characteristic elaboration might be "*This article of the CESCR has been discussed in Paragraph 5 of the Concluding Observation number 4 of the Committee on Economic, Social and Cultural Rights, which states...*"

[51] Klabbers, Jan: 'Glorified Esperanto? Rethinking Human Rights.' In *Finnish Yearbook of International Law Vol. XIII, 2002* (Ed. Tuori, Taina). Martinus Nijhoff Publishers, Leiden, 2004, 63–77.

[52] Merry: Human Rights & Gender Violence, *supra* note 39, 89.

This presentational mode equates 'lawlike' documents to those with a more clearly established juridical status, thus strengthening their role as "spheres of legal knowledge".[53] However, as was mentioned, instead of being matters of uncontested fact, the status of such documents remains the source of intense controversy among international lawyers. These controversies were generally absent from SCANET activities as NAIL scholars seldom visit them; on average each activity included one or two scholars out of a group of eight to ten experts who could be seen as critical legal scholars. Although these encounters often culminated in intense discussions between representatives of different 'schools', discussions commonly remained on a general level, not focussing on such individual details as document legal status. Thus, SCANET activities did not expose their students to the intensity of the ongoing controversies over the legal status of specific documents, instead forming a learning curriculum that offered a more harmonious impression of discussed issues. Many students had received their training in international law primarily from human rights experts also outside SCANET activities, and, as mentioned, the activities included students from numerous disciplines outside international law. Consequently SCANET students would in only exceptional circumstances hold the kind of knowledge that would allow them to position the legalistic presentational mode as a part of the ongoing controversy over legalization. These conditions invest the presentational mode with paramount importance: it becomes the principal medium through which the new generation of human rights experts are socialized into the conception that the legal status of the introduced document *is* what the presentational mode suggests. This transforms the legalistic aesthetic into a pivotal instrument in the process where the human rights phenomenon is transformed through education into a more legalistic direction.

Another example of legalistic emphasis is offered by discussions on the role of human rights treaty bodies in SCANET activities. As was mentioned in Chapter 3, treaty bodies differ from courts both by their juridical status and processes: whereas the members of courts are judges, the members of treaty bodies are independent experts. The terminology utilized to describe the documents produced by the two

[53] Riles, Annelise: 'Anthropology, Human Rights, and Legal Knowledge: Culture in the Iron Cage.' In *108 American Anthropologist 1*, 2006, 52–65, 54.

entities varies. For example the International Court of Justice delivers *judgments* and *advisory opinions* according to a predefined procedure,[54] treaty bodies offer *general comments, concluding observations* or *guidelines* produced through "constructive dialogue".[55] The two also differ in their operations. Courts are more 'legalistic' both by their nature, their process as well as their end result, whereas treaty bodies are not governed by equally clearly established processual rules. Thus treaty bodies have the possibility to function more flexibly and to offer general evaluations, whereas courts usually focus on evaluating specific points of law; a treaty body is, for example, not prevented from reaching conclusions of a given state's human rights record merely because its state report fails to fulfil some formal criteria.[56] The usefulness of treaty bodies could be argued to emerge precisely from their possibility to function 'non-legally' and thus to address human rights issues which cannot by their nature be defined as legal obligations. Although their practices are commonly called "quasi-judicial", it has been argued that treaty bodies were never intended to be considered as courts.[57] SCANET activities offer, however, examples of the reverse, namely of instances where the authority of treaty bodies is defended with the argument that their functioning is 'court-like'. This is a view concurred to by Sally Engle Merry, who describes the system of treaty bodies as "[t]he most lawlike of the human rights mechanisms".[58] In SCANET this applies in particular to the Human Rights Committee which monitors state party compliance with the ICCPR. In SCANET activities the status of the Committee was defended expressly by arguing that out of all the treaty bodies, it most resembles a court. Simultaneously these arguments function as instruments to increase the legality of the human rights phenomenon by assigning treaty bodies the role of courts missing from it.

The third observed technique emerges from the characteristic statement of a predominant SCANET expert: "*I am only a black-letter*

---

[54] International Court of Justice, http://www.icj-cij.org/pcij/index.php?p1=9&PHPSESSID=e8b50769600e3fd2bd724b2b8afedba4 (28.4.2007).

[55] Nowak, Manfred: 'The International Covenant on Civil and Political Rights.' In *International Protection of Human Rights: Achievements and Challenges* (Eds. Isa, Felipe Gómez & Feyter, Koen de). University of Deusto, Bilbao, 2006, 137–154, 149.

[56] See Craven, Matthew: The International Covenant on Economic, Social, and Cultural Rights: A Perspective on Its Development. Oxford University Press, New York, 1995, 31–35.

[57] *Ibid.*, 32.

[58] Merry: Human Rights & Gender Violence, *supra* note 39, 72.

lawyer". This statement was commonly connected to disagreements of philosophical nature as well as to instances where discussion is referred to a person recognized as a black-letter lawyer. This was illustrated by a discussion from the already mentioned SCANET expert meeting on indicators, where uncertainty emerged regarding the suitability of certain treaty provisions to address the topic under discussion. The discussion participants, also holding expert status, paused the conversation and referred it to an expert who was regarded as particularly knowledgeable. The expert opened her comment by stating "*I am only a black-letter lawyer*". This incident signals how being a black-letter lawyer embodies criteria that increases an individual's status in the human rights expert community of practice. This statement entails numerous significant features. First, it creates the impression that the community of practice of human rights experts is characterized by rationality and detachment. Second, the characterization promotes the notion that the human rights regime creates a legal system directly comparable to contract law, for example – a field in which this characterization is easier relatable. Third, the statement defines the field of human rights as creating a 'closed' legal system from which it is no longer necessary to depart as all required answers are already offered by it. This definition reinforces the hierarchy between legal experts and those of other fields.

Legalization as Passionate Engagement

On the surface arguments of legality invest the practices of SCANET experts characteristics similar to those offered by Bruno Latour of the lawyers working at the French Conseil d'état. There the standard professional practice of lawyers is, due to the structure of proceedings, always to prepare for hearings a primary argument and a secondary argument, its potential opposite, in case the first one is rejected.[59] Consequently it is impossible for the lawyers to be passionately engaged in the objects of their work, and their relationship becomes characterized by rationality, bureaucracy and calm detachment. This description resonates with scholarship that views the professional engagements of human rights bureaucrats as reflecting solely the institutional frameworks in which they are carried out, as has been discussed by

[59] Latour: 'Scientific Objects and Legal Objectivity,' *supra* note 32, 86–87.

Tony Waters.[60] Yasushi Uchiyamada discusses the same through his analysis of Japanese body politics, which he describes as being characterized by a powerful void located at its centre.[61] Michael Herzfeld talks of the social production of indifference through bureaucratic practices,[62] and Annelise Riles emphasizes in her research of human rights practices how they form a "set of institutions, knowledge practices, and artifacts thereof that internally generate the effects of their own reality by reflecting on themselves".[63]

Yet such an interpretation appears misguided in regards to SCANET experts and the legality arguments presented above. Here important emerges the controversy, characterized by passion and intensity instead of calm and rational exchange that the process of legalization awakens between different schools of human rights thought. These sentiments were visible in the comments accompanying the student presentation discussed in Chapter 4, in which the student was characterized as being 'tempted' with relativism. Passion and intensity likewise tint the characteristic exclamation of a NAIL scholar: *"I have no patience for the human rights believers"*. SCANET scholars highlight their passionate engagement in the manner they describe their work stating, for example: "*I have failed to find a better way to improve the world than through human rights*". Although such statements may contain self-ironic undertones, simultaneously they convey a genuine belief in the benefits of the expanding – and legalizing – human rights regime.

This connects SCANET experts to Latour's analysis of natural scientists working in the laboratories, whose relationship to their targets of inquiry he characterizes as 'passionate'. He exemplifies this by describing the intense exclamations of joy in instances of success and sentiments of frustration in moments of failure. Latour emphasizes how it would be absurd to expect natural scientists to present arguments contrary to their 'beliefs' merely if their primary findings did not receive immediate favour.[64] This sentiment applies also to SCANET experts. During this study, nothing has emerged to suggest that prominent

[60] Waters, Tony: Bureaucratizing the Good Samaritan: The Limitations of Humanitarian Relief Operations. Boulder, Westview, 2001.

[61] Uchiyamada, Yasushi: 'The Face of the Japanese Body Politics.' In *28 Political and Legal Anthropology Review 2*, 2005, 282–306.

[62] Herzfeld, Michael: The Social Production of Indifference: Exploring the Symbolic Roots of Western Bureaucracy. The University of Chicago Press, Chicago, 1992.

[63] Riles, Annelise: The Network Inside Out. The University of Michigan Press, Ann Arbor, 2001, 3.

[64] Latour: 'Scientific Objects and Legal Objectivity,' *supra* note 32, 75–78.

SCANET experts do *not* view human rights either as sacred, as has been phrased by Michael Perry,[65] or as forming a secular religion. Consequently, although on the surface arguments of legality may convey rational detachment, this analysis suggests that beneath the veneer of professional language prevails a strong sense of passion and activist commitment toward the legalization of the international human rights regime.

Passionate Legitimacy: Introducing Creative Space

In addition to legality, SCANET experts often resort to arguments of 'legitimacy'. The increasing use of legitimacy arguments has been described as a fundamental change in international and human rights law since the end of the Cold War, and its central function has become to defend expansive interpretations on the content of human rights treaties among others.[66] In SCANET activities this rhetoric emerged, for example, in a situation where discussion turned to the juridical status of human rights treaty bodies. I asked how the sources of public international law – 'legalistic' domains – approached the matter. As has been discussed, their authority and functioning had in other discussions been presented as enjoying expansive and unambiguously defined authority in matters related to the interpretation of human rights conventions. This presentation was more unambiguous than that conveyed by the general sources of public international law. For example, Article 38 of the Statute of the International Court of Justice mentions judicial decisions as one of its sources, as well as the teachings of the most highly qualified scholars of various nations. Yet it makes no reference to the documents produced by treaty bodies.[67] In her response the SCANET expert had a different approach: she emphasized that it was not relevant or perhaps even possible to determine the authority of treaty bodies from legalistic sources, as it derived above all from their *legitimacy*. This answer is compelling as it gave rise to a distinct conception of the human rights regime: whereas arguments of legality depict it as a closed system from which it is no longer necessary to

[65] Perry, Michael: The Idea of Human Rights: Four Inquiries. Oxford University Press, Oxford, 1998.

[66] Koskenniemi, Martti: 'Legitimacy, Rights, and Ideology: Notes Towards a Critique of the New Moral Internationalism.' In *7 Associations: Journal for Legal and Social Theory 2*, 2003, 349–373.

[67] International Court of Justice: Statute, http://www.icj-cij.org/documents/index.php?p1=4&p2=2&p3=0 (28.4.2007).

depart, the rhetoric of legitimacy emphasizes that it is, in fact, not complete and certain elements still need to be incorporated into it. Thus, whereas arguments emphasizing legality draw a hierarchy between 'intra' – and 'extra-legal' sources, the rhetoric of legitimacy emphasizes the importance of 'extra-legal' domains.

This rhetoric induces important consequences on the relationship of human rights and law: it introduces extra-legal domains as sufficiently compelling to challenge for example the Statute of the International Court of Justice as an authoritative source regarding the status of human rights treaty bodies. Arguments of legitimacy concretize the already discussed dual character of rights claims as existing both 'inside and outside the law'; as being 'either rules or reasons for rules'. In the present case human rights concerns became the reasons for overriding the sources of public international law – 'rules' – which did not recognize the legal status of treaty bodies; human rights concerns became 'reasons for rules'. For the present analysis such arguments become paramount for two reasons. First, as SCANET experts engage in arguments propagating upon the inclusion of extra-legal domains, it becomes analytically challenging to deduce what kind of conception of human rights they hold, as it clearly exceeds what exists in current legal instruments today. Second, as the experts move to arguments of legitimacy, they expand their systemic agency: in addition to acting as intermediaries who translate the human rights discourse, they become activists who seek to expand the discourse through the incorporation of 'necessary', 'morally right' issues. This gives rise to a realm of personal influence called the *creative space* (Graph 13).

As human rights experts increasingly address matters beyond the scope of law through their creative space, also their systemic agency extends and gains greater societal power. In SCANET activities the experts' creative space gains significance due to the observed learning curriculum: as a consequence of its patterns of flow as well as its conception of knowledge only experts will have the possibility to introduce extra-legal concerns. Many human rights experts are themselves uncomfortable with this characterization, as has been discussed by David Kennedy through his analysis of international humanitarians. He describes how human rights experts are "looking for politics everywhere but in the humanitarian vernacular",[68] and see themselves as intervening only exceptionally in a technical capacity, instead advising,

---

[68] Kennedy: 'The Critique of Rights,' *supra* note 8, 115.

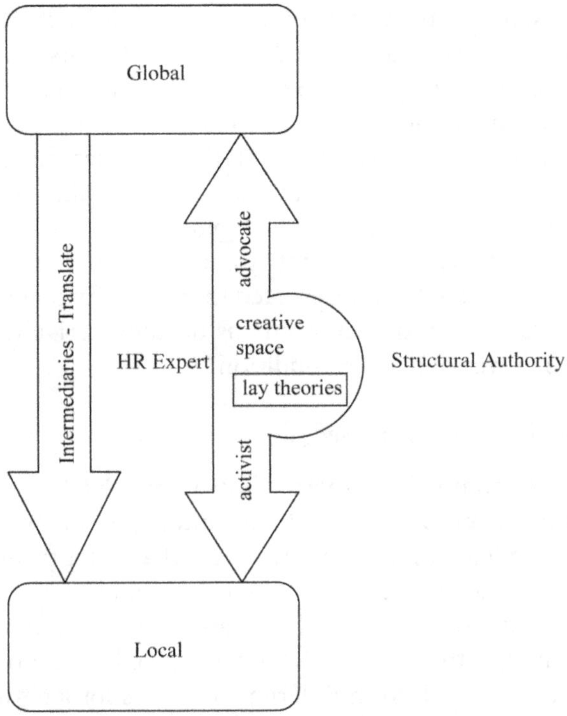

Graph 13: *Creative Space of Human Rights Experts*

interpreting, applying or implementing wisdom originating from elsewhere. These sentiments are interpreted to apply to SCANET experts particularly through the statement of being 'only' a black-letter lawyer. Since the human rights expert community of practice operates on a sharp distinction between law and politics, many find suggestions that their professional capacities entail political elements unwelcome.

As was noted, for most SCANET experts law is their primary source of academic education as well as professional experience. Yet due to the extensive scope of the human rights phenomenon, in their professional capacities experts discuss abundant issues falling outside the realm of law. In this experts resemble lawyers and judges who likewise constantly encounter material from other specialized fields.[69] This

[69] Riles, Annelise: 'Encountering Amateurism: John Henry Wigmore and the Uses of American Formalism.' In *Rethinking the Masters of Comparative Law* (Ed. Riles, Annelise). Hart Publishing, Oxford, 2001, 94–126.

diversity is exemplified by the topics of SCANET activities, which include such events as "Muslims and the Other: Pluralism and Human Rights"; "Muslims and Divorce: Between Sharia and Human Rights" and "Cultural Constraints to Women's Human Rights". As these titles indicate, a significant portion of SCANET activities investigates the 'Other', non-Western cultures, and their compatibility with human rights provisions. Thus it is pivotal to explore, what kind of sources of knowledge experts rely on to identify the 'morally' necessary extra-legal issues that need to be incorporated into the body of human rights knowledge. From what kind of domains do they derive information regarding the universal human condition?

Lay Theories and Expert Knowledge

For this analysis compelling emerges how in SCANET expert profiles absent were mentions of both academic and professional experiences that provide familiarization with ways of life that differ from one's own background. In academic terms this refers to, in addition to anthropology, studies of different religions, geography, history, philosophy and linguistics among others. SCANET expert profiles do not highlight experiences as having lived in different countries for lengthy periods, which might offer in-depth appreciation for previously unfamiliar mode of belief. In SCANET activities, when the compatibility of human rights provisions was discussed in relation to 'Other' cultures, there were no instances in which 'Western' experts shared stories of how unfamiliar ways of life had become known to them through academic endeavours or personal experience. What sources do human rights experts rely in such instances? Two alternatives emerge: either experts consult individuals they consider to hold reliable knowledge, or they utilize some other domains of knowledge embedded implicitly in the knowledge practices of their community of practice. The desirability of the first option was exemplified by the lunch discussions surrounding the submission of China's state report. Treaty body members mentioned as reliable individuals the NGO representatives producing the 'shadow-reports' as well as the "*people who cannot speak English*", the real people.

Gaining knowledge from the 'real people' is, however, problematic. The high intensity of expert work renders exchanges brief, and experts often lack a common language with populations not fluent in English. Perhaps for these reasons SCANET activities did not feature instances where experts highlighted, for example, discussions with the 'common Islamic people' on the compatibility of the Sharia and human rights. A more plausible source of knowledge is formed by the lay theories held by experts. Lay theories have been characterized by Adrian Furnham as the informal and commonsense explanations people give for particular social behaviours; these explanations derive from formal 'scientific' explanations of what actually happens.[70] Furnham describes them as "implicit rather than explicit, with tacit, non-specified assumptions or axioms".[71] He continues by noting how they are frequently "ambiguous, incoherent and inconsistent", translating to the possibility that mutually incompatible or contradictory ideas or beliefs can be simultaneously entertained.[72] Lay theories have also been discovered to hold significance for intergroup relations, as they redefine and uphold relations across racial borders.[73] This study argues that lay theories acquire relevance for the work of human rights experts who belong to the transnational "English-speaking, largely secular, universalistic, law-governed culture" holding its "own norms, values and cultural practices".[74] Since experts lack formal training in disciplines that could offer them more profound understanding of different cultures and societies, the primary source of information becomes the lay theories of the cultural 'other' embedded in the expert community of practice.

Sally Engle Merry discusses how implicit theories were visible in the proceedings of the CEDAW monitoring Committee in their treatment of the Fijian practice called *bulubulu*, a traditional village custom for reconciling differences. Merry describes how the Committee asked the government delegation when they were going to eliminate this custom, and poses the question "[w]hy did the experts assume that the custom itself was the problem rather than its application to court cases?"[75] After observing the proceedings, she came to conclude that this interpretation stemmed from the conception of 'customs' as harmful practices rooted in traditional culture. She notes how "[t]he experts do not

---

[70] Furnham, Adrian F.: Lay Theories: Everyday Understandings of Problems in the Social Sciences. Pergamon Press, Oxford, 1988.

[71] *Ibid.*, 3.

[72] *Ibid.*

[73] Levi, Sheri R.; Chiu, Chi-yue & Hong, Ying-yi: Lay Theories and Intergroup Relations. 9 *Group Processes & Intergroup Relations 9*, 2006, 5–25.

[74] Merry: Human Rights & Gender Violence, *supra* note 39, 37.

[75] *Ibid.*, 4.

have the time to investigate when and how customs such as *bulubulu* are better able to protect women from rape than the courts or how these customs intersect with state legal systems in new ways".[76] As treaty body members lack possibilities to familiarize themselves with individual traditions – they have no time to study extensive ethnographic reports – judgements made on specific cases rely largely on the prior knowledge and assumptions that experts have.

Similar lay theories were visible among SCANET experts. Among SCANET experts 'primitive' or 'traditional' societies are commonly seen as detrimental to the realization of an individual's rights, whereas 'modernity' is desirable; societies organized around the formal principle of equality are preferred to those organized hierarchically, and democracy and liberalism are preferable to all other forms of social organization. In empirical terms such opposition is, of course, only partial. Bruno Latour has challenged the notion that modern societies exist at all,[77] and many formally egalitarian societies are embeded in stark hierarchies based on such features as personal wealth. Consequently this raises the question whether the notion of an egalitarian society remains ideal in nature. Whatever individual scholar may think of such discussions, this study suggests that in the SCANET expert community of practice such distinctions are taken seriously, which leads to circumstances where the work of human rights experts includes the making of value judgements between different societies. This finding connects discussion back to the universalism-relativism debate. In SCANET activities many experts made serious attempts to incorporate greater cultural sensitivity in their scholarship. This awareness channelled itself in interest in the work of such scholars as Ayelet Shachar, who in her book "Multicultural Jurisdictions" attempts to find a middle ground between an absolutist understanding of international human rights norms and cultural difference.[78] Yet these attempts are not without problems, and for example Shachar operates on a fundamentally liberal perspective in which people can 'enter' and 'exit' to and from their 'particular' cultures to a universal, liberal 'non-cultural' space. Consequently such works, despite greater superficial cultural

[76] *Ibid.*, 4–5.

[77] Latour, Bruno: We Have Never Been Modern. Harvard University Press, Cambridge, 1993.

[78] Shachar, Ayelet: Multicultural Jurisdictions: Cultural Differences and Women's Rights. Cambridge University Press, Cambridge, 2001.

sensitivity, end up replicating the above hierarchy between types of societal forms, as has been discussed by Jane Cowan.[79]

Another SCANET expert, upon discovering that I had a background in anthropology mentioned how she had, in a similar effort to broaden her cross-cultural understanding, experimented with anthropological scholarship. The expert commented: "*I read this anthropology book once, thought it was fascinating. But then I discovered it was a hoax and I haven't bothered with anthropology since.*" The book the expert referred to was Margaret Mead's classic work Coming of Age in Samoa,[80] and her classification of the book as a hoax can be interpreted to refer to the critique its ethnography has in retrospect received for the manner it produced Samoan culture as a one-sided idyll. George Marcus and Michael Fischer identify the comments of Derek Freeman as particularly influential in this criticism.[81]

This instance introduces another practice SCANET experts engage in while exploring material that might assign them greater appreciation of cultural diversity: material is processed through the same knowledge practices described in the previous chapter, with great speed and rapidly formed conclusions that do not allow challenges to existing ontological assumptions. This element was summarized by the expert, who characterized how she processed material by stating: "*I go through text very quickly, flicking through the pages. In fact, I can read any book in a day*". In the described instance the expert read Mead's book quickly, reaching a conclusion that the entity was fascinating. This conclusion was contrasted with labelling the book a hoax, a sentiment possibly influenced by Freeman's critique, even though the expert does not identify him by name. However, also this conclusion was reached with speed, subsequently achieving the status of an uncontested fact – that the book is a hoax, and that anthropology is a discipline not to be bothered with. Human rights expert knowledge

---

[79] Cowan, Jane: 'Culture and Rights after Culture and Rights.' In *108 American Anthropologist 1*, 2006, 9–24.

[80] Mead, Margaret: Coming of Age in Samoa: A Psychological Study of Primitive Youth for Western civilization. William Morrow & Company Inc., New York, 1973[1928].

[81] Marcus, George E. & Fischer, Michael M.: Anthropology as Cultural Critique: An Experimental Moment in the Human Sciences. Second Edition. University of Chicago Press, Chicago, 1999, 158–159; Freeman, Derek: Margaret Mead and Samoa: The Making and Unmaking of an Anthropological Myth. Harvard University Press, Cambridge, 1983.

practices do not offer room for a careful investigation of Mead's work and its contribution to ongoing anthropological discussion, nor do they offer possibilities to consider its role as a pioneer study of anthropology's possibilities to offer viable cultural critique.[82] Due to lack of familiarity with anthropological methods, the expert does not have possibilities to assess for herself the merits and shortcomings of Mead's ethnography, nor to explore the subsequent discussion challenging its accuracy. Such phases are dismissed as the work is viewed solely through one perspective: a hoax.

This conclusion confirms the existing ontological assumptions that SCANET experts hold, and introduce circumstances where empirical data is assessed from the perspective of how well or poorly it corresponds with the condition of mankind that has been outlined by international human rights norms. To describe this shift through the terms of theory and empiria, human rights expert knowledge reverse their roles. Instead of being formed on the basis of empirical findings about given contexts, for SCANET experts theory emerges as something that is already embodied in human rights norms. Thus theory is transformed from a description of *how* humans lead their lives into a normative assessment on how they *should* lead their lives. Empiria, in turn, also acquires differing qualitative elements: instead of being received as mere description, it is subjected to normative evaluation on how well or poorly it corresponds with the way matters *should* be; empirical data is not neutral, but instead 'good' or 'bad' for mankind. As was described in Chapter 1, this shift was something that I experienced with puzzlement as I presented my research plan in SCANET activities. This reversal of theory and empiria was further embodied at another SCANET activity by a particularly esteemed expert as she discussed the compatibility of different religions and human rights. After a while the expert appeared to grow weary of the discussion, and stated with emphasis that "*a time will come when all religions will have to yield to human rights*". This comment concretizes the inverse relationship of empiria and theory, as well as highlights why it is unproblematic to SCANET experts. As human rights are fundamentally about global social change, although attempts are made to reach greater cultural sensitivity, this underlying premise remains unchallenged.

---

[82] Marcus & Fischer: Anthropology as Cultural Critique, *ibid.*, 158.

Lay Theories and the Creative Space

A constitutive element remains absent from the present discussion: the fact that no one knows exactly what human rights are, or what exactly forms the theory of human rights. As was discussed in Chapter 2, all kinds of claims are today forwarded through the human rights discourse by both laymen and scholars. This chapter has discussed how in their argumentation SCANET experts move inside and outside the law, framing human rights as both rules and reasons for rules; they argue that the regime of human rights creates both a closed system as well as one that needs to be 'opened up' so that additional elements can be incorporated into it. Importantly, in SCANET activities – as only experts have the possibility to present *knowledge* – decisions over when the body of human rights knowledge needs to be opened up, as well as what kinds of claims need to be incorporated into it, remain within the discretion of the experts' creative space. This transforms the creative space into an important venue through which additional knowledge is offered on human rights. To borrow the terminology of David Kennedy, it is the primary domain of expert 'politics' through which they introduce issues that they construe *should* become integral parts of what are commonly understood as human rights. Through SCANET activities experts socialize students – the next generation of prospective experts – to their own conceptions of what this means. Simultaneously the experts expand the body of human rights knowledge according to their personal understandings of what constitutes universal substance for mankind. Although SCANET experts portray occasional ambivalence toward suggestions of such personal impact, in other instances they celebrate the independence accompanying prestigious expert positions. Thus a SCANET expert characterized her work in a treaty body by stating: "*[a]s an expert, I did not represent my government or check my views from any domain. The view I put forth was my own based on my academic and other experience*".

This chapter has demonstrated that SCANET expert profiles are strongly characterized by legal experience and training. SCANET experts lack the kind of professional, academic and personal experiences that could have assigned them profound understanding of societies and ways of life that differ significantly from their cultures of origin, or from the ontological assumptions embedded in the transnational, secular culture of the human rights community of practice. Thus the creative space of SCANET experts primarily reflects the lay theories they hold of 'primitive' ways of life among others. Simultaneously in their professional practices experts rely on the inside knowledge they hold of the human rights phenomenon, for example a given country's human rights record and its activeness in the human rights *dialogue*. These findings raise the question: how can the knowledge distributed in a context like SCANET incorporate universality instead of particular conceptions of the human condition? This analysis argues that – due to the observed patterns of flow, conceptions of knowledge and the strong influence of lay theories in the creative space of expert – what becomes paramount for global representation is that individuals holding expert positions represent global diversity through their personas. To conclude this study, the next chapter explores the profile of SCANET expertise.

CHAPTER SIX

PROFILE OF EXPERTISE

The Mandates System was created by the League of Nations in 1919 as a response to the changed circumstances of the post-World War I era. As a consequence of the war, former colonies were no longer under the sovereignty of their colonial rulers, yet they were not construed as fully independent either.[1] Instead, as is described by the League's Covenant, they were seen as peoples "not yet able to stand by themselves under the strenuous conditions of the modern world"; they were regarded as "minors".[2] This gave rise to the question of how their political organization should be arranged. The solution became the introduction of the Mandates System, in which former colonies were divided into three stages on the basis of their region's perceived development. It was further argued that "the tutelage of such peoples should be entrusted to advanced nations who, by reason of their resources, their experience or their geographic position, can best undertake this responsibility".[3] In the argumentation explaining the system's necessity and purpose, central emerges the rhetoric of development and progress through education.

This is reflected in a book published by the League in 1945, which describes the System's first three primary aims as "[t]he political and moral education, the improvement of the living conditions and, in general, the protection of the interests of the native population".[4] In addition, education is characterized as a part of the "moral responsibility towards mankind for the treatment of the natives".[5] Read from the perspective of today's egalitarian spirit of global collaboration, these texts embody an embarrassing and patronizing tone. Yet, in the interwar period and up until the founding of the UN, this tone and the

[1] Many thanks to Taina Tuori for discussions and references on this topic. See also Anghie, Antony: Imperialism, Sovereignty and the Making of International Law. Cambridge University Press, Cambridge, 2005.

[2] Covenant of the League of Nations: Art 22, http://www.yale.edu/lawweb/avalon/leagcov.htm (13.12.2006); The Mandates System. League of Nations, Geneva, 1945, 23.

[3] Covenant of the League of Nations, *ibid.*

[4] The Mandates System, *supra* note 2, 50.

[5] *Ibid.*, 11.

Mandates System formed the principal means through which relations were organized between former rulers and colonies. The notions embedded in the Mandates System can be seen to reflect the more general 'civilizing mission' of international law: the responsibility of the 'civilized' world toward the uncivilized, as has been analysed by Martti Koskenniemi[6] – a responsibility that has often also been called the 'white man's burden'.

Officially, the founding of the UN overrode this tradition, introducing to international collaboration for the first time the notion of formal equality between independent nations. This notion was accompanied by a revolutionary new discourse founded on the equality of all peoples, articulated by the UDHR; as has been discussed by Risto Wallin, although various initiatives existed around the human rights discourse in the inter-war period, the discourse did not occupy a decisive role in the operations of the League of Nations.[7] Despite these changes, the UN era entails significant continuity from the League era. This was explicitly stated by the International Court of Justice in its ruling on the South West Africa Case of 1962,[8] and continuity was, among others, reflected in the personnel of the two organizations. The consequences of this continuity have been discussed through vast scholarship on post-colonial studies, in relation to international law particularly by Anthony Anghie.[9] It has often been argued that revolutions, despite their appearance of causing dramatic, all-altering change, even in the most radical of cases induce only minor changes to existing societal structures. These findings pose an important question for the human rights phenomenon: how profoundly have its practices and ideologies changed from those of the League of Nations era embedded in a sharp division of peoples according to their geographic origin? Have they vanished entirely, or become reincarnated in new forms and practices?

---

[6] Koskenniemi, Martti: The Gentle Civilizer of Nations: The Rise and Fall of International Law 1870–1960. Cambridge University Press, Cambridge, 2001.

[7] Wallin, Risto: Yhdistyneet kansakunnat organisaationa: Tutkimus käsittellisestä muutoksesta maailmanjärjestön organisoinnin periaatteissa. Jyväskylän yliopisto, Jyväskylä, 2005.

[8] The continuity of the UN of the 'sacred trust of civilizations' established by the League of Nations was repeated in the 1971 Namibia advisory opinion. Both cases are available at the International Court of Justice website, www.icjcij.org/docket/index.php?+1=38&code=esa&case=468&k=c1 (10.11.2007).

[9] Anghie: Imperialism, Sovereignty and the Making of International Law, *supra* note 1.

Patterns of Flow through Education

The previous chapter concluded by outlining how this chapter would focus on the personas of SCANET experts with the aim of inspecting how, through the experts' creative space, the knowledge distributed in its activities comes to reflect global diversity. In addition, this chapter will explore the profile of expertise to inspect what kind of patterns of flow SCANET activities – commenced over eight decades after the creation of the Mandates System, and over five decades after the adoption of the UDHR – create through the personas of its faculty and students. This analysis is conducted on two levels: first, by setting the observed patterns in the context of global structures and patterns of flow, and second, by setting them in the context of societal structures in Finland. In this focus this chapter continues the analysis of Chapter 4 on the empowering qualities of human rights education by posing the following question: do SCANET activities demonstrate similarity to existing oppressive structures, and if so, do they entail mechanisms that could be seen to render their participants conscious both of these structures and their capabilities of impacting them, thus empowering the participants? The first part of this analysis focusses on the geographic origin of SCANET participants through the categories *North* and *Other*. The second part explores participant gender. *North* and *Other* are borrowed from categories utilized in different UN contexts, for example in the 2006 election for the new Human Rights Council, where geographic areas were divided into Western Europe & Other States, African States, Asian States, Eastern European States, and Latin American & Caribbean States.[10] In this analysis the category North is formed by Western Europe & Other States, whereas all the remaining categories constitute Other. In addition, the category includes members of indigenous peoples originating from the geographic North. As SCANET activities did not feature experts or students from Latin American and Caribbean states, this category does not become relevant.

In addition to UN contexts, these categories are familiar from critical legal scholarship, for example from the analysis of the human rights phenomenon by Makau Mutua.[11] Simultaneously their use awakens

---

[10] Human Rights Council: Elections, 2006, http://www.un.org/ga/60/elect/hrc/ (19.3.2007).

[11] Mutua, Makau: Human Rights: A Political & Cultural Critique. University of Pennsylvania Press, Philadelphia, 2002.

reservation in many human rights scholars as well as anthropologists, as the categories are seen as unsophisticated and politically sensitive. Human rights scholars may question their validity as, although in the UN context geographic origin of persons is essential for securing global representation in its differing bodies, such focus may appear subtly racist. It appears that many human rights scholars construe the universalist ethos of the discourse to have introduced a social space in which such features as geographic origin, religion or race are insignificant and the only relevant characteristic relates to the shared humanity of mankind. Such a notion sounds attractive, yet it ignores the manner in which the human rights phenomenon continues to exist as a part of global and local structures of wealth and social capital among others. It also overlooks the legacy of the Mandates System in which individuals were classified, according to their geographic origin reflecting *North* and *Other*, into 'advanced nations' and 'minors', the latter of whom needed to be educated by the former. By re-introducing these unsophisticated categories, this analysis inquires whether these patterns have vanished through the revolutionary egalitarian discourse of human rights, or whether they find resonance in SCANET activities.

Geographic Profile of Experts and Students

Both permanent SCANET experts and doctorate candidates are required to hold some allegiance to universities and human rights institutes within the Nordic region, yet the geographic origin of participants may vary significantly. SCANET participants' geographic origin has commonly become available from activity programs or informal discussion. This investigation focuses on five SCANET activities which included 148 participants, of whom 42 were experts and 106 students (Table 20). In both groups some participants visited more than one event. Some prominent experts were present in all the examined activities, whereas some participated only in one activity. When all SCANET participants are included 42 participants represent the category Other while 106 represent the category North. When participants are divided into experts and students, these patterns are altered. For experts the portion of North grows while the portion of Other diminishes, for students the reverse occurs. The most salient difference emerges regarding the category of Other: whereas one third of the 106 SCANET students belong to this category, only one in eight of the 42 SCANET experts belongs to it (Table 21). Of all the 148 SCANET participants, one in four belongs to the category of North expert. Simultaneously only one in 25 participants belongs to the category of Other expert. Of the 106 North participants, one in three belongs to the category of expert compared to one in eight of all the 42 Other participants.

This creates a geographic profile of expertise as predominantly Northern: only six of the 42 expert positions, that is one in eight, are held by individuals from the category Other, whereas the remaining 36 expert positions are held by individuals belonging to the category North (Table 22). Emphasizing the importance of this finding is that in the observed SCANET activities, all Other experts participated in the capacity of visiting experts, as permanent SCANET experts included only Northern individuals. Thus permanent SCANET faculty did not include, for example, members of the Sami people, the indigenous population residing in the Northern parts of Norway, Sweden and Finland.

To elaborate this analysis, closer attention needs to be invested on the role of Other males in the categories of experts and students. For experts what emerges as paramount is the discrepancy of quantity

Table 20: Participants in 5 SCANET activities

	N	% of total
EXPERTS	42	28%
STUDENTS	106	72%
TOTAL	148	100%

Table 21: Geographic Affiliation

	EXPERTS	%	STUDENTS	%	TOTAL	%
NORTH	36	86%	70	66%	106	72%
OTHER	6	14%	36	34%	42	28%
TOTAL	42	100%	106	100%	148	100%

Table 22: Geographic Profile of Experts

	N	of all (n=148)	of North/Other (n=106/42)	of experts (n=42)
NORTH	36	24%	34%	86%
OTHER	6	4%	14%	14%

Table 23: Male Experts (N=30)

	N	of all (n=148)	of own (n=106/42)	of all male (n=74)	of male experts (n=30)
NORTH	28	19%	26%	38%	93%
OTHER	2	1%	5%	3%	7%

between North and Other male experts. As is demonstrated by Table 23, of the 42 SCANET participants belonging to the category of Other, only two Other males, in other words under one in twenty, belong to the category of expert. By contrast, of the 106 North participants, 28 Northern males, more than one fourth, belong to the category of experts. Table 23 shows further that whereas 28 individuals of all the 74 SCANET male participants, almost two in five, belong to the category of North male expert, only two individuals, less than one in thirty, belong to the category of Other male expert. Consequently the profile of male experts who participate in SCANET activities almost uniformly represents the North: only one in fourteen male experts belongs to the category of Other.

For male students the patterns are altered. Of the 44 male students, 24 are Other males whereas only 20 are North males; conspicuously, the number of North male experts in the examined activities was 28 (Tables 24a & b). In terms of percentages, males are more prominently represented in the category of Other students than in that of North students. While two thirds of the 36 Other students are male, less than one third of the 70 North students are male. When the profiles of North and Other males are compared to each other, the most decisive element becomes that while participating in SCANET activities, North males are more likely to belong to the category of expert than student, as almost three in five of the 48 North male participants belong to the category of expert. Other males, by contrast, are by overwhelming majority more likely to belong to the category of student; according to this study, of the 26 Other male participants in SCANET, nine out of ten belong to this category (Table 24 a & b; Table 25).

African Participants and Patterns of Flow

Despite such clearly identifiable discrepancies between the geographic profile of experts and students, during this research no instances were encountered where this matter was explicitly discussed in SCANET

Table 24a: Students (N=106)

	N	of all (n=148)	of own (n=106/42)	of students (n=106)	male	% of category	female	% of category
NORTH	70	47%	66%	66%	20	29%	50	71%
OTHER	36	24%	86%	34%	24	67%	12	33%

Table 24b: Male Students (N=44)

	N	of all (n=148)	of own (n=106/42)	of all male (n=74)	of male students (n=44)	of students (n=106)
NORTH	20	14%	19%	27%	45%	19%
OTHER	24	16%	57%	32%	55%	23%

Table 25: Profile of SCANET male participants

	TOTAL	EXPERT	% of all males	% of own category	STUDENT	% of all males	% of own category
NORTH	48	28	38%	58%	20	27%	42%
OTHER	26	2	3%	8%	24	32%	92%
TOTAL	74	30	41%	41%	44	59%	59%

activities. Many experts were likely sensitive to this discrepancy, but saw it to stem rather from developments of past decades, when formal human rights educational contexts were unavailable particularly in Other countries. Thus they saw SCANET activities as a decisive vehicle for future change where expert profiles would become more diverse. Yet, due to the learning curriculum described in Chapter 4 and the manner in which it separated participants into distinct categories, the potency of SCANET activities to induce such structural changes remains uncertain. This matter is elaborated later in this chapter, and for now decisive becomes to explore who the participants belonging to the category of Other students are. Importantly, when compared to the portion of Other individuals in the general populations of the Nordic countries, the portion of Other students is significantly higher in SCANET activities than the portion of Other in the general populations of the Nordic countries. Table 24a demonstrated how one third of SCANET students belong to the category of Other, whereas the portion of foreigners in the Nordic countries ranges between 2.2% for

Finland,[12] 3% in Norway[13] and 10% for Sweden.[14] How can this high percentage of Other individuals among SCANET students be understood; what kind of factors can be seen to contribute to it? To proceed in this analysis, it is useful to distinguish the two primary groups of Other students present in SCANET activities: participants from African countries and those from the Baltic countries and Russia.

To begin with African participants, central becomes that there were no instances in which African, or Asian, participants belonged to the category of expert. Thus these continents were totally unrepresented in the SCANET flow of knowledge which moved from faculty to students. Simultaneously the higher portion of African participants among SCANET students compared to the general populations of Nordic countries appears non-coincidental as the Nordic human rights field has a well-established tradition of inviting representatives from developing countries into the various training programs offered in its region. This is exemplified by the Swedish Raoul Wallenberg Institute. Alongside with its numerous other activities – research, undergraduate and postgraduate courses, technical cooperation, maintaining a human rights library, offering publications – the institute participates in development cooperation through training courses organized in Sweden. These programs, funded by the Swedish International Development Cooperation Agency, annually admit around 25 participants from developing countries to its training programs of 3–5 weeks, with the aim of inducing changes in their home countries by promoting new means of ensuring respect for international human rights standards.[15] The program lists ideal participants as "key persons" in their countries of origin: policy and decision makers, representatives

[12] Sippola, Anna Riitta: 'Suomessa asuu ennätysmäärä ulkomaiden kansalaisia.' In *Helsingin Sanomat* 14.4.2006; Statistics Finland, 2005, http://www.stat.fi/tup/suoluk/suoluk_vaesto_en.html (29.5.2006).

[13] Statistics Norway: 'Differences in education among immigrants,' 2004, http://www.ssb.no/english/magazine/art-2006-05-23-01-en.html (19.5.2006).

[14] However, these figures include all foreigners, with no distinction made on the country of origin. When considering foreigners falling in the category Other, the figures are altered: as an example, in Norway this portion of the general population drops to 1.3%; see Statistics Norway, *ibid.* However, these figures commonly separate European and Baltic countries from non-European countries. As the categories utilized in this study have discussed these countries jointly, these further distinctions are thus not considered.

[15] The Raoul Wallenberg Institute of Human Rights and Humanitarian Law: Training Courses in Sweden, http://www.rwi.lu.se/coop/itp/overview.shtml (10.10.2007).

of institutions with human rights mandates, government institutions involved in the administration of justice, academic staff and NGO representatives. Although the program description emphasizes the importance of networks between present and former participants to facilitate the exchange of ideas, experiences and best practices regionally, it makes no references that the program's educational curriculum would be collaborational, with knowledge flowing both from the Swedish experts acting as educators to participants from developing countries on how their societies can be improved, and from participants of developing countries to the Swedish experts on how the Swedish society could be improved.

This pattern of flow reproduces the ideology embedded in the Mandates System – although with highly different terminology – that the Swedish society can and needs to offer such programs for "[t]he political and moral education, the improvement of the living conditions and, in general, the protection of the interests of the [developing countries'] population".[16] In addition to international diplomacy, the Nordic countries hold another important legacy entailing similar ethos, namely the missionary work by various organizations related to the Lutheran church. These efforts were commonly started during the 19th century, and they have been cited for example by Paul Lauren as precedents of these countries' later activeness in the human rights phenomenon.[17] Yet the rhetoric characterizing missionary work differs significantly from the human rights discourse: whereas the human rights discourse emphasizes the unity of all humanity, the rhetoric accompanying missionary work is founded on the division of individuals into those who have received knowledge of Christianity, been baptized and thus face the prospect of eternal life, and to those who lack them, instead facing the faith of eternal doom. Despite rhetorical difference, both missionary work as well as the Mandates System introduce patterns of flow that are reproduced as well in SCANET activities as in the Raoul Wallenberg Institute training courses. In them knowledge is distributed, for the general well-being of populations, from the North to the Other; from the white faces of the staff pages of the Wallenberg Institute to the diverse-raced faces of the developing countries. Occasional similarity also characterizes rhetoric: upon describing

[16] The Mandates System, *supra* note 2, 50.

[17] Lauren, Paul Gordon: The Evolution of International Human Rights: Visions Seen. University of Pennsylvania Press, Philadelphia, 1998, 46–47.

the overall purposes of its operations, the Wallenberg Institute home page states that it has a "mission" to promote universal respect for human rights.[18]

These patterns of flow find general commonality with the patterns established by contemporary international development and human rights programs. This is exemplified by an expert meeting organized by SCANET. The introduction of the meeting outlined that it was sponsored by the Finnish Ministry of Foreign Affairs, the EU fund ACTE, and the UN High Commissioner for Human Rights as well as SCANET. Thus in this meeting the sponsor domain was predominantly represented by the global North, a finding reflecting commonly established global funding patterns of the human rights phenomenon, discussed for example by Keck and Sikkink.[19] In the SCANET meeting these sponsor countries were distinguished from recipient countries, for the benefit of which the expertise provided with the sponsor country funds were intended. In the SCANET meeting recipients consisted primarily of third world or developing countries. A concrete embodiment of the division was provided by a visiting expert who introduced a new human rights project. The project's sponsors were the Norwegian Foreign Ministry along with the FAO, the UN Food and Agriculture Organization, and the project was intended to find ways to guarantee adequate food for vulnerable groups. The expert introduced the case studies of the project in Uganda and Brazil by explaining:

> We are going to work with local partners. In Uganda we are working both with the government and the civil society, in Brazil exclusively the civil society. In Uganda the work is going to be done by the Ugandans themselves, we are going to help them by financing and organizing seminars. The same thing will occur in Brazil.

This description introduced collaborational patterns in which the North, in this instance Norway, became the sponsor and Uganda and Brazil the recipients. What the North sponsored was both material aid as well as education. The project further held the purpose of guaranteeing food for recipient populations from which it might otherwise be missing. This assigns the sponsor-recipient relationship more dire undertones: it embodies the very survival of the recipients, who are

[18] The Raoul Wallenberg Institute, *supra* note 15.

[19] Keck, Margaret E. & Sikkink, Kathryn: Activists beyond Borders: Advocacy Networks in International Politics. Cornell University Press, Ithaca, 1998.

seen as unable to sustain themselves and thus continue to exist independently of their sponsors.

These findings connect such programs to the former imperialistic arguments that Merry identifies in CEDAW treaty body proceedings.[20] Merry expands this observation by discussing how non-governmential organizations in poorer nations are pushed to adopt human rights approaches to meet the demands of mostly Northern funders.[21] They also resonate with the writings of critical legal scholars,[22] and are visible in Finland through recent emphasis on such programs as the 'Human Rights Based Approach to Development',[23] in which recipient countries are expected to modify their conduct to meet new demands as articulated through the human rights discourse by the Finnish government. The sponsor-recipient relationship can also be approached from another perspective, namely from anthropological scholarship on gifts and exchanges. This vast scholarship has demonstrated how giving and receiving are never simple actions of transferring goods, but instead connected to elaborate systems of reciprocity, politics, lineage systems and social status among others.[24] A gift given initiates an asymmetrical relationship between the donor and recipient, and in order to become normalized again, it needs to be followed by reciprocation, either directly to the donor or to some other domain. In the Native American practice called 'Potlatch' in which property is publicly destroyed by its proprietors, discussed by H.G. Barnett in his classic study from the 1930s, what becomes pivotal, instead of gift giving, is the establishing of social status through destruction, thus attempting to demonstrate greater prosperity than rivals.[25]

---

[20] Merry, Sally Engle: Human Rights & Gender Violence: Translating International Law into Local Justice. The University of Chicago Press, Chicago, 2006, 17.

[21] *Ibid.*, 226.

[22] Mutua: Human Rights, *supra* note 11; Anghie: Imperialism, Sovereignty and the Making of International Law, *supra* note 1.

[23] Seppänen, Samuli: 'Possibilities and Challenges of the Human Rights-Based Approach to Development.' The Erik Castrén Institute Research Reports 17/2005, Helsinki, 2005.

[24] See for example the classic works by Malinowski, Branislaw: Argonauts of the Western Pacific. Waveland Press Inc., Illinois, 1984[1922]; Mauss, Marcel: The Gift: The Form and Reason for Exchange in Archaic Societies. Routledge, London, 2006[1950]; and Godelier, Maurice: Enigma of the Gift. University of Chicago Press, Chicago, 1999.

[25] Barnett, H. G.: 'The Nature of Potlatch.' In *40 American Anthropologist 3,* 1938, 349–358.

The patterns of flow examined in this section introduce and reproduce a continual asymmetrical relationship where the North becomes the donor – of money, food, education and general well-being – and the Other the recipient. Importantly, both SCANET activities as well as the training courses of the Raoul Wallenberg contribute to rather than challenge this relationship. Discussions surrounding the submission of China's state report demonstrated how in their participation in the human rights phenomenon developing countries are often expected to engage in conduct that reinforces this relationship; China's excessively large delegation was construed as a sign of arrogance, as if it were a reckless act of property destruction in a Potlach ceremony by a domain that was generally construed to lack sufficient wealth for it. These relationships of sponsors and recipients stigmatize and condemn underprivileged global domains, Other countries, to "an ambiguous peripheral relation with the existing institutions" which, Ernesto Laclau argues, "can have only paralysing political effects".[26] From this perspective the human rights phenomenon as well as SCANET activities can be construed, instead of being a medium of change, as "part of the problem"[27] that the human rights phenomenon attempts to solve on the level of discourse.

Baltic and Russian Participants and Finland

The other prevalent group of Other students in SCANET activities is formed by participants from the Baltic countries and South-West Russia. Here discrepancy is visible particularly between this group and participants from the Nordic countries – Sweden, Norway, Finland, Iceland and Denmark: as is demonstrated by Table 26, whereas the 27 experts from the Nordic countries constitute almost two thirds of the category of expert – the remaining 9 North experts are visiting experts invited in commonly from European or North American countries – the three Baltic experts account for less than one tenth of the category. Of all the 106 participants in the category North, one fourth are experts from the Nordic countries, whereas only one in fourteen of the 42 Other participants are experts from the Baltic countries. By contrast, although not introduced in a table form, the number of Baltic students

[26] Laclau, Ernesto: Emancipation(s). Verso, London, 1996, 33.
[27] Kennedy, David: The Dark Sides of Virtue: reassessing international humanitarianism. Princeton University Press, Princeton, 2004, 3.

Table 26: Scandinavian & Baltic experts

	EXPERTS	of all (n=148)	of north/other (n=106/42)	of experts (n=42)
NORTH (N=106)	36	24%	34%	86%
OTHER (N=42)	6	4%	14%	14%
SCANDINAVIAN	27	18%	25% (N=106)	64%
BALTIC	3	2%	7% (N=42)	7%

constitutes a much larger portion of all students, also accounting for more than half of the total category of Other students.

These findings repeat the discrepancy in the profiles of expert and student regarding the categories of North and Other. How can this be understood concerning Baltic participants? This section connects this discrepancy to the application guidelines of SCANET as well as the funding guidelines set forth by ScaFund. As was mentioned, in order to gain inclusion in SCANET activities, students require affiliation to the participating Scandinavian and Nordic human rights institutions or universities. Alternately they can hold affiliation to an institution located in the 'adjacent' area of the 'Nordic Region', an expression referring to the Baltic countries and South-West Russia. Particularly the latter inclusion illustrates an expansionistic understanding of the term Nordic, as it is not commonly understood to include these regions. Why has this definition been selected and what is its relevance for the present discussion? An answer highlights patterns of flow emerging from ScaFund activities, which rely on the financial support of the Nordic countries. This establishes again an asymmetrical relationship between Nordic countries and adjacent areas: in activities funded by ScaFund, patterns of flow, in this instance a monetary one, move from the Nordic countries to adjacent areas, establishing a donor-recipient relationship. This asymmetry emerges directly from ScaFund application guidelines, which mention that "[m]any ScaFund activities are open to the adjacent areas, Estonia, Latvia, Lithuania and North-Western Russia", yet for any given activity, "at least 3 Nordic countries (or 2 Nordic + 1 adjacent country) should be represented". This emphasizes the importance of the actual participation of Nordic countries in the activities funded by ScaFund. Description of ScaFund mobility scholarships reproduces the pattern identified of the Raoul Wallenberg Institute training programs by stating that for "young researchers… from the adjacent areas (the Baltic States and North-Western Russia)"

ScaFund offers possibilities for research stays from three up to 12 months in "a Nordic institution associated with a ScaFund network". Thus this reproduces the pattern of flow where participants from Other countries are invited in to the Nordic countries to benefit from the education offered by them.

Also this emphasis has earlier precedents. This is illustrated by the actions of Alva Myrdal, a Swedish pioneer in the field of social reform and one of the first women representatives in UN circles, as is discussed by Doris Linder. Linder describes how, as the UN and its specialized agencies took form, Myrdal, the head of a teacher training and educational research institute in Stockholm who sat on the government's school commission, made known her particular interest in the role UNESCO could play in rebuilding and improving school systems around the world. Linder recounts how at the first general conference of UNESCO in the fall 1946, Myrdal gave a speech explaining that "Sweden wanted to move beyond extending material aid to liberated areas by giving attention to their cultural needs, for example, by printing academic textbooks for Poland and by inviting scholars and adult education leaders to study in Sweden".[28] This instance demonstrates an identical pattern of flow to the one encouraged by ScaFund: a pattern in which a Nordic country – in this instance Sweden – provides both material as well as immaterial aid to a developing Eastern Bloc neighbour – in this instance Poland. In SCANET this pattern of flow gains additional importance from the end of the Cold War, as the consequence of which post-socialist states have rushed to participate in the global human rights regime. Due to their geographic proximity, this has assigned Nordic individuals unique possibilities of acting as educators: to teach what human rights are, and to guide how they should be realized in the post-socialist landscape. Such a relationship increases the status of Nordic countries in the global human rights phenomenon. At the local level, it has expanded the systemic agency of human rights experts into social architects who instruct post-socialist states on how they should be organized to ensure a prosperous future.

This development is not restricted to the relationship of Nordic and Baltic countries. Instead human rights education has become a pivotal

[28] Linder, Doris H.: Equality For Women: The Contribution of Scandinavian Women at the United Nations, 1946–66. In *Scandinavian Studies*, 6/22/2001, 8; Bok, Sissela: Alva Myrdal: A Daughter's Memoir. Addison-Wesley Publishing Company Inc., Massachusetts, 1991.

element more generally in the relationship of post-socialist and particularly Western European countries, as is visible for example in the discussions of new EU membership countries. For Finland these developments create a novel relationship with Russia. As has been discussed, until the end of the Cold War the relationship between the two countries was greatly asymmetrical, with the Soviet Union acting as the donor and Finland as the recipient – of information, cultural impact as well as political influence. The patterns of flow established by SCANET activities reverse this relationship as the representatives of the Nordic countries, including Finnish individuals, act as educators – the donors of knowledge – while Russian participants become its recipients. Other similar examples related particularly to monetary patterns of flow have emerged in the Finnish context in the post-Soviet era. One example of this are the programs initiated by Sitra, an impartial, legally regulated funding agency operating under the Finnish Parliament in association with the European bank of reconstruction and development (EBRD). The programs intend to develop capital investments in Russia with funds originating from Finland, Sweden and Norway, with the aim of helping "privatized healthy corporations to develop, to build international contacts and to survive through the period of economic transition while other corporate funding is nonexistent in Russia".[29] These patterns of flow, both of money and knowledge, embody a new spirit in the collaboration between Finland and Russia. For the first time in history, instead of being a continual and, at times, reluctant recipient, Finland has gained a hierarchically superior, even if occasional, position in an unequal relationship of giving and receiving between the two countries, thus also increasing its status in the new post-Cold War political and ideological order in relation to its former ruler.

Representing Universality

The finding that SCANET faculty is predominantly Northern induces important consequences for the creative space of human rights experts: its content becomes largely determined by individuals whose understanding of what constitutes universal substance matter originates from their own life experiences from the Northern countries. This empirical finding forms a troubling contrast to arguments that, although the human rights discourse may have a Western origin, today,

[29] Norum: 'Norum Oy EBRD:n pääomasijoittajana Venäjällä,' 2002, http://www.sitra.fi/index.asp?DirID=59&DocID=2676 (31.1.2005).

due to its expansive following, its practices embody global diversity. Simultaneously this finding gives rise to the question: from what domains does a context such as SCANET gain its legitimacy? How can it uphold the claim that, despite overt Northern emphasis of expertise, the knowledge distributed in its scope also empirically represents the universal mankind? This issue has been addressed by Immanuel Kant already in the 18th century in his classic piece 'The Idea of a Universal History with a Cosmopolitan Purpose'. In the essay Kant discusses the tendency of the North, or in his writings rather Europe, to see itself as embodying the universal essence of mankind that it then, with both legitimation as well as responsibility, distributes to others.[30] This notion has been since discussed by abundant scholars, of which a recent contribution relating to the argumentation of the European Court of Human Rights has been forwarded by Päivi Leino-Sandberg.[31] Similar ideas were visible in the already discussed instance in which a visiting SCANET expert compared human rights to the facts of natural sciences, asking "*so what if they are of Western origin?*"

As has been mentioned, in discussion SCANET experts often agree with the idea that human rights form a secular religion founded on Enlightenment thought, another origin emphasizing Western background. Thus many human rights scholars do not dispute the existence of such empirically observable Western actors and influences around the human rights discourse and phenomenon. Yet, they invest them differing significance: as human rights are in their *essential* significance construed to form an absolute truth, such external, empirically observable factors are not seen as constitutive to the legitimacy of the human rights phenomenon but instead as coincidental – as if Western actors had simply, through the various developments of history, stumbled across this truth first, and as a consequence it has become natural for them to distribute it to those still lacking it. Simultaneously instances can be observed from SCANET activities that suggest that experts also view the North as capable of embodying the universal in the Kantian spirit. This is reflected in the following example of SCANET student papers produced for one SCANET activity on the manner they

[30] Kant, Immanuel: 'The Idea of a Universal History with a Cosmopolitan Purpose.' In *Kant, Immanuel: Political Writings* (Ed. Reiss, Hans). Second enlarged edition. Cambridge University Press, Cambridge, 1991[1784], 41–53.

[31] Leino-Sandberg, Päivi: Particularity as Universality: The Politics of Human Rights in the European Union. The Erik Castrén Institute Research Reports 15, Helsinki, 2005.

addressed the geographic Other. For this analysis a sample of 15 papers, discussed already in Chapter 4 for their use of acronyms, was further studied to explore whether correlation emerged between the geographic origin of authors and the geographic area in which they focussed their inquiry. Overall surprisingly high correlation was found, meaning that most authors focused on the area of their own geographic origin. The most visible exception from this pattern were four papers by Nordic authors who discussed the problematic human rights conditions of the geographic, Non-European Other. The examined sample of papers featured no instances where students originating from the geographic, Non-European Other focussed on the problematic human rights conditions of the geographic North.

Instead two of the papers making most frequent reference to the geographic Other were both contributed by students originating from the same geographic area. Although this sample of six papers is small in quantity, these findings gain additional weight from the fact that as they were based on research conducted under the supervision of SCANET experts, they can thus be assessed to reflect the implicit assumptions about universal representativeness held by the supervisors. This analysis suggests that the supervising experts construed students originating from the geographic North to have greater possibilities to argue from the perspective of the universal, thus rendering them also well suited to discuss human rights conditions in the geographic Other. As students originating from the geographic Other were viewed to lack similar access to the universal, instead holding greater affinity to their geographic origin, the supervisors guided them to focus their research on their contexts of origin. It should, however, be noted that the ideology of the North as representing the universal is not necessarily exclusive to the field of human rights; Akhil Gupta and James Ferguson claim that they have discovered similar tendencies in the field of anthropology.[32]

Searching for Internal Actors

SCANET expert reactions to the above analysis on the geographic profile of expertise are twofold. On the one hand they may refrain from seeing its Northern emphasis as problematic, as they construe the experts' extensive knowledge of the international human right

[32] Gupta, Akhil & Ferguson, James (Eds.): Anthropological Locations: Boundaries and Grounds of a Field Science. University of California Press, Berkeley, 1997.

framework – assessed to entail universal assertions of universal human substance – to guarantee sufficient access to universal representation. On the other hand the Northern profile might become problematic, as it challenges the notion that the human rights phenomenon creates a forum of cross-cultural dialogue. Thus the described expert profile potentially undermines the phenomenon's global legitimacy. Concern over universal representation is a recurring feature of the human rights field, and it has given rise to ongoing efforts to find 'internal actors' from Other geographic regions to diversify the views of Northern actors. The term 'internal actor' derives from the works of Abdullahi Ahmed An-Na'im, who uses it to discuss the compatibility of the Islamic Sharia and international human rights norms. In these discussions he highlights the importance of actors who are both insiders of different cultures worldwide as well as have access to the expert discourse of human rights.[33] Although this notion sounds attractive, when applied to reality it becomes greatly more challenging. As has been phrased by Sally Engle Merry, since cultural boundaries are always porous, it becomes greatly difficult to determine who is an inside, who an outside actor.[34] She exemplifies this with a discussion from the UN Human Rights Commission in which a Nigerian woman discussed Nigerian widowhood rituals in a tenor Merry describes as "broad condemnation of rituals and cultural practices".[35] This led Merry to ask who the woman spoke for – did all the women in the villages condemn these practices – and to inquire into her work. Merry discovered that the woman was an educated urban woman, a lawyer fluent in English, living in a major urban centre and employed by a US-based human rights NGO. The widowhood rituals she described were a particular concern to women with her profile, as they faced such rituals after their husband's death. The rituals were commonly carried out by relatives who may have disliked the women's life choices or how the urban women had treated the rural relatives while the husband had been alive. Merry adds that in private discussion the Nigerian woman stated that village women do not really mind these rituals.[36]

---

[33] An-Na'im, Abdullah: 'State Responsibility Under International Human Rights Law to Change Religious and Customary Laws.' In *Human Rights of Women: National and International Perspectives* (Ed. Cook, Rebecca J.). University of Pennsylvania Press, Philadelphia, 1994, 167–188, 184.

[34] Merry: Human Rights & Gender Violence, *supra* note 20, 17.

[35] *Ibid.*

[36] *Ibid.*, 18.

Such factors problematise the concept of internal actor. Although a person may represent a certain geography, this does not necessarily translate to representation of an ideology or culture commonly held by people by a particular geographic area – a matter intensified by the fact that ideology and culture are seldom homogenous entities. This issue finds another illustration from the drafting of the UDHR and the writings of Charles Malik, an individual originating from Lebanon and commonly celebrated as representing the 'Middle-Eastern' voice in the negotiations.[37] He also holds a key role in narratives of the drafting efforts emphasizing that "participants came from all parts of the world".[38] Scrutiny of Malik's background and writings, however, challenges the notion that he represents an ideology reflecting the geographic Other of his origins: as has been mentioned, Malik was Harvard educated, and he lived extensively both in Europe and the US. Biographic sketches point out that he was a devoted Thomist, who during negotiations for the UDHR made vigorous attempts to incorporate references to God in the Christian significance into the text.[39] His thinking is more generally illustrated by the 1982 book titled 'A Christian Critique of the University'.[40] In the book Malik discusses the merits of the Western civilization, which he describes as being "*defined* by total fearlessness of and openness to the truth".[41] He celebrates the institution of the university as "more distinctive of Western civilization than any other",[42] and continues by noting how all non-Western universities have modelled themselves after Western universities while the reverse is not true.[43] Malik traces the origins of the University to the ancient Greeks, who to Malik

> More than any other people, displayed an irrepressible and unbounded passion for the exercise of reason and an incredible curiosity to investigate and know anything.

[37] Waltz, Susan: 'Universal Human Rights: The Contribution of Muslim States.' In *26 Human Rights Quarterly 4*, 2004, 799–844, 809.

[38] Alfredsson, Gudmundur & Eide, Asbjorn: 'Introduction.' In *The Universal Declaration of Human Rights: A Common Standard of Achievement* (Eds. Alfredsson, Gudmundur & Eide, Asbjorn). Kluwer Law International, The Hague, 1999, 11.

[39] Biography of Charles Malik, 2003, http://udhr.org/history/Biographies/biocm.htm (23.5.2003).

[40] Malik, Charles: A Christian Critique of the University. North Waterloo Academic Press, Illinois, 1987 [1982].

[41] *Ibid.*, 19.

[42] *Ibid.*, 15.

[43] *Ibid.*, 16.

Consequently "the university is nothing if it is not the home of free inquiry and unfettered curiosity".[44]

Malik wonders why non-Western universities may model themselves after Western universities, but not the reverse. To him,

> The reason is that these non-Western universities (and therefore their own native cultures which they themselves reflect) have not yet sufficiently caught the insatiable original Greek curiosity about all being: they are interested in others only to a degree; for the most part only utilitarianly, only to use them, only to learn from them.

Non-Western cultures

> Are not interested in knowing their essence, their being; they are for the most part wrapped up in themselves; the others are perhaps too strange, too forbidding for them; their original, natural, wholesome curiosity is somehow inhibited.[45]

Written at a time of communism, Malik compares Western and non-western societies by stating that

> Western scientific curiosity is so unquenchable [...] that the West is always complaining against the restrictions the communist and many noncommunist realms impose upon Western scholars and thinkers in their vicarious search for the truth of the histories of those countries and the contemporary conditions of their societies.[46]

Malik discusses the link between Western societies and the truth by stating that

> To the extent this civilization begins to harbor reservations about this fearlessness and this openness, it ceases to be itself; i.e., Western; and to the extent a society, any society, has developed fearlessness of and openness to the truth, it has become Westernized.[47]

He equates Christianity to the truth, discussing how "[a]n inhibition of original curiosity has blunted Soviet universities, for instance, the knowledge of Christianity". To summarize, Malik feels that

> This blunting, inhibiting virus has infected Western universities themselves with respect to the knowledge of Christianity

---

[44] *Ibid.*, 16–17.
[45] *Ibid.*, 18–19.
[46] *Ibid.*, 18–19.
[47] *Ibid.*, 19.

with the consequence that "[t]he non-West is gradually overpowering the West!".[48] These writings are disturbing, as they reflect notions of unilinear evolution found in early anthropological writings.[49] They also idealize Westerness in a manner that would cause uncomfort if presented by a drafter of the UDHR originating from the geographic West. Both these features challenge the notion that in his thinking Malik represents the geographic Other of his origins. Rather they resonate with the characterization of Frantz Fanon of a person with a 'Black Skin, White Masks', an expression he utilizes to describe particularly socially upwardly mobile and educated individuals of former colonies who have lost their native cultural originality and embraced the culture of the former colonizer.[50] Malik's writings suggest that instead of geographic origin, he views Westerness above all as an ideology. Such a definition has prominent consequences on the quest of internal actors in the human rights phenomenon: it portrays attention placed on geographic origin as misplaced, as focus appears more appropriately invested on the exploration of lifestyle choices and ideology held by individuals originating from diverse geographies.

SCANET Indigenous Expert

Also SCANET activities reflect efforts to include 'internal actors' of particularly indigenous peoples. As was mentioned, the observed SCANET activities featured six instances where Other participants belonged to the category of expert. Of these, three originated from Eastern Europe while the remaining three belonged to indigenous peoples: two to the Sami people of the Nordic region and one to indigenous peoples of North America. To inspect whether these Other expert can be held as legitimate 'internal actors' of their geographic Other origins emphasis is invested on issues of lifestyle and ideology. To begin with educational background, the SCANET Other expert backgrounds reproduce the pattern of Charles Malik of being educated

[48] *Ibid.*, 19.

[49] Maine, Henry: Ancient Law: its connection with the early history of society, and its relation to modern ideas. John Murray, London, 1861; Morgan, Henry Lewis: Ancient society. Edited by Leslie, A. Harvard University Press, Cambridge, 1964 [1877].

[50] Fanon, Frantz: Black Skin, White Masks. Grove Press, New York, 1967[1952].

in the geographic North; they have also all pursued their careers in settings that could be characterized as Northern, although some hold strong ties to their geographic place of origin. To explore lifestyle choices, an expert originating from an indigenous group and invited to SCANET activity as an expert on indigenous laws and ways of life merits closer attention. In personal discussion the expert shared details of her life that suggested it had not followed a typically 'indigenous' path:[51] after leaving her community of origin to attend a university located thousands of kilometres away, she had served in numerous consulting positions representing both her community of origin as well as indigenous communities more generally, but made no indication of having lived among her community of origin. Instead her present life was located at a distance of thousands of kilometres, and she had joined a religious sect that was characterized by a specific lifestyle and distinct culture stemming from white Anglo-American heritage. Indigenous members of the sect are highly uncommon. The expert had married another person belonging to the sect and they were raising their children into this religion instead of socializing them into the beliefs of the expert's indigenous background. While these lifestyle choices do not mean that the expert no longer holds an indigenous identity, they do give rise to questions of whether the people of her community of origin would accept her as an internal actor capable of representing their ways. The issue of representativeness, particularly by 'subaltern subjects', has been the topic of vast scholarship asking whether such participation by genuine 'others' is even plausible. Scholars have suggested that the very discourses utilized in such exchanges render real dialogue impossible.[52] In SCANET activities such discussions were not carried out, as the indigenous expert was unequivocally treated as representative of the ideology and customs of her indigenous community of origin.

---

[51] This analysis includes personal information that was not included in formal SCANET activities but instead derived from private discussions. As such discussions did not emerge with all Other experts, the following account presents a sketch from the background of one expert rather than a detailed analysis of the profile of all Other experts. As the purpose of this section is to illuminate features relevant for the present analysis, discussions on what indigenous lifestyle or indigenous identity could constitute of will not be pursued here.

[52] For an introduction into these debates, see the writings of Gayatry Chakravorty Spivak edited by Landry, Donna & Maclean, Gerald (Eds.): The Spivak Reader. Routledge, New York, 1996.

Gender of Expertise

The remainder of this chapter will explore the gender of SCANET expertise as well as how this can be connected to existing societal structures in Finland. For this examination the same five SCANET activities are analysed. In total both males and females are represented by 74 individuals. When participants are divided into experts and students, similar distinctions emerge to those identified in relation to geographic origin. The majority of experts, two thirds of 42, are male, whereas the majority of students, three in five of 106, are female (Table 27). When variables are connected to geographic categories, conspicuous becomes the asymmetry among Nordic experts originating from Finland, Sweden, Norway, Iceland or Denmark: whereas the 26 Nordic males account for three fifths of the 42 experts, the observed activities featured only one Nordic female expert. Also, whereas of all the 30 male experts almost nine of ten are Nordic, only one of the 12 female experts is Nordic (Tables 28 & 29).

These findings differ significantly from those of SCANET students. To begin with all participants, the portions of North males and females

Table 27: Gender

	MALE	% of category	FEMALE	% of category	TOTAL	% of category
EXPERTS	30	71%	12	29%	42	100%
STUDENTS	44	42%	62	58%	106	100%
TOTAL	74	50%	74	50%	148	100%

Table 28: Gender & Geographic Affiliation of SCANET PARTICIPANTS (N=148)

	NORTH	% of all (N=148)	OTHER	% of all (N=148)	TOTAL	% of all (N=148)
MALE	48	32%	26	18%	74	50%
FEMALE	58	39%	16	11%	74	50%
TOTAL	106	72%	42	29%	148	100%

Table 29: Gender & Geographic Affiliation of SCANET EXPERTS (N=42)

	N	of all (n=148)	of own (n=106/42)	of experts (n=42)	male	% of category	female	%
NORTH	36	24%	34%	86%	28	78%	8	22%
OTHER	6	4%	14%	14%	2	33%	4	67%
Nordic	27	18%	25%	64%	26	96%	1	4%

Table 30: Male Students (N=44)

	N	of all (n=148)	of own (n=106/42)	of all male (n=74)	of male students (n=44)	of students (n=106)
NORTH	20	14%	19%	27%	45%	19%
OTHER	24	16%	57%	32%	55%	23%

Table 31: Female Students (N=62)

	N	of all (n=148)	of own (n=106/42)	of all female (n=74)	of female students (n=62)	of students (n=106)
NORTH	50	34%	47%	68%	81%	47%
OTHER	12	8%	29%	16%	19%	11%

in SCANET activities resemble each other, as the 48 North males constitute one third of all the 148 SCANET participants and the 58 North females slightly more (Table 28). When only SCANET students are analysed, the portions again alter: whereas two thirds of the 74 female participants belong to the category of North students, only slightly more than one in four of the 74 males belong to the same category.[53] The 50 North females who participated in the analysed events constitute almost half of all the 106 students, whereas the 20 North males account for less than one fifth (Tables 30 & 31).

[53] Students are here not divided into North and Nordic, as the categories are primarily identical. This is due to the fact that most Northern students come from Nordic countries whereas experts are also invited from other locations.

"Nordic Female Experts Don't Exist"

The finding of the SCANET profile of expertise as distinctly masculine, with particular emphasis on Nordic males, is disturbing and requires closer investigation; how can the observed patterns be understood? I inquired about the scarcity of Nordic female experts in discussion with prominent SCANET experts in two separate instances. In both of them the reason given was identical: "*Nordic female human rights experts do not exist*". This statement is surprising, as examination of both early phases of the human rights phenomenon as well as its current operations suggest Nordic women to be active participants. Early involvement is demonstrated by the already mentioned analysis of Doris Linder, who emphasizes the role of Nordic women through the contributions of Bodil Begtrup of Denmark, Aase Lionaes of Norway, Ulla Lindström and Alva Myrdal of Sweden, and later the contributions of Helvi Sipilä of Finland. Of these Linder construes Bodil Begtrop to have held particular influence over the creation of the United Nations Commission on the Status of Women in 1946, as well as impacting the content of the UDHR on behalf of the interests of women.[54] Prior to the UN era, Paul Lauren highlights the strong involvement of many Nordic women in efforts to develop the social welfare state at the turn of the century.[55] These efforts reflect the active participation of women in the social reform efforts of the 1910s and 1920s in Northeast US; among others, women held key roles in the emergence of the feminist movement[56] as well as the settlement movement; Mina Carson recounts how at least half of the prominent US settlement houses were headed by women.[57]

[54] Linder: 'Equality For Women', *supra* note 28, 5, 8; see also Bok: Alva Myrdal, *supra* note 28.

[55] Lauren: The Evolution of International Human Rights, *supra* note 17.

[56] Cott, Nancy F.: The Grounding of Modern Feminism. Yale University Press, New Haven, 1987.

[57] Carson, Mina: Settlement Folk: Social Thought and the American Settlement Movement 1885–1930. Chicago University Press, Chicago, 1990. The same years also saw more general active participation of women in different domains of the society. According to Ross Wetzsteon, in the US over eight percent of physicians of the time were women, and over fifteen percent of PhDs obtained by the end of the 1910s were by a woman. Both of these figures as well as the percentage of women college students and professors declined in later decades, the last figure being greater in the 1920 than in 1960; see Wetzsteon, Ross: Republic of Dreams: Greenwich Village: The American Bohemia, 1910–1960. Simon & Schuster, New York, 2002, 163.

An overview of the current human rights phenomenon in Finland suggests that women participate actively in it also today. To offer merely a few examples, the current head of the division of human rights affairs at Finland's Foreign Ministry is a female, as is the head of the Finnish Red Cross. Of the board for the Finnish NGO foundation for human rights, only two out of eleven members are male while the remaining nine are female. Of the staff of the Finnish Amnesty International, 14 are female, including its acting executive secretary and the leader of human rights work, while only 4 are male; also the executive secretary of the Finnish League for Human Rights is female. In March 2006 a Finnish woman was nominated as the Deputy Executive Director for the United Nations Population Fund, a position mentioned by a Finnish newspaper as the highest position currently held by a Finn at the UN.[58] In June 2006 another Finnish woman was chosen as a judge for the European Court of Human Rights by the European Council.[59] Also the Finnish press features numerous instances in which females are denoted 'human rights experts'. These findings contrast with the statements of prominent SCANET experts of the non-existence of Nordic female human rights experts. The statement was also contrasted in numerous discussions. Upon being told that according to SCANET experts the lack of Nordic female experts in SCANET activities stemmed from their non-existence, two NAIL scholars commented in separate discussions that "*that is simply not true*". This sentiment was shared by a high-ranking former employer of the Finnish Foreign Ministry. The same conclusion came up in May 2007 in discussions for a conference program addressing the relationship of women's human rights and 'particularism'. The participating high-profile female NGO representative organizing the event was surprised by the statement, and commented instead that in the planning, she had great difficulty to think of male experts who could hold presentations in the conference.

These findings suggest that instead of a lack of Nordic women in the field of human rights, their scarcity in SCANET activities stems from collaborational patterns as well as a conception of expertise that excludes the competences of the women who participate in the human

[58] UNFPA News: 'Mari Simonen Named Deputy Executive Director of UNFPA,' 10.3.2006, http://www.unfpa.org/news/news.cfm?ID=759&Language=1. (18.12.2006).

[59] Ulkoministeriö: Päivi Hirvelä valittiin tuomariksi Euroopan ihmisoikeustuomioistuimeen, http://formin.finland.fi/Public/default.aspx?contentid=70377&nodeid=15145&contentlan=1&culture=fi-FI (27.6.2006).

rights phenomenon in Finland. As was discussed in Chapter 3, in SCANET operations NGO employees and activists, for example, are primarily not construed as experts. As I asked a prominent SCANET expert about the contributions of the mentioned Nordic female human rights actors in the early decades of the human rights phenomenon, she was unfamiliar with their work and instead viewed Nordic female pioneers to remain absent. When I explicitly asked her about the contribution of Helvi Sipilä, the expert stated that she did not view Sipilä primarily as a human rights expert, but instead placed her in the same category as the former UN Secretary General Dag Hammarsköld of UN officials. This formulation differs notably from the assessment of numerous other sources such as Doris Lindner who highlight Sipilä's contributions. It appears as unconventional not to regard her as a human rights expert, as such a characterization is otherwise commonly acceptable. To connect this finding to the profile of expertise, it illuminates the criteria by which a person gains expert status in SCANET; criteria that occasionally exclude individuals whose competences are in other contexts seen to translate to expert status.

Gender of Expertise in the Finnish Context

To explore why a tradition of female human rights expertise recognized in SCANET activities has not emerged, it is useful to place SCANET activities in the wider scope of the Finnish society and the role of women in the labour market as well as the academia. Despite Finland's high international profile as a leader in gender equality and women's rights, reality is more nuanced. The topic was visibly featured in the Finnish press in 2006 due to the 100-year celebration of women's suffrage in the country. In March 2006 the magazine of the University of Helsinki devoted the matter six pages, noting in the ingress how "[l]ong ago Finland was a pioneer of gender equality. Since then we have run out of steam". The article goes on to discuss how the leaders of the three largest political parties are all men, and to note how gender equality rests largely on "myths [...] referring to [...] first female ministers and other heroic women".[60] Although the election of Tarja Halonen as Finland's first female president in 2000 has been celebrated as a significant step toward even greater gender equality, various domains concur that during her two terms, power has increasingly

[60] Engelberg, Mila: 'Keskeneräinen tasavalta.' In *Yliopisto*, 6.3.2006, 14–19.

shifted from the president to the prime minister, a position which, with the exception of a few months, has been held exclusively by men. An article in Finland's largest newspaper from November 2006 continues the theme with a full-page story focussing on the public sector and listing hospitals, courts, the police, banks and numerous ministries among others that are by great majority led by males. The article highlights the prevalence of male leadership with a large photo of three women with the headline "May we introduce Finland's only female hospital district leader".[61] The privileged position of males is emphasized in the private sector, as for example the boards of a hundred largest Finnish corporations have in total 622 positions, of which less than one fifth are occupied by women.[62] Women continue to earn around 20 percent less than men for the same work in Finland, a gap that, contrary to most European countries, has not decreased over the past decade. Consequently, although spring 2007 saw the introduction of a greatly new egalitarian government with approximately half of the ministers female, in autumn 2007 close to 15 000 nurses, the vast majority women, threatened to resign from their jobs as a protest to their low wages and the continued unfulfilled promises by the public sector employer to upgrade their salary level.

These findings also characterize the Finnish academia, a domain a prominent SCANET expert characterizes as "traditionally quite masculine". In December 2006 a daily newspaper reported, based on the 'She Figures' study requested by the European Commission, that the proportion of women as professors in Finland is still low, accounting for only one fifth of all.[63] Another article from the University of Helsinki personnel magazine featured a four-page article titled 'Unwanted doctorates?', discussing the discrimination experienced by females while applying for university positions. The article notes how women are far more likely to hold temporary positions in universities than men, and offers statistics to support these claims: although in 2005 a total of 59% of all doctorates were obtained by women, only 25% of professors are women. The article continues by noting how today many female researchers despair even from applying for permanent positions, as

[61] Hakkarainen, Kaisa: 'Miehet johtavat korkeakouluja, sairaanhoitoa ja oikeudenjakoa.' In *Helsingin Sanomat* A4, 20.11.2006.

[62] Koponen, Kalle: 'Norjalaisten pörssiyhtiöiden hallituksiin tulee sukupuolikiintiöt.' In *Helsingin* Sanomat, B9. 30.12.2005.

[63] Kujala, Liisa: 'Naisia on yhä vähän professoreina.' In *Uutislehti 100*, 5.12.2006, 6; She Figures: 'Women and Science: Statistics and Indicators,' http://ec.europa.eu/research/science-society/pdf/she_figures_2006_en.pdf (27.12.2006).

they have lost all hope of securing them.[64] As one reflection of how wide these sentiments have spread was the December 2006 founding of an association called the Research Women of Helsinki, holding as its specific goal to remove gender inequality in scholarship. Remarkable in the association's founding was that instead of being a new creation, an association with the same name had existed also before, but its operations had been terminated as superfluous in the progressive spirit of the 1990s. Under the current circumstances its revival was perceived as essential – a correct conclusion if judged by the 250 membership applications the organization received during its first months of existence.[65]

Officially gender inequality has emerged as a paramount concern of Finnish academic life, as practically all academic funders require proposals for joint research ventures to entail explicit address on how the research careers of female scholars are to be assisted. Yet daily experiences within university life reinforce the notion that in practice, it continually forms a masculine domain where women are marginalised. This is exemplified by the following personal encounter from the auditing process at the University of Helsinki in autumn 2007 – a cryptic procedure, the outcome of which remains unknown to most personnel but which, it is feared, will find some reflection in funding patterns. I was invited to participate in the auditing session as a member of a three-person team, the two other members of which were male, to represent our research unit; we shared the hour-long session with another three-person, all male team. The auditing team was formed of four individuals, two males and two females. During the session, only the two male members of the auditing team spoke, one of them acting as the session's chair, whereas the two women made no vocal interventions. Instead one of them acted as a secretary and the other as a silent observer. Thus the hour-long session was predominated by the exchanges of the seven participating male members, none of whom had been assigned the role of silent observers, while my own comments became the sole contributions from females. Compared particularly to my earlier mass lecture experiences as a student at the same university where the vast majority of participants were females, this male dominance was striking: somehow, through the complex processes governing advancement in research careers, instead of transforming the silent

[64] Engelberg, Mila: 'Ei-toivottuja tohtoreita?' In *Yliopistolainen* 6/2006, 5–7.
[65] Helsingin tutkijanaiset, www.blogit.helsinki.fi/tutkijanaiset/ (14.3.2007).

mass of female students into active participants in later academic proceedings, women were still denoted the position of silent observers while patterns of vocal exchanges continued to be governed by men – in the lecture room by professors, in the auditing session by representatives of research units and members of the auditing team.

Why does gender inequality continue to exist in the Finnish academia? Various domains have been identified as responsible. Many commentators mention persistent attitudes and stereotypes of males as naturally prone to logical thought and thus well equipped for expert positions, and females as instinctive and less inclined for rational thinking. Another commonly identified source is the school system, which Finnish newpapers claim to "still pushes girls into a narrow women's mould".[66] Childhood experiences more generally have been highlighted by a recent polemic Swedish book by Liza Marklund and Lotta Snickare, who describe how Western mothers differentiate according to gender in the treatment they give to their children already in infancy, spoiling their sons rotten. They point a finger also at women themselves, namely their failure to assist each other – a mistake reflected in the book's title, borrowed from Madeleine Albright: 'There is a special place in Hell for women who don't help each other'.[67] Blame is commonly also invested on men and their discrimination of women from their positions of power. This is mentioned in the discussed newspaper article describing 'unwanted doctorates': men create 'old boy' networks and favour their friends unashamedly.[68] This finding was supported by a 2005 study of certain departments at the University of Helsinki, which discovered that female researchers held frequent sentiments of being marginalised while they felt that male researchers commonly received favouritism from male supervisors. This was reflected among others in opportunities to teach – a manifest expert function, as has been discussed in relation to SCANET. In her study Johanna Kantola found that whereas male researchers were encouraged to teach, female researchers had failed to receive similar encouragement.[69]

---

[66] Leino, Piia: 'Koulu työntää tytöt yhä ahtaaseen naisenmuottiin.' In *Uutislehti 100*, 25.8.2006, 9; Valtioneuvoston asetus lukiokoulutuksen yleisistä valtakunnallisista tavoitteista ja tuntijaosta. 955/2002, http://www.finlex.fi/fi/laki/ajantasa/2002/20020955 (3.6.2007).

[67] Marklund, Liza & Snickare, Lotta: Det finns en särsklid plats i helvetet för kvinnor som inte hjälper till varandra. Piratförlaget, Stockholm, 2005.

[68] Engelberg: 'Ei-toivottuja tohtoreita?', *supra* note 64.

[69] Kantola, Johanna: Mykät, kuurot ja kadotetut: Sukupuolten välinen tasa-arvo Helsingin yliopiston valtio-opin laitoksella. (Translation: The dumb, the deaf and the

Although empirical material is unavailable from the years leading up to the official formation of SCANET, numerous domains suggest that 'old boy' networks – likely formed on implicit collaboration instead of a premeditated design to exclude females – can be associated with SCANET conceptions of expertise. This can be construed as verified by the prominent SCANET expert who explained SCANET's origins by noting:

> It is primarily a question of new names and forms depending on the funding that is currently available. The funding proposals and outlines have in recent years favoured the formation of these kinds of academic networks through the Nordic region, and it is natural that this is the form the SCANET.

Thus, although the official structure of SCANET dates to the year 2000, the collaborational roots behind it are significantly longer, going back to the early 1990s. As is recalled, when describing the emergence of the human rights phenomenon in the Nordic countries, all the pioneers a prominent SCANET expert identified were male, whereas she omitted to mention female experts other sources had highlighted. This can be seen to have contributed to the emergence of a masculine profile of SCANET expertise which has been 'inherited' by the present generation of SCANET male experts from the earlier generation of pioneers. The conclusion on the importance of 'old boy' networks is also supported by an examination of an edited book from 1992 featuring numerous Nordic human rights scholars: although the list of contributors is highly masculine, with only four females among 27 authors, compellingly many contributing male authors have since assumed expert positions in SCANET while the same applies to none of the involved female authors.[70] Without empirical data it remains, of course, impossible to ascertain the other probable impacts contributing to this outcome – such conclusion would require additional examination of the career paths of the female authors who contributed to the book in question – yet this finding cannot be dismissed, as it provides yet another example of the male predominance of SCANET expertise.

---

lost: Gender equality in the Faculty of Political Science at the University of Helsinki) Acta politica 29. Yliopistopaino, Helsinki.. 2005; see also Faust, Maija: Vaatimusten ristipaineessa: Nuoret koulutetut naiset ja kilpailuyhteiskunta. TANE-julkaisuja 8, Tasa-arvoasiain neuvottelukunta, Sosiaali- ja terveusministeriö, Helsinki, 2006.

[70] Eide, Asbjorn et al. (Eds): The Universal Declaration of Human Rights: A Commentary. Oxford University Press, Oxford, 1992.

"The Next Generation Will be Different"

In discussion with SCANET experts the scarcity of North female experts was commonly accompanied with the statement that *"the next generation will be different"*. The ethos of this statement can be connected to the discussed desires that human rights education function as a potent tool for challenging existing oppressive structures. SCANET experts emphasize that they have made distinct efforts to recruit young female researchers and doctorate candidates, thus aiding their research careers. Yet these factors remain insufficient if not accompanied by mechanisms through which the current expert profile would change. Thus the mere increase of doctorates obtained by women fails to ensure that they come to occupy positions equivalent of SCANET expert in the future; as the above figures demonstrated, despite obtaining the majority of PhDs, women still form a significant minority of professors in Finland. These findings are compelling particularly due to the observed patterns of flow of Chapter 4, demonstrating how the SCANET learning curriculum also entails disempowering elements. To proceed in the analysis, it thus becomes vital to observe whether SCANET activities entail points of access that offer potential for change for the next generation of human rights experts. To explore this question through the concept of a community of practice, it becomes pivotal to investigate whether SCANET socializing processes, instead of reproducing the human rights expert community of practice as it is, embody elements that would cause the next generation to differ from the present one.

To find answers to these questions, patterns of flow observable at SCANET activities will be revisited. This analysis continues the study of Chapter 4 on speech acts, namely questions and answers, by inspecting the gender-specific patterns they give rise to, asking particularly whether they reproduce or alter the gender-specific profile of expertise as a masculine domain. The events analysed are constituted of five lectures which occurred in three sessions held during two days of a week-long SCANET activity. Based on the number, gender and status of participants, as well as the number of speech acts, the analysed sessions can be assessed as representative of the general speech patterns of SCANET activities, with the exception that three out of five lectures were held by female experts, a slightly higher than average portion.[71]

[71] I was a participant in the analysed activities, but did not join in the discussions. Thus my input is not reflected in the observed frequencies.

The discussions accompanied lectures that were intended for all SCANET activity participants. In addition to students, they were participated by the experts who were present in the SCANET activity at the time.[72] In total the discussions included 113 speech acts, of which 44 are questions, 56 answers and 13 comments (Table 32). The greater number of answers stems from instances where questions are provided for with more than one answer from different speakers; additional answers are marked as 'answer+'. As is expected, students have been more active in asking questions, accounting for four of five questions, while experts have offered more than nine of ten of answers. Comments, on the other hand, are more evenly divided, with students accounting for almost half of them. In all, experts have occupied a greater role in the discussion, accounting for three fifths of all speech acts (Table 32).

To assess speech acts in terms of gender, male experts come forth as more active, accounting for almost two fifths of all speech acts, while female experts account for one fourth (Table 32).[73] When the categories are explored closer, differences again emerge, as male experts portray a greater readiness in providing answers, offering more than three in five answers while female experts offer one in three. The patterns for asking questions reverses this, with female members asking one question in eight while male experts pose only one question in twenty, translating to two questions of the total of 44 (Table 32). Of these, one was made explicitly in the form "*I have a question to clarify*". To summarize, male experts offer answers twice as often as female experts, who in turn ask questions three times more often than males. The category of 'answer+' shows four instances for both male and female experts occurring in Lectures 1 and 2. Thus both male and female experts show activeness in substituting answers perceived as needing clarification. During Lecture 2, featuring both male and female lecturers, female experts have been particularly active, accounting for three fourths of 'answer+'. In Lecture 1, held by a female expert, there are three additional answers provided by male experts. This is conspicuous, as questions relate primarily to topics covered in the preceding lecture held by the female expert. In these instances additional answers have been offered by male experts to questions stemming from the

[72] For longer, 5–7 day activities, it is common for experts to stay only a part of the time, during which they mostly attend all sessions.

[73] The reviewed session included close to identical numbers of male and female experts present.

Table 32: Summary

	N	Students	% of category	Experts	% of category	Male Experts	% of category	Female Experts	% of category
Questions	44	36	82%	8	18%	2	5%	6	14%
Answer	56 (9 in answer+)	2 (1 in answer+)	4% (11% in answer+)	54 (8 in answer+)	96% (89% in answer+)	35 (4 in answer+)	63% (44% in answer+)	19 (4 in answer+)	34% (44% in answer+)
Comments	13	6	46%	7	54%	5	38%	2	15%
Total	113	44	39%	69	61%	42	37%	27	24%

lecture of female expert; an act that could be interpreted to signal that the answers provided by the female expert were not regarded by the male expert as sufficient. This could also be seen to undermine – intentionally or unintentionally – the authority of the female expert.[74]

Two noteworthy instances in the relationship of male and female experts can be added. The first concluded one of the analysed discussions. A female expert began to answer a question stemming from her lecture. The male expert chairing the session cut the female expert off by saying "*Don't go there, we will cover this topic in the afternoon session*". When this comment was made, the ongoing discussion had neared its finishing time and a great number of questions and answers had already ensued. Thus the intervention could be interpreted to stem from a desire to keep up with the desired schedule. Importantly, this intervention was not made in terms of time but rather of substance. Consequently it became an instance where the male expert established a hierarchy between himself and the female expert by setting limits on the authority of the female expert. As the female expert was not scheduled to lecture in the afternoon session, she would not be the one eventually answering the posed question. To assess the impact of this exchange for the role model of human rights expertise promoted by SCANET activities, decisive was the public nature of this intervention. It conveyed an impression of hierarchy over expertise, with a male expert setting the limits on the realm of the female faculty member's expertise. The second noteworthy instance emerged in a different SCANET activity, following a session in which a female expert had been commenting on student presentations. In a private exchange after the session, the female expert asked if she had talked too much. I said I did not think so. The female expert said that a male expert had told her during the session not to talk so much; her demeanour conveyed a sentiment of displeasure at the incident.

As an isolated incident the latter occurrence is insignificant. However, due to its unusual nature between mutually respecting experts in the prevailing academic climate of politeness, it gains noteworthy nuances, as the occurrence repeats the pattern where a male

---

[74] Here, reactions I received while presenting this point in a speech to the board of the Finnish Women Lawyers' association are noteworthy: the reactions from the audience suggested that this finding was not surprising but rather concurred with their everyday experiences with male colleagues. Of the male expert complementing the answers of a female expert, one audience member stated '*typical*'.

Table 33: Male Experts

	Total	%
Questions	2	5%
Answers	35 (4 in answer+)	83% (10% in answer+)
Comments	5	12%
Total	42	100%

expert establishes a hierarchy between himself and a female expert, effectively setting limits on the latter's sphere of expertise and participation to the SCANET activity in question.[75] To summarize this analysis on the profile of expertise observable in SCANET activities, the following conclusion can be drawn: an analysis of speech acts emphasizes the profile of expertise as a male domain. This is reflected in the greater portion of answers offered by males (Table 32) – more than four fifths of all speech acts forwarded by male experts in the examined sessions (Table 33). This promotes an image of male experts as assuming positions of authority in SCANET activities to emphasize their role as experts. The image of expertise as a male domain is strengthened by the reluctance of male experts to assume a 'student' role by seeking additional information in the form of asking questions. Female experts in their turn contribute to this impression primarily by their lesser activeness in overall participation in speech acts. Although more than two thirds of all speech acts by female experts are in the form of answer (Table 34), these answers constitute only one third of all answers (Table 32). Noteworthy is also the greater tendency of women to engage in speech acts constituted as questions, which account in total for slightly more than one fifth of all female expert speech acts (Table 34), while the same category for men accounts for only one twentieth (Table 33). To summarize, these findings could be

[75] Another interpretation of the incident is to place focus not on the gender but on expertise itself. In other words, that the male expert did not wish to limit the position of authority assumed by the female expert because of her gender but because of the *type* of her expertise. This interpretation emerges as plausible, as the male expert represented 'mainstream' human rights expertise while the female belonged to the group of NAIL experts; a difference that was reflected – in addition to their writings – in their lectures and comments.

Table 34: Female Experts

	Total	%
Questions	6	22%
Answers	19 (4 in answer+)	70% (15% answer+)
Comments	2	7%
Total	27	100%

Table 35: Students

	Total	%
Questions	36	84%
Answers	2 (1 in answer+)	5% (3% in answer+)
Comments	5	12%
Total	43	100%

interpreted to signal greater hesitancy by female experts to assume positions of authority.[76]

However, this model acquires additional nuances through the analysis of student speech acts, simultaneously offering new material for investigating the possibilities of SCANET activities to yield generational change. As has been mentioned, the great majority of student speech acts are in the form of questions, accounting for more than four fifths of both all student speech acts and all questions (Tables 32 & 35). For answers the portion of student speech acts is far smaller, constituting only one twentieth of all student speech acts and even less of all answers (Tables 32 & 35). However, of all the forwarded comments the portion of students is significant, accounting for almost half of them (Table 33). Although the weight of this category is somewhat diminished by the fact that it accounts only for one eight of all student speech

[76] An ironic parallel to this pattern emerged at the Finnish Women Lawyers' association: after my presentation, a chair was needed for the subsequent meeting. This proved significantly challenging, as both of the two candidates suggested demonstrated great reluctance to act as chairs, indicating that '*I have never been a chair, I don't know how I should act*' – a surprising sentiment coming from two professional women with decades of experts as lawyers. In the end a third person was selected.

Table 36: Comments (n=13)

	Expert	% of all	Student	% of all	Total	% of all
MALE	4	31%	2	15%	6	46%
FEMALE	2	15%	5	38%	7	54%
TOTAL	6	46%	7	54%	13	100%

acts (Table 35), its inspection is nevertheless crucial. When all comments are analysed, what arises as distinct is the great activeness with which female students have engaged in making them: they account for more than two fifths of all comments, while female experts and male students account for less than one fifth each, and male experts for the remaining third (Table 36). To connect this finding to the earlier offered characterization of comments as occupying a liminal position between student and expert status, the activeness of female students suggests readiness to experiment with expert positions, a tendency which has potential to translate into more concrete assumption of expert roles in the future. The temporal limits of this research allow no possibilities to follow this matter and to inspect whether the tendency to offer comments will later translate to a more expertly practice of providing answers. Yet this finding exemplifies one significant point of access through which patterns of flow could change as a consequence of SCANET activities.

Subjective Accounts on Human Rights Expertise

The last analysed element are subjective accounts on human rights expertise emerging in SCANET activities. During one of the examined SCANET activities, the topic of gender equality and the treatment of male and female students in their respective research environments came up in an informal discussion among female students. Upon being asked how they viewed gender relations and equality in SCANET, some discussion participants forwarded sentiments of inequality. One female student characterised this by stating that certain male students are selected as apprentices by their supervising male experts, which in practice offered them possibilities for advancement to expert status not offered in equal degree for female students: a sentiment reflecting the study mentioned earlier conducted at the University of Helsinki. Although no starkly contrasting sentiments emerged from the other participants in this discussion, many female students probably had differing experiences – after all, they had voluntarily chosen to pursue their studies in their respective settings, which would have been unlikely had they been entirely unsatisfied with the treatment they received from supervisors. Analysis of SCANET activities, nevertheless, offers subtle support for this subjective sentiment of gender inequality. Three examples illuminate this. In two of these, a student was promoted to expert status and in one, a scholar fulfilling the formal criteria set for SCANET experts assigned student status. The first example relates to a researcher who was invited into a SCANET activity as an expert despite of not having completed a PhD which, as has been discussed, is a customary prerequisite for expert status. Increasing the importance of this invitation was that the researcher was assigned the task of commenting on a number of student presentations based on PhD projects in different stages. Despite the researcher not having completed a PhD, the exchange accompanying student presentations followed the earlier discussed pattern of flow where knowledge moved in the form of comments from the commenting expert to the presenting student with no time allotted for dialogue. Thus, despite the lower formal academic merit of the visiting expert, the predetermined expert-student relationship was upheld.[77]

The second example derives from the already discussed expert meeting organized by SCANET featuring, in addition to SCANET experts, scholars and bureaucrats from different UN human rights offices, research institutes and government representatives. Although the academic and personal profiles of speakers varied – some had just concluded a master's degree and were beginning their professional careers while others had a doctorate degree and decades of professional and academic experience – for the present analysis relevant emerges that all participants were denoted experts status, reflected in unstructured patterns of flow and seating during the activity, as well as lack of predetermined terms accompanying speech acts. Thus instead of being 'raw data', all the presentations held at the meeting are construed as being received as entailing knowledge. Importantly for the present analysis,

[77] Despite not having a PhD, the researcher was highly accomplished in other respects measured, for example, in the number of publications in international journals. However, that such merits were judged to outweigh the lack of the customary formal requirement of a doctorate degree reinforces the importance of non-identifiable factors in determining who is and who is not perceived as a human rights expert.

speakers included one SCANET member who was currently working on a PhD and who on the SCANET website was enlisted in the category of students. Yet in this meeting, reflecting the status assigned to other participants, the student was assigned expert status. The third example depicts an instance where a person listed in the category of senior researchers on the SCANET website was assigned student status in SCANET educational activities. The researcher held a senior researcher position at the respective academic institution, had extensive teaching experience and had co-edited a book with one of SCANET experts. As the researcher had already obtained a doctorate degree, the SCANET presentation focussed on an ongoing post-doctorate research venture. This fact notwithstanding, the presentation was processed identically with PhD presentations: it was appointed two expert commentators, who took the customary time to offer comments without inviting the researcher to join in the discussion. Compared to average students the researcher was more active in offering comments in response, but nevertheless the overall framework established by SCANET experts for the presentation of the paper remained identical with the PhD ventures.

In the above examples the first two instances discuss male researchers while the last concerns a female. Although these incidents offer only glimpses of SCANET activities, they support the subjective sentiments of some female students that male students are offered avenues for expert positions not available to females. However, to complete this analysis, an auxiliary subjective element requires attention, namely the hesitance of females to assume expert positions which was already indicated by the analysis of speech acts. In the last of these three instances also the role of the female researcher was significant – after all, she chose to participate in the SCANET activity in the assigned position. This finding reinforces the earlier conclusion that the male profile of human rights expertise in SCANET activities is reproduced by both participating males and females. It is further probable that both genders are impacted by the stereotypical images of expertise and gender which Sally Engle Merry identifies to have been noted by the CEDAW Committee. She discusses how a treaty body expert noted that gender stereotypes in different countries "including the apparently most progressive Nordic ones" had proved extremely resistant to change.[78]

---

[78] Merry: Human Rights & Gender Violence, *supra* note 20, 75.

Conclusion

This examination of five SCANET activities has depicted the SCANET profile of expertise as predominantly Northern and masculine, whereas the profile of its students is characterized by Other males and Northern, particularly Nordic females (Table 37). Consequently SCANET activities emerge as a context where human rights knowledge – both 'ready' knowledge on the content of human rights documents as well as conceptions of instances where human rights knowledge is not ready and needs to be 'opened up' – flows from Northern males to Nordic females and Other males (Graph 14).

This finding reproduces models observable from other contexts where the white male is construed as having greater access to the position of universality from which to assess the condition and conduct of minorities. Here the analysis of Marianne Valverde of "law's dream of a common knowledge" is illustrative.[79] Valverde discusses an instance from a Canadian court in which homosexual indecent acts were addressed in courts, highlighting how sexual norms in the homosexual community differed from those of the predominant heterosexual community. She notes that the fact that "the investigating officers were all heterosexual was a fact brought out in cross-examination, but this was not interpreted as biassing the officers against gay men despite Greenspan's

Table 37: SCANET PARTICIPANTS (n=148)

	NORTH	% of all	OTHER	% of all	TOTAL	% of all
MALE STUDENTS	20	14%	24	16%	44	30%
FEMALE STUDENTS	50	34%	12	8%	62	42%
MALE EXPERTS	28	19%	2	1%	30	20%
FEMALE EXPERTS	8	5%	4	3%	12	8%
TOTAL	106	72%	42	28%	148	100%

[79] Valverde, Mariana: Law's Dream of a Common Knowledge. Princeton University Press, Princeton, 2003.

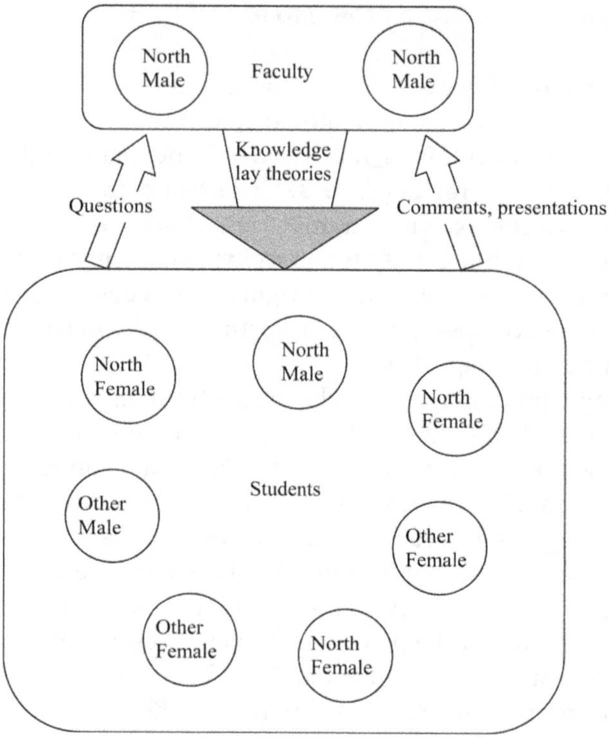

Graph 14: *SCANET Participants & Patterns of Flow*

strenuous efforts to demonstrate that they did not understand gay male sexual culture". She further elaborates how in the court proceedings these heterosexual witnesses "had no trouble discussing female and gay male sexual acts, and interpreting homosexual gestures for the court, with great authority". By contrast, the gay male community leaders "like any other representatives of exoticized minorities, had to take a more humble epistemological standpoint. They could only speak about themselves and their own community".[80] This brought forth a circumstance where "the heterosexual male officers were able to testify from a universal position about gay men, women strippers, and sexual difference in general," whereas "the defence had no possibility of challenging such universal statements by counter-universals; it could only offer the particularistic minority view of gay community members".[81]

---

[80] *Ibid.*, 69.
[81] *Ibid.*, 70.

SCANET activities entail similar features. This is illustrated by the manner in which the already discussed indigenous expert, the 'internal actor', was incorporated into informal SCANET activities, more specifically a dinner following a day of formal activities organized in the regular seminar room setting. By contrast, the dinner was organized in a teepee-like construction erected in the middle of a mountainous scenery about half a kilometre outside the regular activity venue. The dinner was casual, with participants enjoying bowls of soup around a fire, seated on long benches covered in fur. During dinner the expert was invited to share ancestral stories for participants, an activity that resonated with familiar romanticized stereotypes of indigenous pasttime activity. No other experts in SCANET activities were requested to share knowledge of the traditional ways of the people from which they originated by engaging in practices reflecting similar stereotypes. Although the stories of ancestral ways were received with interest by other participants, they simultaneously produced puzzlement and reservation; questions were raised concerning their purpose. Certainly they served to emphasize the difference between this expert of the geographic Other and those representing the geographic North. It could be argued that they made the indigenousness of the expert more tangential to SCANET participants by depicting her as more 'exotic'.[82] Whatever the motivations, this instance served to strengthen the 'particular' identity of the expert: instead of participating in SCANET as a representative of universal mankind alongside other experts, such treatment suggested that her indigenous origin rendered her unsuited for such a position, reducing her realm of expertise instead to the domain of her particular background. This finding is reinforced by the fact that during lectures, numerous prominent SCANET experts held also lectures relating to the position of indigenous peoples whereas the indigenous expert was not invited in to hold lectures on general human rights issues. This contrast reinforced the impression that whereas the experts originating from the North held the kind of competence that allowed them possibilities to move between the 'particular' issues of

[82] This is reminiscent of the criticism Thomas Hyllend Eriksen has forwarded on the concept of culture utilized by UNESCO, noting how "being exotic or different in the eyes of "we" of *our* creative diversity does not qualify for being "cultural" in an analytic sense"; see Eriksen, Thomas Hyllend: 'Between universalism and relativism: a critique of the UNESCO concept of culture.' In *Culture and Rights* (Eds. Cowan et al.). Cambridge University Press, Cambridge, 2001, 127–148, 131.

indigenous groups and the 'general' issues of universal mankind, the indigenous expert lacked insight on universal mankind and instead for SCANET activities only the expertise she held of her particular context was construed as relevant.

Radical feminists have contested the idea that the physical body has an automatic link to ideological representativeness; they have challenged the idea that representation of feminist perspectives requires the participation of biological female bodies. Instead they argue that ideology is disengaged from the physical body and focus on such physicalities is misdirected.[83] These findings could be forwarded to challenge the significance of this chapter's findings – why should it be relevant if the SCANET conception of expertise represents particularly Northern males? Why would this automatically mean that the knowledge distributed in the scope of SCANET would not be representative of universal mankind according to the ideal of the human rights discourse? This analysis does not contest or confirm such claims, as its intent is differently guided. Instead of focussing on issues of representation – perhaps it is plausible that the Northern male experts of SCANET have access to feminist as well as 'Other' epistemologies – it focusses on the structures formed by the patterns of flow identified in SCANET activities. The primary conclusion of this analysis is the manner in which the SCANET conceptions of learning, knowledge and expertise reproduce, rather than provide a radical break from, the very structures of inequality of geographic origin and gender that the human rights discourse attempts to challenge. What becomes salient is how somehow over the past decades, through mechanisms that remain beyond the reach of this analysis, as the systemic agency of human rights experts has become increasingly societally influential and prestigious as well as the subject of professionalization, this position has ended up being occupied by the identical demographic group that is also globally most privileged. This finding forms a stark contrast between human rights in the abstract and in action: whereas in the abstract the discourse is a potent tool of societal change, in the SCANET context it is on the level of action transformed into a tool for reproducing and maintaining the status quo.

It could, of course, be argued that the patterns of flow identified here are not grave enough to warrant cause for dramatic interpretations; the

[83] See for example Butler, Judith: Bodies that Matter: On the Discursive Limits of "Sex". Routledge, London, 1993.

SCANET profile of expertise will hardly become the source of massive human rights violations such as genocide and thus these patterns could be viewed as insignificant in the global mission to advance human rights. While this is true, these findings cannot be dismissed lightly for, as was discussed, for example the gender bias of the Finnish academia continues to provide a source of upset and real life consequences as large quantities of female researchers repeatedly fail to reach their desired career objectives. Six decades after the adoption of the UDHR also the profile of human rights expertise in such an educational context as SCANET has become masculine, with hopes that the next generation 'will be different'. The matter is aggravated by the desires commonly invested in international collaboration that they could transgress such 'particular' features as prejudice and stereotypes, and thus induce for example greater gender equality. Unaccompanied by empirical research testing such optimistic notions, these hopes glorify the domain of international collaboration as a space realizing abstract ideals unburdened by the inequalities, personal biases and prejudices which prevent their realization in 'local' circumstances. This analysis has demonstrated that although the transnational SCANET activities are organized with the intent to contribute to the greater realization of the emancipatory potential of the abstract human rights discourse, its operations have refrained from realizing it. Instead the activities have come to embody the structural biases and inequalities observable in its participant countries, thus reproducing also elements of the civilizing mission.

CONCLUSIONS

Since World War II, the human rights discourse has become synonymous with global good will and promises of a brighter tomorrow. The adoption of the UDHR has come to symbolize a moment when political differences were laid aside and the interests of humanity given centre stage. Against the horrors of World War II, this moment has become a source of assurance that no similar atrocities could ever occur; that as long as people revere the equal value of others, the world will become a better place. No researcher focussing on human rights should allow herself to overlook these sentiments. Simultaneously it is vitally important to explore how these abstract ideals are realized in practice. This study has explored human rights in action in SCANET, a loose network of human rights experts and scholars from the Nordic and Scandinavian region. Through exploration of SCANET educational activities, this study has examined the conceptions of expertise, learning and knowledge created by its patterns of flow. The wider context of this study has been provided by the transformation of values in the Finnish society in the post-World War II era through the diminishment or alteration of religious sentiment; the same era has seen the continual increase of adherence to the human rights discourse. This has led the discourse to move from the *periphery* of the Finnish society to its *centre*. Adherence to the human rights discourse has come to mark the abandoning of old ideologies and the embracing of new ways of thinking. This likewise applies to the state level as human rights are emphasized in policy-making and international relations. Combined with the other political changes particularly after the end of the Cold War, the increased centrality of the human rights discourse coincides with a phase of Finnish history where its desired ideological proximity to the West has continually gained strength over its former connections to the East.

One of the decisive cultural accelerators of the human rights phenomenon pulling people into its incipient community is the radical transformative potential of the human rights discourse. Through its devotion to the equal worth of all, the discourse promises to challenge old oppressive structures and to liberate the individual from them. The paramount tool to realize these desires is commonly construed as human rights education, which renders individuals conscious of the oppression they face and thus empowers them. This promise acquires a distinct meaning in Finland against the legacy of Lutheran ministers acting as educators for the general population; a tradition that embodied a strongly engraved notion of learning as the adoption of knowledge, as well as a strict separation of individuals into those who have divine knowledge and those who lack it. This established a predetermined and rigidly upheld structure between the two groups, subjecting laymen to the authority of the experts. Research has demonstrated how schools utilizing the class-room learning format, in Finland and elsewhere, end up reproducing a similar conception of learning. Through it knowledge becomes conceptualized as 'ready', as a gift bestowed from those holding it to those who are without it. Simultaneously expertise is defined as the individual mastering of skill and knowledge, instead of the result of collaborational activity by a community of practice.

Such conceptions of expertise and learning have been described as particularly ill-suited for human rights education as they stigmatize participants into predetermined positions, and make the outcome of the learning process static instead of empowering. This analysis has identified that these conceptions are applicable to SCANET educational activities, which are characterized by predetermined patterns of flow and the separation of participants into faculty who hold 'knowledge' and students for the benefit of whom knowledge is to be distributed. This finding challenges the capacity of SCANET activities to reproduce the community of practice of human rights experts. Whereas the SCANET learning curriculum teaches its students how to utilize the human rights discourse in their texts, the activities delimit student possibilities to learn to talk as experts, thus restricting the emergence of new identities of mastery. Although SCANET activities render parts of expert knowledge practices transparent, they also leave elements opaque. Consequently the activities entail aspects of socializing their students to become 'expert learners' instead of full members in the expert community.

The importance of these findings was emphasized by the SCANET expert profile, which is characterized by the global North, whereas its students portrayed more diverse alignment. Also, whereas the SCANET faculty is by majority male, SCANET students are by majority female. The SCANET faculty is by contrast formed predominantly by Nordic males, while Nordic females are virtually absent. Nordic females, on the other hand, form the majority of SCANET students whereas Nordic males account for a minority. Thus Nordic males are more likely to participate in SCANET as experts than students. These findings become problematic when connected to oppressive global and local patterns. On the global level troubling becomes the legacy, articulated by the Mandates Commission of the League of Nations, where the 'civilized' world needs to educate the 'uncivilized' world in order to ensure the development and the general well-being of its population, the 'minors not yet able to stand by themselves'. The Nordic countries have an additional legacy for providing education through missionary work by the Lutheran church and, although terminology has changed, SCANET activities entail commonality with these practices. This becomes accessible through scholarship on gifts and exchanges: the transfer of knowledge in SCANET activities moves from faculty to students, which forms an asymmetrical donor-recipient relationship. Scholars have discussed how on the global level such relationships condemn under-privileged global domains, Other countries, to an ambiguous peripheral relation with existing institutions, which induces paralysing effects. This depicts the result of SCANET educational activities again as static instead of empowering, and from this perspective the SCANET profile of expertise and the patterns of flow of its activities form 'part of the problem' the human rights discourse attempts to combat in the abstract.

On the 'local' level problematic becomes the gender of expertise. Here the examined SCANET expert profile gains significance from the wider context of gender relations in Finland and the claims that Finland is a country governed by a poorly realized myth of gender equality. The reality is labelled by male dominance of the public and the private sectors as well as the lower wage levels of women. Gender discrimination plagues many women in the Finnish academia, and despite the fact that today women obtain the majority of doctorate degrees, professors are continually predominantly men. Instead of forming a radical challenge to this structure, SCANET activities reproduce it, and form another contrast to the egalitarian ethos of the abstract human rights discourse. Prominent SCANET experts argue that Nordic female experts do not exist, and emphasize that 'the next generation will be different'. Examination of human rights action in Finland suggests women, by contrast, to be highly active in it. Thus their exclusion from SCANET faculty reflects a distinct conception of expertise held by prominent SCANET experts as well as the collaborational relations formed by its male experts. The argument that the next generation will bring change becomes problematic due to the static elements of the SCANET learning curriculum, rendering dramatic structural change unlikely. Also, why, six decades after the Universal Declaration, should change occur only with the next generation? Why has the male profile of Nordic human rights experts emerged in the first place? These questions gain further importance from the examination of the work by Nordic female actors around the adoption of the Universal Declaration, as well as the strong participation of women in social reform efforts at the beginning of the 20th century. Why has this failed to translate into a well-established legacy of Nordic female human rights experts in SCANET? This analysis has outlined as possible sources for this outcome persistent gender stereotypes, the failure of women to assist each other, their subjective reluctance to assume positions of authority, as well as discrimination and the 'old-boy' networks formed by men.

Importantly, the SCANET profile of expertise and the pattern of knowledge flowing primarily from Northern males to Northern females and Other males finds parallels in the predominant visual imagery of Christianity: in it centre stage is likewise occupied by a white male, whereas the periphery is occupied by women, children, the elderly and the representatives of 'the Others': members of different races as well as hideous heathen figures and the gloomy shadows of doomed souls. Instead of being altered, this visual image has become reproduced in SCANET activities. Most SCANET experts are probably unconscious of this pattern, and may question its relevance, as experts include secularists and members of different faiths. For this study the patterns created by Christianity gain significance from their role as central cultural features in the Finnish society. The legacy of Lutheran ministers acting as educators is further seen as giving rise to another relevant cultural characteristic: the conception that the knowledge disseminated by experts represents *the truth*. In the past the most influential systemic agency of expertise was in Finland largely occupied by Lutheran ministers, who were among the most revered and influential members of society. During the previous decades their position has altered, as instead of reverence, the private lives of ministers have emerged as central sources of 'scandals' sought after by the Finnish tabloid papers. This development has resulted in a vacuum of public role models.

It is overstated to claim this position to be filled by human rights experts. Yet in the Finnish media human rights experts are portrayed as persons of high moral integrity who are committed to reform the world; as individuals to whom others should look up to. Simultaneously the systemic agency of human rights experts has gained greater influence. They are consulted by representatives of the Lutheran church as well as by free-thinkers; by interest groups, policy-makers and laymen. Instead of providing 'points of view', human rights experts are treated as arbitrers of *truth*. This position stems from the continual expansion of the human rights discourse which has transformed human rights into 'free-floating signifiers', concepts that can be filled with any meanings a speaker wishes. This expansion has assigned the systemic agency of experts pivotal importance. To prevent the discourse from becoming synonymous with everything and nothing, the conceptions of experts have become trumps, as offering the truth of what human rights *really* are. However, as has been discussed through the complex relationship of human rights and law, in reality, no one - not even experts - knows exactly what human rights are: on the one hand, they are law, on the other, they are the reason for law. As was demonstrated by arguments of legality and legitimacy in SCANET activities, experts introduce human rights knowledge as being both 'ready' and as unfinished, in need of being 'opened up' so that the missing elements can be incorporated into it.

These latter instances give rise to what has been described as the *creative space* of human rights experts. Through it human rights experts, in SCANET activities members of faculty, incorporate into the body of human rights knowledge elements that they construe vital, yet missing from it. These processes transform the position of an expert into that of an activist. This shift is decisive, as in the Finnish context the status of experts is commonly higher than that of advocates: whereas the latter are construed as biassed by their particular interests, experts are seen to represent solely the interests of universal mankind. Consequently it becomes paramount to explore from what domains the experts acquire their understandings of what the truth about human rights is. This study has demonstrated SCANET expert backgrounds to be characterized by professional and academic experience in law. By contrast, absent were mentions of backgrounds that could be interpreted to provide familiarization with other cultures and ideologies: training in anthropology, studies in different religions, history, philosophy and linguistics among others, as well as experiences of having lived in countries different from one's origin for lengthy periods of time. As the SCANET expert profile represents particularly the global

North, this introduces the question of where they derive knowledge on ways of life differing radically from their own.

This analysis identified as pivotal source of information the lay theories held by experts, meaning the informal and commonsense explanations people give for particular social behaviours. Consequently SCANET experts were portrayed in a contrasting manner: in regards to the body of human rights documents they are experts, but in their understanding of unfamiliar ways of life they remain laymen. This fact is overlooked in instances where human rights experts are called upon as arbiters of truth. Yet it imposes vital consequences on the transparency of the human rights phenomenon, as the existence of the creative space is seldom acknowledged; it has been noted how human rights experts themselves are 'looking for politics everywhere but in the humanitarian vernacular'. Instead of subjecting the beliefs and knowledge practices of experts to empirical analysis, also most anthropologists treat them as individuals providing *knowledge* rather than *data*. This study has approached the human rights phenomenon in Finland as, above all, forming an ideology: a secular religion which entails the aspiration to emancipate the individual inquisitive mind from oppressive structures and religious authority. In action, SCANET educational activities end up reproducing structures and cultural features which are construed as troubling for example in the operations of the Finnish Lutheran church. These findings challenge the notion that the action generated by the abstract human rights discourse could realize the discourse's radical transformative potential in practice. Human rights experts are today increasingly elevated as occupying a moral high ground over laymen. To avoid such elevation from translating into 'the dictatorship of the virtuous', continued critical research is required. This study hopes to contribute to an outcome where human rights action is increasingly subjected to empirical analysis starting from the level of actual practice - from the ground up - instead of from the reverence that the human rights discourse awakens in the abstract.

BIBLIOGRAPHY

AAA (1999): Declaration on Anthropology and Human Rights. http://www.aaanet.org/committees/cfhr/index.htm (2.12.2003).

AAA (1947). American Anthropological Association. 'Statement on Human Rights.' In *49 American Anthropologist 4,* 539–543.

Adams, Francis & Sanders, Barry (2003): Alienable Rights: The Exclusion of African Americans in a White Man's Land 1619–2000. Harper Collins Publishers, New York.

Akhavan, Payam (2001): 'Beyond Impunity: Can International Criminal Justice Prevent Future Atrocities.' In *95 American Journal of International Law 1,* 7–31.

Alexy, Robert (1985): Theorie der Grundrechte. Suhrkamp, Baden-Baden.

Alfredsson, Gudmundur & Eide, Asbjorn (1999): 'Introduction.' In *The Universal Declaration of Human Rights: A Common Standard of Achievement* (Eds. Alfredsson, Gudmundur & Eide, Asbjorn). Kluwer Law International, The Hague, 5–16.

Alston, Philip (1988): 'Making Space for New Human Rights: The Case of the Right to Development.' In *1 Harvard Human Rights Yearbook 3,* 3–40.

Alston, Philip & Crawford, James (2000): Human Rights Reform in the 21th Century. Cambridge University Press, Massachusetts.

American Journal of International Law (2002): 'Agora: Military Commissions.' In *96 American Journal of International Law 2,* 320–364.

The American Law Institute Seventy-fifth Anniversary 1923–1998 (1998). The American Law Institute, Philadelphia & Pennsylvania.

Anderson, Benedict (2003 [1983]): Imagined Communities: Reflections on the Origin and Spread of Nationalism. Revised Edition. Verso, London.

Andreopoulos, George J. (1997): 'Human Rights Education in the Post-Cold War Context.' In *Human Rights Education for the Twenty-First Century* (Eds. Andreopoulos, George J. & Claude, Richard Pierre). Pennsylvania University Press, Pennsylvania, 9–20.

Andreopoulos, George J. & Claude, Richard Pierre (Eds.) (1997): Human Rights Education for the Twenty-First Century. Pennsylvania University Press, Pennsylvania.

—— (1997) 'Preface.' In *Human Rights Education for the Twenty-First Century.* (Eds. Andreopoulos, George J. & Claude, Richard Pierre). Pennsylvania University Press, Pennsylvania, xix–xxii.

Anghie, Antony (2005): Imperialism, Sovereignty and the Making of International Law. Cambridge University Press, Cambridge.

An-Na'im, Abdullah (1994): 'State Responsibility Under International Human Rights Law to Change Religious and Customary Laws.' In *Human Rights of Women: National and International Perspectives* (Ed. Cook, Rebecca J.). University of Pennsylvania Press, Philadelphia, 167–188.

Arat, Zehra F. Kabasakal (2006): 'Forging A Global Culture of Human Rights: Origins and Prospects of the International Bill of Rights.' In *28 Human Rights Quarterly 2,* 416–437.

Barnett, H. G. (1938): 'The Nature of Potlatch.' In *40 American Anthropologist 3,* 349–358.

Bartholomew, Dean & Levi, Jerome M. (Eds.) (2003): At the Risk of Being Heard: Identity, Indigenous Rights, and Postcolonial States. The University of Michigan Press, Ann Arbor.

Bassiouni, M. Cherif & Blakesley, Christopher L. (1992): 'The Need for an International Criminal Court in the New International World Order.' In 25 *Vanderbilt Journal of Transnational Law,* 151–182.

Baxi, Upendra (1997): 'Human Rights Education: The Promise for the Third Millennium?' In *Human Rights Education for the Twenty-First Century* (Eds. Andreopoulos, George J. & Claude, Richard Pierre). Pennsylvania University Press, Pennsylvania, 142–154.

Benhabib, Seyla (2002): The Claims of Culture: Equality and Diversity in the Global Era. Princeton University Press, Princeton.

Blomstedt et al. (1988): Suomen Historia, osa 8: Paasikiven aika, Kekkosen aika, taloudellinen kasvu ja yhteiskuntamurros, massakulttuurin maihinnousu, taistelut kulttuurista. Weilin Göös, Espoo.

Bloed, Arie (Ed.) (1993): The Conference on Security and Cooperation in Europe: Analysis and Basic Documents, 1972–1993. Dordrecht, Boston & London.

Bok, Sissela (1991): Alva Myrdal: A Daughter's Memoir. Addison-Wesley Publishing Company Inc., Massachusetts.

Bourdieu, Pierre (2007 [1972]): Outline of a Theory of Practice. Cambridge University Press, Cambridge.

Boyle, Alan & Anderson, Michael (Eds.) (1996): Human Rights Approaches to Environmental Protection. Clarendon Press, Oxford.

Boyle, James (1985): 'Ideals and Things: International Legal Scholarship and the Prison-House Language.' In 26 *Harvard International Law Journal*, 327–359.

Brenneis, Don (2006): 'Reforming Promise.' In *Documents: Artifacts of Modern Knowledge* (Ed. Annelise Riles). The University of Michigan Press, Ann Arbor, 41–70.

Brett, Rachel (1997): 'Non-Governmental Action in the Field of Human Rights.' In *An Introduction to the International Protection of Human Rights* (Eds. Hanski, Raija & Suksi, Markku). Åbo Akademi University, Åbo, 399–413.

Brettel, Caroline B. (Ed.) (1993): When They Read What We Write: The Politics of Ethnography. Bergin & Garvey, Connecticut.

Bring, Ove (2003): 'Dag Hammarskjöld and the Issue of Humanitarian Intervention.' In *Nordic Cosmpolitanism: Essays in International Law for Martti Koskenniemi* (Eds. Petman, Jarna & Klabbers, Jan). Brill Academic Publishers, Leiden, 485–518.

Butler, Judith (1993): Bodies that Matter: On the Discursive Limits of "Sex". Routledge, London.

Byers, Michael & Nolte, Georg (Eds.) (2003): United States Hegemony and the Foundations of International Law. Cambridge University Press, Cambridge.

Carr, E. H. (2001 [1939]): The Twenty Years' Crisis 1919–1939: An Introduction to the Study of International Relations. Palgrave, Hamsphire.

Carson, Mina (1990): Settlement Folk: Social Thought and the American Settlement Movement 1885–1930. Chicago University Press, Chicago.

Cassese, Antonio (2005): International Law. Second Edition. Oxford University Press, Oxford.

Cassin, René (1972): La pensée et l'action. F. Lalou, Boulogne-sur-Seine.

Chomsky, Noam (1998): 'The United States and the challenge of relativity.' In *Human Rights Fifty Years on: A Reappraisal* (Ed. Evans, Tony). Manchester University Press, Manchester, 24–56.

Cook, Rebecca J. (Ed.) (1994): Human Rights of Women: National and International Perspectives. University of Pennsylvania Press, Philadelphia.

Cooper, John Milton Jr. (2001): Breaking the Heart of the World: Woodrow Wilson and the Fight for the League of Nations. Cambridge University Press, Cambridge.

Cott, Nancy F. (1987): The Grounding of Modern Feminism. Yale University Press, New Haven.

Cottrell, Robert C. (2000): Roger Nash Baldwin and the American Civil Liberties Union. Columbia University Press, New York.

Cowan, Jane (2006): 'Culture and Rights after Culture and Rights.' In *108 American Anthropologist 1*, 9–24.

Cowan, Jane K.; Dembour, Marie-Bénédicte & Wilson, Richard A. (2001): 'Introduction.' In *Culture and Rights* (Eds. Cowan, Jane K.; Dembour, Marie-Bénédicte & Wilson, Richard A.). Cambridge University Press, Cambridge, 1–26.

Craven, Matthew (1995): The International Covenant on Economic, Social, and Cultural Rights: A Perspective on Its Development. Oxford University Press, New York.

Dean, Bartholomew & Levi, Jerome M. (Eds.) (2003): At the Risk of Being Heard: Identity, Indigenous Rights, and Postcolonial States. The University of Michigan Press, Ann Arbor.

Denscombe, Martyn (1982): 'The "Hidden Pedagogy" and Its Implications for Teacher Training.' In *3 British Journal of Sociology of Education 3*, 249–265.

Derrida, Jacques (1984): 'Declarations of Independence', first published in French in Otobiographies: L'enseignement de Nietzsche et la politiqua du nom propre. Galiée, Paris. Reproduced in *Negotiations: Interventions and Interviews 1971–2001*. Stanford University Press, Stanford, 2002, 46–54.

Dezalay, Yves & Garth, Bryant G. (1996): Dealing in Virtue: International Commercial Arbitration and the Construction of a Transnational Legal Order. The University of Chicago Press, Chicago.

Donnelly, Jack (2003): Universal Human Rights in Theory & Practice. Second Edition. Cornell University Press, Ithaca.

(1985): The Concept of Human Rights. Croom Helm, London.

Dresler, Carolyn & Marks, Stephen (2006): 'The Emerging Human Right to Tobacco Control.' In *28 Human Rights Quarterly 3*, 599–651.

Dumont, Louis (1986): Essays on Individualism: Modern Ideology in Anthropological Perspective. The University of Chicago Press, Chicago.

Dworkin, Ronald (1977): Taking Rights Seriously. Harvard University Press, Cambridge.

Eichelberger, Clark M. (1977): Organizing for Peace: A Personal History of the Founding of the United Nations. Harper & Row Publishers, New York.

Eide, Asbjorn et al. (Eds) (1992): The Universal Declaration of Human Rights: A Commentary. Oxford University Press, Oxford.

Engle, Karen (2001): 'From Skepticism to Embrace: Human Rights and the American Anthropological Association from 1947–1999.' In *23 Human Rights Quarterly 3*, 536–559.

Eriksen, Thomas Hyllend (2001): 'Between universalism and relativism: a critique of the UNESCO concept of culture.' In *Culture and Rights* (Eds. Cowan, Jane K., Dembour, Marie-Bénédicte & Wilson, Richard A.). Cambridge University Press, Cambridge, 127–148.

Ervasti, Kaius (2007): Tuomioistuimet ja oikeuslaitos tutkimuksen kohteena: lähestymistavan valinta. http://www.comi.fi/tiedostot/seminaari_2007_02_26_ervasti.pdf (5.6.2007).

Ervo, Laura: 'Förhållandet mellan Europadomstolen och nationella domstolar – findländska perspektiv.' In *JFT 4/2006*, 411–422.

European Journal of International Law (2003): Symposium: 'A War against Terrorism': What Role for International Law? US and European Perspectives. In *14 European Journal of International Law 2*, 209–379.

Evans, Tony (1998): 'Power, hegemony and HR.' In *Human Rights Fifty Years on: A Reappraisal* (Ed. Evans, Tony). Manchester University Press, Manchester, 1–23.

—— (1996) US Hegemony and the Project of Universal Human Rights. MacMillan Press Ltd, Houndmills, Basingstoke, Hampshire and London.

Fanon, Frantz (1967): Black Skin, White Masks. Grove Press, New York.

Faust, Maija (2006): Vaatimusten ristipaineessa: Nuoret koulutetut naiset ja kilpailuyhteiskunta. TANE-julkaisuja 8, Tasa-arvoasiain neuvottelukunta, Sosiaali- ja terveysministeriö, Helsinki.

Ferencz, Benjamin (1980): An International Criminal Court: A Step Towards World Peace – A Documentary History and Analysis. Volume 1. Oceana Publications Inc., New York.

Fortun, Kim (2001): Advocacy after Bhopal: Environmentalism, Disaster, New Global Orders. The University of Chicago Press, Chicago.

Foucault, Michel (1972): The Archaelogy of Knowledge & The Discourse on Language. Translated by A.M. Sheridan Smith. Pantheon Books, New York.

Franck, Thomas M. (1985): Nation Against Nation: What Happened to the U.N Dream and What the U.S. Can Do About It. Oxford University Press, New York.

Freeman, Derek (1983): Margaret Mead and Samoa: The Making and Unmaking of an Anthropological Myth. Harvard University Press, Cambridge.

Freeman, Michael (2006): 'Putting Law in its Place.' In *The Legalization of Human Rights* (Eds. Meckled-Garcia, Saladin & Cali, Basak). Routledge, London, 49–64.

—— (2002) Human Rights: An interdisciplinary approach. Polity Press, Cambridge.

Fried, Gorson (2003): 'Writing for Their Lives: Bentian Dayak Authors and Indonesian Development Discourse.' In *Culture and the Question of Rights* (Ed. Zerner, Charles). Duke University Press, Durham, 142–183.

Fukuyama, Francis (1993): The End of History and the Last Man. Harper Perennial, New York.

Furnham, Adrian F. (1988): Lay Theories: Everyday Understandings of Problems in the Social Sciences. Pergamon Press, Oxford.

Galtung, Johan (1994): Human Rights in Another Key. Polity Press, Cambridge.

Geertz, Clifford (1984): 'Anti Anti-Relativism.' In *86 American Anthropologist 2*, 263–278.

Geison, Gerald, L. (1995): The Private Science of Louis Pasteur. Princeton University Press, Princeton.

Gerlander, Maija; Levander, Lena M. & Repo-Kaarento, Saara (2006): Säpinää seminaareihin: Opas seminaarityöskentelyn kehittämiseen. University of Helsinki, Helsinki.

Ginsburg, Faye (1998 [1989]): Contested Lives: The Abortion Debate in an American Community. Revised Edition. University of California Press, California.

—— (1993) 'The Case of Mistaken Identity: Problems in Representing Women on the Right.' In *When They Read What We Write: The Politics of Ethnography* (Ed. Brettell, Caroline, B.). Bergin & Garvey, Connecticut, 163–176.

Glendon, Mary Ann (2003): 'The Forgotten Crucible: The Latin American Influence on the Universal Human Rights Ideal.' In *16 Harvard Human Rights Journal*, Spring 2003, 27–39.

—— (2001) A World Made New: Eleanor Roosevelt and the Universal Declaration of Human Rights. Random House, New York.

—— (1991) Rights Talk: The Impoverishment of Political Discourse. The Free Press, New York.

Godelier, Maurice (1999): Enigma of the Gift. University of Chicago Press, Chicago.

Goldstein, Daniel M. (2007): 'Human rights as culprit, human rights as victim: rights and security in the state of exception.' In *The Practice of Human Rights: Tracking Law Between the Global and the Local* (Eds. Goodale, Mark & Merry, Sally Engle). Cambridge University Press, Cambridge, 49–77.

Goodale, Mark (2006a): 'Introduction to Anthropology and Human Rights in a New Key.' In *108 American Anthropologist 1*, 1–8.

—— (2006b) 'Ethical Theory as Social Practice.' In *108 American Anthropologist 1*, 25–37.

Goodale, Mark & Merry, Sally Engle (Eds.) (2007): The Practice of Human Rights: Tracking Law Between the Global and the Local. Cambridge University Press, Cambridge.

Gramsci, Antonio (1989 [1971]): Selections from the Prison Notebooks. International Publishers, New York.

Greenhouse, Carol J.; Yngvesson, Barbara & Engel, David M. (1994): Law and Community in Three American Towns. Cornell University Press, Ithaca.
Gupta, Akhil & Ferguson, James (Eds.) (1997). Anthropological Locations: Boundaries and Grounds of a Field Science. University of California Press, Berkeley.
Haavisto, Vuola (2002): Court Work in Transition: An Activity-Theoretical Study of Changing Work Practices in a Finnish District Court. Yliopistopaino, Helsinki.
Halme, Miia (2005): 'Between Culture and Rights - beyond Relativism?' In *28 Polar: The Political and Legal Anthropology Review 2*, 307–315.
—— (2003) The Hidden 'Theory' of M. Cherif Bassiouni. LL.M Thesis, University of Helsinki.
—— (2002) 'The Network Inside Out in Perspective: A Review of the Development of Legal Anthropology.' In *Finnish Yearbook of International Law* (Ed. Petman, Jarna). Kluwer Law International, The Hague, 417–430.
Hancock, Graham (1989): Lords of Poverty: the power, prestige, and corruption of the international aid business. The Atlantic Monthly Press, New York.
Hanks, William F. (1996): Language and Communicative Practices. Westview Press, Colorado.
—— (1991) Foreword. In *Situated Learning: Legitimate Peripheral Participation* (By Lave, Jean & Wenger, Etienne). Cambridge University Press, Cambridge, 3–24.
Hannerz, Ulf (1992): Cultural Complexity: Studies in the Social Organization of Meaning. Columbia University Press, New York.
Hanski, Raija & Suksi, Markku (1997): An Introduction to the International Protection of Human Rights. Second edition. Åbo Akademi University, Åbo.
Hart, H. L. A. (1994 [1961]): The Concept of Law. Second edition. Clarendon Press, Oxford.
Henkin, Louis (1990): The Age of Rights. Columbia University Press, New York.
—— (1981) (Ed.) The International Bill of Rights: The Covenant on Civil and Political Rights. Columbia University Press, New York.
Helminen, Marjut & Lång, K. J. (Eds.) (1987): Kansainväliset ihmisoikeudet. Lakimiesliiton kustannus, Helsinki.
Herzfeld, Michael (1992): The Social Production of Indifference: Exploring the Symbolic Roots of Western Bureaucracy. The University of Chicago Press, Chicago.
Hidén, Mikael (1971): Perusoikeudet Hallitusmuodon II luvussa. Suomalaisen Lakimiesyhdistyksen vuosikirja I, Helsinki.
Hidén, Mikael & Saraviita, Ilkka (1994): Valtiosääntöoikeuden pääpiirteet. 6th, revised edition. Lakimiesliiton kustannus, Helsinki.
Humana, Charles (1983): World Human Rights Guide. Hutchinson & Co., London.
Hurma, Raija; Malin, Riitta-Leena & Syväoja, Olli (1984): Finnish-English General Dictionary. WSOY, Helsinki.
Hyyppä, Markku T. & Kronholm, Erkki (1998): Uni ja vire. Kansaneläkelaitos, Turku.
Ignatieff, Michael (2001): Human Rights as Politics and Idolatry. Princeton University Press, Princeton.
Isa, Felipe Gómez & Feyter, Koen de (2006): International Protection of Human Rights: Achievements and Challenges. University of Deusto, Bilbao.
Jean-Klein, Iris (2002): 'Alternative Modernities, or Accountable Modernities? The Palestinian Movement(s) and Political (Audit) Tourism During the First Intifada.' In *12 Journal of Mediterrannean Studies 1*, 43–80.
Jean-Klein, Iris & Riles, Annelise (2005): 'Introducing Discipline: Anthropology and Human Rights Administration.' In *28 Political and Legal Anthropology Review 2*, 173–203.
Johnson, Paul (1992 [1983]): Modern Times: A History of the World from the 1920's to the 1990's. Phoenix, London.
Johnstone, Andrew E. (2006): Clark Eichelberger, Internationalism and the State, 1941–1948. Ph.D., University of Birmingham.

Josephson, Harold (1975): James Shotwell and the Rise of Internationalism in America. Feirleigh Dickinson University Press, Rutherford.

Joutsamo, Kari (1990): Puolueettomuus ja EY. Euro Consulting Oy, Turku.

Kant, Immanuel (1991[1784]): 'The Idea of a Universal History with a Cosmopolitan Purpose.' In *Kant, Immanuel: Political Writings* (Ed. Reiss, Hans). Second enlarged edition. Cambridge University Press, Cambridge, 41–53.

Kantola, Johanna (2005): Mykät, kuurot ja kadotetut: Sukupuolten välinen tasa-arvo Helsingin yliopiston valtio-opin laitoksella. Acta politica 29. Yliopistopaino, Helsinki.

Kapur, Ratna (2005): Erotic Justice: Law and the New Politics of Postcolonialism. Glasshouse Press, London.

Keck, Margaret E. & Sikkink, Kathryn (1998): Activists beyond Borders: Advocacy Networks in International Politics. Cornell University Press, Ithaca.

Kelsen, Hans (1994 [1934]): Introduction to the Problems of Legal Theory (Translation of *Reine Rechtsteorie*). Clarendon Press, Oxford.

Kennedy, David (2004): The Dark Sides of Virtue: reassessing international humanitarianism. Princeton University Press, Princeton.

Kennedy, Duncan (2002): 'The Critique of Rights.' In *Left Legalism / Left Critique* (Eds. Brown, Wendy & Halley, Janet). Duke University Press, Durham & London, 178–228.

—— (1997) A Critique of Adjudication. Harvard University Press, Cambridge.

—— (1990) 'Legal Education as Training for Hierarchy.' In *The Politics of Law: A Progressive Critique* (Ed. Kairys, David). Revised Edition. Pantheon Books, New York, 38–58.

Kissinger, Henry (2001): 'The Pitfalls of Universal Jurisdiction: Risking Judicial Tyranny.' In *80 Foreign Affairs 4*.

Kitlinski, Tomaz; Leskowics, Pawel & Lockard, Joe (2005): 'Poland's transition: From Communism to Fundamentalist Hetero – Sex,' http://bad.eserver.org/issues/2005/72/kitlinskileszkowiczlockard.html. (11.9.2006).

Kivioja, Pasi (2007): 'Kolmen vuosikymmenen skandaalit'. Julkinen yksityinen seminaari, 23.8.2007, skandaali.files.wordpress.com/2007/08/julkyks.ppt (7.11.2007).

Klabbers, Jan (2004): 'Glorified Esperanto? Rethinking Human Rights.' In *Finnish Yearbook of International Law 2002* (Ed. Tuori, Taina). Martinus Nijhoff Publishers, Leiden, 63–77.

—— (2003) 'Redemption Song? Human Rights Versus Community-building in East Timor.' In *16 Leiden Journal of International Law 2*, 367–376.

—— (1997) Review: The Concept of International Obligations Erga Omnes by Maurizio Ragazzi. Clarendon Press, Oxford. In *The Finnish Yearbook of International Law VIII*. Kluwer University Press, Leiden, 1997.

—— (1996) 'The Redundancy of Soft Law.' In *65 Nordic Journal of International Law*, 167–182.

Klinge Matti (1987): A Brief History of Finland. Otava, Helsinki.

Klug, Francesca (2000): Values for a Godless Age: The Story of the United Kingdom's New Bill of Rights. Penguin Books, London.

Koenig, Shulamith (1997): 'Foreword.' In *Human Rights Education for the Twenty-First Century* (Eds. Andreopoulos, George J. & Claude, Richard Pierre). Pennsylvania University Press, Pennsylvania, viii–xvii.

Kolari, Tuula (2004): The Right to a Decent Environment with Special Reference to Indigenous Peoples. Juridica Lapponica 31, Sevenprint Ltd., Rovaniemi.

Korey, William (1998): NGOs and the Universal Declaration of Human Rights: 'A Curious Grapevine'. St. Martin's Press, New York.

Koskenniemi, Martti (2007): Fragmentation of International Law: Difficulties Arising from the Diversification and Expansion of International Law. Report of the Study Group of the International Law Commission. Hakapaino, Helsinki.

—— (2003) 'Legitimacy, Rights, and Ideology: Notes Towards a Critique of the New Moral Internationalism.' In *7 Associations: Journal for Legal and Social Theory 2*, 349–373.
—— (2001a) The Gentle Civilizer of Nations: The Rise and Fall of International Law 1870–1960. Cambridge University Press, Cambridge.
—— (2001b) 'Human Rights, Politics and Love.' In *Mennesker & rettigheter 4*, 33–45.
—— (1989) From Apology to Utopia: The Structure of International Legal Argument. Lakimiesliiton Kustannus, Helsinki.
Krohn, Claus-Dieter (1993): Intellectuals in Exile: Refugee Scholars and the New School for Social Research (Wissenschaft im Exil). The University of Massaschusetts Press, Massachusetts.
Laclau, Ernesto (1996): Emancipation(s). Verso, London.
Lahti, Minna (2001): Domesticated Violence: The power of the ordinary in everyday Finland. University of Helsinki, Helsinki.
Landry, Donna & Maclean, Gerald (Eds.) (1996): The Spivak Reader. Routledge, New York.
Larson, Edward J. (1997): Summer for the Gods: The Scopes Trial and America's Continuing Debate over Science and Religion. Harvard University Press, Cambridge.
Latour, Bruno (2005): Reassembling the Social: An Introduction to Actor-Network Theory. Oxford University Press, Oxford.
—— (2004): 'Scientific Objects and Legal Objectivity.' In *Law, Anthropology, and the Constitution of the Social: Making Persons and Things* (Eds. Pottage, Alain & Mundy, Martha). Cambridge University Press, Cambridge, 73–114.
—— (1993) We Have Never Been Modern. Harvard University Press, Cambridge.
—— (1987) Science in Action. Harvard University Press, Cambridge.
Lauterpacht, Hersh (1945): An International Bill of the Rights of Man. Columbia University Press, New York.
Lauren, Paul Gordon (1998): The Evolution of International Human Rights: Visions Seen. University of Pennsylvania Press, Philadelphia.
Lave, Jean & Wenger, Etienne (1991): Situated Learning: Legitimate Peripheral Participation. Cambridge University Press, Cambridge.
Leino-Sandberg, Päivi (2005): Particularity as Universality: The Politics of Human Rights in the European Union. The Erik Castrén Institute Research Reports 15, Helsinki.
Leppänen, Sirpa & Nikula, Tarja (2007): 'Diverse uses of English in Finnish society: Discourse-pragmatic insights into media, educational and business contexts.' In *26 Multilingua 4*, 333–380.
Levi, Primo (1986): The Drowned and the Saved. Summit Books, New York.
Levi, Sheri R., Chiu, Chi-yue & Hong, Ying-yi (2006): Lay Theories and Intergroup Relations. In *9 Group Processes & Intergroup Relations 9*, 5–25.
Linder, Doris H. (2001): Equality For Women: The Contribution of Scandinavian Women at the United Nations, 1946–66. In *Scandinavian Studies*, 6/22/2001 http://www.highbeam.com/library/doc3.asp?DOCID=1…)
Lindblom, Anna-Karin (2005): Non-Governmental Organisations in International Law. Cambridge University Press, Cambridge.
Llewellyn, Karl N. & Hoebel, Adamson E. (1941): The Cheyenne Way: Conflict and Case Law in Primitive Jurisprudence. University of Oklahoma Press, Oklahoma.
Locke, John (1698): Two Treatises of Government. Awnsham and John Churchill, Black Swan. Reproduced at http://www.lonang.com/exlibris/locke/loc-001a.htm (12.1.2007).
Luoto, Jari (1997): Ulkopolitiikka ja Ihmisoikeudet: Suomen kansainvälisen ihmisoikeuspolitiikan murroskausi 1985–1995. Gaudeamus, Helsinki.
Macfarlane, L. J. (1985): The Theory and Practice of Human Rights. Maurice Temple Smith, London.

Mahoney, Jack (2007): The Challenge of Human Rights: Their Origin, Development, and Significance. Blackwell Publishing, Malden.

Maine, Henry (1861): Ancient Law: its connection with the early history of society, and its relation to modern ideas. John Murray, London.

Malik, Charles (1987): A Christian Critique of the University. North Waterloo Academic Press, Illinois.

Malinowski, Branislaw (1984[1922]): Argonauts of the Western Pacific. Waveland Press Inc., Illinois.

The Mandates System (1945). League of Nations, Geneva.

Maran, Rita (1997): 'Teaching Human Rights in the Universities.' In *Human Rights Education for the Twenty-First Century* (Eds. Andreopoulos, George J. & Claude, Richard Pierre). Pennsylvania University Press, Pennsylvania, 194–208.

Marceau, Gabrielle (2002): 'The WTO Dispute Settlement and Human Rights.' In *13 European Journal of International Law 4*, 753–814.

Marcus, George E. (1995): 'Ethnography In/Of The World System: The Emergence of Multi-Sited Ethnography.' In *24 Annual Review of Anthropology*, 95–117.

Marcus, George E. & Fischer, Michael M. (1999): Anthropology as Cultural Critique: An Experimental Moment in the Human Sciences. Second Edition. University of Chicago Press, Chicago.

Margalit, Avishai & Halbertal, Moshe (2004): 'Liberalism and the Right to Culture.' In *71 Social Research 3*, 529–548.

Marklund, Liza & Snickare, Lotta (2005): Det finns en särsklid plats i helvetet för kvinnor som inte hjälper till varandra. Piratförlaget, Stockholm.

Marks, Susan & Clapham, Andrew (2005): International Human Rights Lexicon. Oxford University Press, Oxford.

Marsden, George M. (2006): Fundamentalism and American Culture. Oxford University Press, Oxford.

Mauss, Marcel (2006[1950]): The Gift: The Form and Reason for Exchange in Archaic Societies. Routledge, London.

Mazover, Mark (2004): 'The Strange Triumph of Human Rights, 1933–1950.' In *47 The Historical Journal 2*, 379–398.

McGoldrick, Dominic (1994): The Human Rights Committee: Its Role in the Development of the International Covenant on Civil and Political Rights. Oxford University Press, Oxford.

McIntosh, Ian S. (2003): 'Reconciling Personal and Impersonal Worlds: Aboriginal Struggles for Self-Determination.' In *At the Risk of Being Heard: Identity, Indigenous Rights, and Postcolonial States* (Eds. Dean, Bartholomew & Levi, Jerome M.). The University of Michigan Press, Ann Arbor, 293–323.

Mead, Margaret (1973[1928]): Coming of Age in Samoa: A Psychological Study of Primitive Youth for Western civilization. William Morrow & Company Inc., New York.

Meckled-Garcia, Saladin & Cali, Basak (Eds.) (2006): The Legalization of Human Rights. Routledge, London.

Mehlman, Jeffrey (1972): 'The "Floating Signifier": From Lévi-Strauss to Lacan.' In *Yale French Studies 48*, 10–37.

Meintjes, Garth (1997): 'Human Rights Education as Empowerment: Reflections on Pedagogy.' In *Human Rights Education for the Twenty-First Century* (Eds. Andreopoulos, George J. & Claude, Richard Pierre). Pennsylvania University Press, Pennsylvania, 64–79.

Merikoski, Veli & Vilkkonen, Eero (1982): Suomen julkisoikeus pääpiirteittäin. Suomalaisen Lakimiesyhdistyksen julkaisuja. WSOY, Juva.

Meron, Theodor (2006): The Humanization of International Law. Brill Academic Publishers, Leiden.

Merry, Sally Engle (2006): Human Rights & Gender Violence: Translating International Law into Local Justice. The University of Chicago Press, Chicago.

—— (2005) 'Anthropology and Activism: Researching Human Rights across Porous Boundaries.' In *28 Political and Legal Anthropology Review 2*, 240–258.

—— (1990) Getting Justice and Getting Even: Legal Consciousness Among Working-Class Americans. The University of Chicago Press, Chicago.

Messer, Ellen (1997): 'Pluralist Approaches to Human Rights.' In *53 Journal of Anthropological Research 3*, 293–317.

—— (1993) 'Anthropology and Human Rights.' In *22 Annual Review of Anthropology*, 221–249.

Mikkola, Teija; Niemelä, Kati & Petterson, Juha (2007): The Questioning Mind: Faith and Values of the New Generation. Publication 58, Church Research Institute, Tampere.

Montgomery, Heather (2001): 'Imposing rights? A case study of child prostitution in Thailand.' In *Culture and Rights* (Eds. Cowan, Jane K.; Dembour, Marie-Bénédicte & Wilson, Richard A.). Cambridge University Press, Cambridge, 80–101.

Morgan, Henry Lewis (1964 [1877]): Ancient society. Edited by Leslie, A. Harvard University Press, Cambridge.

Morsink, Johannes (1999): The Universal Declaration of Human Rights: Origins, Drafting & Intent. University of Pennsylvania Press, Philadelphia.

Murphy, Paul L. (1979): World War I and the Origin of Civil Liberties in the United States. W. W. Norton & Company, New York.

Mutua, Makau (2002): Human Rights: A Political & Cultural Critique. University of Pennsylvania Press, Philadelphia.

Nagengast, Carole & Turner, Terence (1997): 'Introduction: Universal Human Rights versus Cultural Relativism.' In *53 Journal of Anthropological Research 3*, 269–273.

Nordic Journal of Human Rights (2002). *Mennesker & Rettigheter: Nordisk Tidsskrift for Menneskerettigheter 2*. Symposium: Lovtiltak mot terror.

Nowak, Manfred (2006): 'The International Covenant on Civil and Political Rights.' In *International Protection of Human Rights: Achievements and Challenges* (Eds. Isa, Felipe Gómez & Feyter, Koen de). University of Deusto, Bilbao, 137–154.

—— (2003) Introduction to the International Human Rights Regime. Brill Academic Publisher, Leiden.

O'Flaherty, Michael (2006): 'The Concluding Observations of United Nations Human Rights Treaty Bodies.' In *6 Human Rights Law Review 1*, 27–52.

Ojanen, Tuomas & Haapea, Arto (Eds.) (2006): EU-oikeden perusteita. Edita, Helsinki.

Ojanen, Tuomas (2003): Perusoikeudet ja ihmisoikeudet Suomessa. Forum Iuris, Helsinki.

Ong, Aihwa & Collier, Stephen J. (Eds) (2005): Global Assemblages: Technology, Politics, and Ethics as Anthropological Problems. Blackwell Publishing, Oxford.

Onuf, Nicholas (1985): 'Do Rules Say What They Do? From Ordinary Language to International Law.' In *26 Harvard International Law Journal 2*, 385–410.

Ortner, Sherry (1997) 'Fieldwork in the Postcommunity.' In *22 Anthropology and Humanism 1*, 61–80.

Palonen, Kari (2006): A Struggle with Time: A Conceptual History of "Politics" as an Activity. Lit Verlag, Münster.

Pellonpää, Matti (1988): Euroopan neuvoston ihmisoikeussopimus Suomen näkökulmasta. Oikeusministeriön lainvalmisteluosaston julkaisu 21, Helsinki.

—— (1984) Expulsion in International Law: A Study in International Aliens Law and Human Rights with Special Reference to Finland. Suomalainen tiedeakatemia, Helsinki.

Pelkonen, Heli & Rosas, Allan (Eds.) (1983): Mänskliga rättigheter in Norden. Åbo Akademi, Åbo.

Pentikäinen, Merja (2003): 'The Right to Speak for the Women's Cause: May also Women Participate? The Case of the Holy See in the UN.' In *Nordic Cosmpololitanism:*

Essays in International Law for Martti Koskenniemi (Eds. Petman, Jarna & Klabbers, Jan). Brill Academic Publishers, Leiden, 141–154.

—— (1994) Human Rights Commitments within the CSCE Process: Nature, Contents and Application in Finland. Advisory Board for International Human Rights Affairs No. 3.

Perry, Michael (1998): The Idea of Human Rights: Four Inquiries. Oxford University Press, Oxford.

Petersman, Ernst-Ulrich (2003): 'Human Rights and the Law of the World Trade Organization.' In *37 Journal of World Trade 2,* 241–281.

Peterson, V. Spike & Parisi, Laura (1998): 'Are women human? It's not an academic question.' In *Human Rights Fifty Years on: A Reappraisal* (Ed. Evans, Tony). Manchester University Press, Manchester, 132–160.

Petman, Jarna (2006): 'Human Rights, Democracy, and the Left.' In *2 Unbound Harvard Journal of the Legal Left,* 2006 Spring, 63–90.

Pietilä, Hilkka (2005): Naiset ja YK: vuosikymmenen menestystarina, http://www.minna.fi/minna/artikkelit/ykpietila.html (11.9.2006).

Polvinen, Tuomo (1986): Between East and West : Finland in international politics, 1944–1947. University of Minnesota Press, Minneapolis.

Pottage, Alain & Mundy, Martha (Eds.) (2004): Law, Anthropology, and the Constitution of the Social: Making Persons and Things. Cambridge University Press, Cambridge.

Power, Jonathan (2001): Like Water on Stone: The Story of Amnesty International. Northeastern University Press, Darthmouth.

Powers, Samantha (2003): A Problem from Hell: American and the Age of Genocide. Harper Perennial, New York.

Proskauer, Joseph M. (1950): A Segment of My Times. Farrar, Straus and Company, New York.

Rahkola, Juho (2007): Kirkko median kuvastimessa: Kristinuskon ja kirkollisten asioiden käsittely sanomalehdissä. Kirkon tutkimuskeskus, Tampere.

Rainio, Pauliina (2002): Tietotyön malli koulun kehittämisessä: Muutoksen esteet, edellytykset ja mahdollisuudet opettajien puheessa. Helsingin yliopisto, Helsinki.

Rahkonen, Juho: Kirkko median kuvastimessa: Kristinuskon ja kirkollisten asioiden käsittely sanomalehdissä. Kirkon tutkimuskeskus, Tampere, 2007.

Ranta, Elina (2004): International English – a Future Possibility in the Finnish EFL Classroom? Master's Thesis, University of Tampere.

Rasila, Viljo; Jutikkala, Eino & Kulha, Keijo K. (1980): Suomen poliittinen historia 1905–1975. Werner Söderström, Porvoo.

Redding, Jeffrey A. (2006): 'Human Rights and Homo-Sectuality: The International Politics of Sexuality, Religion and Law.' In *4 Northwestern Journal of International Human Rights,* 436–492.

Redgewell, Catherine (2003): 'US reservations to human rights treaties: all for one and none for all?' In *United States Hegemony and the Foundations of International Law* (Eds. Byers, Michael & Nolte, Georg). Cambridge University Press, Cambridge, 392–415.

Redfield, Peter (2005): 'Doctors, Borders, and Life in Crisis.' In *20 Cultural Anthropology 2,* 328–361.

Relander, Jukka (1997): 'Ulkoinen totuus ja sisäinen kokemus taistolaisessa opiskelijaliikkeessä.' In *Tieteessä Tapahtuu,* 4/1997.

Renteln, Alison Dundes (1990): International Human Rights: Universalism Versus Relativism. Sage Publications, Newbury Park, Delhi and London.

Riles, Annelise: (2006a) 'Anthropology, Human Rights, and Legal Knowledge: Culture in the Iron Cage.' In *108 American Anthropologist 1,* 52–65.

—— (2006b) Documents: Artifacts of Modern Knowledge. The University of Michigan Press, Ann Arbor.

—— (2006c) '[Deadlines]: Removing the Brackets on Politics in Bureaucratic and Anthropological Analysis.' In *Documents: Artifacts of Modern Knowledge* (Ed. Annelise Riles). The University of Michigan Press, Ann Arbor, 71–92.

—— (2002) 'Rights Inside Out: The Uses of Genre in the Women's Human Rights Campaign.' In *15 Leiden Journal of International Law 2*, 285–303.

—— (2001a) The Network Inside Out. The University of Michigan Press, Ann Arbor.

—— (2001b) 'Encountering Amateurism: John Henry Wigmore and the Uses of American Formalism.' In *Rethinking the Masters of Comparative Law* (Ed. Riles, Annelise). Hart Publishing, Oxford.

Roberts, Simon & Palmer, Michael (1998): Dispute Processes: ADR and the Primary Forms of Decision-Making. Cambridge University Press, Cambridge.

Roosevelt, Eleanor (1992 [1961]): The Autobiography of Eleanor Roosevelt. Da Capo Press Inc., New York.

Rosga, AnnJanette (2005): 'The Traffic in Children: The Funding of Translation and the Translation of Funding.' In *28 Political and Legal Anthropology Review 2*, 258–281.

Ruoho, Iiris (2000): 'Double Standards in Evaluating Television: "Peyton Place" and "Dallas" in the Finnish television culture.' In *Inescapable Horizon: Culture and Context* (Eds, Leppänen, Sirpa & Kuortti, Joel). University of Jyväskylä, Jyväskylä.

Rusi, Alpo (2007): Vasemmalta ohi: – Kamppailu Suomen ulkopoliittisesta johtajuudesta rautaesiripun varjossa 1945–1990. Gummerus, Helsinki.

Sahlins, Marshall (2004): Apologies to Thucydides: Understanding History as Culture and Vice Versa. The University of Chicago Press, Chicago.

Sakamoto, Hyakudai (1996): 'The Genome, Artificial Evolution & Human Rights.' In *Protection of the Human Genome and Scientific Responsibility* (Eds. Okamoto, Michio; Fujiki, Norio & Macer Darryl R.J.). Eubios Ethics Institute, 30–31.

Samson, Colin (2001): 'Rights as the reward for simulated cultural sameness: the Innu in the Canadian colonial context.' In *Culture and Rights* (Eds. Cowan, Jane; Dembour, Marie-Bénédicte & Wilson, Richard A.). Cambridge University Press, Cambridge, 226–248.

Sanders, Douglas (2002): 'Human Rights and Sexual Orientation in International Law.' In *25 International Journal of Public Administration 1*, 13–44.

Sano, Hans-Otto & Lindholt, Lone (2000): Human Rights Indicators: Country data and methodology. Danish Institute of Human Rights, Copenhagen.

Sarat, Austin & Felstiner, William L. F. (1995): Divorce Lawyers and Their Clients: Power & Meaning in the Legal Process. Oxford University Press, Oxford.

Saraviita, Ilkka (1989): YYA-sopimus. Lakimiesliiton kustannus, Helsinki.

Scheinin, Martin (2005): Toward a World Court of Human Rights, 2.11.2005, Discussion forum for the Office of the High Commissioner for Human Rights, http://portal.ohchr.org/tbforum/mvnforum/viewthread?thread=981 (28.4.2006).

—— (1996) 'Finland.' In *International Human Rights Norms in the Nordic and Baltic Countries* (Ed. Scheinin, Martin). Martinus Nijhoff Publishers, The Hague, 257–294.

—— (1991) Ihmisoikeudet Suomen oikeudessa. Suomalainen Lakimiesyhdistys, Jyväskylä.

—— (1988) Aseistakieltäytymisoikeus. Hakapaino Oy, Helsinki.

Scheper-Hughes, Nancy (2002): Saints, Scholars, and Schizophrenics: Mental Illness in Rural Ireland. Updated and Expanded Edition. University of California Press, Berkeley.

Sellars, Kirsten (2002): The Rise and Rise of Human Rights. Sutton Publishing, Phoenix Mill.

Seppänen, Samuli (2005): 'Possibilities and Challenges of the Human Rights-Based Approach to Development.' The Erik Castrén Institute Research Reports 17/2005, Helsinki.

Shachar, Ayelet (2001): Multicultural Jurisdictions: Cultural Differences and Women's Rights. Cambridge University Press, Cambridge.

Sieder, Rachel & Witchell, Jessica (2001): 'Advancing indigenous claims through the law: reflections on the Guatemalan peace process.' In *Culture and Rights* (Eds. Cowan, Jane K., Dembour, Marie-Bénédicte & Wilson, Richard A.). Cambridge University Press, Cambridge, 201–225.

Simpson, A. W. Brian (2001): Human Rights and the End of Empire: Britain and the Genesis of the European Convention. Oxford University Press, Oxford.

Skinner, Quentin (2002): Visions of Politics. Volume I: Regarding Method. Cambridge University Press, Cambridge.

Skouteris, Thomas (1997): 'Fin de NAIL: New Approaches to International Law and Its Impact on Contemporary International Legal Scholarship.' In *10 Leiden Journal of International Law 3,* 415–420.

Smythe, Hugh H. (1947): 'The N.A.A.C.P. Protest to UN.' In *8 Phylon (1940–1956) 4,* 355–358.

Sousa Santos, Boaventura de (1997): 'Toward a Multicultural Conception of Human Rights.' In *18 Zeitschrift für Rechtssoziologie 1,* 1–15.

Steiner, Henry J. & Alston, Philip (2000): International Human Rights in Context: Law, Politics, Morals. Second Edition. Oxford University Press, Oxford.

Stephen, Lynn (2003): 'Indigenous Autonomy in Mexico.' In *At the Risk of Being Heard: Identity, Indigenous Rights, and Postcolonial States* (Eds. Dean, Bartholomew & Levi, Jerome M.) The University of Michigan Press, Ann Arbor, 191–216.

Steward, Julian H. (1948): 'Comments on the Statement on Human Rights.' In *50 American Anthropologist 2,* 351–352.

Thomas, Caroline (1998): 'International financial institutions and social and economic human rights: an exploration.' In *Human Rights Fifty Years on: A Reappraisal* (Ed. Evans, Tony). Manchester University Press, Manchester, 161–185.

Toivanen, Reetta; Mahler, Claudia & Mihr, Anja (2006): 'Teaching Human Rights in Europe and its role for minority movement.' In *Human Rights in Europe – A Fragmented Regime* (Ed. Brosig, Malte). Peter Lang Verlag, Berlin, 168–182.

Tomkins, Adam (2001): 'Introduction: On Being Sceptical about Human Rights.' In *Sceptical Essays on Human Rights* (Eds. Ewing, K. D. & Tomkins, Adam). Oxford University Press, Oxford, 1–11.

Tuck, Richard (1979): Natural Rights Theories: Their Origin and Development. Cambridge University Press, Cambridge.

Tuori, Kaius (2006): Ancient Roman Lawyers and Modern Legal Ideals. University of Helsinki, Helsinki.

Tushnet, Mark (1984): 'An Essay on Rights.' In *62 Texas Law Review 8,* 1363–1403.

Turner, Terence (1997): 'Human Rights, Human Difference: Anthropology's Contribution to an Emancipatory Cultural Politics.' In *52 Journal of Anthropological Research 3,* 273–291.

—— (1993) 'Anthropology and Multiculturalism: What Is Anthropology That Multiculturalists Should Be Mindful of It?' In *8 Current Anthropology 4,* 411–429.

Törnudd, Klaus (1986): Finland and the International Norms of Human Rights. Martinus Nijhoff Publishers, Dordrecht.

Uchiyamada, Yasushi (2005): 'The Face of the Japanese Body Politics.' In *28 Political and Legal Anthropology Review 2,* 282–306.

Urban, Greg (2001): Metaculture: How Culture Moves through the World. Public Worlds, Volume 8. University of Minnesota Press, Minneapolis.

Waldron, Jeremy (Ed.) (1987): 'Nonsense upon Stilts': Bentham, Burke and Marx on the Rights of Man. Oxford University Press, Oxford.

Walker, Samuel (1999): In Defence of American Liberties: A History of the ACLU. Second Edition. Southern Illinois University Press, Carbondale.

—— (1998) The Rights Revolution: Rights and Community in Modern America. Oxford University Press, New York.

Wallerstein, Immanuel (2000): The Essential Wallerstein. The New Press, New York.
Wallin, Risto (2005): Yhdistyneet kansakunnat organisaationa: Tutkimus käsittellisestä muutoksesta maailmanjärjestön organisoinnin periaatteissa. Jyväskylän yliopisto, Jyväskylä.
Waltz, Susan (2004): 'Universal Human Rights: The Contribution of Muslim States.' In *26 Human Rights Quarterly 4*, 799–844.
—— (2001) 'Universalizing Human Rights: The Role of Small States in the Construction of the Universal Declaration of Human Rights.' In *23 Human Rights Quarterly 1*, 44–72.
Valverde, Mariana (2003): Law's Dream of a Common Knowledge. Princeton University Press, Princeton.
Washburn, Wilcomb E. (1987): 'Cultural Relativism, Human Rights, and the AAA.' In *89 American Anthropologist 4*, 939–943.
Waters, Tony (2001): Bureaucratizing the Good Samaritan: The Limitations of Humanitarian Relief Operations. Boulder, Westview.
Wells, H. G. (1940): The Rights of Man or What are We Fighting For? Penguin Books, Harmondsworth.
Wells, Jonathan (2002): Icons of Evolution: Science or Myth? Why Much of What We Teach About Evolution is Wrong. Regnery Publishing Inc., Washington D.C.
Wetzsteon, Ross (2002): Republic of Dreams-Greenwich Village: The American Bohemia, 1910–1960. Simon & Schuster, New York.
Vihavainen, Timo (1991): Kansakunta rähmällään: suomettumisen lyhyt historia. Otava, Helsinki.
Viljanen, Anna Maria (1994): Psychiatry and culture. A study of forensic psychiatric argumentation. University of Helsinki, Helsinki.
Viljanen, Veli-Pekka (1996): 'Perusoikeusuudistus ja kansainväliset ihmisoikeussopimukset.' In *Lakimies 5–6*, 788–815.
Wilson, Richard (2007): 'Tyrannosaurus Lex: The Anthropology of Human Rights and Transnational Law.' In *The Practice of Human Rights: Tracking Law Between the Global and the Local* (Eds. Mark Goodale & Sally Engle Merry). Cambridge University Press, Cambridge, 342–369.
—— (1997) (Ed.) Human Rights, Culture and Context: Anthropological Perspectives. Pluto Press, London.
Wiseberg, Laurie S. & Scoble, Harry M. (1977): 'The International League for Human Rights: The Strategy of a Human Rights NGO.' In *7 Georgia Journal of International and Comparative Law*, 289–313.
Woodiwiss, Anthony (2006): 'The law cannot be enough: Human rights and the limits of legalism.' In *The Legalization of Human Rights* (Eds. Meckled-Garcia, Saladin & Cali, Basak). Routledge, London, 32–48.
Zerner, Charles (Ed.) (2003): Culture and the Question of Rights. Duke University Press, Durham.

Documents, Websites & Newspaper articles

Aarnipuu, Tiia (2006). http://www.aarnipuu.net/puheenvuoroja.htm (30.8.3006).
ABCNEWS (2000). '1925 Monkey Trial Still With Us.' 23.7.2000. http://abcnews.go.com/sections/us/DailyNews/scopestrial000723.html (24.9.2003).
Amnesty International
(2007). http://www.jokuraja.fi/ (8.3.2007).
(2006). 'AI's First 40 years.' http://web.amnesty.org/pages/aboutai-timeline-1960s-eng (16.5.2006).
(2006a). 'Report 2006: Finland.' http://web.amnesty.org/report2006/fin-summary-eng (30.4.2007).

(2006b). 'Partners in Crime: Europe's role in US renditions.' 14.6.2006. http://web.amnesty.org/library/index/ENGEUR010082006 (24.8.2006) (2005). 'Joku raja!' http://www.amnesty.fi/jokuraja/svaw.htm (10.11.2005).

(2004). 'Sweden: Concerns over the treatment of deported Egyptians.' 28.5.2004. http://web.amnesty.org/library/index/engeur420012004 (11.9.2006).

Blogspot (2007). 'Naispappi ajettiin kirkosta.' 3.5.2007. http://rankinen.blogspot.com/2007/03/naispappi-ajettiin-kirkosta.html (7.11.2007).

CESCR (1976). International Covenant on Economic, Social and Cultural Social Rights. http://www.unhchr.ch/html/menu3/b/a_cescr.htm (4.4.2006).

Chang (2003). Biography of Peng-Chun Chang. http://www.udhr.org/history/Biographies/biopcc.htm (23.5.2003).

Choike.org. http://www.choike.org/2009/eng/informes/854.html (6.11.2009).

CMI (2005). Chr. Michelsen Insitute. http://www.cmi.no/ (23.9.2005).

Commission to Study the Organization of Peace (1945). Petition to 'The Honorable Edward R. Stettinius, Jr.' March 31, 1945.

Committee on Economic, Social and Cultural Rights (2006). Members. http://www.ohchr.org/english/bodies/cescr/members.htm (21.12.2005 and 31.3.2006).

(2004) State Report of Norway 2004. http://www.ohchr.org/english/bodies/cescr/cescrs34.htm (26.4.2006).

Counterpunch (2006). 'The Human Right to a Nuclear Free World.' By Mairead Corrigan Maguire. 1.3.2006. http://www.counterpunch.org/maguire03012006.html (19.5.2006).

Covenant of the League of Nations (2006), http://www.yale.edu/lawweb/avalon/leag-cov.htm (13.12.2006).

CREDHO (2007). Centre de recherces et d'études sur les droits de l'Homme et le droit humanitaire. http://www.credho.org/enseignts/deadess.htm (6.5.2007).

The Danish Institute for Human Rights (n.d.). http://www.humanrights.dk/frontpage/ (16.5.2006).

Declaration of Commitment on HIV/AIDS (2001). http://www.un.org/ga/aids/coverage/FinalDeclarationHIVAIDS.html (25.9.2006).

DerechosNet (2006). Spanish LLM programs. http://www.derechos.net/links/esp/edu/uni.html (19.9.2006).

Dialogi (2006). 'Lisääntymisoikeus on kiistaton.' http://www.stakes.fi/dialogi/06/d206/44.htm (19.5.2006).

Eduskunta (2006). Täysistunnon pöytäkirja PTK 8/2006 vp. http://www.parliament.fi/faktatmp/utatmp/akxtmp/ptk_8_2006_ke_p_3.shtml (3.6.2007).

EMA (2006a). European Master's Programme in Human Rights and Democratisation. http://www.emahumanrights.org/index.php?option=com_content&task=view&id=12&Itemid=26 Site visited on 18.9.2006.

(2006b). European Regional Master in Democracy and Human Rights in South-East Europe. http://137.204.115.130/activities/education/details-education.php?id=16&noindex=1 (18.9.2006).

EU – China Human Rights Dialogue (2006). http://www.eu-in-china.com/euch_poli3.htm (15.6.2006).

European Court of Human Rights (2007). Ratification of the European Convention on Human Rights. http://www.echr.coe.int/ECHR/EN/Header/Basic+Texts/Basic+Texts/Dates+of+ratification+of+the+European+Convention+on+Human+Rights+and+Additional+Protocols/ (14.6.2007).

FLHR (2006). Finnish League for Human Rights. http://www.ihmisoikeusliitto.fi/tausta/introduction (24.8.2006).

Foreign Affairs Ministry (2005). 'Nellimin metsähakkuut keskeytetään.' Tiedote 358/2005, 16.11.2005. http://www.valtioneuvosto.fi/vn/liston/base.lsp?r=97998&k=fi&old=376 (18.11.2005).

(2004a). 'Foreign Minister Tuomioja on International Human Rights Day: Finland committed to the rights of minorities.' 10.12.2004. http://formin.finland.fi/

public/default.aspx?contentid=62930&nodeid=15630&c ontentlan=2&culture=en-US (29.8.2006).
(2004d). 'Ulkoasiainministeri Tuomioja valtioneuvoston ihmisoikeuspoliittisesta selonteosta.' 31.3.2004. http://formin.finland.fi/public/default.aspx?contentid=61378&nodeid=15631&c ontentlan=1&culture=fi-FI (28.9.2006).
Government Programme (2007). http://www.valtioneuvosto.fi/hallitus/hallitusohjelma/en.jsp (5.11.2007).
Great Ape Project (2006). http://www.greatapeproject.org/ (19.5.2006).
Helsingin tutkijanaiset (2007). www.blogit.helsinki.fi/tutkijanaiset/ (14.3.2007).
High Commissioner
(2006). Working Groups 2006. http://www.unhchr.ch/html/menu2/2/chrwg.htm (27.4.2007).
(2004a). Office of the United Nations High Commissioner for Human Rights. Status of Ratifications of Principal Human Rights Treaties as of 09 June 2004. http://193.194.138.190/pdf/report.pdf (10.5.2005). (2004b). United Nations Decade for Human Rights Education (1995–2004). http://www.unhchr.ch/html/menu6/1/edudec.htm (6.5.2007).
(1994a). High Commissioner for Human Rights. Draft United Nations Declaration on the Rights of Indigenous Peoples of 1994. http://www.unhchr.ch/huridocda/huridoca.nsf/(Symbol)/E.CN.4.SUB.2.RES.1 994.45.En (28.4.2007).
(1994b). High Commissioner for Human Rights. Declaration on the Rights of Disabled Persons. GA Resolution 3447, 9 December 1975. http://www.unhchr.ch/html/menu3/b/72.htm (27.8.2006).
HRO Statement (2006). UN Declaration on the Rights of Indigenous Peoples: Human rights organizations condemn efforts to block vital human rights instrument. http://www.iwgia.org/graphics/Synkron-Library/Documents/Noticeboard/News/International/NGOStatementonDeclarationNov302006.htm (28.4.2007).
HS. Helsingin Sanomat
3.4.2007. 'Simpanssille haetaan ihmisoikeuksia Itävallassa.' By Ilkka Ahtiainen. B3.
20.3.2007. 'Julkilesbo tennistähti: lampailla oikeus homouteen.' By Marko Hamilo.
D2. 10.12.2006. 'Ihmisoikeudet tunnetaan heikosti.' By Kouros, Kristiina; Johansson, Frank &Laukko, Helena. C6.
20.11.2006. 'Miehet johtavat korkeakouluja, sairaanhoitoa ja oikeudenjakoa.' By Kaisa Hakkarainen. A4.
19.10.2006. 'Pienen pieni uutinen.' By Antti Blåfeld. A2.
10.8.2006. 'Puolalainen ääripuolue lähti ristiretkelle homoja vastaan.' By Pilvikki Kause. B3.
27.5.2006. 'Jospa ketään ei lyötäisi – keskustelua verkossa.' C7.
24.5.2006. 'Amnesty moittii Suomea naisiin kohdistuvasta väkivallasta.' By Annamari Sipilä. B2.
Kuukausiliite 5/2006. 'Villivihreat vaistot heräävät.' By Vivi-Ann Sjögren. 95–99.
14.4.2006. 'Suomessa asuu ennätysmäärä ulkomaiden kansalaisia.' By Anna Riitta Sippola.
30.12.2005. 'Norjalaisten pörssiyhtiöiden hallituksiin tulee sukupuolikiintiöt.' By Kalle Koponen. B9.
11.12.2005. 'Inarin mestäkiista kaipaa sovittelijaa.' By Jaakko Tahkolahti. A5.
4.9.2005. 'Aina pienten puolella.' By Anu Nousiainen. D3.
Kuukausiliite 11/1988. 'Pintaremontti riittää.' By Jouni Tervo. 36–38.
Human Rights and Democratisation in Africa (2006). http://www.chr.up.ac.za/academic_pro/llm1/llm1.html (18.8.2006).
Human Rights Committee (2006). Members. http://www.ohchr.org/english/bodies/hrc/members.htm (31.3.2006).
Human Rights Council (2006). Elections. http://www.un.org/ga/60/elect/hrc/ (19.3.2007).

HRW
(n.d.) Human Rights Watch: About HRW. http://www.hrw.org/about/whoweare.html (16.5.2006).
(2006). Resource Library for International Jurisprudence on Sexual Orientation and Gender Identity. http://hrw.org/lgbt/jurisprudence.htm (22.1.2007).
(2005). 'Sweden Violated Torture Ban with U.S. Help.' 20.5.2005. http://hrw.org/english/docs/2005/05/20/sweden10991.htm (28.8.2006).
Human Rights Report (2000). Ihmisoikeudet ja Suomen ulkopolitiikka. Ulkoasianministeriön julkaisuja 9/2000.
Human Rights Report (2004). Valtioneuvoston selonteko Suomen ihmisoikeuspolitiikasta.
Icelandic Human Rights Centre (2005). http://www.humanrights.is/english/about-us/history-and-mandate/ (21.12.2005).
ILGA (2006). International Gay and Lesbian Association. http://www.ilga.org/ (27.11.2006).
Iltalehti (2007). 16.10.2007. 'Seksiskandaali Vatikaanissa: Pappi lähenteli nuorta miestä.' http://www.iltalehti.fi/ulkomaat/200710156719442_ul.shtml (7.11.2007).
L'Institut de Droit International (1929). 'Déclaration des Droits Internationaux de l'Homme.' In *36 Annuaire de l'Institute de Droit International: Session de New York.* Octobre 1929, 110–112.
ICJ (2007). International Court of Justice. http://www.icj-cij.org/pcij/index.php?p1=9&PHPSESSID=e8b50769600e3fd2bd724b2b8afedba4 (28.4.2007).
(2007). Statute. http://www.icj-cij.org/documents/index.php?p1=4&p2=2&p3=0 (28.4.2007). Cases. ww.icjcij.org/docket/index.php?+1=38&code=esa&case=468&k=c1 (10.11.2007).
International Helsinki Federation for Human Rights (2001). Report 2001 (Events of 2000). http://www.ihf-hr.org/documents/doc_summary.php?sec_id=3&d_id=1783 (20.1.2010).
Internet Infidels Discussion Board (2005). 'Using Ockams Razor In An Abortion Debate?' http://www.iidb.org/vbb/archive/index.php/t-130793.html (19.5.2006).
KELA (2003). 'Kela kiintiöi psykoterapiavarat.' 18.12.2003. http://www.verkkouutiset.fi/arkistojuttu.php?id=46356&hakusanat=Hoitosuhde (29.10.2007).
KeskusteluSuomi 24 (2007). http://keskustelu.suomi24.fi/show.fcgi?category=1000000000000003&conference=1500000000000012&posting=22000000027187631 (7.11.2007).
KIOS (n.d.). The Finnish NGO foundation for human rights. http://www.kios.fi/index.jsp (31.8.2006).
Kirkko turvapaikkana (2007). http://www.ekumenia.fi/kirkot_ja_maahanmuuttajat/kirkko_turvapaikkana/ (7.11.2007).
KNAW (2006). The School of Human Rights Research. http://www.uu.nl/uupublish/homerechtsgeleer/onderzoek/onderzoekscholen/rechtenvandemens/english/general/20817main.html (12.11.2007).
Kumppani-lehti (1996). 'Suomi varovainen ihmisoikeussaralla.' By Jari Luoto. 10.3.1996. http://www.kepa.fi/kumppani/513/?searchterm=ihmisoikeudet%20kehitysyhteisty%C3%B6 (5.11.2007).
Legally prepared (2005). The Magazine for Nordic Law Students. 'English is a Must.' By Ida Lindholm. Issue 1, 2005, 63.
LiveJournal (2006). 'How many Polish people does it take to celebrate pride?' 12.6.2006. http://mikeijames.livejournal.com/1385073.html (28.8.2006).
LLM guide (n.d.), online at http://www.llm-guide.com/university/562 (18.9.2006). (2007) LLM guide. Discussion board. http://www.llm-guide.com/board/694/last/ (6.5.2007).
LLM in Human Rights (2006). University of Hong Kong. http://www.hku.hk/ccpl/human_rights/index.html (18.9.2006).

LSE (2002). Profile of Kenneth Roth, executive director of Human Rights Watch. http://www.lse.ac.uk/collections/pressAndInformationOffice/newsAndEvents/archives/2000-2002/Human_Rights_Symposium.htm (30.7.2002).

Malik (2003). Biography of Charles Malik http://udhr.org/history/Biographies/biocm.htm (23.5.2003).

Mediterranean Master's (2006). Mediterranean Master's in Human Rights and Democratisation. http://home.um.edu.mt/laws/entrance/introduction.html (18.9.2006).

MeNaiset (2006). 6.7.2006. 'Tuulen Viemää.' By Bettina Sågblom. 77.

Mennesker & Rettigheter: Nordic Journal of Human Rights (2006). 'Guidelines for Authors' Submissions to Mennesker & Rettigheter: Nordic Journal of Human Rights.' http://www.humanrights.uio.no/forskning/publ/mr/guidelines.html (2.11.2006).

Ministry of Education (2007a). 'Toimenpideohjelma tutkijankoulutuksen ja tutkijanuran kehittämiseksi vuosille 2007–2011.' http://www.minedu.fi/OPM/Julkaisut/2007/Toimenpideohjelma_tutkijankoulutuksen_kehittxmiseksi.html 6.5.2007.

(2007b). 'Opetusministeriön ja opetushallituksen välinen tulosopimus vuosille 2006–2008.' http://www.oph.fi/info/netra/tulossopimus_2006_2008.pdf (3.6.2007).

Minority Rights Group International (2006). http://www.minorityrights.org/ (24.8.2006).

MSNBC (2006). 'Judge rules against "intelligent design".' http://www.msnbc.msn.com/id/10545387/ (2.1.2006).

MTV3 Netti (2007). 'Rusi Rankkana.' 6.11.2007. http://www.mtv3.fi/uutiset/txt/kotimaa.shtml/arkistot/kotimaa/2007/11/578343 (8.11.2007).

Mänskliga rättigheter i Sverige (2001). http://www.riksdagen.se/shopping/R_ShowItem_5715.aspx (2.10.2006).

The New York Times (1995). 'Hillary Clinton, In China, Details Abuse of Women.' By Patrick E. Tyler. September 6, 1995, Section A, 1.

Norwegian Centre (2006). Norwegian Centre for Human Rights. http://www.humanrights.uio.no/english/ (16.5.2006).

Norum (2002). 'Norum Oy EBRD:n pääomasijoittajana Venäjällä.' http://www.sitra.fi/index.asp?DirID=59&DocID=2676 (31.1.2005).

Paris Principles (1993). Office of the High Commissioner for Human Rights. Fact Sheet No. 19, National Institutions for the Promotion and Protecion of Human Rights. http://193.194.138.190/html/menu6/2/fs19.htm (17.5.2006).

Plaza (2007). 'Lyhyestä virsi kaunis, sanoi Iltalehti, kun pappi erotettiin juopottelun takia.' Koko uutinen 30 sanalla. 27.4.2007. ://plaza.fi/ajassa/polttopisteessa/iltalehden-varoittava-esimerkki-typeryydesta (7.11.2007).

Raoul Wallenberg (2006). The Raoul Wallenberg Institute of Human Rights and Humanitarian Law. http://www.rwi.lu.se/institute/aboutrwi.shtml (16.5.2006).

(2007). Training Courses in Sweden. http://www.rwi.lu.se/coop/itp/overview.shtml (10.10.2007).

The Register (2006). 'Google wins SF wireless gig.' By Andrew Orlowski. 6.4.2006. http://www.theregister.co.uk/2006/04/06/google_sf_muni_wifi/ (19.5.2006).

Renewable Energy Access (2005). '"The Human Right to Renewable Energy" Means "Energy Independence for All".' 5.12.2005. http://www.renewableenergyaccess.com/rea/news/story?id=40096 (19.5.2006).

Romulo (2006). Biography of Carlos P. Romulo. http://www.bookrags.com/biography-carlos-p-romulo/index.html (27.2.2006); also http://www.infoplease.com/biography/us/congress/romulo-carlos-pena.html

Scopes Trial (1925). Case Number 5232, the State of Tennessee v. John Thomas Scopes.

SK (2005). Suomen Kuvalehti. 19.8.2005. 'Hän.' By Riitta Kylänpää. 52–56.

She Figures (2006). 'Women and Science: Statistics and Indicators.' European Commission. http://ec.europa.eu/research/science-society/pdf/she_figures_2006_en.pdf (27.12.2006).

Sosiaalifoorumi (2007). Hämeen paino Oy, Forssa.
The Spain Herald (2006). 'Socialists: Give apes human rights.' 25.4.2006. http://www.spainherald.com/3438.html (19.5.2006).
Spiked-liberties (2006). 'There's no human right to wear a jilbab.' By Josie Appleton. 21.3.2006 http://www.spiked-online.com/articles/0000000CAFD5.htm (19.5.2006).
Statistics Finland (2005). http://www.stat.fi/tup/suoluk/suoluk_vaesto_en.html (29.5.2006).
Statistics Norway (2004). 'Differences in education among immigrants.' http://www.ssb.no/english/magazine/art-2006-05-23-01-en.html (19.5.2006).
The Sunday Times
(2006). 'Basic freedoms are being lost in the human rights circus.' By Simon Jenkins. 14.5.2006. http://www.timesonline.co.uk/article/0,,2088-2179499,00.html (19.5.2006).
(2005). 'Woman wins right to wed father-in-law.' By Frances Gibb. 14.9.2005. http://www.timesonline.co.uk/article/0,,2-1779188,00.html (19.5.2006).
Taipei Times (2006). 'Disabled man fights for "human right" to a sex life.' 2.1.2006. http://www.taipeitimes.com/News/world/archives/2006/01/02/2003287074 (19.5.2006).
Tuomioja (2006). Speeches between 1999–2006. http://www.tuomioja.org/index.php?mainAction=listYears&category=4 (30–31.8.2006).
Ulkoministeriö (2006). Päivi Hirvelä valittiin tuomariksi Euroopan ihmisoikeus-tuomioistuimeen. http://formin.finland.fi/Public/default.aspx?contentid=70377&nodeid=15145&contentlan=1&culture=fi-FI (27.6.2006).
Universal Declaration (1948). Universal Declaration of Human Rights. http://www.un.org/Overview/rights.html (4.4.2006).
United Nations
(2006). UN Special Rapporteur. Press Release: 'Statement by UN Special Rapporteur on the Rights of Indigenous Peoples, on the General Assembly's decision not to adopt the Declaration on the Rights of Indigenous Peoples'. http://www.iwgia.org/graphics/Synkron-Library/Documents/Noticeboard/News/International/SRpressreleaseDDDecember2006.htm (28.4.2007).
(2006). Convention on the Rights of Persons with Disabilities. Adopted on 27.8.2006. http://www.un.org/disabilities/convention/conventionfull.shtml (6.11.2009). (2006) Human Rights Council. 3.4.2006. A/Res/60/625. http://www.ohchr.org/english/bodies/hrcouncil/docs/A.RES.60.251_En.pdf (28.8.2006).
(2006). UN Treaty Bodies. http://www.ohchr.org/english/bodies/treaty/index.htm (15.3.2006). (2006) UN Information Centre: 'Rapid Entry into Force of International Criminal Court Statute "a great victory for justice, and for world order", Secretary-General Says.' ' http://www.unis.unvienna.org/unis/pressrels/2002/sgsm8201.html (27.8.2006).
(2001). UN. Year of Dialogue Among Civilizations. http://www.un.org/Dialogue/ (15.6.2006). (1947). Economic and Social Council. Commission on Human Rights. Drafting Committee on an International Bill of Rights. First Session. Report of the Drafting Committee to the Commission on Human Rights. E/CN/21. 1 July 1947.
UNFPA News (2006). 'Mari Simonen Named Deputy Executive Director of UNFPA.' 10.3.2006. http://www.unfpa.org/news/news.cfm?ID=759&Language=1 (18.12.2006).
UNPFII (2004). UN Permanent Forum on Indigenous Issues. Second International Decade of the World's Indigenous Peoples. http://www.un.org/esa/socdev/unpfii/en/second.html (28.4.2007).
University of Essex (2006). Human Rights Centre. http://www2.essex.ac.uk/human_rights_centre/ (25.9.2006).

University of Oslo (n.d.). Human Rights Master of Philosophy in the Theory and Practice of Human Rights launched in 2001. http://www.llm-guide.com/university/463/university-of-oslo-norwegian-centre-for-human-rights (19.9.2006).

University of Oxford (2007). Master's Degree in International Human Rights Law. http://international.conted.ox.ac.uk/mastersdegreeininternationalhumanrightslaw.php (30.4.2007).

US Supreme Court (2005). Members of the Supreme Court of the United States. http://www.supremecourtus.gov/about/members.pdf (23.9.2005).

Uutislehti 100

5.12.2006. 'Naisia on yhä vähän professoreina.' By Liisa Kujala. 6.

25.8.2006. 'Koulu työntää tytöt yhä ahtaaseen naisenmuottiin.' By Piia Leino. 9.

Valtioneuvoston asetus (955/2002). Valtioneuvoston asetus lukiokoulutuksen yleisistä valtakunnallisista tavoitteista ja tuntijaosta. 955/2002. 14.11.2002. http://www.finlex.fi/fi/laki/ajantasa/2002/20020955 (3.6.2007).

Vapaa-ajattelijat (2001). 'Viite: 34/041/1998 Lausuntopyyntönne uskonnonvapauskomitean mietinnöstä (06.04.2001).' http://www.vapaa-ajattelijat.fi/kannanottoja/komitea_lopullinen.html (2.6.2007).

Vienna Declaration (1993). Adopted by the World Conference on Human Rights in Vienna on 25 June 1993. A/Conf. 157/23. http://www.ohchr.org/english/law/vienna.htm (21.12.2005).

The White House (2004). 'President, Mrs. Bush Marks Progress in Global Women's Human Rights.' 12.3.2004. http://www.whitehouse.gov/news/releases/2004/03/20040312-5.html (17.5.2006).

WHRNet (2006). Women's Human Rights Net. http://www.whrnet.org/ (17.5.2006).
(2004). Sexual Rights and the Commission on Human Rights. http://www.whrnet.org/docs/issue-sexualrightscommission.html (28.11.2006).

World Changing (2005). 'Renewable Energy as a Human Right.' http://www.worldchanging.com/archives/003822.html (19.5.2006).

Yle Uutiset (2007). 7.9.2007. 'Häkämiehen Venäjä-kommentit puhuttavat.' http://www.yle.fi/uutiset/24h/id69201.html (29.10.2007).

Yliopisto (2006). 'Keskeneräinen tasavalta.' By Mila Engelberg. Yliopisto 6.3.2006. 14–19.

Yliopistolainen (2006). 'Ei-toivottuja tohtoreita?'. By Mila Engelberg. Yliopistolainen 6/2006. 5–7.

Yliopistolainen (2004). 'Ihmisoikeudet eivät sovi päärakennukseen.' By Henrikki Timgren. Yliopistolainen 7/2004.

Yogyakarta Principles (2007). 'Principles on the International Human Rights Law in Relation to Sexual Orientation and Gender Identity.' March 2007. http://www.yogyakartaprinciples.org/ (6.11.2009).

Åbo Akademi (2006). Institute for Human Rights. http://www.abo.fi/instut/imr/ (16.5.2006 and 12.11.2007).

Appendix 1: Abbreviations in SCANET Student Papers

UN United Nations
UDHR Universal Declaration of Human Rights
UNDP United Nations Development Program
UNICEF United Nations International Children's Educational Fund
UNESCO United Nations Educational, Scientific and Cultural Organization
SC Security Council
GA General Assembly
SG Secretary General
HRC Human Rights Committee
ICCPR International Covenant on Civil and Political Rights
ICESCR International Covenant on Economic, Cultural and Social Rights
CAT Convention against Torture and Other Cruel, Inhuman or Degrading Treatment or Punishment
CEDAW Convention on the Elimination of All Forms of Discrimination against Women
CRC Convention on the Rights of the Child
CERD Convention on the Elimination of All Forms of Racial Discrimination
CMW International Convention on the Protection of the Rights of All Migrant Workers and Members of their Families
ILC International Law Commission
ICJ International Court of Justice
PCIJ Permanent Court of International Justice
ECHR European Court of Human Rights
ICC International Criminal Court
ICTR International Criminal Tribunal for Rwanda
ICTY International Criminal Tribunal for the Former Yugoslavia
EU/EC European Union/European Community/European Commission
TEC Treaty of the European Commission
EC European Constitution
EUCFR European Union Charter of Fundamental Rights
CPT The European Convention for the Prevention of Torture and Inhuman or Degrading Treatment or Punishment
WTO The World Trade Organization
ILO The International Labor Organization
WHO World Health Organization
WIPO World International Property Organization
IPR Intellectual Property Rights
GATT General Agreement on Tariffs and Trade
ICRC International Committee of the Red Cross
NAFTA North-Atlantic Free Trade Agreement
NAALC North American Agreement on Labor Cooperation
NATO North-Atlantic Treaty Organization
MNC Multinational Corporation
IO International Organization
NGO Non-Governmental Organization
DK Denmark
TRNC Turkish Republic of Northern Cyprus
MRT Moldavian Republic of Transnistria
FRY Federal Republic of Yugoslavia
EU-ACP European Union and countries of the Africa, the Caribbean and the Pacific Group
AU African Union

AOU Organization of African Unity
MS Member State
WG working group
IGC inter-governmental conference
GSP generalized tariff preferences
GSP Generalized System of Preferences
NHRI National Human Rights Institution
POW Prisoner of War
GWT Great Western Transmutation
DRC not explained
ASEAN countries not explained
TEU not explained
AFSJ not explained

INDEX

Acronyms 106, 149–152, 156, 217
Activist 15, 18, 20, 30, 63, 95, 98, 100, 114, 171, 191, 192, 227, 251
American Civil Liberties Union (ACLU) 114–115

Baldwin, Roger 39, 114–115
Baltic 33, 52, 112, 117, 208, 212–214
Bill of Rights 39, 41, 104–105, 173
Black-letter lawyer 189, 193

Centre 29, 33–34, 54, 56, 71, 80–81, 95, 97, 103–104, 111–112, 121–122, 168–169, 190, 247, 250
Ceremonial 160, 163–167
Christian 1–3, 13–14, 84, 209, 219–220, 250
Civil and political rights 40, 49
Civilizing mission 6, 18, 202, 245
Cold War 4, 40, 43, 46–47, 49, 51, 191, 214–215, 247
Committee on Economic, Social and Cultural Rights 30, 92–95, 106, 143, 154–155, 160, 182, 186
Community of practice 9–10, 28, 30, 79–80, 86–87, 89, 95–96, 99–100, 112, 124–125, 130, 143, 147–148, 152–153, 159, 164–165, 167–169, 171, 178, 183, 189, 193–196, 199, 232, 248
Conception of knowledge 130, 134–135, 192
Controversy 6, 30, 39, 45, 51, 65, 77, 85, 146, 158, 171, 178–180, 187, 190
Creative Space 30–31, 171, 191–193, 199–200, 203, 215, 251–252

Déclaration des droits de l'homme et du citoyen 104–105
Denmark 1, 12, 44, 48–49, 56, 86, 90, 98, 103, 124, 212, 223, 225
Dezalay, Yves 24, 80, 86
Dialogue 123, 125, 128, 130, 136, 140, 163–164, 188, 200, 218, 222, 239

Economic, social and cultural rights 40, 155
Elite 30, 79, 98, 100, 106, 108, 112–116, 123, 158
Empowering 6, 122, 126, 136, 167, 169–170, 203, 232, 248–249
English 14, 29, 34, 45, 60, 75, 100, 103–112, 115–116, 121–122, 154, 160, 162–163, 181–182, 194–195, 218
European Convention on Human Rights 40, 50, 150
European Court of Human Rights 40, 56, 66, 144, 150, 216, 226
Expansion 8, 29–30, 51, 57–58, 60, 62, 64, 71–72, 81, 105, 121, 171, 213, 251

Faculty 126–132, 137–139, 141–142, 144–145, 147, 150–151, 165, 168–169, 181, 203, 205, 208, 215, 235, 248–249, 251
Finland 1, 3, 6–7, 10, 12, 28–30, 33–34, 42–45, 47–57, 64–65, 67–72, 75, 79, 83, 85–86, 90–92, 97–103, 107–109, 113, 122, 124, 137, 203, 205, 208, 211–212, 215, 222–223, 225–228, 232, 248–250, 252
Finnish academia 228–229, 245, 249
Fundamental rights 52–53, 100, 103, 109

Garth, Bryant 25, 80, 86
Gender 31, 57, 59, 66–68, 70, 101, 149, 203, 223–224, 227, 229, 233, 236, 238, 240, 244–245, 249–250
Generation 2, 25, 108–109, 124–125, 131, 143, 161, 169, 187, 199, 231–232, 244, 249–250

Haavisto, Vaula 136, 138, 185
Hannerz, Ulf 34, 82
Human Rights Committee 67, 85, 92–94, 106, 142, 182–183, 188
Human rights institute 12, 87–88, 90–91
Human rights journal 60–62, 121
Human rights NGO 3, 13, 29, 83, 90, 95–99, 218

Iceland 1, 12, 44, 48, 86, 90, 109, 212, 223
Indicator 175, 189

Indigenous 15, 52, 59, 70–71, 101, 130, 158, 169, 175–176, 203, 205, 221–222, 243–244
Internal actor 217–219, 221–222, 243
International League for the Rights of Man 38, 114

Kennedy, David 18, 85, 180, 192, 199
Kennedy, Duncan 142, 174, 178–179
Knowledge practice 24, 28, 30, 79, 147–148, 152–154, 156–159, 165, 190, 194, 197, 248, 252
Koskenniemi, Martti 179, 202

Latour, Bruno 10, 83, 179, 189, 196
Lave, Jean 9, 16, 79
Legality 138, 178, 186, 188–192, 251
Legitimacy 68, 111, 171–172, 191–192, 216, 218, 251
Legitimate peripheral participant 10, 16, 124–125, 148, 167–170
LGBT-rights 30, 66, 68–69, 83, 96, 147
Lutheran church 1–3, 34, 68, 72, 77–78, 107, 209, 249, 251–252

Magna Carta 104–105
Malik, Charles 38, 115, 183, 219, 221
Merry, Sally Engle 11, 23, 25, 28, 34, 57, 83, 115, 149, 159, 161, 186, 188, 195, 218, 240

NAIL 20–21, 25, 30, 134–135, 140–141, 147, 180, 187, 190, 226, 236
Norway 1, 12, 44, 48, 56, 86, 90, 98, 103, 124, 154–156, 205, 208, 210, 212, 215, 223, 225

Periphery 29, 33–34, 56, 71, 80–81, 103–104, 247, 250

Relativism 13, 16, 23, 144–145, 190, 196
Riles, Annelise 11, 20–21, 25, 27, 38, 98, 106, 149, 159, 190
Roosevelt, Eleanor 36, 38, 46, 95, 183
Russia 37, 42–43, 45–46, 107, 208, 212–213, 215

Sacred 1, 147, 191, 202
Sarat, Austin 179, 185
ScaFund 88–89, 99, 109–110, 112–113, 125, 213–214
Secularization 1–4, 11, 17, 34, 147, 191, 195, 199, 216, 250, 252
Soviet Union 39, 42–46, 49, 215
Speech act 126–130, 134, 149, 232, 234, 236–237, 239–240
Statement of Essential Human Rights 104–105, 115
State report 30, 93, 106, 135, 153–156, 159–160, 162–163, 188, 194, 212
Sweden 12, 42, 44, 48, 51–52, 54, 56, 86, 90, 98, 109, 124, 205, 208, 212, 214–215, 223, 225
Systemic agency 9–10, 30, 79, 82–86, 100, 130, 171, 192, 214, 244, 250–251

Teaching curriculum 10, 124, 171

UN Decade of Human Rights Education 6, 30, 119
Universalism 13, 22–23, 26, 144, 148, 196, 243

Wallerstein, Emmanuel 34
Wenger, Etienne 9, 16, 79

The Eric Castrén Institute Monographs on International Law and Human Rights

General editor
Martti Koskenniemi

1. O. Korhonen: International Law Situated. *An Analysis of the Lawyer's Stance Towards Culture, History and Community*. 2000
   ISBN 9041114521
2. J. Heliskoski: Mixed Agreements as a Technique for Organizing the International Relations of the European Community and its Member States. 2001
   ISBN 904111713X
3. K. Rittich: Recharacterizing Restructuring. *Law, Distribution and Gender in Market Reform*. 2002
   ISBN 9041119353
4. T. Kuokkanen: International Law and the Environment. *Variations on a Theme*. 2002
   ISBN 9041119507
5. L. Mälksoo: Illegal Annexation and State Continuity. *The Case of the Incorporation of the Baltic States by the USSR. A Study of the Tension between Normativity and Power in International Law*. 2003
   ISBN 9041121773
6. T. Långström: Transformation in Russia and International Law. 2003
   ISBN 9004137548
7. M.J. Falcón y Tella: Civil Disobedience. 2004
   ISBN 9004141219
8. J. Summers: Peoples and International Law. *How Nationalism and Self-Determination Shape a Contemporary Law of Nations*. 2007
   ISBN 9789004154919
9. P. Gynther: Beyond Systemic Discrimination. *Educational Rights, Skills Acquisition and the Case of Roma*. 2007
   ISBN 9789004162655
10. M. Letho: Indirect Responsibility for Terrorist Acts. *Redefinition of the Concept of Terrorism Beyond Violent Acts*. 2009
    ISBN 9789004178076
11. M. Halme-Tuomisaari: Human Rights in Action. *Learning Expert Knowledge*. 2010
    ISBN 9789004184459

brill.nl/ilmc

